SUCCESSFUL PERENNIAL GARDENING

A Practical Guide

Lewis and Nancy Hill

A Garden Way Publishing Book

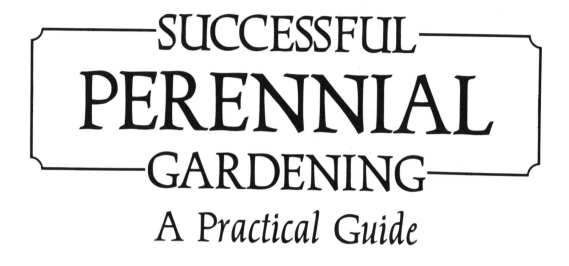

Storey Communications, Inc.
Pownal, Vermont 05261

*The mission of Storey Communications is to serve our customers
by publishing practical information that encourages personal independence
in harmony with the environment.*

Cover and text design by Andrea Gray
Production by Wanda Harper, Beth DiLego, and Cindy McFarland
Front cover photograph by Madelaine S. Gray
Back cover photographs: Cindy McFarland (left), Derek Fell (center and right)
Back cover illustration by Mallory Lake
Typesetting by Accura Type and Design, Barre, Vermont in Garamond

Printed in the United States by Courier
10

The editor wishes to acknowledge the help of Cindy McFarland, who reviewed the manuscript with an editor's care and a gardener's enthusiasm.

Library of Congress Cataloging-in-Publication Data

Hill, Lewis (1924-) and Nancy
  Successful perennial gardening.

  "A Garden Way Publishing book."
  Includes index.
  1. Perennials. 2. Landscape gardening.
3. Gardens—Design. I. Title.
SB434.H55 1988   635.9'32   87-45582
  ISBN 0-88266-473-5
  ISBN 0-88266-472-7 (pbk.)

To our parents,
Dorothy and Warner Davis,
Grace and Alvah Hill,
with love

Contents

PART III
DESCRIPTIONS OF THE BEST GARDEN PERENNIALS

Grateful thanks for inspiration and help over the years to our many gardening friends, among them Barbara, Mary, and Susan Carpenter; Betsey Carrick; Mildred Cook; Gertrude Corwin; Katherine Eisenhart; Elizabeth Hale; Isabel Igleheart; Rosanna and Charlie Jaffin; Flora and Wayne Philbrook; Blanche Pleasants; and Elisabeth Schulz. To horticultural professionals Leonard Perry, Norman Pellett, Bill Uber, and the Vermont Plantsmen. And, most of all, to our very special editor, Sarah May Clarkson.

Introduction

When we were planning our first backyard perennial garden, a visitor from England told us that it takes a minimum of 50 years to create a garden and, if possible, one should allow 200 years. We were still young, but 50 years seemed like a long time and the prospect of a fine border seemed dim. Fortunately, he was wrong. Although our gardens have never rivaled those at Sissinghurst or Kew, they have been a constant joy to us, which was all we asked of them.

In the early years we made many mistakes, and when we were discouraged it was tempting to clean out the beds and plant shrubs instead. In retrospect, we realize that if we'd been better educated on perennial growth and maintenance, we could have avoided most of the problems. We have written this book in the hope that you will not make the same mistakes.

Our gardens have taught us to be patient and tolerant of the whims of nature. We now realize that despite our best intentions, occurrences such as violent storms or other unusual weather, surprise diseases and bugs, as well as unexpected demands on our free time can all ruin the best-laid plans. But like baseball fans, we don't despair—there's always next year! Then everything will grow and bloom to perfection, and we'll be proud to show our backyard to the likes of Gertrude Jekyll herself!

PART I

PLANNING AND PLANTING A PERENNIAL GARDEN

1

Those Fascinating Perennials

From studying the new garden catalogs in mid-January, to tucking in the plants with mulch just before the winter snows arrive, we derive enormous pleasure from our perennial flowers. As soon as the snow melts in the spring we hurry to the gardens to discover which plants are peeping through the wet earth after their winter hibernation. With the first spring shower, many that had seemed dead on first inspection suddenly sprout green buds and we know that more surprises will appear each day until the cycle of seasons brings winter once again.

It is this quality of metamorphosis that attracts us to perennials. The annual flowers that grow, bloom, produce seed, and die the same year are lovely, colorful, and predictable throughout the summer. Herbaceous perennials, on the other hand, are fascinating because most bloom for only short periods and seldom look the same two days in a row, or two years in succession. Our early morning walks reward us with a changing display of blossoms and an endless variation of plant textures, heights, and fragrances. We wait expectantly to see if the new hybrid iris we splurged on last fall will be as spectacular as the catalog description promised, or if the blooms of the peony that were disappointingly small last summer will improve this year.

Sometimes we wonder, nevertheless, why we spend our summers digging, planting, moving plants from place to place, feeding, and spraying while others swim, boat, play tennis and golf, or relax in a hammock. Perennial gardening isn't always fun. In fact,

one gardener has described the struggle with soil, weeds, bugs, and diseases as "war of the (prim)roses."

Our desire to garden, and the pleasure it gives us, no doubt has something to do with the challenge of winning that war, and creating beauty in a spot where only grass and weeds would otherwise be found. It also provides exercise, lovely bouquets, and a good excuse to be outdoors. But the root of our motivation goes deeper, to the peace that subtly creeps over our minds when we are absorbed with our plants. In working with the soil, we join a long procession of humanity tied to the cycle of planting and harvest since the beginning of time.

Perennial gardening was introduced to this country by the first settlers who brought, along with personal necessities, their favorite plants. When we were young our neighbors had a large clump of bluebells in their yard and they often told us how their grandparents had brought a root of the plant from Scotland in a small ship a century earlier. That dark blue campanula seemed to us a living bit of Europe, and we sometimes speculated about how much it must have meant to those homesick settlers during their first difficult years here.

Many of our most common perennial plants were, like the bluebells, imported by immigrants or by returning American missionaries and tourists. Others were discovered by professional horticulturists who visited foreign lands especially to seek new species of plant life. Some imports felt so much at home in this country that they quickly became unappreciated weeds. The common daisy, dandelion, devil's paint-brush, tansy, and many others arrived as garden flowers or medicinal herbs, but rapidly spread throughout the countryside. We've heard that the walled garden got its start in this country when a colonist became suspicious and built a stone wall around his wife's flower garden to keep the plants from spreading into his fields. Not all garden perennials are immigrants, of course. Some were native to North America's fields and woods. Wildflowers such as the lady's slipper, bee balm, and mertensia were admired by the early settlers and transplanted into their yards and gardens.

A great many of today's popular perennials bear little resemblance to those our ancestors grew, due to the work of amateur and professional horticulturists. Dedicated hybridizers have created thousands of new peony, iris, lily, *Hemerocallis*, chrysanthemum, delphinium, and other varieties now available in garden centers, nurseries, or mail-order catalogs. Those first gardeners on our continent would be rightly proud of the descendants of the plants they started and nurtured.

PERENNIALS, BIENNIALS, AND ANNUALS

In horticultural terminology a "perennial" is any plant that lives more than two years. The word encompasses hardy shrubs and trees, as well as tender plants such as geraniums and African violets. This is in contrast to annuals such as cosmos and spinach that grow from seed each spring and live only one season. In this book, however, our use of the word perennial indicates only those hardy herbaceous plants commonly grown in flower gardens—iris, peony, and delphinium, for example.

We also discuss biennials—plants that sprout and grow the first year after seed is planted, then flower, produce seed, and subsequently die the second year. This sequence may vary if a plant sprouts very early and blooms the first year, or if it lives for more than two years, as may happen in areas with a short growing season. Many common varieties of Canterbury bells, sweet William, and foxgloves are well-known garden biennials; burdock, mullein, and bull thistle are common biennial weeds.

The infinite number of perennial varieties may seem overwhelming to new gardeners. Not only are there thousands of genera in endless shapes and colors, but many have a large number of species. To add to the confusion, each species is likely to include numerous varieties (cultivars) that have been developed and named by horticulturists.

Scientific Names

Although you can have a full and successful gardening career without knowing the Latin botanical names of your garden perennials, there are many good reasons for learning them at the outset. Many of us received our plant education at our mother's knee, and find it awkward to call the violet *Viola*, or the bluebell *Campanula*, but we ultimately come to value the scientific nomenclature because it absolutely defines the plant to which we are referring. *Anthemis*, for example, is variously known as yellow daisy, marguerite, and other names in different parts of this country, but *Anthemis tinctoria* identifies a specific plant worldwide. Likewise, honeysuckle is used to describe several different plants—a vine, shrub, wildflower, and flowering perennial—but each has a different, readily identifiable scientific name.

The ability to use the botanical rather than the common name will simplify and expedite the process of buying plants, as well as prevent confusion when you are talking with gardeners from other regions about their experiences. One of our neighbors who grew up in Germany had no difficulty transferring her extensive horticultural knowledge to gardening in this country because of her familiarity with the Latin nomenclature.

The scientific name categorizes a plant into the correct *genus* (the first, and capitalized, part of the name) and, if necessary, the *species* within that genus (the second, descriptive part of the name). All members of the lily genus, for example, are *Lilium*, and the popular Regal Lily is *Lilium regale*, or, after the first reference in a written text, *L. regale*. The species label may describe a particular quality of a plant or indicate its origin, such as *canadensis* for Canada, *japonica* (Japan), *tyrolensis* (the Tyrol), *orientalis* (the Orient), and so on. This specific epithet may distinguish the plant's native habitat: *montana* and *alpina* for mountains, *salvatica* for woods, and *aquaticus* for water. Still others indicate the appearance of the plant—its leaves, stem, blooms, fruit, or habit of growth. *Giganteus* (large), *brevi* (short), *coloratus* (colored), *arborescens* (woody), *mollis* (soft), *annuus* (annual), *nanus* (dwarf), *multiflora* (many flowered), *albus* (white), *trilobus* (three), and *barbatus* (bearded) are only a few of the scientific adjectives you will encounter as you become involved with plants.

In spite of the fact that the scientific nomenclature

may seem as unchanging as the Rock of Gibraltar, don't be surprised if one of your favorite plants is suddenly given a scientific name that's completely different from the one you've learned. Botany, like other sciences, is constantly being reassessed, and botanists occasionally change a label if they find a plant is more accurately described under another category.

Gardeners who wish further information regarding plant families, genus, and species should consult *Hortus Third* (or later versions as they become available). This massive volume (1,290 pages) is universally regarded as the standard reference on horticultural nomenclature.

BECOMING A GARDENER

Like most gardeners, we have moved gradually through several phases that we can see only in retrospect. In the beginning we simply liked flowers and admired perennial gardens with absolutely no idea as to how they were created. People gave us plants, we dug holes, and casually stuck them in the ground without preparing the soil. One by one we learned the names of plant species, but remained unaware of the different varieties. To us, iris were simply white, brown, red, and yellow.

Gradually we came to know more of plant habits —when they bloomed, how high they grew, their vigor, whether their foliage remained attractive throughout the season (peonies are an example) or needed to be cut back (like delphinium and Oriental poppies). We learned to recognize when a plant should be divided and which of the vigorous species

---

AN EXAMPLE OF PLANT CLASSIFICATION: The Felix Crouse Peony

Kingdom: Plantae (plants)
Division: Spermatophyta (plants that produce seeds)
Subdivision: Anthophyta (commonly described as flowering plants)
Class: Dicotyledoneae (seeds with two cotyledons)
Family: Crowfoot
Genus: Paeonia (peony)
Species: lactiflora (Chinese peony)
Cultivar (named variety): Felix Crouse

In a catalog or garden encyclopedia you would find this plant described as *Paeonia lactiflora* 'Felix Crouse.'

---

need to be restrained. It took time, but we finally learned to plan *before* we planted to achieve pleasant color combinations and to arrange the varieties so there would be bloom throughout the garden at every season of the year. We began to set perennials in particular groups and locations, rather than jamming them in arbitrarily. We learned to be ruthless and to actually throw away healthy plants if they had bad habits or contributed little to the garden.

Discerning eyes and a garden regimen developed: we realized that a border didn't look "finished" if an edging was missing, that it was important to weed and fertilize on schedule, and to cut off the fading blooms (known as deadheading). And as we became knowledgeable, we searched for outstanding varieties. A red peony was no longer satisfactory: we ordered a 'Karl Rosenfield' because it had the large, double, dark-red blooms that would look right in the spot we'd chosen for it.

Gardening is not like cooking. You can't just follow a recipe. We are still in the process of learning, and always will be, but the more we know about plants, the more we enjoy the garden experience. No two gardeners want the same thing from a garden, however, and the world is full of people who have never advanced beyond the initial phase of cramming a lot of plants into a small bed. If you are one of these, don't be concerned. A garden should not be such a serious enterprise that it becomes more work than fun, and if you enjoy yours, that should be enough.

CHOOSING YOUR PERENNIALS

It may be tempting to choose perennial species for your garden by looks alone. But, as in choosing a spouse, you need to be aware of what is unseen before you take the plunge. The thousands of different perennial garden species vary widely in their growth and blooming habits, and each has different needs that must be met in order to thrive.

Garden catalogs, with their stunning photos, can be fun and inspirational to read, but with the exception of a few, they are not the best sources of growing information. Extraordinary varieties may be touted which, in fact, have only modest blooms, are weak, short-lived, and demand a great deal of attention. It takes a strong will to resist reaching for your checkbook when the catalogs arrive in the middle of winter, but try to hold off until you are familiar with the varieties. Either read about the plants you'd like to grow in part III of this book, find out if other local gardeners have had success with them, or try to see them bloom at a nursery or neighbor's garden before allotting them space in your own backyard.

Years ago it was common practice for some nurseries to give colorful new names to ordinary plants and then sell them at a high price. Fortunately, this unscrupulous practice does not occur much today, but we still see questionable offerings occasionally in Sunday newspapers, cheap magazines, and direct mail ads. Friends of ours once bought bishop's weed because it was described in this way: Snow-on-the-mountain is a perfect, fast-growing ground cover or edging for your garden. The "fast-growing" description was correct: it took over every nook and cranny of their grounds and gardens, and they'll probably never be entirely rid of it. Like get-rich-quick schemes, if a plant seems too good to be true, it probably is.

Light and Soil Preferences

Although certain plants prefer to grow in partial shade, most common perennials do best in full sunlight. Many, however, can get by beautifully if they receive only a half day of full sun and are exposed to skylight for the remainder of the day. Skylight can be defined as light from an "open" sky, with shading provided by a vertical surface such as a wall, hedge, or building, rather than the canopy of a tree.

The amount of light a perennial needs for good growth and flowering can also be affected by the latitude in which it is found. A variety that needs a location with full sun in the North may do well in a spot with much less light in southern climates because the intensity is greater there. Likewise, a plant that prefers partial shade in the South may not need such protection in a northern valley where there are many overcast days. And in northern latitudes, gardeners may find that plants growing in full sun in June are shaded by trees or buildings in August when the angle of the sun's path is nearer the horizon.

Light exposure affects plants in other ways. Many, like peonies, bloom later in the season when grown on the west side of a building than they would in a sunny southeastern exposure. Plants such as chrysanthemums bloom earlier if they are grown where they get early afternoon shade because their blossoming mechanism is triggered by diminishing light conditions. And the blossoms of some plants are more beautiful when they are grown in shaded conditions. The *Hemerocallis* genus as a whole blooms best in full sunlight, but the blossoms of certain red and pink varieties are brighter when the plants are partially shaded from the bleaching effects of hot afternoon sun.

Most common perennials grow best when planted in the same type of soil you would prepare for a vegetable garden. There are, however, plants that prefer dry soil, others that like it moist, and some which grow only in water. Most thrive when the soil has a pH of 5.5 to 6.5, but there are exceptions. Wild orchids need conditions that would be far too acidic for most plants, and delphinium do best in a more alkaline soil.

The description of each perennial in part III lists any special light and soil requirements it may have.

Weedy Plants

Because we were anxious for quick results when we first started perennial gardening we made the mistake of planting too many *Anthemis, Centaurea,* and old-time daylilies. These fast growers soon crowded out the less aggressive phlox, iris, and *Platycodons,* and caused no end of frustration and work. Now we limit the more vigorous plants, watch them carefully, and don't hesitate to cut them back whenever our flower beds become threatened with unfriendly takeover.

Any plant that people give away in generous quantities should be regarded with mild suspicion. Accept gift plants with caution, even though they may be presented with love and good gardening credentials. One man quite innocently introduced two kinds of *Aegopodium* and an energetic hardy bamboo (*Polygonium sachalinense*) to our community in the early 1900s. Masses of these fast-growing, exotic plants were attractive around his partially shaded lakeside cottage, and he enthusiastically shared divisions with all admirers. Now, nearly a century later, he is immortalized throughout the town by the wretched weeds that new generations of gardeners desperately battle in their flower beds, vegetable gardens, and lawns.

It is unfair to rigidly classify those plants that have the potential of becoming weeds because each can be justified in the proper location for the right purpose. Also, the vigor of a plant may vary considerably according to soil and climatic conditions; plants that have become pirates in our garden might be ideal in yours. We limit the plantings of achillea, *Ajuga, Anthemis, Bellis* (English daisy), *Campanula persicifolia* (peach bells), *Centaurea* (mountain bluet), *Coreopsis, Digitalis* (foxglove), *Hesperis* (sweet rocket), common hosta, *Lupinus* (common lupine), *Lysimachia* (loosestrife), *Monarda* (bee balm), *Sedum, Solidago* (garden goldenrod), and tawny daylily. These have all shown a tendency to take over with only slight encouragement.

New Hybrids

When buying perennials you may sometimes have a choice between new hybrid varieties and the older, tried-and-true kinds. You will want the best for your garden, but how can you know which varieties (especially new ones) will be right for your plan and growing conditions.

Hybrids result from a cross between two different species or varieties. Such crosses are usually possible only within the same genus. Although some new introductions are accidents of nature, most result from the careful scientific planning of horticulturists who attempt to combine the best qualities of different plants. Hybrid varieties often have more spectacular flowers than those of their ancestors, and are well worth seeking out in your garden center or nursery catalogs. In addition to improved color and bloom size, their growing habits may make them more suitable for your garden. A recent favorite of ours is the new Blue Fountain delphinium; it's as attractive as the popular giant Pacific hybrid, but since it is so much shorter, staking is unnecessary even in our windy area.

In spite of their advantages, certain hybrid plants are weaker than their forebears, and less resistant to disease. There are gardeners who prefer old-time varieties because they feel that some new hostas, peonies, and daylilies lack the vigor of the older species, that the hybrid iris are more susceptible to disease than their wild ancestors, and that the newer delphiniums have a shorter lifespan than the original species. And we've heard friends lament that their new *Dianthus*, like hybrid sweet peas and roses, do not have the same delightful fragrance of earlier species.

Perennials for Various Climates

Foresters, farmers, and gardeners rely heavily on the United States Department of Agriculture's planting zone map for choosing the plants that will grow well in their climate. Updated from time to time, it classifies each region according to its annual minimum temperatures (see map), and/or the length of its growing season.

The United States and Canada have a wide range of climates, from areas with year-round ice and snow to semitropical regions. Zone 1 is near-tundra, and zones 2 and 3 have extremely low temperatures and short growing seasons. Much of the continental United States falls into zones 4, 5, 6, and 7 where a wide range of plants can be grown. Since zones 9 and 10 have little frost many semitropical plants can be grown outdoors year-round in these areas.

Gardeners in southern regions face far more problems with heat and drought than their northern neighbors. They frequently need to water daily throughout the summer to keep their gardens thriving, and find it necessary to shade fragile plants during the hottest weather. In some areas, August is a dormant season for plants, and many give up their gardening chores for a few weeks. They return in September to enjoy a long fall season of asters, chrysanthemums, cannas, and similar plants.

Heavy, humus-rich soils are preferable in warm regions because they stay cooler than light sandy ones. Mulches are extremely valuable since they help to keep the soil cool, and prevent moisture from evaporating rapidly. Trees, hedges, tight fences, and walls can give valuable protection from drying winds and, if carefully positioned, can provide light shade during the heat of the day. You can save time and labor if you choose perennials best suited to your particular southern location. Part II lists plants that do best in spots that are dry, as well as suggesting ones for particular types of gardens. To select plants wisely, take advantage of your neighbors' experience, and observe what is thriving in their gardens.

If you garden in the North, in a mountain climate, or a cool weather microclimate that limits the growth of many of your favorite trees and shrubs, it may be an ideal situation for herbaceous perennials. Many such species grow best and bloom over longer periods in areas where summers are cool and evening dews are heavy. Frigid temperatures do not affect them as much as they do woody plants because their tops die down before winter, and snow often mulches the roots. Friends of ours who moved from zone 6 in eastern Massachusetts to our mountain village in zone 3 hardly missed their rhododendrons and laurel because they were captivated by their thriving perennials.

Some plant varieties imported from warmer climates may suffer, nevertheless, when they are exposed over a long period to low winter temperatures. Since the temperature of the soil rather than the air temperature is the critical factor, a plant may survive when the air temperature falls to $-40\,°F$ if there is plenty of snow to serve as insulation, but succumb during a mild winter when there is little snow to prevent the ground from freezing well below the surface. Consequently, if you garden where the mer-

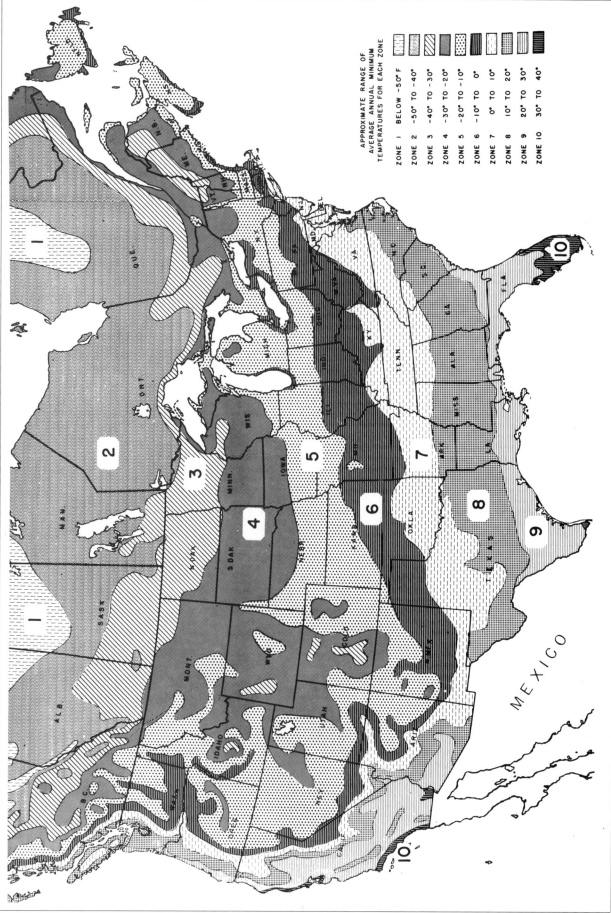

APPROXIMATE RANGE OF
AVERAGE ANNUAL MINIMUM
TEMPERATURES FOR EACH ZONE

ZONE 1 BELOW -50°F
ZONE 2 -50° TO -40°
ZONE 3 -40° TO -30°
ZONE 4 -30° TO -20°
ZONE 5 -20° TO -10°
ZONE 6 -10° TO 0°
ZONE 7 0° TO 10°
ZONE 8 10° TO 20°
ZONE 9 20° TO 30°
ZONE 10 30° TO 40°

SUCCESSFUL PERENNIAL GARDENING

cury drops below zero and a protective layer of snow is not certain, plant only the hardiest of perennials unless you are able to cover them with mulch each fall and uncover them at the proper time in the spring. An insulating material such as leaves, straw, or wood chips around the plants helps prevent excessive fluctuations in soil temperature, but the best insurance is to cover the entire perennial garden with a non-matting and nonsmothering material such as evergreen boughs.

If you are a northern gardener, winter temperatures alone should not govern your choice of plant varieties. Frost is another crucial consideration. Perennials such as anemones, chrysanthemums, gentians, *Hibiscus*, and perennial asters blossom so late in the season that they may flower for only a short time, if at all, where frosts come unusually early.

Certain varieties of the following common perennials are prone to winter loss in subzero climates and protective measures are often necessary. Your northern gardening friends will probably tell you that they have been growing some varieties of these plants for many years without taking winter precautions, however, so don't regard this list as definitive.

Althaea, hollyhock
Anchusa, bugloss
Anemone, Japanese anemone
Aubrieta, rockcress
Bellis, English daisy
Bergenia
Callirhoë, poppy mallow
Ceratostigma, plumbago
Chrysanthemum
Coreopsis, tickseed
Cortaderia, pampas grass
Gaillardia, blanketflower
Helianthemum, sunrose
Kniphofia, torch lily
Lavandula, lavender
Penstemon, beardtongue
Potentilla, cinquefoil
Primula, primrose
Salvia, mealycup sage

Perennial Bulbs

Plants grown from bulbs constitute an important part of any all-season garden border. Spring tulips, daffodils, crocus, *Scilla*, snowdrops, and hyacinths provide bright spots of early color even when the lawn appears dead. And throughout the season *Allium*, *Convallaria*, *Liriope*, lilies, *Lycoris*, *Oxalis*, and *Ranunculus* add interesting blooms and foliage textures.

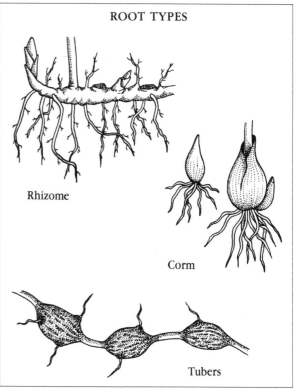

Drawings by Hyla Scudder

ROOT TYPES

Rhizome

Corm

Tubers

The roots of many plants, both hardy and tender, are often called bulbs because they are fleshy, but they do not meet the strict definitions which horticulturists reserve for true bulbs—modified buds with fleshy scales. Iris are among the plants with **rhizomes**: fleshy underground stems that grow close to the surface of the ground and are used for food storage by the plant. Gladiolus have **corms** which are similar to bulbs, but are more solid and don't have scales. Dahlias and Jerusalem artichokes grow from **tubers**: large, fat, underground stems with "eyes" from which sprouts grow. *Hemerocallis* and peonies have thick, fibrous root clumps, which are neither bulbs, corms, rhizomes, nor tubers.

Different types of bulbs vary in lifespan. Daffodils, grape hyacinths, and snowdrops will live for many years if they are planted at the recommended depth, kept fertilized, and divided when they become overcrowded. Tulips and hyacinths are much shorter lived and usually must be replaced every year or two unless they are dug up after they have died down in early summer and stored for replanting in the fall. Lilies may also differ in endurance—many older varieties such as regal, tiger, and *Henryi* live for decades, as do certain Asiatic hybrids such as 'Enchantment.' Most recently developed lily hybrids, however, have short lifespans and must be replaced every few years, although this is not a good reason for omitting them. Some devoted lily lovers treat them as annuals.

Poisonous Plants

Sensational stories occasionally appear in the newspaper about all the deadly plants we grow around our houses. They graphically report that thousands of people, most of them innocent children, die each year from nibbling on delphinium, poinsettia, lily-of-the-valley, iris, columbine, lupine, bleeding-heart, and hyacinth. We do not intend to downplay the possible danger of certain plants, but there is good reason to doubt the accuracy of these articles. The number of alleged poisonings seemed so high that a few years ago some suspicious plantsmen conducted their own investigation. They checked with many large hospitals and found that virtually none had ever recorded a case of fatal poisoning from eating garden perennials or houseplants.

No one questions the fact that some plants are poisonous if ingested. Well-known plants such as *Aconitum* (monkshood) and *Digitalis* (foxglove), both of which have been used medicinally for many years, are known to be extremely toxic when not taken according to prescribed measures. Baneberry, *Colchicum autumnale* (autumn crocus), hellebore, deadly nightshade, and other woods and garden plants can be deadly even in small amounts when eaten, and a few common yard plants such as daphne, English ivy, wisteria, *Lantana*, castor bean, yew, and black locust have varying degrees of toxicity. In some, the entire plant can be toxic, and in others it is only the seeds, roots, or stems. And some plants are poisonous only at certain stages of their growth.

There is little reason not to plant perennials you like because they are poisonous to eat. Handling them is not harmful, and few people are likely to consume them because they're not at all tasty. If small children play near your garden, however, keep them away from the following perennials which are toxic if taken internally.

Aconitum, monkshood
Colchicum autumnale, autumn crocus, meadow saffron
Convallaria, lily-of-the-valley
Delphinium
Digitalis
Helleborus, Christmas rose

Designing Your Perennial Garden

Many years ago a retired farm couple gave us a tour of their perennial "garden." Everything was planted in neat cultivated rows just like their vegetables. As we walked up and down the rows they described each plant's background, told where they had acquired it, and a bit of its lore. There were only one or two plants of each variety, and the garden looked very much like a nursery, quite contrary to all the rules of garden design. But they had spent many hours browsing through catalogs and choosing plants, and proudly displayed their beloved flowers the same way some people show bottles or seashells, not caring a whit about the overall effect. They were so enthusiastic about their plants that we enjoyed the tour as much as they enjoyed giving it. Clearly this was the right garden for them.

During our years in the plant business we have visited hundreds of gardens, and each is as different as the person who created and worked in it. As we observed more and more, and read extensively, it became apparent that there is no one "right" way to design a planting. Still, if you want your garden's overall appearance to appeal to most onlookers, it is essential to follow a few basic guidelines of good design. Generations of gardeners have experimented with positioning colors, shapes, and sizes, and their results can help us as we plan our own.

A perennial garden, like a vegetable plot, is more beautiful, productive, and satisfying when kept to a manageable size. The Chinese have a saying to which all gardeners should pay heed: "Praise large gardens, plant small ones."

If you like flowers and enjoy creating beauty, gardening is undeniably a pleasant way to spend the summer months, but most of us have a great many other demands on our time. As a friend of ours recently said, "I love my perennials, but I'm a 'hack' gardener. I'm away from home every weekday from 7 A.M. until 7 P.M., and there is precious little time for tending the garden." The solution would seem simple: start with a small garden, and stop expanding the minute it becomes more work than fun. Unfortunately, it seems to be just as difficult for an avid gardener to resist setting more plants, as it is for a compulsive eater to go on a diet, or a gambler to give up cards. Tempting new varieties beg to be grown, and the perennials already in the ground must be divided regularly. Who is hard-hearted enough to throw away beautiful surplus plants? It is easy for most of us to decide that a little more lawn must go, to make room for expanding plantings, but hard to find the time to properly maintain it all.

There is no need to replant perennials each year, but they do require a certain amount of regular care and attention if they're going to prosper over time. We often hear our customers state emphatically that annuals are too much trouble: "I want to put in perennials so I won't need to bother with them once they're planted." The implication is that perennials, like roadside trees, will pretty much care for themselves year after year, but this is not the case. Most gardeners spend a lot of time mulching, weeding, deadheading (removing faded blooms), dividing, watering, feeding, coping with insects and disease, and getting the garden ready for winter. Although low-maintenance plants, such as hostas, peonies, and daylilies, need little attention if they have been placed in an ideal spot, even these are not completely care-free.

Whatever your plans for a garden may be, let quality rather than quantity be your guide, especially if you have no plans to hire a staff of professional gardeners!

CHOOSING THE SPOT

Part of the fun of designing a garden is uniting your chosen plants with a unique location. No other garden in the world will be exactly like yours because the design of your home, the natural features of the landscape, and the surrounding vistas will make it distinctive. Even if you live in a city and have little or no choice of garden sites, you can still create a garden that has a character all its own.

If your lot is bare—no trees, pool, hedges, or shrubs there already—you will be able to plan a garden with greater freedom. When such things are already installed, you should choose new plantings that will complement what is already there. A perennial bed always looks best if it relates well in size and design to the buildings and other plantings near it.

Certain spots are natural for a flowering border, so look at fences, walls, hedges, walkways, driveways, terraces, buildings, a brook, a pool, specimen trees, or other defined "edges" that could be used as boundaries. One of our borders snuggles up against a tall clipped arborvitae hedge that surrounds our backyard, and another smaller border lies comfortably alongside an old barn. Take advantage of whatever you've got.

If all gardens followed the example of formal European borders, it would seem that the only place for a perennial bed is a lawn that is as large and level as a ballroom floor. That kind of area can serve as the setting for a magnificent garden, but most of us are neither so ambitious, nor so fortunate, as to garden under such conditions. As the Japanese have demonstrated so well, gardens can fit nearly any available space. Use your imagination, and you may find your grounds are ideal for a colorful flower island, a garden path, a hillside rock garden, a fern bower in the woods, or a tiny cottage garden planted entirely with old-fashioned colonial plants clustered around the back door.

Since flowering perennials need practically full sun throughout the day, choose a sunny spot if you want a wide range of plants to thrive. Ideally, a perennial garden will continue to grow for years in the same location, so make a note not only of present light conditions, but also try to anticipate what may happen in the future. If you or your close neighbors have young trees growing nearby, the amount of shade will increase as they grow, and some pruning, or perhaps complete removal, of trees will be necessary to ensure adequate sunlight for continued good growth and flowering of your perennials. Future growth is hard to predict, however. We have relatives who saw their beautiful backyard garden wither away in deep shade when a six-story apartment building replaced the small house next door. It is interesting to note as well that certain flowers tend to face the source of light when they are planted in a garden that is shaded for part of the day. Daffodils, most daisy-type flowers, pansies, violas, members of the sunflower family, and spiky flowers such as penstemon all have this habit, so if you plan to grow more than a few of these, position your garden to take best advantage of this tendency.

Good soil is basic to a fine garden, but if the site you choose is not blessed with the best, you can either improve it, or grow only those plants that will tolerate your conditions. For instance, water-loving plants may be planted in wet spots; rock garden or desert-type plants prefer dry, gravelly soil. A more complete discussion on soils and soil improvements can be found in chapter 4.

Whenever possible, avoid placing plants too close to trees and shrubs, not only because of the shade, but also because their large roots will creep into your beds and rob your plants of nutrients and moisture. It may be difficult to gauge what an adequate distance will be since the roots of a large shade tree can extend 100 feet or more from the trunk. It *is* possible to garden near trees, large hedges, and shrubs if the lot gets plenty of sun, and if you provide enough fertilizer and water so that both your garden and the larger plants will be nourished. Some gardeners bury a metal or concrete barrier 2 or more feet deep between a newly planted hedge or shrub border and the garden to keep the roots from venturing where they are not wanted.

If wind is a problem where you live, choose a sheltered spot for your perennials, or create a protected area with hedges or fences. We are pleased with the 7-foot evergreen hedge that serves as our back border because it allows us to grow tall and fragile plants such as delphinium, hollyhocks, and Oriental poppies even on our windy hilltop. A basket weave or picket fence will also offer protection, but unless the confined area is tiny, a tight board fence or one made of fiberglass panels can create powerful downdrafts and cause winds to swirl among the plants, which can inflict as much damage as a direct gale.

Positioning Perennials

The concept of clumping is basic to good garden design. When each plant grows separately and does not touch its neighbor, the garden has an orderly look, and each plant is allowed to reach its full potential. To create the masses of color and the shapes that make perennial borders so attractive, plant clumps of the same variety at intervals throughout the garden. The eye of the observer is drawn from one to the next and a pattern is created. One large peony, shasta daisy, or lupine clump is often large enough to establish a block or mass of the same color and height; but with smaller plants, such as *Primula* (primrose) and *Heuchera* (coral bells), three, five, or even seven may be used. Odd numbers seem to work best in garden design.

When spacing the plants allow plenty of room for the healthy expansion of each clump so that it will not impinge on neighboring plants. This takes some discipline because we all have a tendency to put new small plants too close together. It is difficult to know the amount of space a mature plant will need because each one grows so differently, but as a rule allow at least 1 foot between every plant in a clump, and 2 or more feet between each clump. One vigorous-growing plant, such as daylily, peony, or gloriosa daisy, may fill an area 3 or 4 feet in diameter within just a couple of years. After a few years of gardening experience, you will be better able to judge how plants grow in your locality, and can decide with assurance how far apart each should be planted.

Even with generous spacing most perennials will need to be divided from time to time and the clumps reduced to a manageable size. Overgrown gardens not only appear messy and lose their charm, but even more important, plants that are crowded do not grow or blossom well.

PLANT SIZE

Common sense dictates that plants must be arranged according to height, so that plants such as sweet William and pansies will not be completely hidden behind a tall clump of foxglove. We have met gardeners so impressed by this reasoning that their borders are rigidly arranged according to height: tall plants in the back row, medium-sized ones in the middle, and low-growing ones in front. They plant island gardens the same way, in tiers like a wedding cake, with the tallest plants in the center. But such inflexible arrangements seem almost artificial. A garden is more pleasing to the eye if plants of different heights, colors, and varieties are arranged as if they're growing naturally throughout the garden. An irregular arrangement of heights is made easier and more attractive by the fact that perennials bloom at different times. You can place a Blue Fountain delphinium near the front of a bed with the confidence that it will have finished blooming and can be cut

---

TALL-GROWING PLANTS

Certain varieties of these plants grow to 4 feet or more.

Aconitum, monkshood
Althaea rosea, hollyhock
Aster
Astilbe, spirea
Boltonia, starwort
Campanula pyramidalis, chimney bellflower
Cassia marilandica, senna
Cimicifuga, bugbane
Delphinium
Digitalis, foxglove
Echinops, globe thistle
Eremurus, desert candle
Eupatorium purpureum, Joe Pye-weed
Helenium autumnale, sneezeweed
Hemerocallis, daylily (especially *Altissima* hybrids)
Hibiscus, rose mallow
Inula helenium, elecampane
Lilium, lily (Black Dragon, Burgundy, Copper King, Moonlight, Sentinel, and others)
Macleaya cordata, plume poppy
Rudbeckia laciniata, golden glow
Thalictrum, meadowrue
Valeriana officinalis, valerian

DWARF PLANTS

The following grow to a maximum height of less than 1 foot.

Ajuga reptans, bugleweed
Alchemilla, lady's mantle
Alyssum saxatile compactum, dwarf goldentuft
Arabis alpina, alpine rockcress
Armeria, thrift
Bellis perennis, English daisy
Campanula carpatica, Carpathian bellflower
Cerastium tomentosum, snow-in-summer
Ceratostigma plumbaginoides, Larpente plumbago
Dianthus barbatus, dwarf sweet William
D. plumaris, grass pink
Dicentra eximia, fernleaf bleeding-heart
Dryas
Festuca glauca, blue fescue
Filipendula hexapetala, dropwort
Geum, avens
Heuchera sanguinea, coral bells
Iberis sempervirens, candytuft
Iris pumila, dwarf iris
Nepeta mussinii, flowering catmint
Papaver nudicaule, Iceland poppy
Phlox subulata, moss pink
Primula, primrose
Sedum, stonecrop
Tunica saxifraga, saxifrage tunic flower
Veronica incana, wooly speedwell
V. rupestris, rock speedwell
Vinca minor, myrtle, periwinkle

back before the shorter penstemon behind it starts to flower.

Figuring heights as you design the garden is a tricky business, even for an experienced gardener. Often the different varieties of one species grow to varying heights, and identical varieties may also grow to different sizes, depending on the particular soil, light conditions, and climate. You'll find that plant descriptions should be used only as guides. The plants may behave quite differently given the conditions in your garden.

FLOWERING TIMES

The sequence of bloom is a major factor in the design of a perennial garden since it is hoped that there will be blossoms throughout the bed from early spring until fall frosts, unless a seasonal garden is planned. Most perennials bloom for only a limited period in their annual life cycle, so both new gardeners and long-time horticulturists complain of "gaps" when the garden produces few, if any, flowers.

Just as it is difficult to estimate the height of perennials, it is also hard to tell exactly when each species will blossom. Various soils, light conditions, and climate variations can cause identical plants to flower at different times. In addition, identical plants may behave differently from one year to the next. A warm spring may accelerate the blooms, or an unexpected late winter or cool spring is likely to delay the flowering period. In our short growing season, spring often arrives late, and some years the daffodils, *Doronicum, Pulmonaria*, and tulips all bloom at the same time along with the lilacs and apple trees.

Although charts are useful as broad guidelines, the expertise of neighboring gardeners will be more precise and valuable. After a season or two of observing perennial plants in your area you will better understand how they are likely to behave in your garden. Even so, like us, you will probably shuffle plants around for as long as you grow perennials in order to achieve a satisfying design and attractive garden appearance. We keep a notebook handy to record not only blooming times, but also plant heights and combinations that we like. We place plastic tags or signs next to those that are to be moved when the time is right. Each spring we get plenty of exercise rearranging our plants.

PLANT SIZE AND BLOSSOM CONSIDERATIONS

A garden is easier to plan if you first select a few basic or accent plants for each of the four blooming seasons outlined below. Accent plants are those prominent perennials that form the backbone of your display—strong growers that are durable, have attractive blooms, and furnish interesting foliage for most of the season. You can plant your entire garden with such plants, of course, but most growers like to set some of the smaller, less robust plants among the stronger growers to supply additional beauty and interest to the garden. The accents may even find a special place in your heart. One lady we knew gave individual names to each of her favorites and would sometimes call our nursery to ask why 'Lady Macbeth' and 'Don Quixote' weren't doing well.

If you are unsure of the best choices for accent plants in a new garden, the following list may help.

Spring Bloomers

Tall

Aquilegia, columbine
Dicentra spectabilis, common bleeding-heart
Doronicum, leopard's bane
Iris sibirica, Siberian iris

Medium

Dicentra eximia, fernleaf bleeding-heart
Dianthus barbatus, sweet William
Hemerocallis, daylily; early varieties

Short

Phlox subulata, moss pink
Viola, violet

Early Summer

Tall

Delphinium
Iris germanica, German iris
Lupinus, lupine
Paeonia, peony

Medium

Anthemis, golden marguerite
Campanula, bellflower
Centaurea, cornflower
Chrysanthemum coccineum, pyrethrum
Hemerocallis, daylily
Lilium, lily
Penstemon, beardtongue

Short

Bellis, English daisy
Campanula carpatica, Carpathian bellflower
Heuchera, coral bells

Mid- to Late Summer

Tall

Aconitum, monkshood
Echinops, globe thistle
Gypsophila, baby's-breath
Hemerocallis, daylily
Hosta
Liatris
Lythrum
Monarda, bee balm
Phlox

Medium

Astilbe, spirea
Chrysanthemum maximum, shasta daisy
Gaillardia, blanketflower
Lychnis, campion

Kniphofia, tritoma
Rudbeckia, coneflower

Short

Geranium, crane's bill
Limonium, sea lavender
Platycodon, balloon flower
Stokesia, Stokes' aster
Stachys, betony

Late Summer and Fall

Tall

Anemone japonica, Japanese anemone
Aster
Hibiscus, rose mallow
Salvia, sage

Medium

Chelone, turtlehead
Chrysanthemum

Short

Aster, dwarf varieties
Chrysanthemum, dwarf varieties
Sedum

ANNUALS IN THE PERENNIAL GARDEN

Many gardeners plant annuals (bedding plants) to provide bloom throughout the season in their perennial beds. They are handy as "fillers" among the sparse plants in a new bed and provide additional color during times when perennials are not blooming in an established bed. We also use them to fill the bare spots left after the spring bulbs have bloomed and died down.

Most gardeners plant started annuals rather than seeds because they begin to bloom soon after being set out. Unless they are used as an edging, annuals should be clumped like perennials and given lots of space so they will be able to grow to their full beauty without crowding. Ten to 12 inches apart is seldom too much and large-growing types, such as *Cleome* or 'Crackerjack' marigolds, need even more room.

Choose annuals with heights and colors that will complement the established perennials in your garden. A single color is most effective, but if you mix them, choose colors that are compatible. Annual blossoms must be picked as soon as they fade or they will go to seed and stop blooming. Petunias need this treatment on a daily basis, but others, such as impatiens and marigolds, need less frequent attention.

PLAN A SUCCESSION OF BLOOM

The blooming times noted here are for zones 5 and 6. If you garden in a warmer or colder zone, the plants will bloom at different times, and you will need to adjust the schedule accordingly. Check with experienced local gardeners or nurserymen to find out when the plants in each category are likely to blossom. In our zone-3 climate, for example, almost nothing blooms until May, and all spring- and early-summer-blooming perennials flower a few weeks later than noted in the list. By midsummer the long days have enabled most of the summer- and fall-blossoming perennials to catch up, so their flowers appear in the North at nearly the same time as they do further south.

Plants marked with an asterisk are especially good choices for beginning gardeners because they are easy to grow and are desirable in the border. Some are extremely vigorous, however, and must be kept under control (see the section on weedy plants, pages 6–7, chapter 1). Note too, that some species, such as *Veronica*, include many varieties that may bloom at different times.

Perennials That Bloom Over a Long Season

Campanula carpatica, Carpathian bellflower
Centaurea montana, mountain bluet
 Coreopsis grandiflora, tickseed
 Dianthus latifolius, long-blooming sweet William
Dicentra eximia, fernleaf bleeding-heart
Gaillardia aristata, blanketflower
Heuchera sanguinea, coral bells
 Kniphofia uvaria, torch lily
 Myosotis alpestris, alpine forget-me-not
 Physostegia virginiana, false dragonhead
Viola cornuta, horned violet

February/March

Crocus angustifolius, crocus
 Eranthis hyemalis, winter aconite
 Erica carnea, spring heath
 Helleborus, Christmas rose
 Iris reticulata, netted iris
Narcissus, daffodil, jonquil, narcissus
 Scilla siberica, squill

April

 Ajuga reptans, bugleweed
 Alyssum saxatile, goldentuft
Aquilegia, columbine
 Arabis alpina, rockcress
 Aubrieta deltoidea, purple rockcress
Bellis perennis, English daisy
 Caltha palustris, cowslip, marsh marigold
Centaurea montana, mountain bluet

Dicentra eximia, fernleaf bleeding-heart
D. spectabilis, bleeding-heart
 Euphorbia polychroma, spurge
Iberis sempervirens, candytuft
 Iris chamaeiris, Crimean iris
 Mertensia virginica, Virginia bluebells
Nepeta mussinii, flowering catmint
Papaver nudicaule, Iceland poppy
 Phlox divaricata, blue phlox
Phlox subulata, moss pink
Primula, primrose
 Saxifraga cordifolia, saxifrage
 Thalictrum dioicum, meadowrue
 Veronica pectinata, early veronica, speedwell
Viola, violet, pansy

May

 Achillea tomentosa, wooly yarrow
 Actaea, baneberry
 Ajuga reptans, bugleweed
 Armeria, thrift
 Aurinia saxatilis, goldentuft
 Asperula odorata, sweet woodruff
 Aster alpinus, mountain aster
Bellis perennis, English daisy
 Cerastium tomentosum, snow-in-summer
Chrysanthemum coccineum, pyrethrum, painted daisy
Convallaria majalis, lily-of-the-valley
Dianthus barbatus, sweet William
 D. plumarius, grass pink
Dicentra, bleeding-heart
Doronicum, leopard's bane
 Epimedium, bishop's hat
 Euphorbia cyparissias, spurge
Geranium, crane's bill
Helenium, sneezeweed
 Hesperis, sweet rocket
Iberis sempervirens, candytuft
Iris, bearded iris
 Linum perenne, flax
Lupinus, lupine
 Lychnis chalcedonica, Maltese cross
 Malva moschata, musk mallow
Mertensia virginica, Virginia bluebells
Nepeta mussinii, flowering catmint
 Paeonia suffruticosa, tree peony
 Polemonium caeruleum, Jacob's ladder
Primula, primrose
 Ranunculus repens, dwarf buttercup
 Saxifraga, saxifrage
 Sedum, stonecrop
 Thymus, thyme

Trollius, globeflower
Veronica, speedwell
Viola, violet, pansy

June

Achillea tomentosa, wooly yarrow
Althaea rosea, hollyhock
Alyssum rostratum, yellowhead alyssum
Asclepias tuberosa, butterfly weed
Callirhoë involucrata, poppy mallow
Campanula, bellflower
Chrysanthemum coccineum, pyrethrum, painted daisy
Coronilla, crownvetch
Delphinium, larkspur
Dianthus barbatus, sweet William
Dictamnus, gas plant
Digitalis, foxglove
Echinops ritro, globe thistle
Erodium manescavii, heron's bill
Geum, avens
Gypsophila, baby's-breath
Hemerocallis, daylily
Heuchera, coral bells
*Iris
Lychnis, campion
Lythrum, loosestrife
Monarda, bee balm
Paeonia, peony
Papaver, Iceland and Oriental poppy
Penstemon, beardtongue
Thermopsis, false lupine
Veronica, speedwell

July

Achillea, yarrow
Aconitum, monkshood
Adenophora confusa, ladybells
Althaea rosea, hollyhock
Anchusa italica, bugloss
Anthemis, yellow daisy
Aruncus sylvester, goat's beard
Chrysanthemum coccineum, pyrethrum, painted daisy
C. maximum, shasta daisy
Delphinium, larkspur
Digitalis, foxglove
Filipendula ulmaria, meadowsweet
Gaillardia, blanketflower
Geum, avens
Hemerocallis, daylily
Lychnis, campion
Penstemon, beardtongue
Phlox maculata, 'Miss Lingard'
Platycodon, balloon flower
Scabiosa caucasica, Caucasian scabious

Stokesia, Stokes' aster
Tradescantia virginiana, spiderwort
Veronica, speedwell

August

Anthemis, yellow daisy
Artemisia, silvermound
Boltonia
Chelone, turtlehead
Cimicifuga, bugbane
Coreopsis grandiflora, tickseed
Gypsophila, baby's-breath
Helenium, sneezeweed
Heliopsis, false sunflower
Hibiscus moscheutos, rose mallow
Hosta, plantainlily
Liatris, gayfeather
Linum, flax
Lobelia, cardinal flower
Macleaya cordata, plume poppy
Monarda, bee balm
Phlox paniculata, border phlox
Physostegia, false dragonhead
Platycodon, balloon flower
Scabiosa, pincushion flower, scabious
Veronica, speedwell

September

Aconitum autumnale, autumn monkshood
Anemone japonica, Japanese anemone
Artemisia lactiflora, white mugwort
*Aster
Boltonia, false starwort
Chelone, turtlehead
*Chrysanthemum
Cimicifuga, bugbane
Echinacea purpurea, purple coneflower
Eupatorium, mistflower
Gaillardia aristata, blanketflower
Helenium, sneezeweed
Helianthus, sunflower
Heliopsis, false sunflower
Hibiscus, rose mallow
Lathyrus, flowering pea
Liatris, gayfeather
Lobelia, cardinal flower
Phlox paniculata, border phlox
Physostegia, false dragonhead
Rudbeckia, gloriosa daisy
Salvia, sage
Sedum, stonecrop
Stokesia, Stokes' aster
Veronica, speedwell

Annuals, like newly planted perennials, need more watering in dry periods because their roots do not go as deep as those of established perennials, and they may need occasional applications of a liquid fertilizer or manure tea (an explanation of which appears on page 59).

There are plenty of annuals available in innumerable colors, shapes, and sizes. We tuck in asters, bachelor buttons, calendulas, zinnias, and many others to provide color throughout the summer. Annual alyssum and dwarf marigolds are attractive when planted as a low-growing edging. We often use marigolds as fillers because they need less deadheading than most other annuals and are good for repelling insects from the garden. Petunias are beautiful in planters and in large beds of a single variety, but they are not our first choice in the perennial bed because, as we mentioned, they stop blossoming almost immediately if the faded blossoms are not picked frequently. *Pelargoniums* (geraniums) brighten up a border nicely when used as annuals although they are actually tender perennials. *Cleome* and *Lavatera*, which grow up to 3 feet in height, make striking accent plants as well as fillers.

Even though our border is filled to overflowing with perennial clumps each spring, we always move out a few plants to make room for several flats of colorful, long-blooming annuals. Our garden seems incomplete without them.

FOLIAGE

Blossoms in a garden, just as in a bouquet of cut flowers, seem barren without a background of attractive foliage. Hedges and shrubs make effective backdrops, and masses of green within the garden serve to separate the different colors of flowering plants. Clumps of various leafy textures add beauty, too, when the plants are not in bloom. Greens are predominant in most gardens, and the gray foliage plants such as silvermound or lamb's ears (*Stachys*) can also be used to provide striking contrast. A few perennials have variegated leaves or foliage in red, blue, or yellow hues. Certain plants, such as hosta, are grown more for their interesting foliage than their flowers, as are annuals like coleus and *Caladium*, which is a tuberous plant. Ornamental grasses with unusual textures, colors, and shapes are also widely planted.

Some plants with "golden" foliage (hostas are an example) and perennial grasses with variegated leaves appear to be sick and undernourished unless they are used skillfully. Always put in more than one plant of each variety to indicate that the planting is deliberate, and separate each grouping of such plants with those of green foliage for contrast. The massive blue-leaved hostas, for example, are much more striking when interplanted with the green-leaved varieties.

When we first started gardening, we chose our perennials primarily because we liked their blooms. Now we consider plants for the appearance of their foliage as well. Many form clumps with interesting and attractive leaves. Even when there are few or no flowers, the masses of lacy, delicate maidenhair fern, rubbery sedums, and sturdy *Rudbeckia* contrast nicely with the spiky foliage of the iris and daylilies. The foliage clumps of massive peonies and lupines are quite unlike the shapes and textures of phlox and the tall globe thistle. Although we enjoy their blossoms in season, we have also discovered that the widely different leaf clumps of the mounded crane's bill (*Geranium*), the speckled lungwort (*Pulmonaria*), and the scalloped coral bells (*Heuchera*) all make beautiful front-of-the-border plants throughout the summer. A seasoned gardener, like a stage director or artist, gives attention to the mood created by the *background* of the scene.

HOW BEST TO USE COLOR

As in interior decoration colors can be used to create special effects and moods. Blue, green, white, and pale shades of lavender and yellow are cool colors; orange, red, and bright yellows are warm. Red and other vibrant colors make a display of perennials seem closer than it is, and can create the illusion that the garden is larger. Blues, on the other hand, make a garden appear smaller and more distant.

Our perception of each color changes according to whatever shades surround it and, of course, according to the amount and quality of lighting it receives. Plants can look quite different in sunlight than they do in shade. Bright hues appear less brilliant on a sunny day than on a cloudy one, and colors seem to change considerably, no matter what the weather, from morning, to high noon, to the dusk of evening.

A bed of annuals is easy to arrange according to color because the same plants stay in bloom all season, but in a perennial border the colors constantly change as different plants come into blossom. It would seem challenging enough to design a perennial garden that appears full of bloom throughout the season, while keeping plants of different heights from obscuring each other. But we should, in addition, arrange the plants so their colors remain harmonious even though the blossoms change from week to week!

It has been said that Mother Nature can throw together flowers of any color and they don't clash as they would in a man-made environment. In our early gardening days we took those words to heart and paid no attention to the color scheme of the garden. We planted bright orange and pink lilies side by side, and seed mixtures with a jumble of reds, oranges, and yellows. As we visited gardens that had been color coordinated, however, it became obvious that our capricious methods were not the best. Even in nature colors clash. Gardens that have been planted in thoughtful color combinations have an overall beauty that a hodgepodge can't match. If you have any doubts, take a color photo of both types of borders and compare them.

In a color-coordinated garden the clumps of each color group should not only be of the same variety but also the same shade, rather than a mixture of shades. A dozen pink *Primula* planted together, for example, have a more impressive visual impact than a multicolored clump. The validity of this concept is obvious in parks where large beds of the same varieties of geraniums, petunias, or marigolds are so effective.

When you have chosen the colors for each grouping arrange them so they don't clash with their surroundings. A simple way to do this is to use white flowers as mediators—they will "cool" and separate the brilliant shades. Masses of white also make bright colors appear even brighter and create the illusion that the bed is larger than it is.

To achieve a harmonious color design your good sense will often tell you what goes best with what, or, like Gertrude Jekyll, the great English gardener and writer, you can scientifically plan the bed according to the color spectrum. Nearly a century ago she established an enduring reputation as the leading authority on color by creating long color masses in her huge gardens which she termed "drifts." Using the spectrum, she arranged the reds followed by orange, yellow, blue, and violet. She never planted primary colors side by side, but separated each with paler shades of the same color or white so that each led into the next without a sharp contrast. One way to use this concept in a border is to plant the blue/purple/violet flowers at one end, followed by increasingly pale shades of blue; then pale yellows, bright yellows, pale yellows, bright oranges, pale oranges, red-oranges, and bright reds.

To include the entire color spectrum a garden would need to be large, and most of us obviously cannot duplicate Miss Jekyll's 300-foot-long, 14-foot-wide borders (or afford her seventeen assistants!). For a smaller version, choose whichever parts of the spectrum appeal to you. Position pale colors to flow into vivid, then progress back to pale or white shades. The drifts do not need to be huge to be effective, but if drifts of more than two colors are used, they should be proportionate to each other and to the garden as a whole.

Our own border is small with a large variety of plants, so like most gardeners, we cannot use the color drifts that Jekyll recommends. We modify her methods by separating the clumps of more vivid hues with groupings of white or pale-colored flowers in the same part of the color spectrum. Farther along the border we try to duplicate a similar grouping of the same plants. Thus, when the eye falls on one group of red sweet William it is drawn along to an identical group farther on, and then another in a continuing scheme throughout the garden.

The symmetry of such a planting should not be as repetitive as a wallpaper pattern, but orderly enough so the design provides continuity. Showy accent plants such as deep blue delphinium, bright-red Russell's hybrid lupine, gloriosa daisy, or others of special size, brilliance, or beauty make good focus plants, and the smaller plants with more subtle shades can be interspersed among them.

Color in Seasonal Gardens

Seasonal gardens are much easier to design with color in mind since you do not need a lot of space for great numbers of plants that will blossom throughout the season. Spring tulips, for instance, are especially attractive when grouped in a mass of a single eye-catching color. In our community some residents who only spend August here have a garden filled entirely with brightly colored phlox that are separated by clumps of phlox in paler shades or white. It makes a beautiful sight. We've seen other gardens planted entirely with two or three colors of chrysanthemums or with lilies.

Color Gardens

Once we had the pleasure of helping an elderly lady with her gardening chores for the summer. Of her several small perennial gardens, her special favorite was a blue and white border enclosed by a low stone wall. Delphinium provided accent points at the corners, and masses of *Polemonium*, campanula, *Cerastium*, iris, shasta daisy, hosta, *Iberis*, and others bloomed at various times throughout the spring, summer, and fall. Since that pleasant introduction to a color garden we have admired many other effective beds created with a single color such as pink, red, yellow, or blue, combined with white. Some were planned with the gardener's favorite color in mind, and others with colors that complemented their backgrounds—an aging shed of weathered boards, a tall stone foundation where a barn once stood, a sheared evergreen hedge, a wooden fence, or a reflecting pool.

Since blue flowers are scarce, and therefore particularly prized, we list some of the most common here. Note that we have also included a list of white-flowered plants to be used in combination with brightly colored ones. Check out each variety before you plant it to be sure it's the shade you prefer since colors vary greatly even within the same species. Some of these plants are, of course, available in many other colors.

Blue-Flowered Plants

Anchusa italica, bugloss
Aquilegia caerulea, blue columbine
Aster
Baptisia, wild indigo
Campanula, bellflower
Centaurea montana, mountain bluet
Ceratostigma, plumbago
Delphinium
Echinops, globe thistle
Eryngium, sea holly
Hosta, plantainlily
Iris
Linum, flax
Lobelia, cardinal flower
Lupinus, lupine
Mertensia, Virginia bluebells
Myosotis, forget-me-not
Nepeta mussinii, flowering catmint
Polemonium, Jacob's ladder
Pulmonaria, lungwort
Scabiosa
Tradescantia, spiderwort
Veronica, speedwell

White-Flowered Plants

Achillea, yarrow
Althaea rosea, hollyhock
Anemone japonica, Japanese anemone
Aquilegia, columbine
Arabis, rockcress

Aster
Campanula, bellflower
Cerastium, snow-in-summer
Chrysanthemum maximum, shasta daisy
Clematis
Delphinium
Filipendula, meadowsweet
Gypsophila, baby's-breath
Hibiscus, rose mallow
Hosta, plantainlily
Iberis, candytuft
Iris
Lysimachia, loosestrife
Paeonia, peony
Phlox
Papaver orientale, Oriental poppy
Valerian
Yucca

DESIGNING THE GARDEN ON PAPER

If arranging the plants tastefully according to height, bloom sequence, and color seems puzzling, treat it like a game. Designing a plant chart can be as much fun for the gardener as doing a crossword puzzle, and the results are much longer lasting. It can simplify the buying process, pinpoint potential mistakes, and speed up planting because you avoid last-minute decision making in the spring. The chart also provides a permanent record of your garden, and by making notes on it throughout the summer you can correct any errors of the previous season when you redo it the following winter.

The first step is to list all the perennials you intend to grow according to their blooming season. Next, divide each of these blooming categories into color groups, and you're ready to begin.

One way to construct a garden plan is to use cutouts of appropriately colored paper to represent each plant grouping or large clump. Place a coded number on each indicating its height and a letter designating the blooming period. Lay out these pieces on graph paper and move them around, trying out various combinations. When you are satisfied, paste the pieces in place and you'll have an accurate planting chart.

Another method, especially good for large borders, is to set up your garden blueprint as follows. 1.) On a sheet of graph paper sketch in "plots" where your

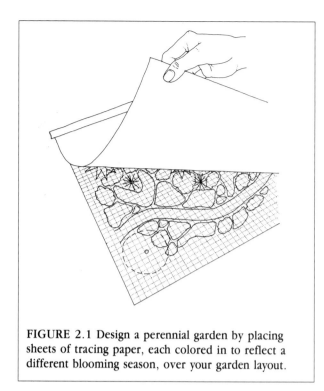

FIGURE 2.1 Design a perennial garden by placing sheets of tracing paper, each colored in to reflect a different blooming season, over your garden layout.

plants will grow. Allow 2 to 3 feet for each ordinary-sized clump and 3 or more feet for each large accent clump. 2.) Tape tracing paper over the garden plots and draw in specific plant locations. Make four such tracings; mark one for April/May, one for June/July, one for August/September, and another for October until frost. 3.) Use the tracing paper overlays to fill in each chart with the plants that bloom that season, arranged according to height and color combination, until each plot is filled. 4.) Combine all the seasonal plantings in one chart. They will not overlap, and you'll have a clear plan for planting. See Figure 2.1 for a better idea of how this method works.

When a garden is planted haphazardly, without design or blueprint, the results can be disappointing. Colors will probably clash, and plants positioned too close together will keep small plants hidden behind their tall neighbors. An evening at the drawing board can net beautiful dividends in your garden, save lame excuses to fellow gardeners, and prevent some future backaches.

3

Soils and How to Improve Them

When we were growing up we often heard the proverb, "Well begun is half done." This bit of wisdom can be applied to any type of garden, but it is particularly fitting for a perennial bed which is expected to last for years without annual tilling and replanting.

If you're lucky, the location you choose for your perennials will be covered with rich topsoil. But it is more likely that you'll be faced with converting a grassy lawn, former hay field, sand dune, or other challenging site into a perennial bed. If it is covered with grass and weeds you must get rid of the green tops and weed roots before you plant or you will be confronted with a monumental weeding task forever after.

Because most perennials develop huge root systems, a deep, rich, lightweight soil is necessary if they are to thrive. If the soil in the spot you have chosen for your garden is poor, worn out, and lacks humus and nutrients, the perennials will probably struggle, and never achieve the results you want. Moist, well-drained soil is recommended for growing most perennials. The earth should never dry out completely, nor be soggy for extended periods. A gardener's dream soil is a deep, light loam well supplied with moisture-retaining humus. Sandy soils dry out too quickly, which causes the plants to suffer from lack of moisture; heavy, wet soils compact easily and force out the air that is necessary for good root growth.

Dig up a spadeful or two of your topsoil and squeeze it with your hands. Does it feel like model-ing clay or does it slide, like sand, through your fingers? Hopefully its texture will be somewhere between the two, with particles of mineral matter, such as sand, mixed with organic matter, to create a light, spongelike material when moist. If you are uncertain about its quality ask a successful gardening friend to examine your soil and help you decide whether it is in good shape for planting or needs improvement.

The basic formula that nurserymen use for the soil mixture in pots and containers is one-third (by volume) each of humus, sand, and ordinary soil. Garden soil ideally contains a similar proportion: one-third each of fertile humus, sand, and fine clay particles.

PREPARING THE BED

Although a garden can be started from scratch in the spring, the ideal time to prepare a new bed is in early fall. By tilling it deeply then and again in the spring you can eliminate most of the weeds before planting.

A small plot can be spaded up by hand, but for a large one you'll need to use a garden tractor or roto-tiller to break up the soil. Avoid using a large farm tractor, either to till or spread fertilizer, because heavy machinery compacts the soil nearly as much as a tiller loosens it. Since the root systems of many perennials grow deep, work the soil to a depth of at least 2 feet. Remove all weed roots and rocks at this time because

CLAY. Lighten heavy clay or clay-loam soil by tilling in sand. A large amount may be necessary if your soil is extremely heavy, and additional sand may be needed every few years as it gradually disappears into the subsoil. Humus is likely to be lacking in such soils. Add manure, peat moss, or compost, if necessary. It may also be helpful to grow a cover crop such as oats or rye for a season and till it into the soil before planting.

GRAVEL OR SANDY. Dry, light soil needs compost, manure, or peat moss in greater than normal amounts. Till in one or more cover crops, too. If you don't want to take the time to improve the soil in this way, or if it is in particularly bad condition, spread rich topsoil on the spot 6 to 12 inches deep and till it thoroughly.

SWAMPY WET. If there is low ground nearby consider draining the area with ditches or drain tile, then add sandy topsoil to raise the low-lying beds a foot or more. The easiest option, of course, is to leave the area as it is and grow some of the interesting plants that thrive in water or damp spots. See the section on water gardens (pages 84–87) for more information.

it will be much more difficult, if not impossible, to get rid of them after the garden has been planted.

Tilling in topsoil is the fastest way to remedy a bad soil condition, but obtaining good topsoil is difficult in many areas and it may be very expensive. Fortunately there are other methods. Our favorite takes time, but we feel the results justify the effort: till the site thoroughly in the fall and sow a cover crop of winter rye. The thickly planted grain stalks not only

choke out weeds, but add humus to the soil when it is tilled under in the spring. An alternative is to plant rye, buckwheat, oats, or millet in the spring, and till it under in the fall. A second tilling the following spring thoroughly pulverizes the soil and breaks down all the green material.

If your soil appears to be in good shape it may only need enriching with compost or manure. Simply apply the manure or compost after the first tilling, and till or spade it thoroughly until the sod is broken into fine particles and the humus is well mixed into the soil.

If your plot is not large, and you have time and a strong back, the old-fashioned "double dig" method is the best way to prepare the soil for a long-lasting perennial bed (see Figure 3.1). With a spade, at one end of the garden plot, dig a trench about 2 feet wide along the width of the bed, to a depth of 1 foot. Place the sod and soil on a sheet of plastic. Add to the hole a mixture of compost-manure or plain compost, and thoroughly mix this with the soil at the bottom to a depth of another foot. Then dig up the next 2-foot width. Place the sod from the second hole upside down into the first hole and spread over it a balanced dry organic or chemical fertilizer. Use 3 pounds for each 100 square feet of garden, or the equivalent of a 5-foot by 20-foot plot. Cover it with the remaining soil. Continue in the same manner throughout the garden and in the final hole place the sod and soil you had saved from the first dig.

Since heavy sod is difficult to spade or till you can save work by first covering the site with clear plastic to kill off any existing plant life. The sun will bake the plants under the plastic, as well as germinate and kill most of the dormant seeds, all within a few weeks. It is also possible to destroy the grass and

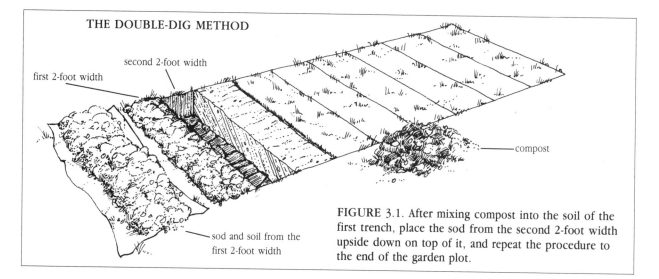

THE DOUBLE-DIG METHOD

second 2-foot width

first 2-foot width

compost

sod and soil from the first 2-foot width

FIGURE 3.1. After mixing compost into the soil of the first trench, place the sod from the second 2-foot width upside down on top of it, and repeat the procedure to the end of the garden plot.

weeds with an herbicide. Chemicals are fast and efficient, but unless you use the right products and application methods they can have a detrimental effect on the soil and be harmful to future plant life. If you opt for herbicides, ask your garden store or county agent which ones are currently recommended, read the label carefully, and follow the directions exactly.

Nutrients

Although improving the texture of the soil by the addition of humus is important we also have to be concerned with its fertility. At first, nothing could seem much duller than a discussion of soil nutrients, but try to think of them in the same way you'd think about a diet for yourself. Without good nourishment your health would suffer; plants have the same problem when they are not fed properly. Although some people would advise you to plant your perennial garden first and fertilize it later, it is far better to have plenty of nutrients mixed throughout the soil initially so they will be available to each plant during all stages of its growth.

Whether you garden organically or rely on chemicals will determine which steps you take to improve the soil's fertility. Well-rotted farm manure and compost not only add humus, but like other organic fertilizers—kelp, fish emulsion, dried manure, and bonemeal—also supply nutrients. Manure often carries weed seeds, though, so it's best to let it sit for a year before adding it to the soil. Organic fertilizers are less likely than chemical fertilizers to "burn" the plants if you give them an overdose, but unless you have a good supply nearby, or gather your own materials, organic plant food is apt to cost more than the chemical kind. In addition, the nutrient value of organic products can vary widely. We prefer to use organic fertilizers, but sometimes find we have barely enough for our vegetable garden and orchard so we occasionally use chemical plant food on our perennials and ornamentals.

Chemical fertilizers contain nutrients that are absorbed by most plants in sufficient quantities, but many of them are so soluble that they leach away quickly in the soil. Therefore, subsequent applications throughout the season may be necessary. Determining the correct amount is tricky: when too much is applied the rapid availability of chemicals can cause the fertilizer to "burn" a plant (browning of the leaves) which stunts growth and often kills it outright. The stimulation of too much rapid growth can also produce weak, unhealthy plants that are susceptible to insects and diseases. In an attempt to overcome the problems of leaching and plant burn, manufacturers have developed a variety of slow-release fertilizers that safely provide food for the plants all summer with only one application in early spring. When using chemicals of any kind be sure to follow the directions exactly and remember that more is almost never better.

The primary elements needed for good plant growth are nitrogen (N), phosphorus (P), and potash (K). These three minerals are listed in the above order on the packages of chemical and natural fertilizers, both in dry and liquid forms. When a fertilizer label reads 5-8-10 it means that the fertilizer contains 5 percent nitrogen, 8 percent phosphorus, and 10 percent potash. The other 77 percent is inert filler. Dry fertilizers are often pelletized, which makes them easier to pour and spread.

Organic gardeners use manure and compost as basic soil conditioners. They supply humus and nutrients to the soil as well, but additional fertilizer is often necessary for successful plant growth. Many organic fertilizers, such as cottonseed meal, bloodmeal, and tankage (animal wastes from butcher shops), are used to supply nitrogen and other nutrients. Greensand, wood ashes, and granite dust provide potash; bonemeal and rock phosphate furnish phosphorus. Seaweed and fish oils are rich in the most necessary nutrients and also provide trace elements such as boron, manganese, and others that are necessary in minute amounts for good growth, but are occasionally lacking in worn-out soils. You can have a sample of your soil tested by your local extension service agent to see if it is deficient in these trace minerals. If you use manure, composted leaves, and similar materials, the small amount of trace minerals necessary should already be available to the plants.

If you use commercially dried cow or sheep manure, spread at least 10 pounds over each 100-square-foot plot (10 feet by 10 feet) before the final tilling. Farm manure in its natural state can be used safely in varying amounts, but since it has a much higher moisture content than dried manure, 100 pounds per 100 square feet is the recommended ratio. Poultry manure is richer, but it can "burn" plants and should be applied at only one-third of the above rate.

To prepare the soil in an existing garden to which you are adding new perennials (rather than establishing an entire garden bed), dig a large hole deep enough for each plant and add a shovelful of farm

FIGURE 3.2. The left side of this compost pile has been covered with lawn clippings and is "fermenting" while the right side is in use.

manure (or a cup of dried manure) to the bottom. Cover it with a thin layer of soil and then plant the perennial. Water thoroughly and fill in the rest of the hole with rich topsoil or compost.

Humus

Humus is partially decayed organic matter—it is the "life" of your soil. It stores moisture and nutrients, keeps the soil loose, allows aeration, and encourages the bacterial and earthworm activity necessary for healthy plant growth. Although setting a plant into a material that is 100 percent humus such as peat moss or rotted manure is not recommended, it is well known that a soil rich in humus will make perennials thrive. Homemade compost is an ideal source of humus, but if you don't have enough, the next best thing is to substitute a mixture of peat moss and manure. An organic mulch will also add a continuing supply of humus as it decays.

MAKING COMPOST

The words *compost pile* have a different meaning for each gardener. It can run the gamut from a heap of rotted wood shavings in a back corner of the yard, to a scientifically layered pile of various organic materials placed in an elaborate container made of wood, fiberglass, or cement blocks. Much has been written about how best to build a compost pile, and how to encourage the materials in it to rot faster without odor.

We use a simple method. Near our vegetable garden we have constructed two bins side by side, each 6 feet square, with cement blocks piled on three sides. Both are approximately 3 feet high. In one bin we alternate layers of organic material (table scraps, garden wastes, weeds, leaves, grass clippings) with layers of soil and layers of manure; and we keep it moist so the fermenting materials won't get too hot and allow valuable nitrogen to escape. Figure 3.2 shows this type of compost pile. The heap soon fills with earthworms, which help the materials to settle and decompose rapidly into a rich, black humus. As soon as one enclosure is filled we cover it with lawn clippings, let it rest until the composting process is completed, and start filling the second bin. It takes about a year for the materials to decompose, and if it isn't completely finished we dig compost out from the bottom.

SWEET OR SOUR SOIL?

If your soil is well supplied with organic matter and nutrients the plants will probably grow well, and soil acidity (pH) shouldn't be a concern. But if the soil is extremely acidic (sour) or alkaline (sweet), nutrients are "locked" into the soil and the plants may be unable to utilize them. If you suspect that the pH of your soil is at one extreme or the other, buy a small soil test kit and check it yourself, or ask your county extension agent about a test.

The pH scale chemically measures acidity on a scale

of 1 to 14 as shown in Figure 3.3. One is the most acid, 14 the most alkaline, and 7 is neutral. The mineral and organic matter present in the soil determine its pH. Soils containing aluminum, sulfur, iron, peat, decayed pine needles, or oak leaves are acidic. Those with calcium are more alkaline. Most perennials grow best in soil with a pH that ranges from 5.5 to 7, although heaths and heathers prefer one of 4.5 to 5, while delphinium and clematis favor a pH of nearly 7.

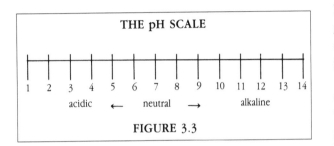

THE pH SCALE

1 2 3 4 5 6 7 8 9 10 11 12 13 14
acidic ← neutral → alkaline

FIGURE 3.3

To make acid soil more alkaline add 10 pounds of lime, or 20 pounds of wood ashes, per 100 square feet of soil to raise the pH one point. Since lime leaches away in the rain, you'll need to repeat the application every two or three years. When the pH has to be lowered add peat moss, cottonseed meal, sulfur, or an acid fertilizer of the type used for blueberries and azaleas. Three to 4 pounds of sulfur per 100 square feet will lower the pH one point.

Edgings

Just as important as the preparation of soil is the establishment of proper garden edgings. They are needed to protect the perennial bed from weeds which can invade the garden either by dropping seeds lifted in by the wind, or by sneaking their roots in subversively from the sides. Although airborne weed seeds are nearly impossible to keep out, edgings are a good way to check the growth of the root-penetrating kind. An edging serves other worthwhile purposes. It defines exactly what is garden and what is not, and gives a bed a finished appearance, often making the difference between a fine garden and a mediocre one.

Install an edging when you first prepare the bed. If you want a straight-edged border use a taut string tied to stakes at each end as a guide. An irregular or curved bed can be created by using a rope, clothesline, or garden hose in a similar way.

In many gardens the edging is simply a narrow strip of bare earth about 8 inches wide between the flowers and lawn. These were once very popular and the edging tool used to create them—a sharp blade on a straight handle—was an indispensable piece of equipment for the serious gardener. Such a cut-out edging is attractive, but because it must be recut frequently it is less used today.

Plastic, steel, or aluminum edgings take longer to install initially, but they make effective, long-lasting barriers. They are available at most hardware and garden stores, and can be bent easily to fit beds of any shape, which makes them useful for an island garden or a pathway, as well as for a straight border.

The depth of edging you need depends on the type of growth that surrounds your garden. A 4-inch depth will keep out shallow-rooted weeds and most lawn grasses, but 8 inches will do the job even better. Edgings that are 2 or more feet in depth are necessary to halt the deep-roving roots of shrubs and hedges. To install one—after marking the edge of the border—dig a ditch straight down to the necessary depth. Sink the edging vertically, but make sure the top edge is level with the soil so it won't be visible or interfere with mowing the lawn.

Many perennial beds are delineated with visible edgings, which are intended to add beauty to the garden. Bricks (placed either horizontally or at an angle), flagstones, paving blocks, tiles, concrete, wooden timbers, stone chips, and similar products are all used. If you decide to use a wood edging choose cypress, redwood, or another long-lasting type. Treat less durable woods with Cuprinol or another nontoxic preservative. Avoid using timbers such as railroad ties that have been soaked in creosote or other chemicals, such as Pentachlorophenol, that are toxic to plants.

Attractive edgings can also be made with living plants such as a low, tight hedge of dwarf shrubs, perennials, or annuals. Boxwood, barberry, ivy, lavender, *Pachysandra*, candytuft, thyme, thrift, alyssum, and alpine strawberry are often used as edgings, especially in large formal gardens. Though beautiful, they require more maintenance than an inanimate edging, and they are not effective in keeping out weed roots.

You will find that a well-planned and maintained edging gives a finished touch to a garden, much as the right frame or matting enhances a fine painting or photograph.

4

Planting the Perennial Garden

fter the bed is prepared and the edging in place you're ready for the fun—planting the perennials. To help transfer your design from graph paper to soil in the correct dimensions, you may want to use a bit of ordinary flour or garden lime to mark the spots where you will set the plants. A 50-foot metal measuring tape will help to measure lengthwise, and a short carpenter's folding rule works well to mark the distances from front to back.

You want to keep the soil loose to allow plant roots to grow easily, so try to compact it as little as possible when working in the garden, both at planting time and later. Don't walk on the soil unless necessary, especially when it is wet. You can reach into a narrow bed from the outside, but in a wide one you may want to lay down boards to absorb the pressure of your weight.

Be faithful to your plan and resist the temptation to fill up the bed quickly with easily available perennials that you may not like in the future. There is rarely any reason to do all your planting the same day; rather, do it in stages as you acquire new plants. Most newly planted borders look sparse, but if you want a full bed the first season stick in annual bedding plants as fillers.

Because potted perennials can be planted successfully throughout the season, it's best to buy the varieties you want in containers: they suffer no transplant shock because every root stays intact. Mail-order plants that are shipped bare rooted, and other bare-rooted perennials, are best planted during spring in northern zones so they will have time to become well established before winter. South of zone 5, either fall or spring planting is equally good.

Plants that are freshly dug from a nursery or a friend's garden can be moved easily in the spring, although most perennials can be transplanted all summer if they are handled carefully (see below). Those that go into a short, partly dormant period directly after blooming—bearded iris, bleeding-heart, peonies, Madonna lilies, *Doronicum*, and Oriental poppies, for instance—are best moved at that time. Fall is the ideal time for planting lilies and the early-blooming spring bulbs.

BARE-ROOTED PLANTS

When a bare-rooted plant arrives from a mail-order nursery the roots are usually covered with sphagnum moss or other moisture-retaining material. Unpack it immediately and if it looks dry soak it in a pail of water for a few minutes. Then plant it according to the enclosed directions. If you must wait a few days before planting store it in a cool, dark place in the packing material, but never leave it soaking in water for long periods.

Evenings or cloudy days are the best times to plant bare-rooted stock because it won't dry out quickly. Treat plants that are out of soil like fish out of water.

Always keep the roots covered with moist burlap or a wet towel to avoid the drying effects of sun or wind. Careless treatment of bare-rooted plants is responsible for more unnecessary casualties than all other poor planting techniques together!

When examining your new bare-rooted perennial, you'll notice that the roots extend from the top part known as the crown. Set the plant into the soil by positioning its roots according to their apparent growth habit, either by spreading them outward or downward (see Figure 4.1). Most perennials should be set at the same depth they were previously growing. It is easy to find this level if the old soil line is visible on the stem (or stems). If you aren't sure about the proper depth, arrange the plant so that the top of the root area—the bottom of the crown—is an inch below the soil. Notable exceptions to this rule are peonies and bearded iris. Set peonies so that the base of the red sprout on the uppermost part of the root is *not more* than three-quarters of an inch to an inch below the soil's surface. If it is deeper the plant will not produce flowers for many years. Since iris roots, too, must be barely covered for best results, set the crown at ground level.

Our favorite planting method is to dig a hole that is twice as large as the root ball with a spade or trowel; never try to squeeze the roots into a small hole. Mix a small amount of compost and a few tablespoons of manure with the soil you removed from the hole, and half fill the hole with water. This old-time practice—called "puddling"—assures that crucial moisture will reach the bottom of the roots, and is shown in Figure 4.2. Put a little of the soil you have prepared into the hole and set the plant into it. Finish filling the hole with the soil mix. The muddy mixture will force out any air pockets that might dry out the roots. Firm

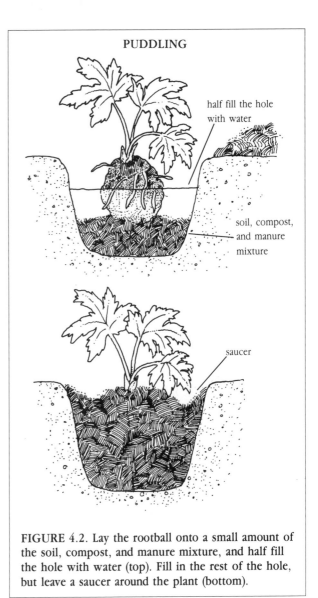

PUDDLING

half fill the hole with water

soil, compost, and manure mixture

saucer

FIGURE 4.2. Lay the rootball onto a small amount of the soil, compost, and manure mixture, and half fill the hole with water (top). Fill in the rest of the hole, but leave a saucer around the plant (bottom).

the soil carefully, but leave a slight depression, or saucer, around each plant to catch the rain and future waterings.

Not everyone uses the puddle method, preferring to simply set the plant in loosened soil and water it well. Whichever method you choose, create a saucer around each plant to assure that water will reach the roots, and tamp the soil firmly by stepping on it to ensure there will be no air pockets.

POTTED PLANTS

If the soil in the pot is dry, water it thoroughly so that the plant roots will be completely soaked. Dig a hole somewhat larger and deeper than the pot size to accommodate a compost and soil mix around the root ball that will encourage new root growth. Then proceed to plant.

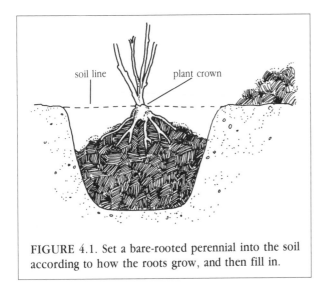

soil line   plant crown

FIGURE 4.1. Set a bare-rooted perennial into the soil according to how the roots grow, and then fill in.

Usually the plant will pop out of its container easily if you turn it over and tap it gently on the bottom, but if it sticks insert a knife around the edge, just as if you were taking a cake from its tin. Keep the root ball intact and set it in the hole so the top of the root ball is just beneath the surface of the soil.

Watering

Water both bare-rooted and potted plants immediately after planting. Add a bit of liquid seaweed, fish emulsion, manure, or liquid chemical fertilizer with the water to get the plant off to a fast start. After the initial watering, continue to water every day thereafter for a week or two, unless it rains hard. Once the plants are well established, water them only when the soil is dry.

Lupines serve as a good water register before and during their blooming period because, even though they have very deep roots, they are particularly sensitive to lack of water. You might want to plant a clump to provide a signal. When they begin to wilt, the garden needs watering.

MOVING DORMANT CLUMPS*

1.) Prepare a hole, as for potted a plant.
2.) Cut back tops to 2 inches.
3.) With spade or fork, cut vertically, deep into the soil, encircling the plant, and taking with it a good-sized ball of soil.
4.) Move clump to a new hole. If not planted immediately, keep the roots moist, and do not expose the clump to wind or sun.
5.) Once in place, treat as a potted plant.
* For summer transplanting, see pages 59–60.

BULBS

Most bulbs need to be in a cultivated, weed-free bed if they are to thrive. Spring-blooming bulbs should be planted in early fall so they will have a chance to develop roots before the ground freezes, but lilies and summer-blooming bulbs can be planted in either spring or fall. Use a trowel, dibble, or bulb

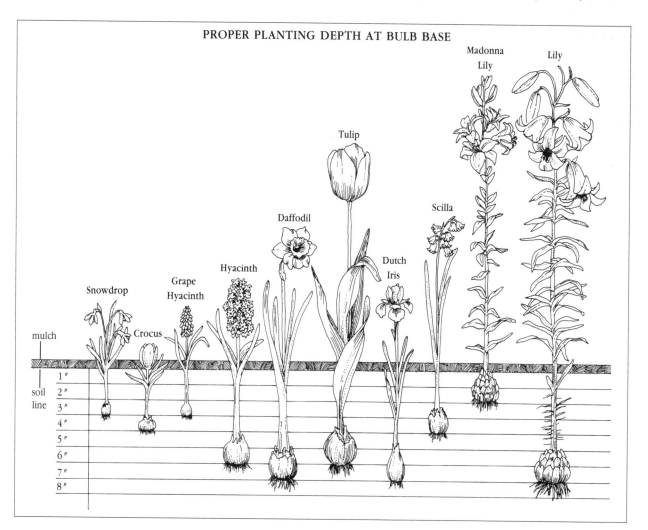

PROPER PLANTING DEPTH AT BULB BASE

planter, and set them, pointed side up, at the appropriate depth (see chart). Keep in mind that even though bulbs bloom and remain green for only a short time, they need regular fertilizing, dividing, and care like other perennials.

Crocus and most common varieties of daffodils (narcissus) are more vigorous than most other bulbs, so they are often planted in a semiwild area for naturalizing. Don't set them out in a place that will need early weekly mowing and trimming, such as the middle of the lawn. The fragrant, old-fashioned double daffodils and King Alfred trumpets will flourish and compete well with grass if it is kept mowed *after the foliage dies down* in early summer. Such varieties bloom profusely for years if they are fertilized lightly and the bulbs are divided and replanted every six to ten years.

When clumps of spring bulbs and other perennials are planted in a border, care must be taken to keep track of their location and not dig into them after their foliage has disappeared. To avoid this we reserve an area about 2 feet wide in the front of the bed for bulbs and annuals. After the daffodils have bloomed, the foliage turned yellow, and the nutrients have returned to the bulb, we cut off the tops. Then when the threat of frost is over, we carefully plant begonias, marigolds, *Calendulas*, and other annuals in the soil above the spring bulbs.

Most tulip varieties don't usually thrive the following spring if they are left in the ground through the summer, so as soon as their leaves turn brown we dig them up and dry them for a few days, then store them in a cool, dry closet until it is time to replant in the fall.

If snowdrops and crocus are not disturbed, they will continue to come up for several years. They can be planted along the front of the border, or naturalized in the lawn or in woodland areas beneath trees and large shrubs. Because of their low cost, however, many gardeners treat them as annuals and plant new ones each fall.

Labeling

Directly after planting, place an unobstructive labeled stake near each perennial plant. The labels will clearly identify the perennials when the graph plan is not handy, and they mark the spot so you won't absentmindedly dig into a plant when it is dormant. After years of using wood, plastic, and aluminum labels, we've settled on the latter: they are the most permanent because the imprint of the pen lasts indefinitely on the soft aluminum, and is not affected by weathering. You'll find them in most garden centers and nursery catalogs.

THE MANY ADVANTAGES OF MULCH

Since new plants are likely to be small, your garden will have a great deal of bare soil after planting. If left exposed to sun and wind, the soil will soon dry out and erode. The solution is mulch. After using it for many years we would never attempt to garden without it. Mulch not only protects the soil, but improves the garden's appearance, checks the growth of many kinds of weeds, and keeps the plants clean by preventing soil from splashing onto them during a hard rain. A layer of mulch preserves moisture, saves watering chores, and helps protect plant roots from sudden changes of temperature. Earthworms work busily in the moist, cool soil beneath the mulch, aerating it and creating a loose medium where roots can grow easily. Mulches are also useful for protecting the roots of tender perennials over the winter (see Fall Chores, page 60). And if these reasons for mulching don't convince you, organic mulch materials gradually decompose and add valuable humus and fertilizer to the soil.

Many different materials can be used. We cover our gardens with lawn clippings an inch thick in early summer when we have a good supply: they decompose nicely and don't scatter weed seeds. Each fall we tuck a layer of newly raked leaves, 3 to 4 inches thick among the plants after they've been cut down. If it doesn't rain right away we water them, so the leaves will become compacted and won't blow away in the first wind. If we need additional mulch at other times of the year we use partly composted bark, peanut shells, chopped hay, or whatever other suitable organic material is readily available, and apply from 1 to 2 inches. Experiment to find the mulch that works best for you because in some areas slugs will hide under a cool layer of mulch (such as woodchips) during the day, and make a feast of your garden at night.

Gardeners in other regions have a variety of materials from which to choose. Those near farms can often buy spoiled hay, ensilage, or straw; a woodworking mill may provide partly rotted shavings, woodchips, or shredded bark; and in some areas, marsh hay, citrus, or beet pulp may be available.

Not all organic materials are ideal. Sawdust packs down too hard and locks up nitrogen if it mixes with the soil. Paper doesn't let water pass through easily and can look unsightly.

REVIVING AN OLD PERENNIAL BED

A perennial bed that is overgrown and neglected can be hard to face, and like the old woman who lived in a shoe, a gardener who has acquired one may not know what to do. Whether such a spot came with the property, or your border has simply gotten out of hand because you haven't had time to care for it properly, don't despair. There is probably a good chance that it can be salvaged and become a thing of beauty once again.

Your first decision must be whether to restore it, or to rip out all the plants and start over. If you can't identify the plants or tell which are the weeds, ask another gardener for help and tag them if you have a short memory. A neglected bed will most likely consist of weeds and the more vigorous perennial varieties, such as yellow loosestrife, lavender phlox, daylilies, and lupines gone wild.

Remaking an old bed is usually easier than starting from scratch, and it is exciting to find treasures hidden among the weeds. The plants you salvage are likely to be larger than those you would buy, fully acclimated, and waiting for a chance to grow. Furthermore, the only expense will be your labor!

If you decide things aren't out of hand, and suspect your neglected border could thrive if given the right encouragement, decide which plants are worth saving and which should go to the compost pile. After you have made a list, draw a garden design, just as if you were building the bed from scratch; sketch in the plants you intend to leave in place, those you want to move to a new location, and those to discard.

Although remaking a bed can be done almost any time of the year if you do it carefully, the best time is early spring, as soon as you can identify the plants, but before much growth has taken place. Plants reestablish themselves quicker at this time.

The first task calls for a sturdy back—most of the weeds and perennials you intend to assign to the compost pile will be robust after years of neglect. Choose a day for digging when the soil is fairly dry, because it will be easier to shake valuable soil from the roots.

Nutrients and humus in the bed will probably have been depleted, so you may need to supply additional topsoil after you have dug out the unwanted plants. If the remaining plants look healthy and the soil seems in good condition, however, a few bales of peat moss and some manure or compost may be enough. Spade the additives into the soil around the plants you are leaving, and into all the empty spots where you plan to set new ones.

Although this method works well if your garden has not fallen too far into disrepair, it will not be worth the trouble to save a border if it has become hopelessly overgrown. You'll have better results if you dig everything out and start over. Sort out the plants as you dig, shaking off all the soil from the weeds and unwanted perennials before placing them in the compost pile for recycling. Carefully dig up the treasures you want to save; keep their root balls intact, set them close together in a shady spot, and cover them with damp cloths (old quilts, towels, burlap, or anything else that holds moisture well). Then prepare the empty bed as if you were starting from scratch: meticulous weeding to remove all weed roots, deep tilling or spading, and then adding fertilizer as described in chapter 3. Finally, with your garden plan in hand, replant all the clumps you have saved. Your border will be good as new, and quite possibly even better than the original.

Although inorganic mulches such as coarse gravel, flat stones, fiberglass- and plastic-weed-check fabrics, and marble chips do not add humus or fertility to the soil they do have other advantages: they contain no weed seeds, last for a long time, and some are attractive. Black polyethylene can be laid between the rows in cutting or collection gardens, but is not practical in perennial borders, because it is difficult to fit around the clumps, and makes dividing and moving plants difficult.

The organic or "natural" gardening movement has introduced many excellent alternatives to the use of chemical fertilizers and herbicides. Mulches, we feel, are one of the very best of these. They offer so many benefits to plants and gardeners, we would not want to garden without them.

5

Dividing Your Perennials

Plant division is a skill every perennial gardener has to learn early, even though you may be hesitant at first.

Each spring after the bed has become well established, some clumps need to be split up for a variety of reasons. First, the health of many types of plants will suffer if they become too large. As a plant expands, its outer roots may remain healthy, but the middle portion will become crowded and starved for nutrients, moisture, and light. A plant in such condition is called a "doughnut," and it is easily recognizable because the new, stronger roots and stems are visible on the outside (see Figure 5.1). The roots of shasta daisies, phlox, and chrysanthemums deteriorate in the center as they grow larger, and others, such as iris and coral bells (*Heuchera*), push themselves out of the ground if they are too crowded. Another important reason for dividing is to control growth. Certain plants spread rapidly by nature, and the clumps must be divided regularly to prevent them from crowding out their companions. A third reason for division is that you get lots of new plants to expand your own plantings, share with friends, sell, or donate to a community plant sale.

Perennials vary a great deal in their need to be divided, and after a short period of gardening you will easily recognize when the time comes for action. Most should be separated every two to four years, but some, such as chrysanthemum, *Monarda*, and *Anthemis*, need dividing every spring. Well-behaved species—*Dictamnus*, peony, hosta, and others—may

thrive for many years in a clump without showing signs of deterioration.

There is some disagreement among gardeners as to what is the best time of year to divide, but those of us who live in the North (zones 3, 4, and 5) usually divide plants in early spring. They are still partially dormant then, so suffer less shock, and they'll have a long growing season ahead to become well established in their new location before winter. There are exceptions, however. *Doronicum, Primula, Pulmonaria*, daffodils, and other early-blooming plants are best divided immediately after their flowers have faded. The time to separate peonies, iris, and Oriental poppies is likewise, after their flowering period.

In warmer areas of the country the general rule of

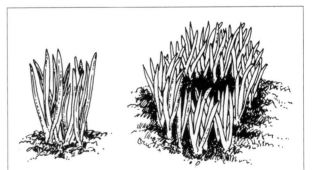

FIGURE 5.1. A plant that develops a "doughnut" condition starts out looking normal (left), but then feeds so heavily for nutrients that new, strong roots develop away from the root core so that the plant forms a doughnut (right).

thumb is to divide the spring-blossoming plants after they have bloomed, the summer bloomers in late summer or fall, and the fall bloomers in the spring, with the same exceptions as noted for peonies, iris, and Oriental poppies.

Some gardeners pay no attention to the guidelines, and divide plants whenever the spirit moves them. At a small nursery near us the owner sells perennials by chipping off large pieces of his clumps whenever anyone wants a new plant, even if they are in full flower. Although such a practice would seem somewhat risky, he has operated a successful business for years, and credits his success to dividing the plants in larger pieces than is usually done and instructing his customers how to plant them properly.

HOW TO DO IT

Think of division as a simple form of pruning. It is as essential to good perennial gardening as the pruning of a fruit tree is to a productive orchard, but fortunately, much easier.

Perennials are divided differently depending on how they grow. Most perennials fall into one of the following five categories.

Compact, shallow-rooted plants such as Primulas (Figure 5.2). Dig up the entire clump and, with your hands, pull it apart into smaller plants. Pry them carefully so the roots will not be injured.

Solid clumps such as Aconitum, Centaurea, daylilies, Dicentras, peonies, phlox (Figure 5.3). When

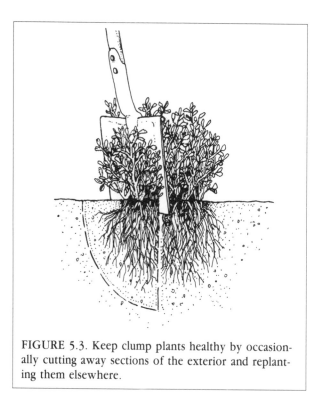

FIGURE 5.3. Keep clump plants healthy by occasionally cutting away sections of the exterior and replanting them elsewhere.

the purpose of your division is simply to make a healthy clump smaller, or to propagate one or two new plants, the easiest way is to cut away sections of the exterior with a spade so as not to disturb the interior. If the center of the clump is unhealthy and dying, however, the entire clump must be dug up and cut into pieces (or pried apart with a spading fork if the roots are intertwined). Discard the weak or diseased section and replant the good portions.

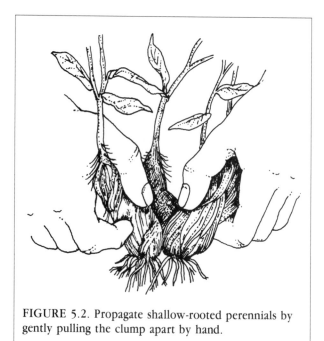

FIGURE 5.2. Propagate shallow-rooted perennials by gently pulling the clump apart by hand.

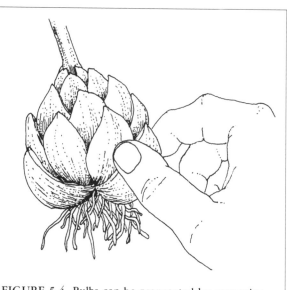

FIGURE 5.4. Bulbs can be propagated by separating and replanting them, or by removing bulblets and setting them out in a transplant bed.

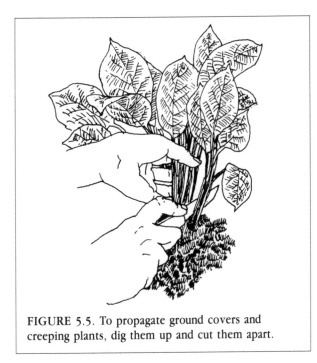

FIGURE 5.5. To propagate ground covers and creeping plants, dig them up and cut them apart.

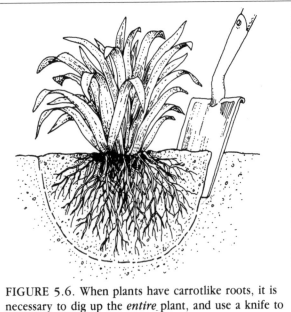

FIGURE 5.6. When plants have carrotlike roots, it is necessary to dig up the *entire* plant, and use a knife to cut it into a number of smaller plants.

Bulbs, including lilies and spring-blooming bulbs such as daffodils (Figure 5.4). Dig them up, separate by hand, and replant them at the proper depth. Place any tiny bulblets in flats or transplant beds (see page 36) for one season to allow them to come to maturity before they are planted permanently.

Ground covers and creeping plants such as Vinca and Phlox subulata (Figure 5.5). Dig the plants up and cut them apart nearly anytime.

Plants with carrotlike roots such as lupine and Dictamnus (Figure 5.5). Dig the entire plant in early spring, and cut apart each section with a sharp knife; if you do it carefully, the injured plants will heal quickly.

In the spring you will find buds or sprouts on the crowns of perennials. Leave two to four in each division, as you split the clump apart. If you are dividing later, when the plant has live stems, cut them back by at least one-half so there will be less foliage for the roots to support. Don't worry about the way they look: new stems and foliage will grow.

In order to start many new plants, nurseries will frequently divide a clump into very tiny sections, and nurse them carefully until they reach a healthy size. In a home garden it is unnecessary to make the divisions small since large ones will grow far better and produce more blooms the following season. Unless the plants are huge most are best divided into only two or three new plants. If you decide to produce a lot of plants instead, you can grow these small plantlets in flats or small pots for a few weeks until they have developed good root systems. Then they can be safely planted in a bed.

Handle your divisions with care and don't leave them out of their element for long. Replant them as described in chapter 4.

A successful businessman who dabbles in the stock market tells us that propagating plants is the gardening chore he most enjoys. He happily compares dividing plants to the splitting of stocks, and the volunteer seedlings that appear in his border are his dividends!

6

Starting Your Own Perennials

One of the nice things about perennials is that most of them multiply so rapidly. From only a few iris or hosta you can get enough new plants to start another garden in only a few years. Sometimes the rapid proliferation of perennials creates a dilemma—how to dispose of overabundant plants without setting out additional acres of them or tossing them out. If you are a beginning gardener and need plants, however, such a situation can work to your advantage. By attending plant sales or visiting friends' gardens, you can often find outstanding plants. Be careful, though, that you don't pick up undesirable varieties. Check each one for weeds, diseases, and bugs that could later create problems in your garden.

Perennials can be propagated either sexually, by seeds, or asexually by division, cuttings, grafting, or tissue culture. Although planting seeds is the best way to start annuals, biennials, and certain perennials, the seedlings of most named varieties of perennials do not come "true." Instead, the resulting plants may resemble some of the plant's many ancestors rather than its parent, and be quite different in terms of color, size, or shape. If you were to plant every seed on a Glacier chrysanthemum, for example, the results would yield an interesting assortment of plants, but none would be exactly like the Glacier. To get the real thing you'd need to propagate it asexually.

In part III, beginning on page 135, you will find the best method to propagate each kind of perennial. On the pages that follow we describe those methods.

SEEDS

Fortunately, garden/seed catalogs identify the perennials that *do* come true. We grow from seed *Bellis*, canterbury bells, delphiniums, *Dianthus*, foxgloves, gloriosa daisies, forget-me-nots, *Hibiscus*, hollyhocks, lupines, shasta daisies, pyrethrums, and others. The seed catalogs brighten up many a stormy winter day as we dream over the colorful photos in Park's, Thompson and Morgan, and other beautiful catalogs (the addresses of these and other seed catalogs can be found in the appendix). Selecting seeds to plant in our border is always fun, but frustrating because we invariably covet far more varieties than we have the space to grow.

Order your seeds early, before the choice varieties are sold out. If you don't plant them at once, store them in a plastic bag in a cool, dry closet, with the exception of delphinium seeds, which start better if they are kept cold in the refrigerator until they are planted.

If you decide to save your own seed, forego deadheading a few flowers and let them form seeds. They are ripe when they have dried and turned brown. Pick them before the seeds begin to drop and self-sow.

We save seed from some of our favorite plants, including delphiniums, and the biennial hollyhocks, foxgloves, and gloriosa daisies. We plant them where it's not important to have a specific color, because we aren't always sure what color will result. When we want plants of a particular shade, such as the Newport Pink sweet William, we buy the seeds. Although we grow several named varieties of sweet William in our garden, we don't save seed from any of them because the bees mix the pollen among the various plants. As a consequence, the seedlings have a wide variety of colors. The seeds we buy have been produced by a grower who raises each variety well isolated from other closely related plants. He can guarantee that both parents of each seed will be of the same variety, and the colors will come true.

Soil

It is possible to successfully start perennial seeds in ordinary garden soil that has been finely tilled, but you will have far better results, and less trouble with disease, if you use a sterile, weed-free starting medium. This is true whether you plant indoors or in flats, cold frames, or shade beds outside. Soil can be sterilized with heat or chemicals, but as an alternative we strongly recommend that you use a pre-mixed artifical soil such as Pro-Mix, Gro-Mix, or Metro-Mix that are readily available in garden centers and farm stores. Don't use commercial potting soil: it is good for repotting houseplants, but not for starting seeds.

Starting Seeds Outdoors

The easiest way to start seeds is in a cold frame as shown in Figure 6.1. If you are planting seeds you have saved from your own plants, it's best to sow them at the same time that nature does. This is usually in mid- to late summer, as soon as the seeds are ripe and ready to drop from the plant. If you buy the

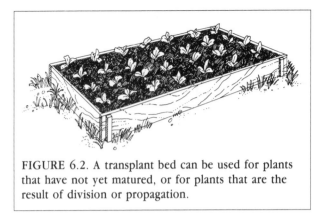

FIGURE 6.2. A transplant bed can be used for plants that have not yet matured, or for plants that are the result of division or propagation.

seed, spring is a good planting time—the seed germinates well during the cool spring days. The extra months give the plants time to become larger and well established before winter.

Most perennial seeds germinate best when not subjected to direct sunlight, so if the frame is not in a shady spot, cover it with laths—narrow strips of wood, such as a section of snow fence—or a white sheet. Put chicken-wire netting or a window screen over the frame to keep out seed-eating birds, and add a few mothballs to discourage mice, moles, and ants.

Keep the bed under the cold frame watered, but don't oversoak. Usually it is best to water in the morning, so the surface of the soil will dry out quickly, and disease is less likely to proliferate on the moist stems. When the seedlings are well established and have developed their second set of leaves, remove the shade if you have used one, and either thin the seedlings so they are 2 inches apart, or transplant them to a new bed that has been thoroughly tilled and fertilized. Space them 2 or more inches apart each way. Whichever cultural method you choose, fertilize the plants with liquid fertilizer, every two or three weeks until Labor Day. Any plants that are large and healthy can then be planted in their permanent location in the border. Small plants should be mulched and left in the transplant bed until spring. You can also use a transplant bed as a temporary home for plants that are the result of cuttings or division (Figure 6.2).

Starting Seeds Under Grow Lights

Although we prefer to plant perennial and biennial seeds outdoors, we always start a few in mid-winter along with the annuals and tomato seeds because some plants, such as pansies, gloriosa daisies, and chrysanthemums, will bloom the same year if planted early. Over the years we have started seeds in hot beds (cold frames with heating cables in the

FIGURE 6.1. Start seeds outside by planting them in well-prepared garden soil protected by a cold frame.

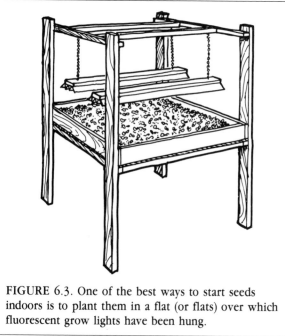

FIGURE 6.3. One of the best ways to start seeds indoors is to plant them in a flat (or flats) over which fluorescent grow lights have been hung.

bottom), greenhouses, and sunny windows. But fluorescent grow lights have consistently given us the best results: it is easy to maintain the proper temperature and light conditions with grow lights, the plants need less attention, and disease problems are nearly eliminated (Figure 6.3).

Whether you start seeds indoors or out, disease is likely to be the worst problem. Damping-off diseases can affect new seedlings especially, if you use garden or field soil in which disease-causing organisms may be present; they are also likely to occur if the seedlings are moist or cold for several hours at a time.

Soak the artificial soil thoroughly with slightly warm water until it is completely moist. Then plant the seeds over the top of the mix as sparsely as possible. We usually plant them in rows. It is difficult not to spread seeds too thickly, especially the fine varieties, but they grow much better and transplant easier if they are not crowded. Finally, cover the seeds with a thin layer of fine perlite. This material dries out rapidly after waterings and helps to prevent damping-off disease.

Leave the grow lights on twenty-four hours a day until the seedlings are well started. Keep the temperature at whatever is recommended on the seed package, usually between 70° to 80° F. Water them once or twice each day, using a gentle spray that will not hurt the delicate seedlings. A bulb sprinkler, such as the type used for laundry, is ideal (see Figure 6.4). The water should be warm enough to avoid chilling the seedlings—room temperature or warmer. Water

when the grow lights are first turned on, and try not to water too heavily: overwatering and cool temperatures are the primary causes of seedling failure.

After the seedlings are well developed (two to three weeks), gradually lower the heat to room temperature, and leave the grow lights on for about twelve hours daily or set them in a sunny window. Apply a liquid fertilizer once a week, but at only one-half the normal strength recommended on the label.

Transplant the seedlings to flats or small pots that are filled with good soil as soon as they have developed their first set of true leaves. Space them 2 to 3 inches apart in flats; there should be only one seedling to each pot.

If you have a large number of seedlings you may prefer to move them into an outdoor transplant bed, as described above.

DEVELOPING YOUR OWN HYBRIDS

A popular hobby among perennial growers is the creation of a new variety by crossing two existing ones. If the results are successful, the plant is named and introduced to the public as a hybrid. Among the well-known successes are Russell's lupines, Pacific Hybrids delphinium, and thousands of named varieties of chrysanthemums, daylilies, hosta, iris, and lilies.

Bees pollinate by transferring pollen from the male *stamens* of one flower to the female *pistil* (usually a long green tube with an enlarged cap at the end) of another flower (see Figure 6.5). If you intend to hy-

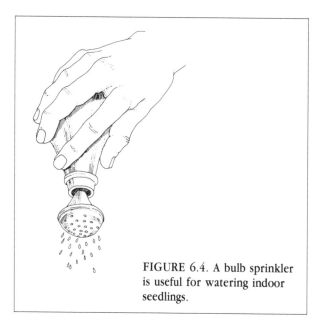

FIGURE 6.4. A bulb sprinkler is useful for watering indoor seedlings.

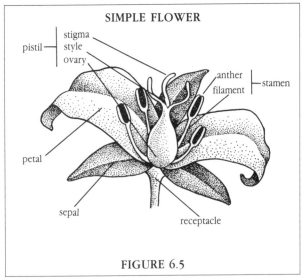

Drawing by Hyla Scudder

SIMPLE FLOWER

pistil — stigma
style
ovary

anther
filament — stamen

petal

sepal
receptacle

FIGURE 6.5

bridize you must get to the flower before the bees. Cover the bud, before it opens, with a small paper bag. After the flower opens, transfer the pollen from another flower to the pistil of the flower that was covered. Use a brush, or pinch off one of the stamens and brush the pollen from it directly onto the pistil. Then tag the flower so you can identify the seed later, and record the names of both parents in a notebook.

Hybridizers try to combine the best qualities of different plants into an outstanding new specimen. They work to improve size, color, vigor, disease resistance, hardiness, or fragrance. Although much plant breeding is done by universities and large nurseries, amateur horticulturists have introduced many outstanding new plant varieties in the past century. Most amateur breeders belong to a plant society that specializes in the species they are hybridizing, and these organizations help with the registration, naming, and introduction of new varieties.

ASEXUAL PROPAGATION

Most perennials are propagated in ways other than by seed, since very few named varieties come true from seed. If you want a replica of your Crimson Star phlox or Stella d'Oro daylily, for instance, you must start it asexually. As we've mentioned, there are several ways that perennials may be propagated from a portion of the parent plant.

Dividing Perennials

Dividing a clump into two or more plants is the most common way to propagate asexually, and with most perennials it is easily done. Division is an impor-

tant part of general garden culture, and necessary even when no extra plants are needed (see pages 32–34).

Stem Cuttings

Certain plants can be propagated by taking stem cuttings (see Figure 6.6). This method of propagation is particularly useful when you don't want to disturb a valuable plant by digging it up.

Spring is the best time to take cuttings from plants that bloom in the summer, and early summer is best for spring and fall bloomers. Choose a healthy, vigorous plant, and cut off the top of a stalk with hand pruners or a knife. Cuttings should be from 6 to 8 inches long in order to encourage the development of a good root system before winter. It should be easy to get cuttings from a tall-growing plant, such as phlox, but those from low-growing plants—silvermound and thyme, for instance—may have to be shorter. On plants such as old-fashioned bleeding-heart, look for a sliplike portion with a side shoot coming from it, rather than a stem with a single leaf.

Although a cutting will usually produce roots no matter where you make the bottom cut, the root formation tends to be heavier if you make the cut about one-quarter of an inch below a node (the joint where a leaf sprouts from the stem). Pinch off the very tip of the cutting to encourage the development of roots rather than top growth.

Dip the base of each cutting first into water and then into a rooting hormone such as Rootone or Hormodin. Make a hole about an inch deep with a thin dowel or pencil in a pot or flat filled with a moistened mixture of perlite and vermiculite (half and half by volume). Stick the base of each cutting into a hole and firm the mixture around it. Cover the pot or flat with a sheet of clear plastic (food wrap) if the cuttings are small, or a plastic lid of some kind, and place it in a warm, shady spot out of direct sunlight.

Never let the perlite-vermiculite mix dry out: spray or sprinkle the cuttings lightly with water several times a day, and roots should begin to form within two to six weeks. Check their progress by pulling very gently on the cutting to see if it is still loose. As soon as they root remove the plastic cover and treat them as you would any new seedlings. After a few more weeks, when they are well rooted and new leaves have started to grow, transplant them to pots or a transplant bed.

Each genus of perennial below grows well from stem cuttings.

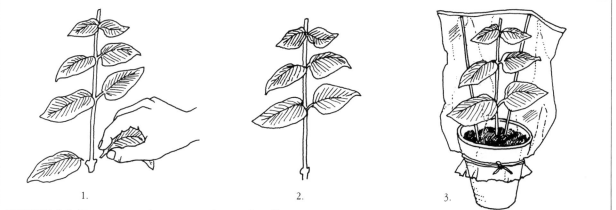

FIGURE 6.6. To propagate by stem cuttings, snip off a plant stem one-quarter of an inch below a node (1), pinch off the very tip of that stem as well as the lower leaves (2), dip in rooting hormone, and plant in the appropriate starting mix (3).

Achillea, yarrow
Alyssum
Arabis, rockcress
Artemisia, silvermound
Asclepias, butterfly weed
Aster
Aubrieta, rockcress
Campanula, bellflower
Centaurea, cornflower
Cerastium, snow-in-summer
Chrysanthemum
Clematis
Coreopsis, tickseed
Delphinium, larkspur
Dianthus, pinks
Dicentra, bleeding-heart
Dictamnus, gas plant
Eupatorium, boneset
Gaillardia, blanketflower
Geum, avens
Helenium, sneezeweed
Helianthus, sunflower
Heliopsis, sunflower
Herbs
Iberis, candytuft
Linum, flax
Lobelia, cardinal flower
Lupinus, lupine
Lychnis, campion
Lythrum, loosestrife
Monarda, bee balm
Myosotis, forget-me-not
Nepeta, catmint
Oenothera, evening primrose
Penstemon, beardtongue
Phlox
Platycodon, balloon flower
Potentilla, cinquefoil
Rudbeckia hirta, gloriosa daisy

Salvia, sage
Saponaria, soapwort
Sedum, stonecrop
Silene, catchfly
Verbascum, mullein
Veronica, speedwell

Root Cuttings

Root cuttings are used primarily to obtain a large number of plants from the parent. We accidentally used this form of propagation once when we were trying to get rid of old *Hemerocallis dumortieri* clumps that we had raised as foundation plants around a greenhouse. Even two years after we had carefully dug them out, hundreds of new plants kept springing from the tiny roots we had accidentally cut off and left in the ground. Although very few fine perennials start as easily from root cuttings as *Hemerocallis*—or dandelions, quack grass, and Canadian thistle —some species do very well. Huge numbers of new phlox, achillea, and *Monarda*, for instance, are produced in this manner by nurseries each year.

Early spring is the best time to take root cuttings. It is possible to cut off some of the outer roots from the parent plant without greatly disturbing it by cutting around the perimeter of the roots with a spade; but ordinarily the entire plant is dug up and pieces of root are cut from it. If you want to save the parent plant don't entirely dissect it, but leave about half of the roots intact before replanting it. If saving the original is not important, you can cut up the roots of the entire plant into smaller pieces, and start a new large family. The roots are treated in one of two different ways, depending on the growth habit of the plant.

Plants with fine roots (Figure 6.7). Cut the roots into pieces that are 1 to 2 inches long and scatter them

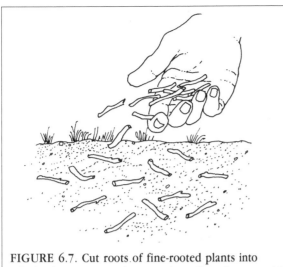

FIGURE 6.7. Cut roots of fine-rooted plants into 1-inch pieces, scatter them on the soil, and cover with a light layer of soil.

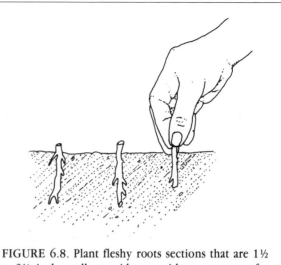

FIGURE 6.8. Plant fleshy roots sections that are 1½ to 2½ inches tall, top side up, with one-quarter of an inch protruding from the soil.

horizontally over the surface of well-prepared, rich, sandy soil. Cover them with one-half inch of sifted soil. Fine-rooted plants include phlox, achillea, crown-vetch, sea holly, flowering spurge, *Gaillardia*, soap-wort, salvia, Stokes' aster, and *Verbascum*.

Plants with fleshy roots (Figure 6.8). Cut the roots into pieces from 1½ to 2½ inches long (peonies should be 3 inches long). When cutting, be sure to lay them down with all the top ends facing the same way so you can later plant them vertically, topside up. Place them about 3 inches apart with the top of the root protruding about a quarter of an inch above the soil. *Acanthus*, bee balm, *Dicentra spectabilis, Gypsophila*, Oriental poppies, and peonies fall into this category. Use a light sandy soil or a mixture of perlite and a plant starting medium such as Pro-Mix (half and half by volume), either in the ground or in a deep flat.

Keep the cuttings moist, but not waterlogged, and if the weather is cool a protected cold frame or greenhouse will give the best results. After they begin to grow, treat them just as you would seedlings. Once they have become well established, you can either plant the root cuttings where they will grow per-manently, or cover them with leaves or other organic mulch for the winter and plant them out in the spring.

Below are some perennials that start well from root cuttings.

Anchusa, bugloss
Anemone japonica, Japanese anemone
Asclepias, butterfly weed
Dicentra spectabilis, old-fashioned bleeding-heart
Dictamnus, gas plant
Echinops, globe thistle

Gypsophila, baby's-breath
Oenothera, evening primrose
Papaver orientale, Oriental poppy
Phlox
Sedum, stonecrop
Stokesia, Stokes' aster
Trollius, globeflower
Yucca

Layering

Some perennials, especially the vine types and those used as rock plants and ground covers, form new plants by developing roots wherever their spreading tops touch the soil. There is a simple way

FIGURE 6.9. One way to propagate is to encourage root growth from stems that have been layered into small pots which are adjacent to the mother plant.

for you to speed up the natural rooting process of plants such as campanula, *Cerastium*, creeping phlox, periwinkle, vinca, thyme, and others. Simply loosen the soil a few inches from a stem that is close to the ground with a hand trowel or garden fork, and bury that portion of the stem about one-half inch deep in the soil (Figure 6.9). Roots will form where the stems are covered. *Dianthus* and many other upright plants can be bent over and treated in a similar manner. Layering may be done successfully anytime during early summer and most vine-type perennials will root quickly. The new plants can be cut from their parent in late summer or the following spring and transplanted.

Grafting

Grafting—the process of joining two separate plants to form a new plant—is used to start only a few species of perennials because easier methods of propagation work just as well for most plants. It is practical only for starting varieties that do not come true from seed, do not root well from cuttings, and are difficult to divide.

The transplanting of one variety of plant onto another by surgery is a tricky process, and it is feasible to graft only those plants that do not produce suckers or offshoots that would outgrow the grafted portion. Large double-white or pink-flowering varieties of *Gypsophila* (baby's-breath) are commonly grafted on seedlings of ordinary *Gypsophila* by joining the two parts in a cleft graft (see Figure 6.10). The union is then covered with tape or wax and planted so the graft union is about an inch below the surface of the soil. You may want to try this interesting procedure to test your skill, but don't expect perfect results every time. You may have noticed that grafted varieties of *Gypsophila*, such as Bristol Fairy, are expensive, which testifies to the difficulty of successful grafting.

Tissue Culture

Plant cloning has moved out of the experimental stage and is now widely used to propagate plants all over the world. If you have recently purchased geraniums, berry plants, or orchids, it is likely that they were started in this manner. Tissue culture is so productive that in less than a year it is possible to start over a million plants from a single piece of stem, and in a relatively small space. Not only can tissue-cultured plants be propagated quickly, but because of the sterile laboratory techniques employed, they

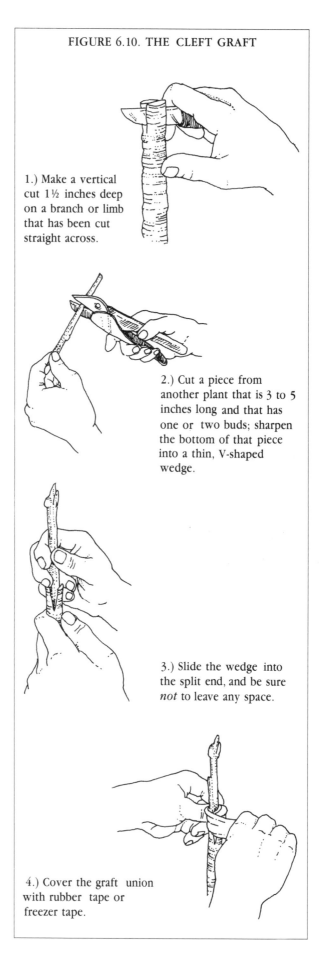

FIGURE 6.10. THE CLEFT GRAFT

1.) Make a vertical cut 1½ inches deep on a branch or limb that has been cut straight across.

2.) Cut a piece from another plant that is 3 to 5 inches long and that has one or two buds; sharpen the bottom of that piece into a thin, V-shaped wedge.

3.) Slide the wedge into the split end, and be sure *not* to leave any space.

4.) Cover the graft union with rubber tape or freezer tape.

are free from disease. Quite often they are lower in price, too.

Laboratory cloning of plants is not yet feasible for most home gardeners, but experimental kits are available for amateur horticulturists. The equipment necessary to maintain the absolutely sterile conditions required is expensive, and the cultural methods are complicated; growing media must be measured precisely, and the temperatures and pH kept at exact levels. Each species, and often each variety within the same species, requires a special formula.

Among the problems with tissue culture are the mutations that sometimes occur in the laboratory, causing a change in plant characteristics during the cloning process. A popular variety of daylily, for instance, can develop into a quite different variety in the test tube, and thousands could be sold before the error is noticed. Although progress is continuous, tissue culture will probably never make other methods of propagation obsolete, especially for those of us who are home gardeners.

We have no plans to put in a tissue culture laboratory, and will continue to increase our plant supply by conventional methods. Although our garden is overflowing, we always need new plants to replace varieties that have died, or to fill the spaces left by ones we no longer want. We use plants as gifts, too, but most of all, we propagate because we enjoy creating new plants, particularly the ones that are especially challenging to reproduce.

7

Coping With Disease, Insect, and Animal Pests

ew gardens stay problem free for long, and what would gardeners talk about if nothing ever went wrong? Such frustrating diseases as mildew or rust can strike your best specimens the day before the garden club is scheduled to meet in your backyard. Ravaging insects lurk, from the tiny cyclamen mites—those great deformers of delphinium—to huge Japanese beetles that devour nearly every green thing in sight. Weeds can wrestle down the strongest garden plants if they are not controlled. Even the weather often seems to work against us—a sudden storm can devastate an entire garden in a few minutes. In a humid or cool growing season, diseases attack; when the weather is hot and dry, insects flourish. It may seem, at times, like a no-win situation.

Then there are the animals. We speak kindly to the toads that snack on bugs, and try to accept the nocturnal bats that are said to consume tons of insects. We live on the edge of a large tract of forest land so a wide variety of wildlife comes to visit our gardens, but not to admire the flowers. Mice, chipmunks, rabbits, and deer chew on everything, including plants that are allegedly poisonous. Skunks, woodchucks, and moles dig large holes, and even the birds we love so much often roost on the taller plants and break them. Please don't let our grumbling discourage you. Many of the pests we'll discuss will never bother your plants. But if a problem appears, we hope to help you identify and cope with it.

Because the control of disease, insects, and weeds is difficult, aggravating, and expensive, we try to prevent their occurrence from the outset. When we started our nursery many years ago, we were often careless about where we got our plants since we wanted to have a big variety available in a short period of time. Consequently, we picked up a distressing assortment of insects, diseases, and weeds, all of which took years to eradicate. We finally made the reluctant decision not to accept gift plants, no matter how tempting, and to buy stock only from certified pest-free sources.

Unless you're in the nursery business too, you won't need to be as meticulous about accepting gifts, but *do* try to look each gift horse in the mouth. If you have suspicion about a plant, wash all the soil off the roots and set it in an isolated spot until you are satisfied that it is not harboring any weed seeds or bugs that might infect your garden.

There are a number of easy ways to avoid garden problems:
- Keep your perennials healthy and vigorous, and leave plenty of space around them for proper air circulation. Overcrowded, undernourished plants are more likely to have trouble.
- Avoid species that are particularly vulnerable to pests. Check the detailed description of each variety you are considering in part III, for more information on plant pests and diseases.
- Disease and insects often overwinter in old leaves and stalks, so cut the stems off every plant in late fall (leave about 2 inches of stubble), and remove them from the garden.

Few gardeners want to cover their plants with foul-smelling sprays and dusts that kill both the bad and the beneficial insects. Any natural control is preferable and there are many:

- Inspect the plants frequently. If you notice the beginning of a problem, act at once to snip off the spotted leaf or stem, and remove any plant that looks hopelessly sick.
- Plant a few marigolds and *Alliums* (onion-type plants) throughout the garden—marigolds have been found to repel many insects and nematodes, and *Alliums* discourage ants and Japanese beetles, for example.
- Pick off bugs and drop them in a can of kerosene, or wash them off with soap (not detergent) and water.
- Fight back with natural enemies. Buy and distribute insects such as ladybugs and praying mantis that eat aphids. Distribute milky disease spore dust, which attacks the larvae (grubs) of chewing insects, but does not harm the plants.
- Collect earwigs and slugs overnight by laying wide boards on the ground; they can be crushed or shaken into a pan of kerosene in the morning.
- Whenever possible, use only those sprays that are known to be less toxic. These include insecticidal soap, Thuricide, pyrethrum, and rotenone.

PESTICIDES

We would prefer never to use chemical pesticides on our gardens, but resort to them occasionally to control such difficult pests as cyclamen mites, rusts, and mildew. One by one many of the sprays we had been told were safe have been banned from use, and even such commonly recommended chemicals as captan, and so-called natural products such as pyrethrum (made from native *Chrysanthemum coccineum*) and rotenone, are now suspected of causing cancer.

Because of increased concern, chemicals known to be dangerous are being taken off the market, and new safer ones are being developed. If you have a weed, disease, or insect problem that you can't control by recommended "natural" methods, check with your garden center to find the safest treatments available. If you do spray or dust with pesticides, "spot" spray as much as possible, apply them exactly as recommended on the label, use only as much as is necessary, and store them in a secure place. Be sure to protect yourself: wear gloves, a hood, long pants and

INSECT CONTROL

Chemicals: Diazinon, malathion, methoxychlor, Sevin (carbaryl)
For Organic Gardeners: insecticidal soap, pyrethrum, rotenone, Thuricide

DISEASE CONTROL

Fungicides: benomyl, copper sulfate, Lesan, sulfur

a long-sleeved shirt (old clothes to which you have no attachment). Never buy chemicals in large amounts —they may subsequently be declared unsafe, and furthermore many products deteriorate in storage and lose their effectiveness after a few years. Gardeners with small children should be especially careful when using and storing pesticides and herbicides, just as you would with drugs and medicines. And, finally, keep in mind that chemical pest and weed controls could influence the whole ecology of your garden through their effects on the natural habitats of both good *and* bad bugs, bees, butterflies, and hummingbirds.

For those with small gardens who decide to use chemicals, all-purpose sprays or dust containing several different pesticides are convenient because they are formulated to take care of most disease and insect problems, but whenever possible, use a chemical designed to handle the specific situation, and don't apply a general pesticide if it is needed only to control one problem.

Pesticides are sold in powder and liquid form. The powders can be applied with a hand duster, mixed with water and sprayed, or sprinkled on with an old watering can (that won't then be used on vegetables). *Never* spray chemicals on plants that are in bloom because bees may take the poisons back to their hive. The "flit gun," or hand-held sprayer, is an excellent tool for pest control in a small garden because it is easily directed and uses a minimum amount of spray. If your garden is larger you may want a small tank sprayer or one that attaches to a hose.

DISEASES

Fortunately, perennials are not as vulnerable to disease as potatoes and fruits, but they are by no means immune. Diseases can be caused by fungus, bacteria, or virus. They are also spread from plant to plant by the wind, by insects such as aphids and leafhoppers, transferring soil and compost, and by tools such as trowels and spades. Below are some of the most common diseases and popular methods of control.

ANTHRACNOSE or LEAF SPOT. This fungus usually manifests itself by a dying back of new growth and by leaf spots with slightly raised borders. Not too common on perennials, it does appear often on annuals, vegetables, and shrubs, particularly during wet seasons. Occasionally it hits chrysanthemums, delphinium, and monkshood. Most fungicides give effective control.

BLIGHT. There are many kinds of blight: they show up as spots or lesions that disfigure the leaves, sometimes with a gummy substance issuing from them, and are especially prevalent in damp weather. Botrytis, sometimes called gray mold, is most common in greenhouses, but can also attack chrysanthemums, lilies, primroses, and other plants in the outdoor garden. Anemones, lupines, *Pachysandra*, and poppies may also be affected by blight. Suspect blight, also, when peony buds wither and do not open. Remove and destroy diseased parts as soon as you notice them to help prevent its spread. Benomyl and ferbam are useful chemical controls.

CANKER. These are not common on perennials, but bleeding canker can affect peonies, tulips, and some others. Remove the oozing portion and destroy it.

CLUB ROOT. This fungus disease affects members of the cabbage family, sweet alyssum, and some perennials. Roots develop gall-like swellings and growth is stunted. It is most prevalent in acidic soils, and can often be prevented by adding lime.

LEAF TROUBLES. Besides anthracnose, there are many other leaf diseases that can affect perennials. Among them are leaf blotch, leaf scorch, yellows, and various other leaf spots. Fungicides can help, but the best remedy usually is to remove the infected part immediately and destroy it.

MILDEW. Phlox is a primary target of this fungus which covers the leaves and blossoms with a whitish powder; it can also hit chrysanthemums, delphinium, and others. Try to buy only disease-free plants, don't set them in a location where air circulation is poor, and never allow foliage to become so thick that air movement is impeded and sunlight blocked out. Sulfur dusts have long been used for mildew problems, but benomyl gives better control.

MOLD. These fungi (including botrytis) grow on leaves and stems, and are often closely related to blight. Plants that are overcrowded and growing where air circulation is poor are most susceptible. Most of the molds, such as those that grow on decaying organic matter, are harmless. Those affecting living plants may be gray, white, dark colored, or in the case of lawn grasses, even pink. Fungicides help, but sometimes fail to completely control a bad infestation. If the problem persists, the plants should be destroyed.

MOSAIC. Symptoms of this and similar viruses are yellow spots on the leaves, which sometimes give them a mottled effect. Another sign may be a dwarfing of both the plant and its blooms. Even if only a few leaves show symptoms the entire plant will become infected and eventually die. This ailment is primarily spread by aphids, and it affects chrysanthemums, *Dianthus*, delphinium, iris, lilies, *Primula*, and others. Mosaic diseases are not completely understood and there is no effective remedy, but the best control is to quickly remove and destroy any plant that shows signs of it.

ROT. This wet-brown condition resembles rot and can be seen on stems, leaves, roots, and occasionally even flowers. Crown rot sometimes appears at the base, or crown, of *Aconitum*, *Ajuga*, delphinium, iris, lilies, and some of the spring bulbs. The only sure way to eradicate the disease is to destroy the affected plants and sterilize the soil where they grew with a chemical such as Vapam. However, fungicides such as Banrot help keep it under control.

RUST. Because they look exactly like their name, rusts are easy to identify. Unfortunately, they are not easy to control, and when weather conditions are favorable they can disfigure an entire planting. Various rusts are known to hit chrysanthemums, *Dianthus*, hollyhocks, and mints, including bee balm. Plant only disease-free stock and destroy any infected plants as soon as you notice them. Sulfur dusts provide partial control, as does ferbam.

SCAB. This fungus shows up on plant leaves as spots with white centers. Pansies and violets are fairly susceptible. Regular spraying with a fungicide, and removal of the infected parts should keep the problem in check.

VIRUS DISEASES. There are many virus diseases in addition to mosaic, including some of the so-called diebacks. They can be spread by close contact with an infected plant, but are usually passed around by sucking insects, and there is no effective treatment. The best control is to plant virus-free varieties, and whenever possible, virus-resistant ones. Plants infected with virus have discolored leaves, and growth is often stunted. Deterioration may be fairly

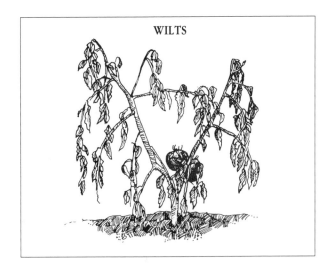

WILTS

rapid, or it could take place over several months. Remove any suspicious looking plant as soon as you notice virus-related symptoms and plant it in an out-of-the-way place, until you can determine whether or not the problem is a virus.

WILTS. The wilting of a perennial may be caused simply by lack of moisture in the soil, or it can be from one of the serious wilt diseases that suddenly cut off the supply of water to a part, or sometimes an entire, plant. The two most common wilts, fusarian and verticillium, affect many vegetables, perennials, and trees, and pruning off the affected part, which is sometimes the entire plant, is the only treatment. Since the disease may remain in the soil for months, and sometimes longer, it is best not to grow perennials on land used the previous two or three years for raising potatoes, tomatoes, strawberries, roses, or other plants that are especially susceptible to wilt.

INSECTS

The list of insects that have a taste for perennials may seem endless, but like diseases, most never become a serious problem. There are many exceptions, however, and among them are Japanese beetles —an overwhelming problem in some areas—and gypsy moths, which can devour practically everything when they fall from the trees they have been consuming.

Three types of creatures may invade your garden: sucking aphids and mites; chewing caterpillars, beetles, and grasshoppers; and borers that work on the interior of stems and roots. The most prevalent garden pests and reasonable solutions follow.

ANTS. These do not usually afflict the plants themselves, but they do spread both aphids and scale by "herding" these insects to obtain their honeydew secretions. It is not pleasant to dig into an anthill or to import them into the house on your peony blossoms. To get rid of them, find their home and soak it with an insecticide or use ant traps or other bait.

APHIDS. These tiny lice suck the juices from a plant, especially its new growth, and cause its leaves to curl. The damage is not as noticeable as with chewing insects, but they can greatly weaken a plant without it being obvious. Malathion is a popular remedy, as are methoxychlor, rotenone, and Sevin, or you could simply wash them off (perhaps only temporarily) with your garden hose and a high-pressure nozzle.

BEETLES. Beetles come in numerous shapes, sizes, and colors—a fascinating assortment of specimens, both beneficial and harmful. The most common are the Asiatic garden beetle, blister beetle, and flea beetle, but the most destructive and potentially deadly to plants are Japanese beetles. Small numbers can be controlled by using beetle traps, and by picking them off and dropping them into a jar of kerosene. Malathion and Sevin are known to be effective on large infestations of beetles.

BORERS. Borers are small caterpillars that winter over in old stalks and garden debris. They are not easy to spot, and are therefore hard to reach with a spray. Look for small holes in any iris rhizomes (roots) you plant and cut them out. Stalk borers may bother delphinium, lilies, peonies, phlox, and certain annuals and vegetables. Because they will die if their winter habitat is destroyed, the best control is to remove all dead plant tops and any other garden wastes in late fall. Soak the ground around the plants with Sevin or malathion at the same time.

CATERPILLARS. The larvae of various moths, butterflies, and certain sawflies are likely to appear in a variety of sizes and colors. They are vigorous eaters, and the holes they make in leaves can be readily identified. Cutworms cut off small plants entirely. Most insecticides and dusts will control them.

EARWIGS. These evil-looking pests can be nearly as invasive in homes as in gardens, and are difficult to eradicate from either. They sometimes feed on chrysanthemums and other perennials. Spraying with an insecticide will provide some relief, but the most effective method seems to be trapping. One trick is to invert a flowerpot filled with hay, held off the ground a little bit by a short stake. Earwigs will gather under the flowerpot and can be shaken out several times a day into a can of kerosene. They will also gather under boards or sheets of cardboard and can likewise be thrown into kerosene.

FLIES. Whiteflies are more of a problem in greenhouses than in outdoor beds. Usually they are introduced by plants purchased at an infected nursery, and are more of a nuisance than a danger to your plants. Often they disappear by themselves outside, but if you have a greenhouse or houseplants be careful not to get any of your infected plants near them or you may have a serious problem for years to come. Most of the treatments used by commercial operators are not safe for homeowners to use.

The narcissus bulb fly can greatly damage spring-flowering bulbs. The fly lays its eggs in the soil near the bulb and the larva then eats the bulb. Whenever plants appear to be growing poorly, the bulbs should be dug up and inspected. Any that show signs of being mushy should be discarded. To ensure fly-free plantings, sprinkle any new bulbs with all-purpose garden dust before planting.

GRASSHOPPERS. In late summer grasshoppers and locusts appear. Ordinarily they are a problem only during those years when large infestations occur. Spraying with malathion or Sevin will give good control.

LEAFHOPPERS. These small, active insects can be as destructive in the perennial garden as in the vegetable patch. Most garden insecticides control them, but repeat applications are usually necessary.

LEAF MINERS. These minuscule insects feed on interior leaf tissue leaving tiny trails, blotches, and blisters. Leaf miners seldom afflict perennials as much as lilacs and birch, and can often be controlled by picking off the damaged leaves. If you have a problem with them year after year, spray plants in the spring when the adults emerge and lay their eggs. Malathion or an all-purpose spray can be used.

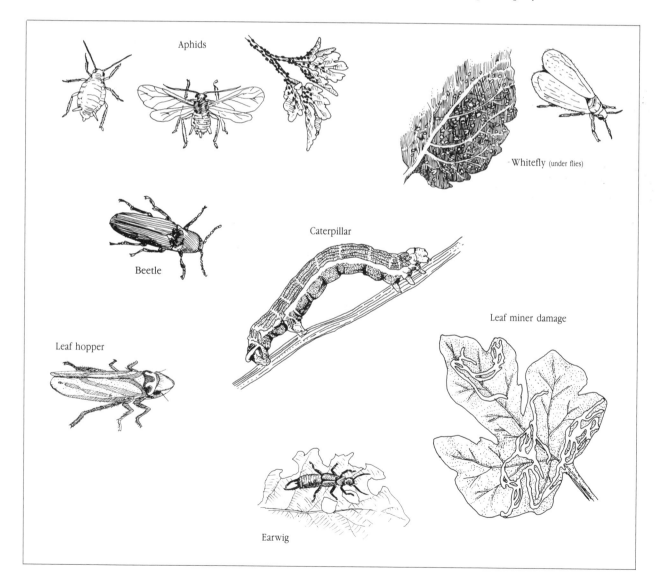

Aphids

Whitefly (under flies)

Beetle

Caterpillar

Leaf miner damage

Leaf hopper

Earwig

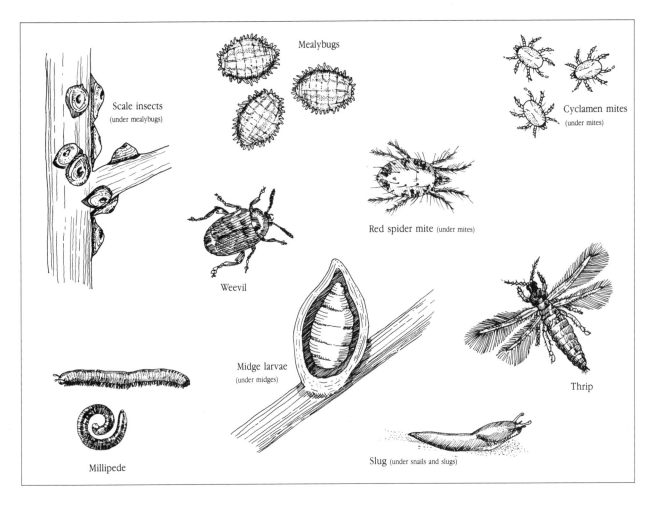

Mealybugs

Scale insects
(under mealybugs)

Cyclamen mites
(under mites)

Red spider mite (under mites)

Weevil

Thrip

Midge larvae
(under midges)

Millipede

Slug (under snails and slugs)

MEALYBUGS. Probably the best known of the scale insects, the cottony looking egg clusters of mealybugs make them easily recognizable. It is a common pest in milder climates, but in the North it is usually confined to greenhouses. Garden insecticides are used for control.

MIDGES. Galls, an abnormal growth on plants, are caused by these small flies, which are sometimes called gnats. The chrysanthemum gall midge is orange-colored and disfigures leaves, stems, and flower buds. Small infestations can be controlled by picking off the damaged parts. Malathion is effective if there are large invasions.

MILLIPEDES, CENTIPEDES, AND WIREWORMS. These are not true insects, and they are not usually a problem in perennial plantings except during the years when they may appear in large numbers. Diazinon gives good control.

MITES. Mites cause a blistered, rough appearance on leaves and often prevent flowers from opening. They are not true insects, but have eight legs like a spider, so are called spider mites. Because they are very tiny their damage may go unnoticed until it becomes extensive. The red spider mite and the two-spotted spider mite are common, as is the cyclamen

mite which can decimate delphiniums. Malathion is an acknowledged remedy.

NEMATODES. These microscopic insects live in the soil and in decaying organic matter. They feed on plant leaves and roots and are especially prevalent in cultivated soils. More of a menace in warm climates they attack a variety of bulbs and perennials such as anemones, campanula, *Dianthus*, *Digitalis*, hyacinths, narcissus, primrose, and phlox.

In areas where nematodes are known to be a serious problem, the soil of a newly prepared bed should be sterilized with Vapam or methyl bromide before planting. Both are restricted chemicals, so a licensed professional will have to perform this procedure. When buying new plants try to buy only from certified nurseries since your sterile beds can be easily reinfected. Some gardeners report good luck controlling nematodes by interplanting the tall, old-fashioned, strong-smelling marigolds among the plants. But if a garden is badly infected the only certain remedy is to dig out the plants and destroy them, sterilize the soil, and start again.

SAWFLIES. The large violet sawfly eats holes in violet and pansy leaves, most often at night. It also attacks poplars and willows, so their highest concentrations are often found in the vicinity of those trees. Most ordinary garden insecticides will control them, but several sprayings may be necessary.

SNAILS AND SLUGS. Though not insects, snails and slugs are serious garden pests because they chew large holes in plant leaves. They like cool, moist places and an acid soil, and usually feed at night. If slugs are a problem in your area use mulches judiciously, remove rubbish and other breeding places, and sprinkle alkaline materials such as lime or ashes about the garden to help control them. Slugs can't crawl well over rough material, so layers of sand or gravel will discourage their movement. Some gardeners lay a board on the ground to attract slugs that are seeking a cool place to hide during the day, then turn the board over and crush them with another board. Commercial slug bait may also help; the saucer-of-stale-beer trap method is more colorful than helpful.

THRIPS. These minute insects attack perennials by sucking out the sap in the leaves, which results in a silvery, mottled appearance. They are most active during hot, dry years. Pyrethrum, rotenone, and Sevin can be used to control them.

WEEVILS. Weevils attack *Althaea* (hollyhock), *Primula* (primrose), and some other perennials, but are not usually a serious problem in the border. All-purpose garden dusts and sprays give good control.

Physiological Problems

Plants can suffer from a host of environmental hazards that are often mistaken for disease or insect troubles. Perennials can look distressed because of too much or too little water, sun, fertilizer, or lime; as well as from overcrowding, growing in soil that has been compacted, or damage from wind, frost, or hail. Before reaching for the spray can, or calling the extension service, check out these possible causes.

ANIMAL SCOUNDRELS

Recently we received a frantic phone call from our neighbor down the road. She had spent the entire previous day separating her daylilies and had replanted them, carefully placing ¼ cup of bonemeal in each hole. The next morning not a single plant was still in the ground. It was clear that a skunk, fox, or coyote looking for dinner got on the scent of the bonemeal and carefully dug up each one, searching for the bone. We suggested that when she reset the plants she throw in a few mothballs to confuse the critter.

Wild animals aren't the only creatures that can devastate perennial beds. We've had pigs and cattle run through ours with disastrous results; dogs, goats, sheep, and ponies can wreck a garden in short order, too. Even cats seeking a cool place to nap on a hot day can crush small plants. We wish we could give you a surefire method of coping with animals in the garden, but after years of trying we can report only partial success. Wild animals are not only larger than bugs, but much more crafty because the less intelligent among them were destroyed by the selection process centuries ago. Guns, traps, and poisons are either illegal or unwise in many locations, so deer, woodchucks, and rabbits often have the upper hand.

Growers use flashing lights, noisemakers, human hair and urine, rotten eggs, mothballs, bloodmeal, and other foul smells, but get only mixed results because the animals discover over time that these tactics pose no real threat. Strong, tight fences—including electric ones—offer the best security; though they are fine around a vegetable garden or orchard, they can spoil the appearance of a perennial garden that is intended primarily for beauty. A dog is also good protection if it's smart enough to frighten off the pillagers without killing deer or getting involved with skunks or porcupines.

Gardeners formerly used chlordane to kill the grub that attracted moles and skunks to lawns and flower beds, but its use is now restricted. If skunks are your problem, and you have the nerve, set a Have-a-Heart-type box trap, bait it with cat food, and wait until morning. Then carefully throw a dark blanket over the trap, transport it far into the countryside, and let the animal go. Hopefully the skunk won't get home before you do!

Moles don't eat plants, but their burrowings are unsightly and let air into the roots which dries them out. Mice and voles also use these underground passageways, and they *do* eat roots and bulbs. Cats and traps are useful in combating these pests, but the best mole remedy we have tried is to drop rolled-up sticks of unwrapped Juicy Fruit gum into mole burrows. The moles love the gum, but apparently haven't learned to chew it without swallowing, which results in their premature demise. Use plastic gloves when handling the gum, so you won't leave a human smell on it.

The huge list of possible pests and hazards to perennial plants can appear distressing, but as we said earlier, most of them may never trouble you. Actually, the surprises that appear each season can not only provide a challenge, but also make for hot topics for discussions with fellow gardeners.

8

The Fine Art of Weed Control

Weeds, in spite of their bad reputation, do have a worthwhile purpose. Nature abhors barren earth nearly as much as it does a vacuum, and quickly works to cover any nude soil with weeds that will protect it from erosion, build up the soil, and make it productive once more. Although this works to the benefit of us all, we often wish, as we're on our knees in the perennial bed, that weeds didn't do their jobs quite so efficiently.

If you garden in a city or well-groomed suburb the weeds in your garden will be easier to control than those in a rural area where every breeze seems to be full of dandelion, grass, goldenrod, thistle, or milkweed seeds. Whenever you use raw farm manure, compost that is not fully decomposed, or spread straw and hay for mulch, you can add thousands of ambitious weed seeds to your garden soil.

KNOW YOUR ENEMIES

Even experienced gardeners sometimes have trouble differentiating between a plant and a weed. One grower told us that if a plant looks especially healthy and vigorous she assumes it must be a weed, but waits a few weeks before pulling it up, just to be sure. Whether you garden in the city or country, the seashore or the mountains, you will find weed species that are common to all areas and those that are restricted to a particular locale. If you learn to identify the most common weeds early in your gardening experience, and find out how they grow and reproduce, you'll be better able to control them.

Weeds are classified either as broadleafs or grasses. Broadleafs range from low-growing, creepy invaders such as wild veronica, chickweed, and purslane, to tall monsters like burdock and bull thistle. One of the worst weeds we face is quack grass, which you probably battle too, no matter where you live. In New England it is known as witchgrass, our Canadian friends call it twitch grass, and colorful adjectives often precede it in both regions.

Both grasses and broadleafs may be either annuals or perennials. Perennial weeds, such as quack grass, live for years and may spread over many acres by sending up new plants from their far-reaching roots as well as by scattering seeds. In only a few months one tiny horsetail plant (which produces spores as opposed to seeds) growing in lightweight soil can spread roots 40 feet in every direction and create a new plant every inch or two. Perennials like goldenrod reproduce rapidly by scattering seeds, as do annual weeds such as the vigorous lambsquarters, *Kochia*, and crabgrass. Scientists tell us it is possible for a single tiny groundsel to produce one billion seeds a year. A gardener's work is never finished!

WEED CONTROL

Controlling weeds is an exercise in persistence. If you spend a few minutes each day, or even twice a week, in your garden attacking the weeds they will be unable to get a foothold and reproduce. Deep, rich, loose garden soil makes weeds easy to pull before they become well anchored and, as we said before, a mulch discourages the sprouting of seeds that have been scattered by plants in the area, or blown in from afar.

Some gardeners prefer the chemical approach to weed control by relying on herbicides. In the past half century a great many weed killers have been developed; gardeners were told that chemicals would solve all their weed problems. But, like insecticides, some herbicides cause more problems than they solve, and the long-term effects of their accumulation in the soil and groundwater are still unknown.

The battle with weeds, as with bugs, will probably never be won, and each gardener has a sneaking suspicion that weeds would take over the world without his or her efforts. We recommend controlling weeds by hand whenever it is feasible. Weeding is good therapy, cheaper than an analyst, and a great way to get rid of aggression. There are even some gardeners who claim to derive great pleasure from wolfing down a meal of dandelion greens or lambs-quarters, like cannibals eating their enemies.

If you decide to use chemicals for some of your weed control, however, it is important to understand how they work. Herbicides are selective or nonselective. The selective types kill only certain weeds or grasses and are commonly used on farm crops. The nonselective destroy all vegetation: they are sprayed on driveways and paths, under fences, on rights-of-way, and to "clean up" areas before planting. The most common herbicides, both selective and nonselective, work in one or more of the following ways.

FOLIAR. When sprayed on foliage the chemical is absorbed by the plant. Among the herbicides that kill plant life in this manner are Roundup, which is effective on most growing plants, and Fusilade, a grass killer.

SOIL-ACTIVATED. Herbicides such as Princeps (simazine) and Aatrex (atrazine), when sprinkled, sprayed, or otherwise applied to the soil, are absorbed through the roots of certain weeds which destroys them.

PREMERGENT. When applied to the soil, herbicides such as Dacthyl and Treflan prevent the sprouting of seeds already in the soil, as well as those that blow in during the time that chemical is still active. Premergents do not kill established plants, but are effective in suppressing the growth of seeds in manure or mulch. They also prevent the sprouting of seeds self-sown by perennials and biennials. Although some are considered safe to use in established perennial beds, these herbicides may damage young perennials or annuals that are not well established.

If you feel that chemicals are the best method of weed control for you, contact your garden or farm store and explain your problem. Then follow directions carefully. Even when you use herbicides according to instructions, the results may vary each time. Their effectiveness depends greatly on the stage of growth of the plant, the type of soil, the rainfall, and the air temperature on the day you apply them.

We often dream of the day our plantings will be free of quack grass, purslane, and dandelions, but in our more logical thinking realize that, like bugs, all these nuisances will be around much longer than we will. As we continue in the struggle to keep them a safe distance from our perennial plantings, we'll try instead to appreciate their tenacity at what they do best, which is to serve as ground covers for wastelands and worn-out pastures.

WHY PLANTS MAY BE GROWING OR BLOOMING POORLY

- Clumps are too large and need dividing.
- Plants are set too deep or too shallow.
- Plants are too small or too young.
- Possible damage from frost.
- Soil is too wet or too dry.
- Plants need fertilizer or lime.
- Too much fertilizer or lime.
- Injury from careless use of garden sprays or weed killers.
- Injury from diseases such as wilts.
- Injury from insects, including tiny ones such as mites and aphids, or soil pests such as nematodes.
- Wilting from hot weather; drying winds.
- Damage from animals such as moles, gophers, woodchucks, deer, or even domesticated pets!

9

Garden Accessories and Lighting

Recently we visited an interesting small garden near a restored farmhouse. The owners had used the granite foundation of the former barn as a backdrop and combined it successfully with a stone statue they had picked up on a visit to Spain (which served as the focal point) next to a tiny pool. The colorful perennials were complemented by the man-made objects and the spot was charming.

The inanimate objects you insert can either enhance or detract from the overall effect of a garden. Small-scale statuary, planters, urns, sundials, and garden furniture should blend into the landscape rather than stand out as prominent features that distract you upon entering the area. Fortunately, most people today prefer a natural look to the once-popular painted rocks, pink flamingos, gazing globes, and plastic animals.

If you're starting from scratch, install first any walls, terraces, patios, pools, large fountains, pathways, steps, bridges, or other basic features that will become part of the overall landscape design. Be sure not to place such permanent fixtures in a spot where it may be necessary to eventually disturb them. We know of people who have had to dig up beautiful perennial beds, paths, and terraces to get at their water, sewage, or power lines.

It can be a pleasure to select ornaments to enhance your garden, and you probably have certain spots that suggest a particular object: perhaps a bench placed where the garden opens with a view to the sea or mountains, a rail fence lining a country pathway, Grecian urns to flank the entrance of a formal garden, or an arched rose arbor to connect two gardens. Another approach is to build your garden around a particularly impressive ornament as our friends did with their Spanish statue. A sundial makes an ideal center for an herb garden, or you might use a fountain or waterfall as a focal point that will add movement and a soothing sound. To introduce another kind of motion and sound, hang wind chimes or bells unobtrusively from the branch of a nearby tree. A few birdhouses, feeders, or a birdbath will attract motion and sound of yet another sort.

Whatever fixtures you choose should be appropriate to your home if it is nearby. A contemporary sculpture that would be suitable for a modern home would seem out of place near an early American homestead. Likewise, a flagstone pathway and rail fence would be in character near a colonial-style home, but a path of modern paving blocks or a basket weave fence would not.

Choose objects that are proportionate to your garden and its surroundings. At the Huntington Gardens in San Marino, California, rows of large classical statues flank a long lawn with a view to the hills, making an impressive and memorable scene. Even one of those statues would be completely out of place in our small backyard garden, just as our tiny sundial would be lost in the broad expanse at Huntington Gardens.

Everyone has an opinion about the tastefulness—or lack of it—of using small ornaments in the garden. We feel that they can be fun as long as they're not overdone. A cast iron frog or an earth-tone gnome in the right place can add a touch of whimsy to a bed of perennials, but if the garden is full of brightly colored plastic ducks and "Snail Crossing" signs, your attention is likely to gravitate toward them rather than to the flowers. We have a classic stone statue of Saint Francis, 18 inches tall, which was given to us by friends when they had to move their garden. It hides unobtrusively in the midst of our lavender each summer where one can come upon it quite unexpectedly.

As with interior decorating, the inanimate objects you use should contribute to an integrated whole in the garden. Experiment, if possible, with any unusual new object before you make it permanent. View it from various spots around the grounds and from indoors if it will be visible from the home. Earth-tone objects, weathered materials, and rocks blend into the landscape better than anything covered with white paint, or other articles with materials or colors that detract from the garden setting. Wood is especially attractive and appropriate, but must be treated with a wood preservative or sealer unless it is known to be durable like redwood or cypress.

ILLUMINATING YOUR GARDEN

Except for occasional moonlit walks most of us never see our perennials at night unless we hunt up a flashlight and make a special effort. If you entertain a great deal on summer evenings, however, or use your garden areas at night—near a swimming pool, tennis court, or patio—you may want to cast light on your perennials.

To illuminate a garden attractively is quite different from installing lights for safety or security. A professional outdoor lighting expert will spend many hours moving lights around to achieve just the right balance between light and shadow. Of course, there's no reason why you can't do the same thing by experimenting with portable floodlights.

It will help to visit other lighted landscapes before you invest heavily in such a project so you can compare the type of light each kind of bulb gives. Mercury vapor, quartz, incandescent, fluorescent, and others each shine with a different quality of light and distort to some degree the natural colors of foliage and flowers.

Because lights in the summer are likely to attract clouds of moths, and they in turn may attract swooping bats, you may want to consider using lights that are less inviting to insects, or setting up electric bug killers in unobtrusive spots.

Be certain that the wire you or your electrician uses is of a gauge that is heavy enough for everything on that system, as well as for any extra fixtures you might want later. Bury the wires deep enough so that they are not likely to be disturbed, make a chart so you can locate them if necessary, and be careful to avoid them when digging or driving metal posts.

Gardens that are illuminated by nonelectric lights have an entirely different quality. Gaslights, Kon Tiki kerosene torches, or Japanese stone lanterns are all used for evening entertaining. It is not easy to achieve unusual lighting effects on flowers without electricity, but the charm and mystery of a garden in flickering light cannot be duplicated by an incandescent bulb.

SUGGESTIONS FOR THE PLACEMENT OF LIGHTS

- Hide the light source. Obscure the bulbs high in the foliage of trees, or low, behind shrubbery. If you set up a high overhead light shining downward, use a second light beamed upward so the source of the upper one will be hidden. Downlighting emphasizes the foliage of trees and illuminates nicely the perennials, paths, pools, or the garden decorations.
- Light a terrace, patio, or path from a spot high enough that the light does not blind or glare. Add a dimmer switch if you want to adjust the lighting and make it more subtle.
- Illuminate a garden outside a picture window with floodlights mounted on the house which will shine toward the garden.
- Place submerged pool lights on the side from which the pool is seen so they won't shine in the viewer's eyes. Reflecting pool lights should be situated in such a way that only the plants to be reflected are illuminated.
- Light a rock garden from front and above, or from lights placed behind large rocks or shrubs at the sides of the garden like footlights.
- Illuminate running water in a fountain or waterfall either from behind or below to highlight the shimmering effect.

The Effect of Light on Plants

When you plan your garden lighting, it is important to realize that lights can sometimes affect the growth and flowering habits of nearby plants. If they are left on all night, or even for several hours in the evening, the plants will experience what amounts to a long summer day. This extension of light encourages faster growth and earlier flowering of certain plants such as carnations and many annuals, but it delays the blooming of chrysanthemums, fall asters, poinsettias, and others that flower only as the days get shorter. Small amounts of light have no effect on most perennials.

If you install bright lights in your perennial garden, and keep them on for long periods, it may also have a detrimental effect on certain shrubs and trees nearby which have their various stages of growth triggered according to the amount of light they receive. Some plants, if they get extra light in the fall when daylight hours would ordinarily be shortened, may not realize winter is coming and fail to develop their leaf and flower buds for the following spring. Many trees also need a shortened day to stop growing and harden their new growth before the first frost. If the growing season is artificially lengthened such trees may be full of sap and in lush growing condition when the first cold snap comes, and the entire tree can be killed. Careful gardeners use their garden lights only occasionally, if at all, during the month preceding the first likely fall frost.

Garden lighting enables people who work during the day to enjoy their plantings once the sun goes down. Although our garden is not fully lighted, we're glad to have our floodlight and post lantern when we entertain in the backyard, or when we want to show our perennials to evening guests. One friend told us she especially enjoys entertaining in her lighted garden, because the semidarkness effectively conceals many of the weeds that show so glaringly in bright sunlight!

Garden Culture

Everyone approaches gardening chores differently. The enthusiastic gardener, like an avid fisherman, feels that life is enhanced by such a pleasure-filled occupation. The garden is a spot for relaxation, an oasis in a worrisome world. Another gardener may regard the digging, watering, and weeding as a series of necessary tasks, comparable to housework, cleaning the garage, or painting the house. He or she tends to ignore the garden, and may only rush out to groom the plants before entertaining guests. We, and most other gardeners, fall somewhere between these two extremes. We enjoy our time in the garden, but sometimes feel pressured to fit the necessary chores into busy lives that are filled with other activities.

However you may feel about your garden tasks, it's important to stop clipping and weeding occasionally and appreciate your handiwork. Try not to focus only on the problems like one perfectionist we know who stalks his beds like Sherlock Holmes—magnifying glass in hand—looking for anything out of place. When he discovers a weed, insect, or disease he is ready for battle, before anything can proliferate. He snips off the lupine blossoms the day after they are past their prime, rescues the frail astilbe from its aggressive bee balm neighbor, and notes in his little book that the large clump of white peonies needs dividing as soon as they finish blooming. When we compliment him on such meticulous beds, he invariably points out some small detail that isn't quite perfect, and we suspect that he may never actually see the beauty of the garden because he concentrates only on the weak spots. Happy gardeners notice the flowers as well as the weeds, and see both the butterflies and the slugs.

SPRING CARE

Without the respite that winter affords, most of us would lose interest in an avocation as intensive as gardening. But each spring our vigor is renewed, along with the unrealistic hope that *this* year both our gardens and the weather will be perfect. By the time the snow has melted and the crocus and snowdrops have faded, any disappointments from the previous season are forgotten, and we are eager to dig in the soil once more. Early spring is a perfect time to be outdoors: the days are not yet too hot, the evenings are long, and the black flies and mosquitos are still asleep.

The first spring job is always to remove any mulch that is covering the tender perennials. You may want to remove mulch in two stages: first, push away the mulch from the *crown* of the plant for a week or two, then clear it all away (see Figure 10.1). The advantage of this system is that if there is the threat of a hard frost, you can easily cover the plants again with mulch until the danger is past. But at any rate, be sure to wait until a cloudy day to clear all the mulch away

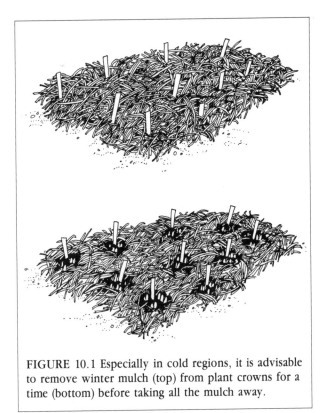

FIGURE 10.1 Especially in cold regions, it is advisable to remove winter mulch (top) from plant crowns for a time (bottom) before taking all the mulch away.

so the plants will have time to adjust to daylight before bright spring sunshine can "burn" any pale new growth.

The vigorous weeds always seem to appear first and grow faster than perennials, so as soon as their sprouts poke through the earth be ready to attack. We begin the cleaning out job armed with a trowel, clippers, and dandelion digger. For light spring jobs we've found that plastic laundry baskets are more convenient than garden carts for carrying tools, moving plants, and transporting weeds to the compost pile.

In addition to eliminating the weeds, it is usually necessary to reset a few *Primulas* and other shallow-rooted plants that frosts have popped out of the ground. Occasionally some of the young plants, such as daylilies, sink into the soil over the winter and must be raised up a few inches if they're going to grow well.

When everything has sprouted, look for empty spots. Some years every plant survives, but other springs you may need to consult the stake labels or your garden plan to discover which plants have died over the winter, and make a note to replace them. Although losing choice plants is tough, sometimes it is inevitable. Even if you do everything right, and the winter has been mild, certain varieties are naturally short-lived. And there may also be casualties among any new experimental plants. When there is a puzzling demise, we suspect the plant may have died out

of pure cussedness. A cynic once told us that the secret of successful gardening is to pretend you don't care whether a plant lives or dies, and it will usually live, just out of spite.

Early spring is a good time to move those plants that were blooming in the wrong place the previous year and to divide clumps that are too large (see Moving page 29, and Division pages 32–34). Only the spring bloomers, and a few others, such as iris, peonies, and Oriental poppies, which prefer to be moved during their dormant period after they have blossomed, are safe from this springtime shuffle. Dig the plant with a ball of soil and plant according to the directions on pages 59–60.

As the days get warmer, set out the new perennial varieties you couldn't resist in the garden catalogs last winter and the treasures you have discovered at local nurseries. This is also the time to transplant any perennial and biennial seedlings started in the seedbed last summer.

As soon as the foliage of daffodils and other spring bulbs has turned yellow or brown, clip it off. Sometimes daffodils stay green for what seems an abnormally long time, so we braid the tops together to make them more compact and less visible until the foliage looks dead (see Figure 10.2). If it is necessary, this is a good time to divide or move them. Also in late spring, dig up and store hyacinth and tulip bulbs for fall replanting.

If you used a mulch, earthworms will have worked beneath it to keep the soil loose and aerated. If you did not use mulch, the soil in your bed will probably have hardened, and spring is a good time to aerate it. Use a small spading fork and carefully cultivate around the plants to a depth of about 8 inches.

FIGURE 10.2. Braid green daffodil foliage after the flowers die to keep the plants from looking messy.

After the garden maintenance and planting tasks are done, cultivate small amounts of manure, compost, or a commercial fertilizer into the soil between the plants. If you use commercial fertilizer, mix one level tablespoon of 5-10-10 into the soil around each medium-sized clump. Adjust the amount accordingly for smaller or larger plants and clumps. Nutrients in the soil must be replaced each year because they are continually being depleted by plant growth and leaching.

EARLY SUMMER CARE

In addition to the fall or spring feeding, we give our plants a weak solution of liquid fertilizer once or twice during the early summer, especially if growth appears to be weak. This may not be necessary if they are thriving, but after a few seasons of gardening you'll know what your plants need and when to adjust their feeding schedules accordingly.

A good time to replenish mulch is after the soil has been fertilized and the spring moving and dividing chores are over. Apply 1 to 2 inches of mulch after a hard rain when the soil is well soaked. Tough weeds can still penetrate the mulch, but they can be pulled out easily.

Staking

No one enjoys having to use artificial supports in the garden, but perennials that become floppy or break easily in a wind or rainstorm must be staked. In an informal garden that is protected from the wind, it may be necessary to stake only those plants with large, heavy blooms such as peonies and tall-growing delphiniums, hollyhocks, and golden glows (*Rudbeckia laciniata*). But if your garden is formal, or in a windy spot, you may need to stake plants such as lilies, lupine, foxglove, and other flowers of medium height.

Bamboo, wood, plastic, and metal stakes of various sizes, and plant ties (heavy green twine or yarn) are all available commercially. Pieces of cloth torn into strips can also be used for tying and staking. To make homemade ties as inconspicuous as possible some gardeners rub them in soil or dye them green. Don't use ordinary string or wire because it will cut into the plant stems.

The trick to effective and inconspicuous staking is timing. Do it early, as soon as the stems are sturdy enough, but before flower buds form and the plants actually need it. That way the stakes and ties will be

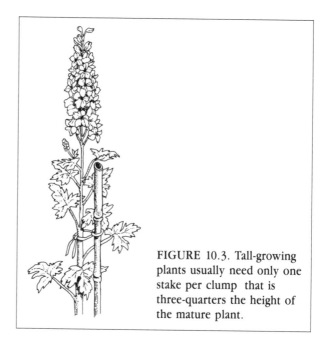

FIGURE 10.3. Tall-growing plants usually need only one stake per clump that is three-quarters the height of the mature plant.

hidden behind the new foliage as it grows. Some plants, such as *Aconitum* and *Digitalis*, need only one stake per clump at a height about three-quarters that of the mature plant (see Figure 10.3). Loop the tying material around the entire clump and secure it by wrapping it around the stake two or three times.

A large clump, such as hollyhocks or delphinium, must be treated differently. The traditional method is to place three or four stakes at intervals around the exterior of the clump. Wrap twine or yarn around the stakes at 1-foot intervals up from the soil as the plant grows. The foliage will intertwine with the support, thereby making it less visible. In recent years we have used 4-foot, three-sided, metal "tomato" fences to support these large clumpy plants (see Figure 10.4). As the plant grows, the foliage surrounds the supports

Drawing by David Sylvester

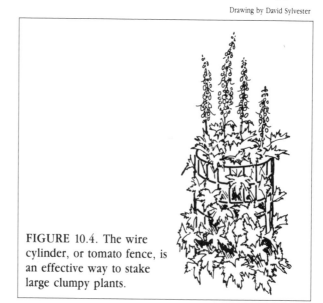

FIGURE 10.4. The wire cylinder, or tomato fence, is an effective way to stake large clumpy plants.

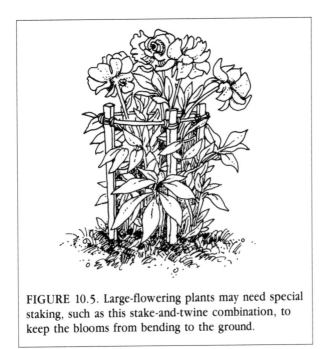

FIGURE 10.5. Large-flowering plants may need special staking, such as this stake-and-twine combination, to keep the blooms from bending to the ground.

and they become nearly invisible. Their greatest advantage is the ease of installation, but we have friends who live near a windswept lake who are even more efficient. They built two parallel rustic rail fences 2 feet apart, at the back of their border, and plant their giant Pacific hybrid delphinium between them.

Peonies and large flowering mums need special staking—not because of their height, but because of their extraordinarily heavy blossoms. Ring-type supports on wire stakes suitable for these plants are available at garden centers and in catalogs. Or you can make your own by welding a heavy ring such as wreath wire to metal garden stakes. The ring supports the stems, yet allows the foliage and blossoms to bend over it naturally. Figure 10.5 shows another option using wooden stakes and garden twine tied at a height appropriate to keep the heavy blooms from falling over.

SUMMER GROOMING AND CARE

After new perennials are well established and deeply rooted they need less attention, but the garden must not be left unattended—the frequent footsteps of the gardener are the best fertilizer. Summer grooming is similar to tidying up a room, only more fun. Most jobs are obvious: remove the weeds as soon as they appear, and cut off any broken, dead, or injured stems as well as all diseased or insect-damaged leaves.

The most frequent summer activity is *deadheading*. This aggressive verb seems to be peculiar to

gardeners since it is not listed in our unabridged dictionary, but it describes perfectly the act of snipping off faded flowers with your pruning scissors, a knife, or even your fingers (Figure 10.6). This habit has become so established in us that more than once we've found ourselves in the embarrassing position of deadheading when we visit a friend's garden!

Faded flowers should be removed not only for appearance's sake, but because seeds will form if they are not removed. Seed development weakens the plant, causes it to stop blooming early, and sometimes even shortens its life. Certain biennials such as foxgloves and forget-me-nots produce an abundance of seeds in order to perpetuate their kind, and these can grow into horrendous weeds. Other plants, if allowed to procreate, produce vigorous, but inferior, seedlings which crowd out their hybrid parents. All over the countryside there are phlox seedlings of a dull magenta color that have taken over the beds of their brightly colored ancestors.

In climates with a long enough growing season, cutting back lupine, phlox, *Anthemis*, and delphinium plants directly after blooming will often encourage a second flowering in late summer.

It is during the warmth and humidity of summer days that diseases and insects are most likely to proliferate, so watch for them during your regular garden inspections. At one time gardeners were urged to spray early and often to prevent any possible troubles, but in today's chemically conscious world most of us don't spread pesticides without good reason. For more on pest control, please refer to chapter 7.

If the perennials appear to need additional fertilizer, give them a liquid feeding of fish emulsion, seaweed, a chemical fertilizer such as Miracle-Gro, or a light

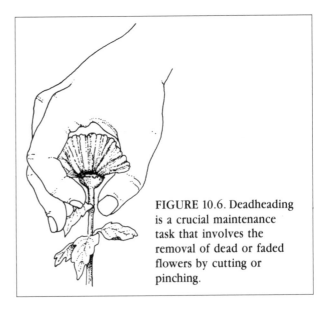

FIGURE 10.6. Deadheading is a crucial maintenance task that involves the removal of dead or faded flowers by cutting or pinching.

sprinkling of 5-10-10. One of our favorite summer dressings is *manure tea*. In a large, covered plastic garbage can that is filled with water we keep a burlap bag of manure gleaned from a neighbor's barnyard. As we remove "tea," we add more water. The resultant liquid solution gives plants a good balance of fast-acting nutrients.

Be careful not to overfeed perennials. Too much fertilizer is likely to stimulate lush foliage growth, but could result in fewer blooms.

At one time or another watering becomes a necessity. New plants and seedlings without a heavy root system need extra water, and in a dry climate or drought period you may need to irrigate the entire garden. Don't provide water unless there is good reason, however, because the plants will become dependent on it and fail to develop the deep roots they need for good growth.

During a dry spell, a heavy soaking about twice a week is more beneficial than a light daily watering. Water moves through the soil slowly, and a short, heavy shower or watering may not reach the roots before it evaporates. At least 1 inch of water, either rain or irrigation, is the minimum amount necessary to provide sufficient moisture to soak through mulch and soil and reach the roots. A rain gauge is a helpful piece of garden equipment, but judging how much is the *right* amount of water for your garden is often a matter of "by guess and by gosh."

Because moisture evaporates rapidly in the heat of the day, do not water when the sun is high unless the plants are obviously wilting. Some gardeners feel that the best time to water is early morning because the sun will quickly dry any moisture on the leaves; whereas watering in the evening keeps the foliage wet all night and can encourage disease. We prefer evening irrigation because less evaporation takes place at that time and the results last longer. We have heavy dews in our area, which also keep the plants moist throughout the night.

If you use lawn or irrigation-type sprinklers check the results occasionally. Water from them falls like a light shower and may never even reach the soil under plants with heavy, umbrellalike foliage. For this reason, we prefer to use a soaker hose rather than a lawn sprinkler so that the water goes to the soil rather than the foliage.

Pinching and Thinning

Home gardeners sometimes wonder why their plants aren't as impressive as the magnificent specimens in the garden catalogs. The secret is not a magic fertilizer or mystical incantation, but simple pinching or thinning which anyone can do as well as the professionals.

To grow chrysanthemums as compact and bushy as those at the florist's, pinch the ends of the new sprouts once a week or so in early summer. This pinching will stimulate the growth of side branches, make them produce more blooms, and prevent them from becoming tall and leggy.

Another technique to get larger flowers on certain perennials, is to disbud or pinch off part of the flower buds to make the remaining flowers much bigger. To get giant-sized peony blossoms, for example, pick off all of the small side buds in early summer. The plant's energy will be forced into the one fat bud at the end of each stem. Later in the season you may want to repeat this procedure on your large-blooming *Hibiscus* and chrysanthemums. Just as with thinning carrots, the results will be well worth your trouble.

You can encourage better blossoms on perennials that produce numerous shoots per clump, such as phlox, delphinium, *Helenium*, hollyhocks, daisies, and hardy asters, by thinning out some of the stalks when they are about 4 or 5 inches tall. Thinning also allows better air circulation within the clump, which discourages rusts and mildews.

Summer Transplanting

There are gardeners who like to move things about and there are those who never disturb a plant—no matter how out of place it may look. Years ago we gardened for a lady who moved the furniture so often her husband was never sure where he would sleep at night, and she frequently rearranged her flower border with the same restless energy. She employed another part-time gardener, and since we all worked on different days and didn't see each other, we never knew where any perennial might be the next time we appeared! The poor plants never had a chance to adjust and grow well.

For your sake and the sake of the plants, a weekly shuffling of the garden is not recommended, but occasionally a perennial does need to be moved. You can transplant successfully—even when the plant is in bloom—if you are careful. Problems may occur when a clump is very large; and certain plants suffer when they are dug up out of season—the gas plant or Oriental poppy, for instance.

Choose a rainy or cloudy day, or the cool of the evening, for transplanting. If the soil is dry, water the plant thoroughly before you uproot it so the soil will stick firmly to the roots. Dig it up carefully in order to keep the entire root ball intact, and follow the rules given earlier for planting. Be generous with water, and add a small amount of liquid fertilizer to the first watering. If you notice it is wilting, shade it from the sun for a few days with a basket, pasteboard carton, paper bag, or white sheet.

FALL CHORES

Gardeners disagree about how to treat their perennials in the fall, such as how to mulch, and whether or not to cut plants back to the ground after blooming. We feel it makes sense to let the plants die down naturally so that all the nutrients in the leaves and stems can return to the roots to be stored for the winter. After a light frost or two, we do cut off the dead stems. Because we live in snow country we leave about 6 inches of old stem to catch and hold the winter snow for additional insulation. If your garden will not be covered with snow, cut the stems back to about 2 inches from the ground.

Mulching in the fall helps to protect dormant plants during the winter months. Tender plants, if unprotected, are likely to die during extremely low temperatures, and shallow-rooted perennials are often heaved out of the ground by the alternate freezing and thawing of the earth. We have found that a 3- to 6-inch mulch of leaves, or other organic material, tucked around our perennials each fall will help to prevent most winter losses.

As extra insurance for the tender varieties (plants such as chrysanthemum, *Kniphofia*, and *Hypericum* in our climate), we cover them with several thicknesses of evergreen boughs. If you don't live in evergreen country, use other insulating materials such as straw, salt hay, or the foam blankets sold in garden stores. Do not completely cover the plants with boughs or any other insulating material until after the ground begins to freeze a bit at night and you are sure they are completely dormant. Otherwise, the perennials may continue to grow under the cover, and the new growth is likely to be killed when the cold finally penetrates it.

With the coming of winter, gardeners should pause for a while. A garden is never finished, but late fall is the closest we come to feeling that it is. That is the time to clear out the brain and rest the gardening muscles for a while. By late January we will have forgotten about weeds and bugs and be eager once again to make plans for spring.

A Perennial Gardener's Calendar

Obviously one garden calendar will not fit all the planting zones of the United States and Canada. Spring arrives in each zone at various times, as does the first fall frost, and each of these may differ from year to year even in the same locality. Therefore, the suggestions below—given for zones 5 through 7—can serve only as a general guide, and must be modified to accommodate the area in which you live.

January/February

- Read inspiring and helpful garden books. Study the catalogs.
- Review your perennial record book.
- Design a perennial garden.
- Order plants, seeds, flats, starting mix, pots, labels, and stakes. Inspect new tools and equipment in hardware stores and garden centers.
- Plant perennial and biennial seeds in flats under grow lights.

March/April/May

- Clean up the garden as soon as the snow is gone.
- Uncover tender plants when the threat of hard frosts is past.
- Replant any plants that were heaved out of the ground by frost.
- Start weeding. If you use herbicides, apply the pre-mergent kinds early before new weed seeds sprout.

- Divide fast-growing perennials (*Bellis*, chrysanthemum, *Gaillardia*, geranium, *Hemerocallis*, *Kniphofia*, lily-of-the-valley, phlox, *Salvia*, shasta daisy) and others that are becoming too large.
- Transplant any perennials that you want to relocate.
- Expand the border, if necessary, and build any new gardens.
- Set out any seedlings and cuttings you started last summer, and when the weather warms up, all those you grew inside over the winter. Plant any newly purchased perennials. Be sure to label everything.
- Cultivate around the clumps and fertilize everything.
- Add mulch if the old layer is getting thin.
- Keep notes in your record book about new plantings, successes, and failures, and include comments and ideas for the future.
- Take cuttings from the tips of chrysanthemums and delphiniums to propagate new plants.
- Use a good fungicide to spray or dust hollyhocks, phlox, and any other plants that are susceptible to disease.
- Cut back the wilted flowers of early-blooming plants. Divide daffodils as soon as they die down if they are too crowded. Dig and store tulip bulbs in a cool closet for fall replanting.
- Ventilate greenhouses, cold frames, and hotbeds.
- Watch for early signs of aphids and other insects, and launch an attack if they appear.
- Stake tall-growing plants.

- Pinch back chrysanthemum sprouts to promote bushiness.
- Pick some of the buds off peonies for larger blooms.

June

- Keep fading flowers picked so the plants will continue to bloom longer, except for those you have chosen to produce seed.
- Cut back delphinium after they have blossomed to encourage a fall bloom.
- Continue to pinch back chrysanthemums.
- Weed, spray, and water as needed.
- Layer the creeping phlox, dwarf pinks, and ground covers if you want more plants (see pages 40–1).
- If you wish, take photos of the garden in bloom every two weeks throughout the summer.

July

- Plant newly gathered seeds as soon as they ripen, or dry and save them for late winter planting indoors.
- Continue to weed, water, spray, and cut off all faded blooms.
- Apply liquid fertilizer or manure tea if plants are not growing well.
- Make a list of those things you wish that you'd done last winter when you were less busy and file it away for January reference.

August

- Continue weeding and deadheading as needed. Discontinue feeding.
- Be especially watchful for disease and insects; take steps to control them if necessary.

- Fill your home with perennial bouquets, share them with your friends.
- Divide and replant iris, Oriental poppies, and peonies if the clumps are too large.
- Transplant any seedlings into pots or transplant beds; or into the garden if they are large enough.
- Stake tall-growing chrysanthemums and other fall-blooming plants.

September/October/November

- Continue watering and insect and disease control as long as necessary.
- Dig out, give away, or discard any plants that you want to replace.
- Prepare the soil for any new plantings.
- Cut back all perennials for neatness, disease control, and to prevent seeding. Leave a few inches of stem to hold snow for winter protection in northern climates.
- Do some final weeding; mulch between the plants with newly fallen leaves or other mulch.
- Cover tender perennials with evergreen boughs as soon as the ground starts to freeze lightly.

December

- Clean, oil, and store all your garden tools. Take an inventory of supplies so you can order necessary items before spring.
- Buy gift certificates for plants, seeds, or gadgets as Christmas gifts for your gardening friends, and drop gentle hints concerning the garden supplies and books you've been coveting.
- Finally, sit down a few minutes and enjoy the pictures you took last summer of those plants now sleeping comfortably under the mulch and snow.

PART II

A FEAST OF GARDENS

When we hear the words "perennial garden" most of us envision a border: a bed where an everchanging panorama of attractive flowers blooms throughout the spring, summer, and fall. But perennials are not limited to borders—some of the myriad species can be found planted alongside garden paths, in collections consisting of many varieties of a single species, in pots and planters, or on a rocky slope. Perennials are also at home in water gardens, shady woodland glens, country cottage gardens, wildflower beds, herb patches, foundation plantings around a house, and in other specialty gardens. On the pages that follow we hope you will find ideas and inspiration to create gardens that will give you perennial pleasure.

Illustrations by Elayne Sears

12

The Perennial Pathway

"To lead her down the garden path" is likely to connote something quite different to a gardener than to the rest of the world. When we lead someone in that direction the purpose is innocent: to show him or her a new bloom perhaps or to enlist suggestions for improving the garden layout. A pathway makes an ideal setting for perennials whether you use a modest row of chrysanthemums to line a short, straight walkway from the porch or garage, or an elaborate path through meadow and woods bordered by shrubs, trees, annuals, and herbaceous perennials. Planted pathways can add character to your landscaping, too, by dividing a large garden into interesting smaller plots. From a practical point of view, a path is not only a good place to view the plants, but makes it easier to haul along a garden cart as well.

A perennial path has added impact when it leads to a spot of interest. In a flat or formal garden, a sundial, gazebo, or statue might be a fine focal point, and in a more natural setting the path might lead to another garden, a small pool, or simply to a bench where you can sit and enjoy the beauty.

A path may be as simple as a strip of mown grass, or it can be crushed rock or shell, gravel, bark nuggets, flagstone, slate, or elaborately designed brick. It may also be paved with asphalt or concrete. Investigate the choices thoroughly before deciding what best fits your needs because the construction and maintenance of each type of surface is quite different. A poorly paved pathway may crack where frosts go deep, and even flagstones, bricks, and slate should be laid on a base of gravel or coarse sand to provide proper drainage and prevent heaving. If you use crushed rock or a similar material, install an edging to border it so that perennial roots will not infringe on the path. An edging will also keep loose path materials and garden mulches separate from each other. Make the path wide enough (a minimum of 3 or 4 feet) so that it will invite strollers and won't disappear as the plants grow larger. Use clothesline or rope to define the edges before you start to dig.

Your choice of perennials for lining the path may be limited by climatic, soil, and light conditions. Spring bulbs, rock plants, ground covers, and other low-growing plants make good choices for sunny paths. A woodsy lane might be lined with wildflowers, hostas, ferns, or other shade-loving foliage plants. One of the most charming garden paths we've ever had the pleasure to walk along meandered beside a small brook and ascended a hillside. Tucked into narrow beds were colorful *Primulas* of every shape and size. Another one of our favorite paths winds through a friend's backyard to her vegetable garden and is bordered with edible herbs.

If your area is open, a few shrubs or small trees might be planted as a background in addition to the perennials. Select evergreen or flowering plants that

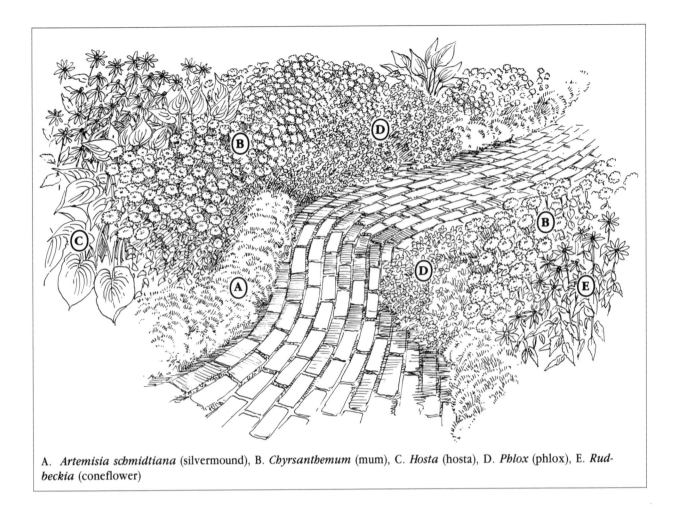

A. *Artemisia schmidtiana* (silvermound), B. *Chyrsanthemum* (mum), C. *Hosta* (hosta), D. *Phlox* (phlox), E. *Rudbeckia* (coneflower)

will not grow too large and overhang the path and its flower border—or be prepared to prune them back severely forevermore.

There are no hard rules for choosing the plants to be used along a pathway, but tall-growing species, such as delphinium, and sprawlers like Oriental poppies, are not recommended. As in other borders, a mass of similar plants is more effective than a mixture of one-of-a-kinds. Attractive foliage plants can be as effective as a collection of flowering perennials. Some gardeners change their pathway plantings throughout the year: daffodils and other bulbs in spring, annuals for summer bloom, and chrysanthemums for autumn.

It is difficult to say how wide the plantings on each side of the path should be. Usually they are narrower than a normal border planting. If you use only *Primula* or other compact plants, a 2-foot width might be enough; but for hostas, ferns, and larger plants a minimum of 4 feet would be necessary.

13

The Seasonal Garden

A garden that blooms only during specific times of the season is ideal if you have a vacation cottage, or spend part of the year away from home. People who leave suburban homes or city town houses during the summer may choose to create a spring and fall garden at their year-round home, and one filled with summer-blooming perennials at their mountain or lakeshore retreat. Vacationers who spend June and July in our community fill their gardens with delphinium, lilies, peonies, Oriental poppies, sweet William, and other early-blooming varieties. The August residents plant shasta and gloriosa daisies, campanula, phlox, daylilies, and similar perennials that bloom during that time.

Even if you never leave home you may enjoy a seasonal garden, especially if you have limited time or a very small area. Many northerners have unsettled spring weather—tulips and other early perennials can be ruined in a late snowstorm or subzero temperatures. Although few of us would forego the pleasures of growing daffodils for this reason, it makes sense to concentrate more effort on perennials that bloom after the weather has stabilized, and avoid fussing with plants that often have their blooming period cut short. Likewise, those who live where late summer is extremely hot may wish to avoid plants that bloom in August, and devote their time, instead, to the early summer and fall bloomers.

Even when none of these reasons prevail, some gardeners prefer the fun of seasonal beds. Many people plant spring bulbs, but have no garden the rest of the year; others have collection gardens (see chapter 28), or simply masses of a chosen perennial such as iris, peonies, or chrysanthemums. We have seen large gardens separated by walls into a series of small plots, each representing a few weeks of the season. Even though only one section of the garden would be blooming at a time, it was interesting to wander through them at different times of the spring, summer, and fall.

Chapter 2 provides a list of perennial blossoming times to help you make the best choices if you want flowers for only one or two months of the year. To choose even more precisely, buy plants in bloom from your local garden center during the weeks in which you want your best display.

14

A Garden For Bouquets and Arrangements

When gardeners want a bouquet of fresh flowers they generally pluck some from a border, choosing each bloom carefully so as not to spoil the current display. If you need large quantities of cut flowers—for your own pleasure, or to exhibit, give away, or sell—they should be grown separately in what the Victorians called a "cutting garden." In such a garden you can pick to your heart's content without concern about the effect on the bed when you've finished.

A cutting garden is not designed to be a spot of great beauty throughout the season, so it shouldn't be located in immediate view. We keep a small cutting bed in one corner of our vegetable garden where it is accessible and easy to tend. The plants are set like the vegetables so we can use a push cultivator and pick them easily. With the bed in that location we are unconcerned about plant heights, color clashes, or blooming times.

Even though the appearance does not matter as it would in a show garden, it is essential to weed frequently so the perennials won't be crowded or deprived of nutrients and moisture. Provide adequate water and fertilizer to obtain the maximum number of flowers, and deadhead regularly to prevent seed formation.

CHOOSING VARIETIES

By selecting perennials that bloom at different times, you can have cut flowers from early spring until the first light frost, and even after if hardy asters and chrysanthemums are among your choices. Although almost any perennial may be used in a flower arrangement, some are far better than others—not only because of their beauty, but also because they last longer after arranging. Certain varieties of *Astilbe* shatter immediately after picking, for instance, and an arrangement of daylilies will not look at all the same on the second day. Our list of the best perennials for cutting is below, but yours will undoubtedly be somewhat different after you've been growing flowers for a while.

Achillea, yarrow
Aconitum, monkshood
Anemone japonica, Japanese anemone
Anthemis, marguerite
Aster
Campanula, bellflower
Carnation
Centaurea montana, mountain bluet
Chrysanthemum
Chrysanthemum coccineum, pyrethrum
Chrysanthemum maximum, shasta daisy
Coreopsis, tickseed
Crocosmia, montebretia
Delphinium
Dicentra, bleeding-heart
Doronicum, leopard's bane
Echinops, globe thistle
Gaillardia, blanketflower
Gypsophila, baby's-breath
Helenium, sneezeweed
Helianthus, sunflower
Iris

Kniphofia, torch lily
Liatris, gayfeather
Lupinus, lupine
Paeonia, peony
Penstemon, beardtongue
Physostegia virginiana, false dragonhead
Rudbeckia, gloriosa daisy
Salvia, flowering sage
Trollius, globeflower
Veronica, speedwell

Suggestions For Miniature Bouquets

Convallaria, lily-of-the-valley
Heuchera, coral bells
Iberis, candytuft
Myosotis, forget-me-not
Viola, pansy, viola

In addition to perennials, most cutting gardens include a generous number of colorful annuals and bulb-type plants that make good cut flowers. A few daffodils, narcissus, tulips, grape hyacinth, and fragrant freesia are welcome in the spring; asters, bachelor buttons, calendula, celosia, zinnia, stocks, snapdragon, *Lavatera*, sweet peas, dahlias, gladioli, and other bouquet favorites are good choices as the season progresses. Even herbs make good bouquets—we use Italian parsley as greenery for small-scale bouquets, and dill for its large, showy flower heads.

Picking

It is best to pick in the morning when the stems are filled with water and the plants covered with dew. Take a pail full of tepid water to the garden, along with *sharp* scissors, clippers, or a knife. Select only prime flowers: those that are just opening or have recently opened. Cut the stem on a slant or straight across—we've found it doesn't matter which, as long as the instrument is sharp and does not crush the stem tissue. Take stems that are as long as possible to give yourself more latitude in arranging, and remove the bottom leaves so they won't pollute the water. Store the pail and flowers in a cool place until you are ready to use them.

Arranging

Anyone can pick perennial flowers and stick them in a vase, but it's just as easy to *arrange* them using a few devices purchased from a garden shop: an instant oasis which is reusable, a pinholder (or needlepoint holder), and floral clay. An oasis makes all the difference because it will hold the stems wherever

you want them. Never let one flower depend on another to hold it upright. Cut the oasis slightly smaller than the container and put it on a needlepoint holder that you've covered with a piece of nylon panty hose as shown in the illustration. That way the oasis can be easily removed later. If the holder doesn't stay in place, fasten it to the bottom of the container with floral tape or clay. Soak the oasis in lukewarm water for a minute before you set any flowers in it.

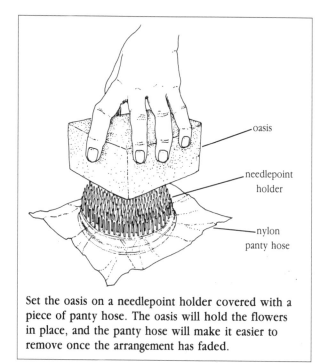

oasis

needlepoint holder

nylon panty hose

Set the oasis on a needlepoint holder covered with a piece of panty hose. The oasis will hold the flowers in place, and the panty hose will make it easier to remove once the arrangement has faded.

The container you choose should be clean so the flowers will stay fresh, and the flowers you use should relate well to it. Neutral-colored containers are usually best and even plain jars and cans can be hidden in baskets, an antique kettle, or other imaginative receptacle.

If you are arranging for a flower show there are any number of rules to follow, but for a home arrangement only a few of them need apply. First, consider where the arrangement will go, so you can design it to fit in the intended space. Will it be seen from one side only—perhaps on a mantel or wall nook, for example—or from all sides as a table centerpiece? Second, arrange the height of the bouquet in proportion to the height of the container. Inexperienced arrangers tend to use vases that are too tall and it is common to see flower heads barely peeking out over the top. The container should be no more than one-third the height of the arrangement. Third, decide the shape of the arrangement *before* you begin, whether triangular, circular, or something else. Then use the heavier flowers—those that are larger or darker in

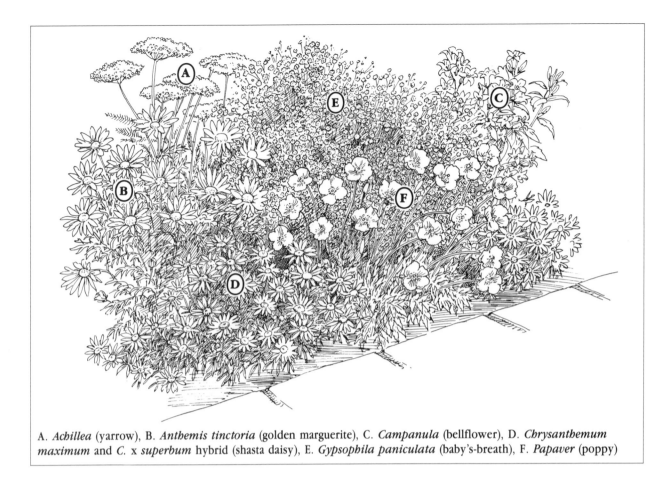

A. *Achillea* (yarrow), B. *Anthemis tinctoria* (golden marguerite), C. *Campanula* (bellflower), D. *Chrysanthemum maximum* and *C.* x *superbum* hybrid (shasta daisy), E. *Gypsophila paniculata* (baby's-breath), F. *Papaver* (poppy)

color—in the center, and the lighter, smaller ones near the perimeter. And finally, cover the oasis completely with greenery so it will be invisible. You'll then be ready to arrange your flowers into a blue-ribbon bouquet.

FLOWERS FOR DRYING

We went to colonial Williamsburg once in November and regretted that we were unable to view the gardens when they were in bloom. But the beautiful dried arrangements in each home nearly compensated for what we missed in summer. As long as people have gardened they have dried flowers to enjoy during the cold seasons, and modern techniques make it easy to dry even those species that were once difficult to dry successfully.

Some of the loveliest dried perennials, such as the *Physalis alkekengi* (Chinese lantern) and *Lunaria* (money plant), do not make much of a splash in the summer garden so are good plants to raise in a cutting garden. Other varieties grown especially for easy drying are achillea, artemesia, *Echinops ritro* (globe thistle), statice, and annuals such as strawflowers.

Many of these can be dried easily the old-fashioned way by stripping off the leaves, tying them together by the stems, and hanging them upside down out of the sunlight, in a dry, warm attic or garage for 2 to 4 weeks. The dried flowers are then stored in paper bags. The best and fastest method of drying garden perennials is by packing the blooms carefully in silica gel. This product evaporates the moisture so rapidly that the plant's form and color are retained extremely well. It is available, with directions for use, at garden centers and from seed companies.

Enjoying Your Cut or Dried Perennials

A friend astounded us recently by saying that she never picked any flowers to bring indoors because they were so messy and covered with ants, earwigs, and slugs. Her argument does not deter us from enjoying fresh bouquets in the kitchen, dining room, living room, bedrooms, and even the bathroom from early spring until fall frosts. Blooms from our garden go into church arrangements, wedding and anniversary bouquets, corsages, decorative dried bunches, and to sick friends in the hospital and nursing homes. We use them as hostess gifts and cut impulsive bouquets for our visitors. They make us feel wealthy!

15

A Foundation Garden

There was a time when no one would think of buying anything but tightly clipped evergreens for foundation plants around their home. Not anymore. Flowering shrubs, food plants, and planters filled with annuals are now popular, and many homeowners like us use perennial flowers for this purpose—they are far less expensive than shrubbery and easier to bring home and plant. But we grow them primarily because here in the North tons of snow and ice either fall or must be shoveled from rooftops every winter. The weight of winter precipitation has devastated our evergreens and flowering shrubs, and although we have built structures to cover the few we have, we now grow mostly herbaceous perennials around the house. They solve our problem easily by hiding underground for the snow season.

Even where heavy snows are not a problem, perennials are popular for foundation planting because they add such interesting foliage textures and an ever-changing variety of colorful blooms to an otherwise green landscape. Hollyhocks seem to belong next to a shingled country cottage, and plantings of peonies, daylilies, and monkshood look natural around a Cape bungalow. Our neighbors have a narrow perennial bed bordering the front of their white clapboard New England home; it provides them and all passersby with a constant change of blooms from the earliest spring bulbs to late-fall chrysanthemums.

The best perennials to use near a house are those that will develop into good-sized plants, but not spread out too much. Because they are always on display, they should have attractive foliage and look nice even when not in bloom. We use several varieties and heights of daylilies for this purpose, as well as large clumps of pink peonies, which people often mistake for rhododendron. Hostas are excellent, especially for shady spots, and the aromatic *Dictamnus* (gas plant) also works well in the shade. Plants such as *Dicentra spectabilis* (old-fashioned bleeding-heart), lupines, delphinium, and Oriental poppies are all attractive when they're in bloom, but look sad after their blossoming period is finished and the foliage has died back. If you use them, do it sparingly, and tuck in tall-growing annuals or brightly colored geraniums to camouflage their messy postbloom foliage.

If your building is white, brown, gray, or another neutral shade, you will not need to be fussy about choosing flowering plants of the proper color; but if it is red, blue, yellow, or an unusual tone, select plants that will have compatible blooms. Those with pale or white blossoms may be your only option.

You can plant large clumps of the more massive perennials just as you would evergreens or flowering shrubs, with tall ones at the corners and on each side of the front doorways, and with lower-growing kinds under the windows. Or you may decide to grow a narrow perennial border or cottage garden next to the building instead.

If your building has wood siding, leave a space between your perennials and the structure so the moisture-holding plants won't rot the wood or deteriorate the paint. Unless you plan to water frequently, set the perennials outside the drip line of any overhanging roof so they will get the benefit of rainfall. We have found that the more rugged varieties of hosta and daylilies grow well even under the eaves without drain spouts, but it is not advisable to set plants where they might drown in a downpour.

As in any planting, provide good topsoil, proper drainage, and a location that will provide enough sunlight. Mulch the area around the plants with bark, woodchips, or another attractive material: it will prevent rain from splashing dirt on the house, help control weeds, and conserve soil fertility. Add fertilizer a couple of times during the summer if rain from the roof is likely to wash out fertility, and add a sprinkling of lime each year for the same reason. A weed-check fabric (available from most garden supply stores) that allows moisture to penetrate, placed under the mulch, will save a lot of weeding time.

Shaded areas that receive only a few hours of direct sunlight, but are still exposed to bright skylight the rest of the day are not a good spot for sun-loving plants. Best plant choices for these spots are *Aquilegia*, *Dicentra eximia*, ferns, hosta, *Hemerocallis*, monkshood, and trollius. For the difficult-to-grow north side of a building and other areas that get little direct sunlight try ferns, hosta, and beds of *Convallaria* (lily-of-the-valley). For a list of other shade-loving perennials see page 94.

Perennials often used as foundation plants include:
Althaea rosea, hollyhock
Chrysanthemum
Chrysanthemum maximum, shasta daisy
Dictamnus, gas plant
Gaillardia, blanketflower
Hemerocallis, daylily
Hosta, plantainlily
Lavandula, lavender
Oenothera, evening primrose
Paeonia, peony
Phlox
Potentilla, cinquefoil
Rudbeckia hirta, gloriosa daisy

16

The Wildflower Garden

To design a garden of wildflowers might seem to be a contradictory exercise since such plants thrive when uncultivated, unarranged, and untouched by man. It is difficult to improve on Nature and her methods, so the goal of a wildflower gardener is to make a planting look attractive and unaffected. We know of one such successful garden near a lake where flowers bloom continuously beginning with a lush carpet of bloodroot and spring beauties, continuing with colorful lady's slippers and other wild orchids, followed by summer flowers such as daisies and Queen Anne's lace, and topped off with deep purple asters and fringed gentians in late autumn. It took many years for the couple who established this plot to achieve an unstudied, natural appearance there. Considerable expertise was required as well since each wildflower is particular about its home and is happy only when living in its favorite type of soil with the right amount of sun.

When the term wildflower is applied to a garden it suggests that only native plants would be included, but such a garden may also contain varieties with a natural, uncultivated appearance. Achillea, various daisies, *Thalictrum*, liatris, campanula, and *Dianthus* fit nicely into such plantings, whereas delphinium, peonies, and tall phlox would appear out of place, as would plants with double blooms and the giant flowering hybrids of such species as iris, daylily, and *Digitalis*.

Since the most desirable wildflowers are fussy about where they grow, it is necessary to select plants according to the soil, light, and moisture conditions you have available, or be prepared to modify your conditions to those the various species demand. Some can be very particular about soil. Many forest wildflowers, such as wild orchids, *Dicentra*, *Trillium*, and others, need the same conditions found under deciduous trees in the woodland—bright full sun in early spring, but medium to heavy shade during the summer months. *Caltha palustris* (marsh marigold), *Impatiens pallida* (jewelweed), and *Typha* (cattail) grow only in sunny, moist locations.

Although it is possible to create the environment that wild plants like, it is easier and the results will probably be better, if you choose plants for the conditions that already exist. Rather than try to drain a marshy area, for instance, plant aquatic, semiaquatic, or bog specimens that prefer such a spot. If the area is so heavily shaded, either by dense trees or buildings, that few wildflowers will grow, ferns, hostas, and other foliage plants would be an acceptable option. In a hot, sandy location choose cactus, yucca, and aloes. Hal Bruce, author of the excellent book, *How to Grow Wildflowers and Wild Shrubs and Trees in Your Own Garden* advises that we change our mentality rather than our garden terrain. He suggests, too, that if we have a problem spot where cultivated varieties will not grow, it may be the perfect place for native wildflowers. By looking to see what flourishes locally in the wild (and in soil similar to yours), you will be able to create a natural-looking garden without a great deal of work or discouragement.

A MEADOW OF WILDFLOWERS

Meadow wildflowers such as daisies, black-eyed Susans, buttercups, and asters are easier to grow than woodland species. Most like full sun and thrive even in poor soil. Unfortunately, as gardeners well know, some grow so prolifically that they become weeds.

An open landscape such as a meadow or a hillside that is a bother to keep mowed is a good spot for a wildflower planting. Many garden catalogs and specialty stores offer a premixed selection of wildflower seeds for various climates in different parts of the country. Usually these packets contain a mixture of annual, biennial, and perennial varieties, including some grasses. The mixtures may be formulated either for a sunny field or a shady spot in or near a forest.

In spite of the alluring ads that promise wonderful wildflower meadows by the mere scattering of seed over an open field, the results of such a sowing are less than certain. Nature can toss seeds over hayfields and some will thrive, but the chance of success is better if the soil is prepared first. Wildflower gardens don't need to be cultivated and fertilized as thoroughly as a perennial border, but if the seed is to germinate and start well, it should be sown in soil that has been tilled to a depth of at least 6 to 10 inches.

You will achieve the best results if you remove all the turf, rather than till it under, so that your seeds will escape competition from weed roots and seeds in the top layer of soil. If you'd rather not do this, you can cover it with clear plastic for a few weeks before planting. The weeds will germinate and be burned by the heat that is generated and trapped underneath the plastic. Another method is to spray an herbicide such as Roundup to kill existing growth. New seedlings may need to be killed off with later sprays as they germinate. Don't expect a weed-free planting, whatever method you choose, because some seeds lie dormant for years waiting for the right opportunity to grow.

Spring is the best time to plant most seed mixtures, although they can also be sown in the fall where winters are not too severe. A good method of sowing the seeds over a large area is to mix them thoroughly with sand so you won't plant them too thickly. Scatter the mix by flinging it outward by hand, and rake it into the soil. *If* the weather is dry, you may need to sprinkle it heavily twice a week during the germination period, which may take as long as six weeks.

The annuals in your planting will bloom the first year and drop their seed for next year's flowering; but the biennials and most of the perennials will not blossom until the second year. An annual mowing in late summer, after the annuals have gone to seed, will help keep the meadow from growing up to weeds, hay, and brush.

WOODLAND WILDFLOWERS

One wildflower gardener in our community announces in church each spring when his collection of lady's slippers is in bloom, so we can all view the large, beautiful display at its peak. Although he is very modest, we all know it is his skill and knowledge that makes the plantings flourish. In his small backyard, he has successfully duplicated the various conditions that each of his woodland flowers love.

You won't need to be a specialist to grow woodland wildflowers in your own shady border, but reading a good book about them—and providing the environment each requires—will help ensure your success. Most need at least partial shade, and deep, rich soil. Each, too, has its own preference in regard to moisture conditions and soil pH. Weather can affect them so much that their annual flowering time may vary each year by as much as two or three weeks depending on the degree days.

You can grow woodland wildflowers from seed, but it is far easier to buy plants from one of the many wildflower mail-order nurseries and gardens where they are grown under ideal conditions. Although some people collect plants from the wild, the chances for success with them are limited, and many feel that disturbing wild plants is unethical. Furthermore, it may even be criminal if you move some of the rare varieties that are considered endangered. These species are protected by law unless their habitat faces certain destruction because of construction or development work. It is also illegal to poach on private or public lands without permission.

You may be able to find nonendangered specimens on your own land. Use great care in digging them because they often have deep or very fragile root systems (see Transplanting, pages 59–60). Wildflowers will have a better chance of survival if they are planted in early spring, just as they are starting to grow.

Since most bloom for only a short time and then die down, you must plant a few of many different varieties to enjoy blooms throughout the summer.

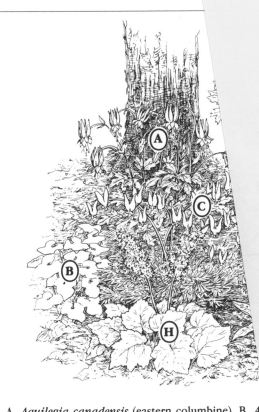

A. *Aquilegia canadensis* (eastern columbine), B. *As____ _____ ____* (wild ginger), C. *Dicentra cucullaria* (Dutchman's breeches), D. *Erythronium americanum* (east___ ____ ___). E. *Hepatica acutiloba* (sharp-lobed hepatica), F. *Podophyllum peltatum* (mayapple), G. *Sanguinaria _____ ____* odroot), H. *Tiarella cordifolia* (foamflower), I. *Trillium erectum* (purple trillium), J. *Viola papilion___* _____ ____ lue violet)

Even so, it may be best to establish your wildflow___ _____ ___ e listed in part III, so for more information garden in a place where it can be enjoyed at its pea_ _____ ____ a garden encyclopedia or books such as *A* but won't be highly visible at a time when bloom__ ___ _____ *f Wildflowers* and *The Wildflower Garden-* are scarce. We know a couple who have made num___ ___ ____ *e: Northeast, Mid-Atlantic, Great Lakes,* erous pathways through the maple woods behinc ___ ___ *rn Canada Edition*, both by Henry W. Art their home and planted a variety of wildflowers along ___ ___ *ay* Publishing). the borders of each path. During different times of the year visitors get invited to walk along whichever path is in its blooming period.

The soil in woods is likely to be loose and shouldn't need much preparation, so spot planting usually works well. Wildflowers don't require the care that cultivated ones do, but an occasional removal of weeds and bushes will probably be necessary.

In addition to reading some of the books on wildflower identification and culture (see the list of books for further reading in the appendix), you may want to visit display gardens where wildflowers are featured. These can be found at many botanical gardens, arboretums, and nature centers.

Among the plants worthy of a place in a wildflower garden are those listed below. Use the codes to locate the proper ones for your locations. Not all of these

_____il

_____ moderate shade
_____ wet soil

_____gue, trout lily, *Erythronium americanum*
_____ *Agrimonia*
_____ ood, *Anemone quinquifolia*
_____butus, trailing, *Epigaea repens*
#Aster, *Aster*, var.
*Baneberry, *Actaea rubra, A. alba*
  Bearberry, *Arctostaphylos uva-ursi*
#Bee balm, *Monarda didyma*
#Bellflower, bluebells, *Campanula*, var.
*Bloodroot, *Sanguinaria canadensis*
*Bluet, *Hedyotis*
*Bottle gentian, *Gentiana andrewsii*

* Bouncing bet, *Saponaria officinalis*
Bugbane, *Cimicifuga racemosa*
+ * Bunchberry, *Cornus canadensis*
Butterfly weed, *Asclepias tuberosa*
Calypso, *Calypso bulbosa*
#Cardinal flower, *Lobelia cardinalis*
@Cattail, *Typha latifolia*
#Coltsfoot, *Tussilago farfara*
Dutchman's breeches, *Dicentra cucullaria*
#Evening primrose, *Oenothera biennis*
#Everlasting, *Anaphalis margaritacea*
False Solomon's seal, *Smilacina racemosa*
Foamflower, *Tiarella cordifolia*
#Forget-me-not, *Myosotis verna*
#Geranium, wild, *Geranium maculatum*
* Goldthread, *Coptis trifolia*
Hepatica, *Hepatica triloba*
Indigo, false, *Baptisia australis*
@Iris, flag, *Iris versicolor*
* Jack-in-the-pulpit, *Arisaema triphyllum*
@Jewelweed, *Impatiens pallida*
#Larkspur, *Delphinium tricorne*
Lavender, sea, *Limonium*
* Lily, Canada, *Lilium canadense*
#Lobelia, *Lobelia*
#Loosestrife, *Lythrum*
#Lupine, sundial, *Lupinus perennis*
Mallow, *Malva*

@#Marsh marigold, cowslip, *Caltha palustris*
#Mayapple, mandrake, *Podophyllum peltatum*
#Milkweed, *Asclepias*
Moonseed, *Menispermum*
+ * Orchid
grass pink orchid, *Calopogon pulchellus*
lady's slipper pink, *Cypripedium acaule*
orchis, showy, *Orchis spectabilis*
yellow, *Cypripedium pubescens*
white, *Cypripedium candidum*
Partridgeberry, *Mitchella repens*
Pennyroyal, wild American, *Hedeoma pulegioides*
Periwinkle, *Vinca minor*
#Queen Anne's lace, *Daucus carota*
•Saxifrage, *Saxifraga vorgomoemsis*
Shooting star, *Dodecatheon meadia*
#Speedwell, *Veronica*
* Spiderwort, Virginia, *Tradescantia virginiana*
* Spring beauty, *Claytonia virginica*
Squirrel-corn, *Dicentra canadensis*
Starflower, *Trientalis americana*
* Trillium, *Trillium*, var.
* Turtlehead, *Chelone glabra*
#Violet, *Viola*, var.
* Wild ginger, *Asarum canadense*
Windflower, *Anemone*, var.
+ * Wintergreen, *Gaultheria procumbens*
#Yarrow, *Achillea*

17

The Rock Garden

When a newcomer from a large city moved to our small town many years ago and started to create a rock garden, a lot of spirited discussion took place among our neighbors as to how large a crop of rocks the lady planned to grow. Rocks were something our ancestors had spent several generations removing from the fields—making a garden of them was unimaginable. Since then, the local people have become more enlightened about rock gardens, but some still wonder at the wisdom of spending a great deal of time and money to haul back all those rocks that the original settlers dragged away.

If your property has a slope dotted with interesting or weathered rock formations, it may be an ideal spot for a rock garden or rockery, as it is sometimes called. But any garden that features rocks prominently can be called a rock garden. It is not even necessary to have a slope—one can be created on a flat location with just a few loads of topsoil and a pile of rocks. In very different locations—Swaledale, England and Miami, Florida, for instance—we have seen attractive rockeries that were built on what was originally level ground.

Whatever your terrain, this specialized form of gardening can be fascinating. Some purists feel that a rock garden should contain only those plants which grow naturally on rocky slopes in poor soil, but most rock gardeners use a wide variety of low-growing perennials, annuals, bulbs, and shrubbery. The term "rock plants," however, usually refers to species that grow in temperate areas rather than subtropical desert spots, and it is those species that we describe here.

If you want the overall effect to be beautiful, a rock garden must be carefully designed rather than aimlessly constructed. Yet even though it may have been weeks in the planning, it should look as if it evolved naturally.

Because rockeries must be planted and cared for by hand, it is best to start with a small area unless you have lots of time, interest, and skill. If you have the perfect spot, you may not need to do more than choose plants, locate paths, and create level outcroppings as kneeling places. But if you must bring in rocks and soil you'll have more planning and work ahead. Choose rocks that are compatible with the landscape, if they are available, rather than those that are quarried, highly colored, or polished. If excavating is necessary, dump the topsoil in piles close by while the work is being done, so that you can replace it later. Set the rocks in the lowest, front part of the garden first and work upward, burying more than half of each rock firmly so it will be well anchored. After the rocks are in place, let the soil settle around them for a few days before planting. Check your construction frequently at the early stages by viewing it from a distance as well as close up, to be sure the positioning is aesthetically pleasing.

Most rock garden plants need full or nearly full sun, and although they do not require extremely fertile soil it should be at least 8 inches deep and have excellent drainage so that water pockets will not form. To

A. *Campanula caespitosa, C. cochleariifolia,* or *C. garganica* (bellflowers), B. *Iberis saxatilis* (rock candytuft), C. *Iris chamaeiris* (Crimean iris) or *I. cristata* (crested iris), D. *Thymus serpyllum* (mother-of-thyme)

accomplish this, spread a layer of crushed rock between the rocks before putting back the topsoil, and if the soil is heavy mix in some sand and peat moss to lighten it. If any of the plants you are using need more fertility than ordinary rock plants, mix a little compost, leaf mold, or manure into the soil where these will be planted.

CHOOSING PLANTS

A rock gardener has a wide variety of plants to choose from, which makes it a challenge to find the perfect species for your site and combine them aesthetically. The best plants are compact, low-growing perennials. To achieve pleasing combinations, consider not only plant color and mature height, but also form: are they rounded (crane's bill), spiky (iris), or prostrate and spreading (thyme or ground phlox)?

The size of the plants should be on the same scale as the garden itself. Tiny plants look best in a small space; taller perennials, dwarf evergreens, and low-growing shrubs, such as potentilla or spreading cotoneaster, are more appropriate to a long wide hillside. And because so many of the plants best suited to a rock garden bloom only in the spring, you may want to consider strategic placement of summer-blooming heaths, heathers, and perhaps some annuals to add more color during the rest of the growing season.

Select those plants that are best for your climate and exposure—whether it is a cool, north-facing hillside or a dry, sunny slope. If you live where winters are long and the growing season short, you may be able to establish a true alpine garden of plants that are native to the European mountain ranges, Rockies, White Mountains, or other high elevations. Most of these are small or compact with rugged root systems that enable them to live in poor soil and under severe weather conditions. They need cool weather

—especially cool summers—and perfect drainage to do well.

Certain nurseries specialize entirely in alpine and rock garden species and their catalogs are good sources of planting ideas (see Sources of Perennial Seeds and Plants in the appendix). The American Rock Garden Society can be an invaluable resource, too. The members, as in other plant societies, swap seeds, plants, and ideas. For further inspiration, visit the beautiful rockeries in botanical gardens. Among the best are the Denver Botanic Garden's Alpine Garden, the Thompson Memorial Rock Garden at the New York Botanical Garden, and the University of British Columbia Garden in Vancouver. A few of the most popular alpine plants are listed below.

Anemone alpina, alpine anemone
Aquilegia alpina, alpine columbine
Arabis alpina, alpine rockcress
Aster alpinus, alpine aster
Dianthus alpinus, alpine pink
Hymenosys grandiflora, alpine sunflower
Leontopodium alpinum, edelweiss
Myosotis alpestris, alpine forget-me-not
Papaver alpinum, alpine poppy
Satureis, alpine plant easily grown from seed
Silene quadrifida, alpine catchfly

CARE

Your rock garden could be compared to a collection of potted plants, and they will grow best if you tend them accordingly. Be sure each "pot" is well drained so that water will not collect there and drown the plant. Loosen the soil in each pocket occasionally with a small garden fork. Although most rock plants do well in poor soil, add dry manure or liquid fertilizer if the plants seem weak.

Housekeeping chores include cutting back any leggy plants after flowering, clipping off dead portions, and dividing any plant that becomes rootbound or too large for its space. Check for insects and diseases as in any other bed; slugs may be especially pesky because they enjoy the shelter found among rocks. Never let weeds grow in the nooks and crannies, not only for appearance's sake, but more importantly, because they will quickly crowd out the other plants. Whether it is weeds or vigorous plants that are allowed to take over, an unkempt rockery is a sad sight. Only a few minutes of daily care will prevent the need for a future overhaul.

Winter weather can be hard on tender plant varieties because they are more exposed to cold winds and dehydration in a rock garden than when growing in level beds. Alpines on their native mountaintops have become toughened, but are also accustomed to a heavy snow cover. If you don't get much snow, a mulch will help protect both hearty and more tender plants. In particularly exposed regions of this continent it is a good idea to cover the entire bed with evergreen branches or straw as well just after the ground starts to freeze.

Water in a Rock Garden

A waterfall or stream is a natural addition to a rockery, providing both musical sounds and a cooling effect. If you do not have a small natural stream already running among your rocks, you can build your own by installing a small submersible circulating pump designed especially for fountains and waterfalls. These pumps require little electricity and permit a large range of water rhythms: the best are those that make everything appear as natural as possible.

Especially effective in the right location is a series of short waterfalls that drop from one rock-formed pool to the next below it, then finally to the bottom pool from which the water is recirculated back to the top.

If you have no suitable natural rock formations, pools as well as complete waterfall units made of fiberglass or other materials are available from garden supply catalogs. Or you can construct your own pools and waterfalls by using real rocks and the premixed concrete available in bags at most hardware stores. You'll also need plastic hose or pipe to return the water to the uppermost level, and electric wire suitable for underground burial to supply power for the pump.

SOME TRADITIONAL ROCK GARDEN PLANTS

Below is a list of perennials best suited to rock gardens. For a more detailed description see the general list of perennials in part III beginning on page 135.

Achillea tomentosa, wooly yarrow. Yellow, flowering dwarf plant about 12 inches tall.
Adonis amurensis plena, amur adonis. Early blooming, with yellow-green flowers 6 inches tall.
Aethionema coridifolium, Lebanon stonecress. Dwarf plant, seldom over 3 inches tall, with blue foliage and soft pink blossoms.
Ajuga, bugleweed. Fast-growing, dwarf ground cover.

A. reptans rubra has purplish-red flowers and purple foliage. *A. reptans alba* has dark green foliage and 6-inch white spikes for blooms.

Alchemilla, lady's mantle. Good ground cover that spreads rapidly from seed. Grows 8 to 12 inches tall.

Alyssum saxatile, basket of gold. Excellent for edging perennial borders and rock gardens. The varieties *A. s.* 'Citrina' (pale yellow), *A. s.* 'Compacta' (dwarf with bright yellow blooms), and *A. flora plenum* (yellow double blooms) are all better than the common variety.

Anchusa, summer forget-me-not, bugloss. *A. myosotidiflora* is a dwarf variety suitable for rock planting.

Anemone pulsatilla, pasque flower. Eight to 12 inches tall with finely cut grayish leaves and purple flowers. Needs acid soil; blooms in spring. *A. p. alba* is a white-blooming form; *A. magellanica* also has white blooms and is recommended where winters are too severe for *A. pulsatilla* varieties.

Aquilegia, columbine. Native wild varieties are best for rock gardens. Has red, white, blue, or yellow flowers, sometimes in combinations. Grows about 15 inches tall.

Arabis, rockcress. *A. caucasica* is the common form, but *A. alpina* blooms better; both have white flowers. 'Flor-pleno' has double-white blossoms, and 'Rosabella' has rose-pink ones.

Arenaria, sandwort. *A. montana*, or mountain sandwort, grows to a height of 4 inches and is one of the best of this genus for rock gardens.

Artemisia. Usually planted for its silvery-gray foliage rather than its bloom. *A. schmidtiana* (silvermound) is one of the best for rock gardens.

Asarum, wild ginger. Low-growing plant with fragrant rootstocks and attractive foliage. Likes woodsy soil filled with leaf mold.

Aster. Many dwarf kinds are suitable for rock gardens.

Aubrieta deltoidea, purple rockcress. Grows well in the poor dry soils characteristic of rock gardens. Many hybrids, some of pink, red, and lavender.

Bellis perennis, English daisy. Low-growing, free-flowering dwarf plants with daisylike blooms. Spreads rapidly both by division and by seed.

Bergenia cordifolia, heartleaf bergenia. Thick, rosettelike leaves with pink flowers on 12-inch stems. They prefer afternoon shade and sandy soil combined with lime.

Cactus. The hardy cacti, *Opuntia*, are good rock garden plants. They need light soil with lots of leaf mold, loam, sand, and enough lime so that it's not at all acidic. Extra water is required during the summer.

Campanula, bellflower. Dwarf bellflowers make good rock garden plants. Among the best are *C. carpatica*, *C. garganica* with star-shaped blooms, *C. glomerata*, *C. portenschlagiana*, and *C. rotundifolia*. They do best when mulched over the winter and should be divided at least every three years.

Catananche caerulea, cupid's dart. Attractive blue or white flowers, excellent for drying, and easily grown.

Cerastium tomentosum, snow-in-summer. A low-growing plant with pure white flowers, that looks like a snowy carpet.

Ceratostigma plumbaginoides, bunge (sometimes called plumbago). Valuable for its blue flowers that appear over a long season, and also for its glossy-green foliage. Needs winter protection in cold regions.

Corydalis lutea. These small plants (up to 12 inches high) are ideal for the rock garden. They grow well in light, dry soils and can tolerate both sun and shade.

Dianthus, garden pinks. Many species of *Dianthus* are appropriate for a rock garden. Their free-flowering habits add color when little else is in bloom. Among the best are sweet William, the grass pink, and maiden pink, although there are many more. They need a well-drained soil to ensure a long growing period and must be divided often. The sweet William should be treated as a biennial and planted each year, even though it may live longer.

Dicentra eximia, fernleaf bleeding-heart. This neat little plant blooms for most of the summer. It has attractive foliage, does best in light shade, and should be divided often.

Dracocephalum ruyschiana, Siberian dragonhead. Purple flowers in spikes that grow about 12 inches tall. Easy to grow from seed.

Epimedium, bishop's hat. Twelve inches tall with a variety of blossom colors. Likes moist, sandy loam and light shade; must not be allowed to dry out.

Euphorbia, spurge. There are over a thousand species of this one plant, many of which are suitable for rock gardens. Most like sandy, dry soils; some have brightly colored blossoms.

Ferns. Although most ferns like moist soil, a few thrive on dry, rocky land. Four of the most useful in a rockery are common polypody, hayscented fern, sensitive fern, and rusty woodsia. A description of each will be found in the chapter on shade gardening, pages 96–97.

Festuca glauca, blue fescue. A silvery-blue, tufted

grass that grows to a height of 10 inches.

Filipendula, meadowsweet. *F. hexapetala* 'Flora Pleno' grows to 18 inches, has double blooms, and attractive foliage.

Gaillardia, blanketflower. One of the best varieties is known as 'Goblin'—it grows only 12 inches tall and has red and yellow blooms from July until frost. This genus likes warm, sandy soils and full sun; should be divided annually.

Galium boreale, northern bedstraw. Feathery leaves and tiny flowers resembling wild baby's-breath. Grows easily, but is too tall for many places.

Galium odoratum (Asperula odorata), sweet woodruff. Good ground cover. Grows well in the tiny crevices between rocks, but can become weedy.

Geranium sanguineum, crane's bill. There are many varieties of this low-growing plant; they like moist, cool places and are easily grown from seed.

Geum, avens. Double and single flowers of good size on 12-inch plants. They grow best in sun or light shade in nearly any kind of soil, but should not be in a wet place over the winter.

Gypsophila repens, baby's-breath. The dwarf varieties *G. alba* and *G. rosea* are both excellent for the rock garden. Plant in full sun and water frequently.

Helianthemum, sunrose. Shrubby plant, good for hot, dry places and a limestone soil. Needs winter protection in the North.

Hemerocallis, daylily. The dwarf kinds add summer bloom when the flowering season of many rock plants is over.

Heuchera sanguinea, coral bells. These small and dainty flowers bloom all summer in pink, red, and white.

Hosta. Miniature varieties such as 'Pinwheel' are recommended.

Iberis, candytuft. Low-growing, evergreen, shrubby with white blossoms. Likes full sun, plenty of moisture, and once established should not be disturbed.

Iris. Dwarf iris are ideal for rock gardens—they like sun and need little care. 'Sea Jewell' and 'Aqua Star' are outstanding new introductions.

Leontopodium alpinum, edelweiss. One of the best known and beloved of all alpine plants, it is easily grown in the rock garden. Likes rich, somewhat sandy soil with a little lime, and enjoys growing among rocks.

Limonium, sea lavender. Grows well nearly everywhere if the soil is not too heavy.

Linaria alpina, alpine toadflax. One of the best *Linaria* for the rock garden.

Linum, flax. These blue-flowering perennials make ideal rock plants.

Lychnis, campion. Many of these are ideal for the rock garden.

Mertensia virginica, Virginia bluebells. Early pink and blue blooms.

Myosotis, forget-me-not. Allow them to go to seed, which will keep new plants coming.

Phlox. Dwarf, creeping kinds are best as rock garden plants; they need full sun. *P. subulata* comes in several bright colors.

Polemonium, Jacob's ladder. Does best in rich soil and light shade.

Primula, primrose. These prefer heavy, rich, slightly acidic soil, and plenty of moisture.

Ranunculus, buttercup. Easy to grow, but may not overwinter well in the North.

Saponaria, soapwort. Fast-spreading, creeping plant with pink flowers; blossoms in early spring.

Saxifraga, saxifrage. These come in many forms, which are ideal for the rock garden because they grow easily in tough places.

Sedum. Old reliables of the rock garden. They grow fast, and some kinds can quickly take over an entire slope. Plant in sandy soil and full sun for best results.

Sempervivum. The hen-and-chickens and houseleek varieties are ideal.

Silene schafta, moss campion. Summer-blossoming dwarf plant with pink blooms.

Stachys lanata, betony. Lavender flowers that appear in summer.

Thymus, thyme. Some of the thymes make thick mats that are ideal for the rock garden. An added attraction is their heavy bloom of pink and lavender flowers.

Tunica saxifraga (also called *Petrorhagia*), tunic flower. Makes a thick mat with pale pink blooms that last throughout the summer.

Veronica, speedwell. The low-growing kinds are best for rock gardens. They like sun, moist soil, and occasional feeding.

Viola, violet. An easy-to-grow perennial. Choose varieties carefully—some like sun, others do best in shade.

Two recent books that make good reading are *Rock Gardening* by H. Lincoln Foster, published by Timber Press, and *Alpines for Your Garden*, by Alan Bloom, available from International Specialized Book Services, Inc., Portland, Oregon.

18

The Fragrant Garden

During the busy summer season we need to remind ourselves occasionally to stop and enjoy our garden, so we post a small sign: "Don't Forget to Smell the Flowers." No reminder is necessary to sniff certain fragrant species such as regal lilies, but sometimes we need to get so near a delicately scented flower that our noses become covered with yellow pollen. Once we had to administer first aid to a young visitor who didn't notice a bee hard at work within the bloom he was examining!

The scented garden is often one of the most popular in large arboretums. Planted exclusively with perennials, annuals, herbs, and shrubs chosen for their aromatic characteristics, these gardens are filled with delicious scents blown by the breeze or released as visitors brush past herbs and other plants with fragrant foliage. Sometimes these gardens are in raised beds, so they can be more easily enjoyed by the blind and elderly.

In most backyard gardens, the fragrant plants are interspersed with unscented specimens, but it can be fun to create a garden dominated by plants with pleasant aromas. If the garden is near the windows of a home, the fragrance can be enjoyed indoors as well as out. An added bonus is that many fragrant flowers can be cut, dried, and used in potpourri.

Because the list of sweet-scented perennials is not long, and most flowers bloom only for limited periods, they are often used in combination with other fragrant plants. Such a perennial border is often bounded by shrubs or small trees such as lilacs, shrub roses, mock orange (*Philadelphus*), or flowering crabs. Annuals with scented blooms, including annual heliotrope, mignonette, nasturtium, pansy, petunia, scabiosa, stock, sweet alyssum, sweet peas, sweet sultan, and verbena, are often used as edgings or interspersed with perennials. Popular too are such aromatic herbs as borage, lavender, rosemary, sage, tarragon, thyme, and members of the mint family.

When designing a fragrance garden you may want to avoid any plants with scents that don't appeal to you. Gas plant (*Dictamnus*), for instance, has a pungent medicinal odor that some people find offensive. Another strong scent is that of *Valeriana officinalis* (garden heliotrope or common valerian), which is beloved by some, but not all.

Old-fashioned flower varieties are often more fragrant than new hybrids since breeders, in their search for larger and "double" blooms, have sacrificed the original fragrance. Many carnations and pinks, for example, no longer have the rich, spicy scent of their forebears, and the original lemon lily is sweeter than most of its descendants.

Don't expect the fragrance of such a garden to be obvious throughout the season—many scents are so light that they are noticeable only in the evening or on cloudy days with no wind. Even so, you may want to follow the example of the experts and use unscented flowers to separate the plants of different aromas that bloom at the same time. Each can then be savored by itself.

Among the perennials with fragrant blooms are:

Aloysia citridora, lemon verbena
Asperula odorata, sweet woodruff
Centaurea moschata, sweet sultan
Chrysanthemum—only a few are fragrant.
Clematis paniculata, sweet autumn clematis
Convallaria majalis, lily-of-the-valley
Dianthus, garden pinks and carnations
Hemerocallis, 'Hyperion,' lemon lily, and others
Hesperis matronalis, sweet rocket
Hosta grandiflora, funkia, plantainlily

Iris, bearded iris
Lavandula vera, lavender
Lilium, regal, Madonna, olympic, and others
Lycoris, magic lily
Monarda, bee balm
Narcissus, daffodil
Nymphaea odorata, water lily—many varieties are fragrant.
Oenothera, evening primrose
Paeonia, varieties such as 'Avalanche,' 'Jules Elie,' 'Sarah Bernhardt'
Primula, primrose, many varieties
Valeriana officinalis, garden heliotrope or common valerian
Viola, certain pansies, Canada violet, sweet violet, and white violet

19

The Water Garden

fter trying unsuccessfully to drain a small swamp near his home, a friend of ours read an article about water gardens, and subsequently hired a bulldozer to dig a shallow pool there instead. Now he is developing a small garden reminiscent of Monet's at Giverny, with pink, red, and white water lilies.

Water gardening is a fascinating and unique hobby. Although it may include growing plants around a fountain or pool, a bona fide water garden contains aquatic plants such as water lilies that are grown entirely in water, and semiaquatics (the moisture-loving shrubs and perennials such as pitcher plants) that grow well in natural bogs or swamps.

One of the nice things about gardening with water is that minimal work is required after the initial construction and planting has been completed. As long as the ecological balance of the area is maintained, there is no hoeing or cultivating, little weeding, and of course, no watering!

For several years we had a small pool in our backyard planted with red and white water lilies. It was much enjoyed both by us and a friendly green frog who spent a lot of time sitting on the pads, catching insects, and being photographed by visitors. We made our garden by sinking a child's plastic wading pool into the ground and filling it with water. We then placed several pots in it, each containing one lily planted in soil. Water trickled in slowly through a camouflaged inlet pipe and the small amount of overflow spilled into the lawn. It could not have been

more simple or carefree, which was its undoing. We became so accustomed to ignoring it, that during a dry spell one summer we forgot to check the water inflow. It had stopped, and we lost all the plants.

You may not need to construct a pool to grow water lilies if you already have a shallow pond or slow-moving stream. Those with a naturally wet area, like our friend, can scoop out part of it to create a pond about 2 feet deep. In these kinds of ponds the water lilies can be planted directly in the muddy soil at the bottom, provided the water isn't more than 2 feet in depth. Most farm and fish ponds are much too deep and many are too cold for successful water lily culture. If you raise water plants in your pond, don't try to keep ducks or geese there because they'll rapidly wreck the plantings.

AQUATIC PLANTS

The term "aquatic" usually refers to all plants that live in water, whether they are free-floating or rooted in soil, with submerged or floating leaves. Those most cultivated are members of the Nymphaeceae family which includes water lilies, lotuses, and similar plants. The *Nuphar* and *Nymphaea* genera are the common pond lilies in this country. The *Nymphaea* both hardy and tropical, have been widely hybridized. Water lilies range in size from the *Victoria* genus, one of the largest, with flowers that are 15 inches in width, to tiny pygmy varieties that are only 1½ to 2 inches across. Of the fifty or so cultivars and species of water lilies available today, the Marliac hybrids are among the best for home growers. See the appendix for the names of garden suppliers.

Examples of many of the best varieties can be seen at the following water gardens.

Balboa Park
San Diego, California

Brooklyn Botanic Garden
Brooklyn, New York

Longwood Gardens
Kennett Square, Pennsylvania

Kenilworth Aquatic Gardens
Washington, D.C.

New York Botanical Garden
Bronx, New York

St. Louis Botanical Garden
St. Louis, Missouri

THE POOL

Water lilies need at least five hours of full sunlight each day, so select a spot for your pool that will provide it, and make sure the location is away from trees that might drop leaves or needles into the water and contaminate it. The pool should be from 2 to 2½ feet deep for best results. Formerly, most were built of reinforced concrete, but now fiberglass or heavy polyvinyl plastic are most often used because they are easier to install and less likely to crack in freezing temperatures. Nurseries that sell water plants frequently stock preformed pools and liners in many sizes.

Although a pool does not need fresh water running through it all the time, plumbing should be installed so that additional water can be added whenever evaporation makes it necessary. Since it needs cleaning occasionally, a drain and plug at the lowest end of the pool will save you the trouble of pumping out the water.

PLANTING

You will want the water in your garden pool to remain somewhat clear, so set your plants, as we did, in containers rather than in soil at the bottom. The size of the container should correspond to plant size. A 10-inch pot is suitable for the small pygmy water lilies, but the huge tropical varieties will need at least a bushel-size tub.

Place only one plant in each container. Water plants are heavy feeders—the soil mix should contain at least one part well-rotted manure to four parts fertile garden soil. Mix in a small amount of commercial fertilizer, such as 5-10-10, too. Water lilies grow from rhizomes, which should be placed in the container so that the crown is barely exposed. Cover the top of the soil with coarse sand to keep it from clouding the water. Then water the pot thoroughly before submerging it; otherwise it may float back to the surface.

For best results, place the containers so that the rims are 4 to 8 inches under the surface of the water. Adjust the height, if necessary, by placing rocks, bricks, or concrete blocks under the containers. Space them according to the size of the mature plants, from 3 to 5 feet apart. Most water lilies need at least 10 square feet of water surface when mature, except for the pygmy size, which take up only about 4 square feet. Plant hardy water lilies in early spring, but tropical varieties should not be put outside until the water temperature is a minimum of 70°F. Don't be alarmed if the leaves stay submerged for the first few days before they rise and float to the surface.

The fragrant flowers of the hardy water lilies and certain tropical varieties do not stay open round-the-clock, but usually unfurl on a summer day at 8 A.M. and close about ten hours later at 6 P.M. The length of the daily bloom depends on the amount of light and the temperature (some of the tropical types, however, are night bloomers). One of the fascinating things about these unusual plants is the slow, hour-long unfolding—one by one—of the petals each day. When they close, the same process repeats itself in reverse. You'll also notice that the color of certain varieties will change considerably from day to day.

Hardy varieties will survive even a northern winter as long as their roots remain below ice level. If your pool is likely to freeze almost or completely solid, remove the containers and store them in a cool root cellar or basement until spring. Tropical varieties require a completely frost-free environment—they *must* be taken inside except in those regions where no frost is likely. Never let the stored plants dry out during the winter.

Water gardening in earthen ponds is most successful when everything is ecologically balanced among the plants and other living organisms. Pond expert Bill Uber is the owner of Van Ness Water Gardens in Upland, California. To achieve an ecological balance in an earthen water garden he recommends that, for each square yard of water surface, you should add:

- 1 large water lily (for beauty, and also because the lily pads prevent loss of pond oxygen)
- 2 bunches oxygenating grasses (they replace oxygen and prevent algae formation)
- 2 fish (goldfish or koi, about 5 inches long to eat flies, mosquito larvae, algae)
- 12 snails (they consume algae)

Within two to three months a balance will become established in the pond and the organisms will support each other.

CARING FOR THE POOL

Although a water garden requires less care than one planted in soil it cannot be completely neglected. Remove any unsightly yellowed foliage and seed pods as they appear, and if the plants are not thriving, place soluble fertilizer tablets around their roots every two weeks. Water lilies grown in the soil bottom of a shallow pond can be left undisturbed, but those in containers should be divided every two to five years. If the plants get too large, the flowers will become fewer and smaller, but if they are given proper care the plants may live for fifty years or more.

Like their soil counterparts, aquatic plants are affected by pests. The water lily aphid (*Ropalosiphum nymphaeae*) is the most common insect. It can be controlled by spraying; when the flowers are closed, use a solution of kerosene emulsion and water (1:15). The Japanese beetle, the leaf-eating beetle, and caterpillars of the *Noctuid* or *Hydrocamp propalis* moths may also feed on the plants, but can be controlled by pyrethrum or rotenone. Never use chlorinated hydrocarbon insecticides as pest control in ponds, especially if you have fish or frogs there. In hot, humid weather a fungus disease sometimes develops on the leaves of water lilies if conditions in the pond are crowded. It can be controlled by a careful, limited application of a fungicide, but be careful not to spill any into the water.

BOG OR SWAMP POSSIBILITIES

Few people choose to deliberately create a swamp or boggy area in their backyard, but if you already have one somewhere on your property, it can be made into a spot that is more interesting than annoying. The aquatic and semiaquatic plant life that grows in such places is unique and endlessly fascinating.

You may want to investigate the possibility of scooping out a portion of your swamp to make a small, year-round pond. If it is dug to a depth of 1½ to 2 feet, with a greater depth in the middle, you will be able to raise *Nymphaea* as well as those that grow upright, with their roots submerged in water. Part of the earth moved from the bottom can be used to build small low islands or hummocks where water ferns, mosses, pitcher plants, and other bog plants can be grown. Such plants need little care or fertilizer, and because most like an acid environment, lime or wood ashes shouldn't be used on them.

Below are some of the plants you may want for your wetland garden.

Acorus calamus, sweet flag
Arundo, giant reed
Iris pseudacorus, yellow flag
Iris versicolor, blue flag
Marsilea, water clover
Nelumbo lutea, lotus
Nuphar, cow lily
Orontium, golden club
Osmunda regalis, royal fern
Peltandra virginica, arrow arum
Pontederia cordata, pickerelweed
Sagittaria, arrowhead
S. sagittifolia 'Flore Pleno,' swamp potato
Sarracenia purpurea, pitcher plant
Typha angustifolia, narrow-leaved cattail

PLANTS FOR MOIST/DRY PLACES

You may own land that is not only moist for much of the year, but fluctuates occasionally between being covered with water during prolonged rains and drying out during hot or arid spells. These areas are difficult to plant because most common garden perennials and wildflowers won't tolerate these conditions. The following plants, however, can stand considerable moisture as well as dryness for short periods.

Aletris farinosa, star grass
Asclepias incarnata, swamp milkweed
Aster novae-angliae, New England aster
Boltonia asteroides, starwort
Caltha palustris, marsh marigold
Eupatorium perfoliatum, boneset
E. purpureum and *maculatum*, Joe Pye-weed
Ferns, cinnamon, royal, and sensitive varieties
Gentiana andrewsii, closed gentian
Hibiscus moscheutos, rose mallow or swamp mallow
Hosta, plantainlily
Iris sibirica, Siberian iris

Lobelia cardinalis, cardinal flower
L. siphilitica, blue lobelia
Lychnis flos-cuculi, ragged robin
Lysimachia terrestris, swamp candles
Lythrum salicaria, purple loosestrife
Mertensia, Virginia bluebells
Miscanthus, zebra grass
Monarda didyma, bee balm
Myosotis, forget-me-not

Phlox maculata, summer phlox
Pontederia cordata, pickerelweed
Ranunculus, swamp buttercup
Rhexia, deer grass, meadow beauties
Sagittaria latifolia, duck potato
Solidago graminifolia, lance-leafed goldenrod
Typha latifolia, cattail
Veronicastrum virginianum, culver's root
Viola cucullata, blue bog violet

20

Gardening on a Hillside

hen we were starting our first perennial bed, an experienced local horticulturist dropped by and remarked that it would be difficult to create a worthwhile garden on our uneven backyard lawn. She advised that we bring in several loads of topsoil to do it right. Since neither our time nor budget would allow that, we worked with what we had and have not been sorry. There is no doubt that many of the world's great formal gardens are on level ground, but our sloping country border makes no pretense to being either formal or great. We've found that an informal hillside garden has a character of its own.

Whether your hillside is a gentle slope or a near precipice, and whether it is sunny and dry or shaded and cool, it is possible to make it attractive with plants. In addition to the aesthetic consideration, there may be a practical reason for planting perennials on an incline: many slopes are difficult and even dangerous to mow. Hillsides present a special problem, however, since even more than level gardens, they are constantly in full view. If the plantings are poorly planned, or unkempt, the results will be plainly visible.

PLANT POSSIBILITIES

The species you choose will depend on the light and soil conditions, the angle of the slope, and your own inclinations. A rocky, gravelly, eroded slope might be converted to a lovely rock garden if you want to spend time with it. To dispense with fussy gardening, however, it would be best to spread a mulch on such a slope, and plant either a ground cover or clumps of easy-care plants. Three years ago we covered a steep slope at one end of our property with a mulch of wood shavings and planted a variety of colorful daylilies 3 feet apart. The plants have become more beautiful each year and are growing so fast that the mulch is barely visible.

It is usually more convenient to feature existing formations such as rocks and crevices, than to conceal or remove them. If your slope is wide, you may choose to design paths that meander through it gradually, with stepping stones from the bottom to the top. Perennials and dwarf shrubs that will stay low and compact are attractive along such paths. On a very steep slope where paths would erode badly, and it would be difficult to navigate, heavily rooted ground covers may be the only solution unless the hillside can be made into narrow terraces. They can be held in place by retaining walls of stone or rot-resistant wood timbers, planks, or logs.

Ground Cover-Type Plantings

If you have the room consider planting several varieties of these, both for interest and to ensure against choosing a kind that might not do well. Each variety should cover a good-sized area so that interesting patches result, rather than mixing the various kinds together. Keep them separate by edgings or paths to ensure that the effect won't be lost as they intermingle in future years.

In light to medium shade use *Asperula* (sweet wood-ruff), *Asarum* (wild ginger), *Convallaria* (lily-of-the-valley), *Pachysandra*, *Vinca minor* (myrtle, peri-winkle), or some of the dwarf ferns. In full sun, good possibilities are *Aegopodium* (bishop's weed), *Ajuga* (bugleweed), *Cerastium* (snow-in-summer), *Coronilla varia* (crownvetch), *Dicentra eximia* (fernleaf bleeding-heart), *Gypsophila repens* 'Rosea' (creeping baby's-breath), *Phlox subulata* (moss pink), thyme, and veronica. Spring-flowering bulbs such as crocus, grape hyacinths, and daffodils are attractive when planted among them.

Herbaceous Perennials

Many garden perennials are suitable for planting on sunny slopes if the soil is rich and deep. The best choices are rugged varieties with heavy, vigorous root systems that hold the slope well and prevent erosion, and those with foliage that will stay in good condition throughout the summer.

Our favorites are vigorous varieties of *Hemerocallis* (daylily) for sunny and lightly shaded spots, and hostas for planting in moderate to heavy shade. Both bloom over a long period, and even when they are not in bloom, their foliage is attractive. Achillea, *Anthemis*, chrysanthemum, *Convallaria*, *Digitalis*, lythrum, *Lysimachia* (loosestrife), *Monarda*, wild phlox, *Oenothera*, *Pulmonaria*, *Rudbeckia*, sedum, shasta daisy, and Siberian iris also do well on slopes, but you may want to experiment with various species in your location before planting large amounts.

Wildflower seed is often planted on highway slopes in many areas of the country with great success. Lupine has become naturalized and can be seen on roadside banks all over our area. When it is in bloom, people drive for miles to admire the hillsides of lavender, purple, and pink.

Rock Garden and Alpine Plants

On pages 79–81 you will find suggestions for rock garden plants, and on page 79 a list of alpine plants.

PLANTING

On a bank that is completely naked, perhaps as a result of grading, the task of preparation will be easier, but cover it as soon as possible so it won't erode and so the birds won't plant it with seeds of junky plants you don't want. If it is mostly gravel or rocks, spread some topsoil first to get the plants off to a better start. Fertilize it well with manure or a commercial mix that you rake in. Then seed the bank with an annual grain such as rye, oats, or millet and spread a layer of hay over it before the grain sprouts. Set the perennials or ground covers among the grain just as it is beginning to sprout. As the plants become established, cut back the grain around them and apply a mulch around each plant.

If you prefer, and there is no rush to get the slope planted, let the grain grow throughout the summer undisturbed. Leave it there uncut over the winter. It will freeze and become a strawlike mulch; in the spring the perennials or ground cover can then be set into the soil. Add more mulch to help hold the soil until the plants become well established and to check any weed growth. If you use herbicides to keep new weeds from sprouting, apply them two or three weeks after the plants are set in and growing; or weed by hand until the plants have completely covered the slope.

If the bank is not bare initially, getting it ready may be a long-term project. Till or spade it thoroughly to completely pulverize the sod of the whole area. If you must cope with poison ivy, thistles, blackberry canes, sumac, or honeysuckle, it will be necessary to dig out the roots of such plants or use a herbicide such as Roundup before you till. After tilling, spread additional topsoil, if necessary. Then fertilize and seed the area as described previously.

For further information we recommend *Hillside Gardening* by William Lake Douglas, with photographs by Derek Fell (Simon & Schuster). It contains many inspirational illustrations and worthwhile ideas from different parts of the country.

21

Gardening in Containers

Some people, of necessity, must do all their outdoor gardening in containers—those who live in high-rise apartment buildings or have only paved courtyard areas, for example. Even people with plenty of space for an outdoor garden like to brighten up the exterior of their homes with potted perennials on a porch, patio, deck, around a paved pool or play area, or in an atrium or sunroom.

Only your imagination need limit what will serve as a container. We have plants growing in hollow stumps, iron kettles, the center of an old gristmill stone, a watering tub originally used for cattle, as well as in pottery, wood, and plastic hanging pots, and window boxes. We know others who use whiskey barrels, cut-off water tanks, stone urns, and planters of wood fiber, concrete, brick, stone, clay, fiberglass, metal, or glass.

Houseplants and annuals such as petunias come first to mind when we think of container growing, but many hardy perennials, including lilies, hosta, day-lilies, Japanese iris, chrysanthemums, spring bulbs, and ferns thrive in pots, too. Both hardy and tender perennial herbs such as lavender, bay, and rosemary also do well in containers. In a mild climate, rock garden species are often planted in ornamental urns with holes in the sides or in strawberry barrels. Unless your planters are large, choose compact, clump-type plants rather than tall, upright specimens. Those that bloom over a long period and have attractive foliage, such as coral bells, shasta daisy, and fernleaf bleeding-heart, are better than kinds that bloom for only a short period and then die back.

One of the obvious advantages of using containers instead of planting directly in the ground is that unless the planters or pots are permanently installed, the perennials are portable. You can rearrange the display to show blossoms at their best, and even create the effect of continuous bloom throughout the season, just as public gardens do: grow all your plants in an out-of-the-way spot and move them into the garden area as they bloom. By rotating the pots, you can enjoy bulbs such as daffodils, hyacinths, and tulips in the spring, followed by plants such as *Primula*, pansies, and viola. Later, a multitude of summer bloomers can be brought out, and in the fall, hardy chrysanthemums. The plants can also be moved, when necessary, to spots with more favorable sunlight conditions, or to a place that is sheltered from a torrential rain or windstorm.

There are other advantages to container growing. Even in close quarters, it is easy to grow a wide variety of plants that prefer different conditions. You can regulate the moisture, soil fertility, and acidity to suit each individual plant, whereas in a garden bed it would be difficult to grow an acid-loving heather next to a lime-loving delphinium. Also, because the foliage of container-grown plants is exposed to less ground area, soil-borne diseases and insects are not as easily spread to the plants. Weeds are less likely to be a problem in pots, and invasive plants, such as bee balm, can be kept under control easily.

Except for watering, plants in containers require

less care than those in a bed, which makes this type of gardening ideal for people who do not enjoy digging and weeding. Anyone who cannot bend or stoop easily appreciates container gardening since the pots can be placed at a height convenient for inspection and care.

Plastic pots, although not as beautiful as clay, wood, or stone, have many advantages. They are easy to clean and the soil in them does not dry out as fast as that in clay pottery. They are also lightweight, an asset when you rearrange the terrace furniture, need to turn them so they won't lean toward the light, or move them into a greenhouse or root cellar for the winter. They are available in an array of colors and sizes, which can fit inside other types of containers if you wish.

Choose sizes that are big enough to allow your plants to grow to maturity, keeping in mind that perennials have large root systems. A 10-inch pot is a minimum for all but the tiniest kinds; a bigger size is preferable for most. Be certain that the planter you use has large drainage holes, so the soil won't become waterlogged during a heavy rain.

PLANTING

Since the soil in a container is limited, and roots cannot search any further for nutrients, the soil must be of particularly good quality. Commercial potting soil is not only more convenient, but it is also sterile—less likely to contain diseases, insects, and weed seeds. If you need a great deal of soil, as we do because we grow potted plants to sell, make your own by mixing one-third each of peat, rich loamy soil, and either sand or vermiculite (by volume, not weight). We sometimes substitute compost for peat or vary the formula in other ways.

Whether you mix your own soil or buy it, dump it into a clean wheelbarrow or other large container. Then blend in a few cups of dried manure and bonemeal, plus a small amount of slow-release commercial fertilizer, following closely the directions on the bag. Add lime only if it is needed by the plants you intend to grow.

Before putting the soil mix into the pots, place a thin layer of small rocks or broken clay fragments at the bottom of each container so the soil won't pack too tightly over the drainage holes and plug them.

Put enough soil into the bottom of the container to position the root ball of the plant at its original depth; then add soil until the pot is filled to within a half-inch or so of the top. This will allow room for watering. Firm the soil so no air is left to dry out the roots, and then add a thin layer of mulch. Water it thoroughly.

Container plants should be repotted each spring, and if the clumps are large, they should be divided so they don't become rootbound. Use new soil and additional slow-release fertilizer when you repot them.

CULTURE

Plants growing in containers are more like pets than those in a garden because they are so dependent on you. Most will need watering every day, and in hot, dry, or windy weather they may need it more often.

Whether you use a sprinkler can or hose, do not pour water haphazardly over the plants. Since the foliage may act as an umbrella, it is easy to water the leaves but not the soil. When plants are in the ground, the surrounding soil absorbs the runoff so it can still reach the roots; in a container any water that splashes off is lost. A light rain can be diverted in the same way. If you water with a hose, use low pressure so the force of the stream will not damage the plant or wash a hole into the soil and expose the roots.

Since daily watering is likely to leach away nutrients rapidly, in addition to the slow-release plant food you applied in the spring, every few weeks you should add small amounts of dry or liquid fertilizer. Lime is also depleted quickly in containers, leaving the soil too acid for fertilizer to be absorbed by the plants. If you have container plants that are not flourishing, test the pH of the soil and add lime if necessary.

WINTERING

In warm climates or in areas where thick layers of snow cover the ground, perennials will winter safely outdoors with no protection. Where there is little or no snow cover and the temperatures fall below freezing for long periods, the soil is likely to freeze solid which can dessicate plant roots. Few perennials can survive such treatment and those on a paved terrace, deck, or growing in an elevated planter or urn are particularly vulnerable.

One way to protect perennials in moveable pots is to move them to a cool greenhouse or cold frame for the winter. Since most need a dormant period, don't try to overwinter them in a greenhouse. Another method is to pack the pots close together

A. *Geranium* (crane's bill), B. *Achillea* (sneezeweed), C. *Hemerocallis* (daylily), D. *Oenothera* (sundrop), E. *Viola* (violet)

in a sheltered place on the ground so they can absorb heat and moisture from the soil. We tip the pots on their sides so water won't collect in them during a spring thaw and drown the plants when the drainage holes are still frozen. After a few hard frosts, cover the pots with evergreen boughs or one of those specially made foam insulating blankets that are available from garden supply stores. If you have only a few pots and a convenient place, burying them for the winter gives good protection. Each fall we sink several large clay and plastic pots of herbs in our vegetable garden after they have spent the summer on our backyard terrace.

The following plants do well in containers.

Early Flowering

Aquilegia, columbine
Centaurea montana, mountain bluet
Daffodils, and other spring bulbs
Dicentra, bleeding-heart
Doronicum, leopard's bane
Primula, primrose
Viola, pansies and violets

Summer Flowering

Achillea, yarrow
Aconitum, monkshood
Anthemis, marguerite
Chrysanthemum coccineum, pyrethrum
C. maximum, shasta daisy
Dianthus, pinks, sweet William
Gaillardia, blanketflower
Geranium, crane's bill
Gypsophila, baby's-breath
Hemerocallis, daylily
Heuchera, coral bells
Kniphofia, torch lily
Liatris, gayfeather
Lythrum, loosestrife
Monarda, bee balm
Oenothera, sundrop, evening primrose
Penstemon, beardtongue
Phlox
Rudbeckia, gloriosa daisy

Fall Flowering

Anemone japonica, Japanese anemone, windflower
Aster
Chrysanthemum

22

Gardening in a Shady Nook

The term "shade" encompasses so many different light conditions that it's hard to describe gardening techniques that will fit every situation. Shade can range from the dense darkness of a pine forest where only plants such as Indian pipe will grow, to the light-dappled shade under birch trees which allows a great deal of sunlight to filter through. It may also connote an area that gets strong skylight but no sun, such as the north side of a building. The intensity of light and shade also differs at various latitudes and at different times of the growing season. In the North, for instance, the northeast side of a building might get an abundance of sun in early June, but as the sun rises more toward the southeast and sets earlier in August, it may get little or none. Another factor that will affect the amount of light is the growth of nearby trees and bushes. We have met many gardeners who were puzzled because a garden that once bloomed prolifically ceased to grow well. When we checked it out, the culprit was often increased shading from nearby trees.

If you are not already familiar with light conditions in your prospective garden spot, it will be helpful to observe that area for one entire growing season to determine the quality of shade at various times of the day and year. If deciduous trees are the source, note whether the shade is dappled when they are in full leaf, as it is under the poplar family, or very dense, as under an oak or maple. If the shade seems too heavy for the proper growth of most plants, cutting off a few lower limbs from the offending trees will sometimes allow more light to enter from the sides.

The amount of moisture a shady spot receives may affect what you can grow there as much as the amount of light. The soil under pine trees is usually dry because the tree acts as an umbrella and falling rain seldom reaches there. It is just as likely, however, for a shaded spot to be excessively moist. If you hope to grow any plants when the soil is soggy for most of the summer, you must either drain it, build it up by adding topsoil, or choose only those specimens that do well in both bog and shade conditions.

Where the soil is thin and tree roots completely fill the area, even strong plants may not survive such competition. If you run into roots when you dig, either add a thick layer of topsoil or plant only shallow-rooted ground covers such as English ivy, myrtle, *Pachysandra*, and other woodland plants that normally grow under such conditions.

CHOOSING PLANTS

To grow plants successfully in the shade, you must choose varieties appropriate to the type of shade you have. Most plants need at least a few hours of direct sun, and filtered light or full skylight (known as light shade) for the rest of the day. There is a long list of perennials that will grow in places which get little or no sunshine, but have an abundance of filtered light (medium shade). Only a few plants can thrive in the darkness of an evergreen forest (dense shade), although *Pachysandra*, English ivy, myrtle, the Canadian mayflower (*Maianthemum*), and moneywort (*Lysimachia nummularia*) are worth a try in the slightly open areas where small amounts of light filter through to ground level.

In light shade it is possible to have continuous bloom beginning with a carpet of spring bulbs such as snowdrops, *Scilla*, *Muscari*, and daffodils, and continuing into the spring with lily-of-the-valley, violets, and similar species. Plants such as *Dicentra eximia*

(fernleaf bleeding-heart) that blossom throughout the growing season, and different varieties of hosta and *Hemerocallis*, will provide bloom for a long period. See the box below to find the season of bloom of various perennial plants. Shade-loving, continuous-blooming annuals such as *Impatiens* and begonias add color when the perennial blossoms are scarce.

Ferns are especially useful plants for shady areas, not only because they thrive there, but because they are so beautiful. They're ideal as border plants along a shady path, clumped in sunless garden corners, or on the north side of a building or high fence where

PERENNIALS FOR SHADY SPOTS

SP = Spring blooming
ES = Early summer blooms
SU = Summer blooming
L = Late summer or fall blooms
No * = full sun to light shade
* = light to medium shade
** = medium shade to dense shade
*** = dense shade

*Aconitum, monkshood, SU
Aegopodium, bishop's weed or goutweed, SU
*Ajuga, bugleweed, SU
Alchemilla, lady's mantle, SU
Anaphalis, pearly everlasting, SU
Anemone, wood anemone, SU
Aquilegia, columbine, ES
**Arenaria, sandwort, ES
Aruncus, goat's beard, SU
**Asperula, sweet woodruff, SP
Aster, L
Astilbe, perennial spirea, SU
Aubrieta, purple rockcress, ES
Baptisia, wild blue indigo, ES
*Bergenia, SP
*Brunnera, ES
Campanula, bellflower, SU
*Cimicifuga, bugbane, snakeroot, SU
Clematis, SU
**Convallaria, lily-of-the-valley, ES
*Corydalis, SU
*Dicentra eximia, fernleaf bleeding-heart, SP, ES, SU, L
Dictamnus, gas plant, SU
*Digitalis, foxglove, SU
*Doronicum, leopard's bane, SP
*Epimedium, SP
Euphorbia, spurge, SU
*Gentiana, gentian, L
Geranium, crane's bill, SU

*Helleborus, Christmas rose, L
Hemerocallis, daylily, SU, L
*Hesperis, sweet rocket, SU
Heuchera, coral bells, SP, ES, SU, L
Hibiscus, L
**Hosta, plantainlily, SU
Iberis, candytuft, ES
*Iris cristata, crested iris, ES
I. foetidissima, Gladwin iris, ES
Lamium, dead nettle, ES
Ligularia, golden-ray, SU
*Lilium, lily species including *L. canadense*, *L. martagon*, *L. aurelian*, and Oriental hybrids, SU
**Liriope, lily-turf, SU
*Lobelia, cardinal flower, SU
**Lysimachia, loosestrife, SU
Lythrum, purple loosestrife, SU
***Mertensia virginica*, Virginia bluebells, SP
*Monarda, bee balm, SU
*Myosotis, forget-me-not, SP
Omphalodes, navelwort, SP
**Pachysandra, spurge, SP
*Phlox divaricata, wild blue phlox, ES
P. subulata, moss pink, SP
**Polemonium reptans*, Jacob's ladder, ES
*Polygonatum, Solomon's seal, SP
*Polygonum affine, fleeceflower, SU, L
**Primula, primrose, ES
*Pulmonaria, lungwort, SP
**Rodgersia, Rodger's flower, ES
Stachys byzantina, lamb's ears, SU
*Thalictrum, meadowrue, SU
*Tiarella, foamflower, ES
**Trillium, SP
Trollius, globeflower, ES
Veronica, speedwell, SU
**Vinca, myrtle, periwinkle, ES
*Viola, woods violet, ES

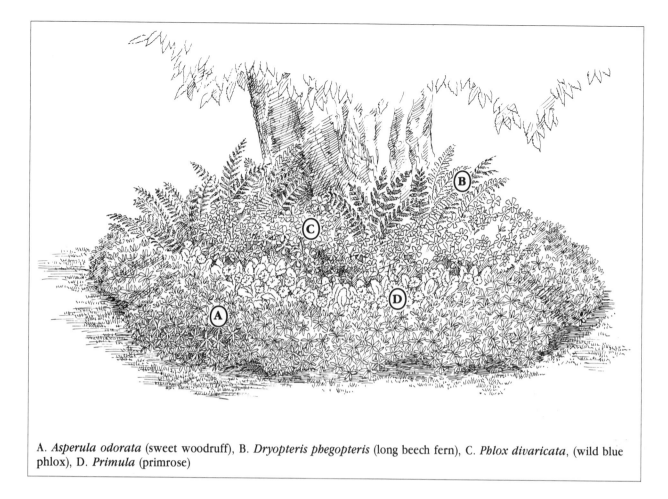

A. *Asperula odorata* (sweet woodruff), B. *Dryopteris phegopteris* (long beech fern), C. *Phlox divaricata*, (wild blue phlox), D. *Primula* (primrose)

even grass doesn't grow well. Most prefer the dappled shade created by deciduous trees to that of an evergreen forest, and most also like a woodsy, acidic soil, and benefit from a mulch of rotting leaves or needles.

Ferns can be transplanted from the wild in very early spring or late fall, but you will undoubtedly establish a more successful fern bower if you buy mature potted plants from a nursery or garden center.

Lycopodium (club mosses) are mosslike evergreen plants, such as ground cedar, princess pine, and reindeer moss, usually found in or near evergreen forests. They make interesting ground covers in shallow, acidic soil, and should be planted in light to medium shade where they get little competition from other plants. They can often be purchased from wildflower nurseries.

DESIGNING A SHADE GARDEN

If your perennial bed gets mostly light shade, simply choose the proper plants for that area by using the chart above, and coordinate their colors and heights the same as you would in any other bed. We have a light-shade situation in our backyard where a tight cedar hedge keeps the sun out of a small corner of the garden for much of the day, although abundant skylight is still available. Many perennials will grow there, such as delphinium and *Rudbeckia*, but since they get only a bit of afternoon sun, they tend to bloom later than those in full sun and for a longer period. This shaded corner gives us a chance to grow *Primula*, hosta, and woods plants such as lady's slippers and ferns that do not enjoy full sun.

The design of a medium-shade planting is more challenging. To grow a conventional perennial garden in an area partially shaded by trees, or on the north side of a house, is well-nigh impossible. But a woodland garden is ideal for such a spot. (Although the name suggests a forest area, a woodland garden can flourish even in the shadow of tall city buildings, if the right soil and moisture conditions exist.) Foliage plants are especially attractive, the different colors of which can be combined to add interest and unusual textures. The large hosta leaves contrast pleasantly with the delicate, lacy green of ferns, for example.

If the area is large, design pathways through it, and plant borders of *Ajuga*, *Pachysandra*, ivy, hosta, daylilies, Christmas fern, or primroses. Light-colored bricks or stones will contrast nicely with plant greenery, but a less formal, well-worn path of bare dirt is more natural looking.

The colors of a shaded garden may in actuality appear quite different from those you had carefully planned on paper since our perception of color differs according to the quality of the light that falls on it. In general, white and pastel blooms provide a bright, glowing quality in a sunless garden. More vivid colors may appear dim or, in certain shade situations, shine brilliantly and clash so much that they must be shifted from one spot to another.

In a shady planting, as in a rock garden, running water, old stumps, stones, and pools add greatly to the atmosphere. If there are no natural features in the area, you may be able to design substitutes and add such welcoming features as benches or other garden seats.

PLANTING AND CARING FOR A SHADE GARDEN

Planting a graden in the shade is not much different from planting an ordinary border in the sun. Soil acidity may be more of a problem, however, so test the soil before planting. Add lime only if the pH is below 5.5, and only in spots where you plan to grow perennials rather than acid-loving wildflowers and ferns. Allow more space for each plant in the shade than you would in full sun—the foliage will then have room to spread out and absorb all the available light.

Plants in woodland locations must compete with trees for nutrients, so fertilize them more heavily than you would those in a conventional garden. A thick mulch of organic material helps to create the woodland conditions they like. Check plants growing under trees each spring to see if fallen leaves or needles need to be cleaned away—such debris could smother the plants. In addition, make sure that plants under a canopy of trees, or sheltered from wind-driven rains by buildings, walls, or tight fences, are getting the moisture they need.

Ferns

Because ferns are so popular for shady gardens, we list here some of the most suitable.

Adiantum, maidenhair. These lacy ferns are among the most beautiful of all and are not difficult to grow. They like an area that gets only a little morning sun and a bit of skylight during the day. Often abundant in the rich, moist, well-drained, leaf-mulched soil of maple woods. An acid soil is not required. The native *A. pedatum*, the most recommended, grows to a height of about 20 inches.

Athyrium, glade fern, lady fern. This is another large group of ferns, *A. filix-femina* (the lady fern) being the best known. It, too, is not fussy about soil pH, grows in sun or shade, but needs adequate moisture or the leaves become brown. Grows to a height of 30 to 36 inches. *A. goeringianum*, Japanese painted fern, is a colorful import, with 2-foot fronds of gray-green and wine red; it needs moisture, lots of organic matter, and partial shade to grow to its best color and vigor.

Botrychium, rattlesnake fern. There are several common varieties of this species, growing from 5 to 24 inches tall. It likes moderately acid soil, sun, and is unique because it produces seeds in small clusters on the fronds.

Camptosorus rhizophyllus, walking fern. A creeping fern, less common than many of the others, it is found growing near rocks where the soil is moist and relatively sweet. Useful in rock gardens if enough moisture is present.

Cystopteris bulbifera, bladder fern. Grows from 12 to 24 inches tall and produces small bulbs along the stem at the base of the leaves. Likes moist soil, is not particular about acidity, and grows into a dainty attractive plant.

Dennstaedtia, cup fern. These evergreen ferns grow in full sunlight, although some kinds do well in shade. So vigorous it can become weedy and cover entire pastures of worn-out soil. Does especially well in a less acid soil, but this is not imperative. *D. punctilobula*, hay-scented fern, is one of the more attractive varieties. Grows 1 to 3 feet tall and smells of hay when crushed; serves as a useful ground cover, but will probably need to be controlled.

Dryopteris, wood fern. There are over a thousand varieties in this genus, many of which are especially attractive. They like shade, are not particular about soils. *D. crispa*, the crested wood fern, grows to 30 inches, stays evergreen in the warmer parts of the country, but dies down in the North although it is hardy. *D. marginalis*, leather wood fern, has a maximum height of 2 feet and is used in floral displays. *D. spinulosa*, often called fancy fern or toothed fern, is semievergreen, very attractive, and often collected for florist use because it is so long lasting; it is also outstanding in the landscape.

Lygodium palmatum, Hartford fern. A climbing plant that grows to about 4 feet. Prefers moist, acid soils and a shady location.

Matteuccia, ostrich fern. This massive plant grows up to 6 feet tall, likes moist soil, shade, and should not be planted too deeply. *M. pensylvanica* may grow to 10 feet in a wet location and spreads rapidly.

Onoclea sensibilis, sensitive fern. Grows fast enough to become weedy especially in moist locations. Grows in sun or light shade, is very tender to fall frosts, and reaches a height of 30 inches. Produces interesting fruits that are widely used in dried flower arrangements.

Osmunda, flowering fern. *O. cinnamomea*, cinnamon fern. About 3 feet tall with spores borne on cinnamonlike sticks in the center of the fronds. Likes moist places, sun, or shade. *O. claytoniana*, interrupted fern, another impressive specimen, is happy in moist spots, grows in sun, but seems to be at its massive best in light shade. It gets 36 inches tall, with spores growing about midway in the middle of its large fronds. *O. regalis*, royal fern, grows in very moist places, sometimes even water, likes partial shade, and somewhat acid soil. Up to 6 feet tall, but usually less.

Polypodium virginianum, common polypody. Small evergreen fern, 6 to 12 inches tall. Grows in sun or shade, acid or sweet soils. Good for rock gardens where it will develop into a thick mass.

Polystichum, holly fern. One of the best is *P. acrostichoides*, Christmas fern, a beautiful evergreen resembling the Boston fern. It likes the shade of deciduous woods, but can be grown in the sun if kept well watered; 1 to 3 feet tall.

Woodsia. *W. obtusa*, woodsia fern, is a small fern, up to 12 inches, that likes dry, shady places. Since they thrive in difficult places where there is little soil, they are useful in the shady parts of a rock garden. *W. ilvensis*, rusty woodsia, is a small fern about 6 inches tall with dark brown new growth; good ground cover.

Shade gardens offer refreshing relief on a hot summer day, and a completely different assortment of plants than those that grow in a sun-drenched border. In addition to these bonuses, the trees and shrubs that provide the shade also furnish protective shelter to a wide range of birds and small animals such as chipmunks, which can further enhance the garden with sound and motion.

23

Seashore Plantings

If you live or vacation near the shore, you know that growing plants there is not easy. Strong winds, glaring sun, sandy soil, and salt spray present a constant challenge to gardeners from New Brunswick to Key West on the Atlantic, and from British Columbia to southern California on the Pacific. Nevertheless, spectacular perennial borders flourish on each coast, nestled near sand dunes and alongside sea walls. If you are skeptical that a beautiful garden can be built near the ocean, a glance at the photos of Lee Bailey's gardens in Bridgehampton, Long Island, from his book *Lee Bailey's Country Flowers*, will dispel your doubts and inspire you to start a seaside garden.

If you have a choice of shore locations, choose a place for your bed that is protected from the wind and away from the salt-loaded splashes of the highest tides. Wind not only breaks fragile plants and bends sturdy ones, but it also rapidly dries out all growing things, a condition that is aggravated by bright, glaring sunlight. Because of the glare, many plant species that demand full sun inland, do better in light shade when grown near the shore. Buildings, hedgerows, walls of brick or stone, and board fences are all effective as windbreaks and shade providers. The barrier does not need to be high in many locations; even a low wall provides some protection.

Any trees or shrubs used as an oceanside windbreak should, of course, be salt-tolerant. Certain varieties are sensitive to salt spray on their foliage and others are killed by salt water on their roots. Arrowwood viburnum, Austrian pine, amur and California privet, Colorado spruce, shore pine, old-fashioned lilac, mountain *Andromeda*, Russian olive, juniper, and white spruce are fairly resistant to both spray on their foliage and salt damage on their roots. Canadian hemlock, Scotch pine, yews, arborvitae, and most other hedge-type evergreens are extremely susceptible to salt spray on their foliage.

Since soil along the shore is usually sandy and poor in quality, it is necessary to enrich it. Mix compost, topsoil, peat moss, manure or, even better, all three, into the soil before planting. Seaweed, too, is an exceptionally good soil conditioner and enricher. Because it contains no weeds, and is disease free, it can be used in making compost, as a mulch, or even spread on the beds and tilled in as you would manure. It provides humus and nutrients like manure, but is even richer in trace elements. Gather seaweed during the winter and let the rain wash off the salt and other debris before using it on the bed.

You will probably find it necessary to water seaside plants frequently during hot, dry spells and to wash residual salt off the plants after a high wind. A built-in sprinkler or trickle irrigation system can save a lot of time if you garden in an area where the summer weather is particularly dry and hot. Mulch around your plants with salt hay, seaweed, woodchips, shredded bark, cocoa hulls, or whatever organic material is available. This will help protect the soil against moisture loss and erosion, and should cut down on weeding.

PLANTS

For the basic plants in your garden, choose sturdy perennials that will thrive in sandy soil, full sun, and salt-laden air and wind. We recommend the following for seaside locations, but don't hesitate to try others that appeal to you, including annuals, especially if your garden is sheltered and some distance away from the surf and spray. The plants with asterisks are particularly effective in a dry location.

Achillea tomentosa, yarrow
Ajuga, bugleweed
Althaea rosea, hollyhock
Anchusa azurea, Italian bugloss
Anthemis, marguerite
Aquilegia, columbine
Arabis, rockcress
Armeria maritima, common thrift
Artemisia stellerana, Dusty Miller
Asclepias tuberosa, butterfly milkweed
*Aster
Astilbe*, spirea
Baptisia australis, wild indigo
Catanache, cupid's dart
*Chrysanthemum
Cimicifuga*, snakeroot
Coreopsis, tickseed
Delphinium, larkspur
Dianthus, pinks, sweet William
Digitalis, foxglove
Doronicum caucasicum, leopard's bane
Echinops, globe thistle
Erigeron, fleabane

Eryngium maritimum, sea holly
*Euphorbia
Gaillardia*, blanketflower
Gypsophila, baby's-breath
Hemerocallis, daylily
Heuchera sanguinea, coral bells
Hibiscus moscheutos, rose mallow
Hosta, plantainlily
Iberis sempervirens, candytuft, evergreen
Kniphofia, torch lily
Lathyrus littoralis, beach pea
Lilium superbum, turk's cap lily
Limonium, sea lavender, statice
Liriope spicata, lily-turf
Lychnis coronaria, rose campion
Lythrum salicaria, loosestrife
Monarda didyma, bee balm
Papaver orientale, Oriental poppy
*Phlox
Rudbeckia, coneflower
Sedum, stonecrop
Sempervivum tectorum, hen-and-chickens, houseleek
Stachys, lamb's ears
Viola cornuta, tufted pansy
*Yucca

The challenge of transforming what may be a barren landscape into a colorful garden in a hostile environment may seem formidable. But anyone who feels that sandy soil and harsh climatic conditions make beautiful plantings impossible should be encouraged by the fact that ever since colonial times the village gardens found along the coast have been considered among the most attractive on the continent.

24

The Herb Garden

The first year we had an herb garden it was a great success. Each little plant flourished and by fall had filled the spot we'd allotted to it. By the middle of the next summer, however, it was clear that we had a problem. The spearmint, sweet woodruff, and thyme were running wild and crowding out other plants such as rosemary and sage. The garden had to be completely revamped. We learned the hard way that when certain invasive herbs are happy with their bed and board, they must be severely disciplined and kept in their place, if the garden is to remain attractive.

Herbs are often grown more for culinary, medicinal and aromatic purposes than for their beauty. People who enjoy cooking, plant those that are used for flavoring and savoring, such as sweet basil for pesto, tarragon for vinegar, and spearmint for tea. Others concentrate on plants for medicinal salves and ointments; and still others choose to specialize in the fragrant herbs. Our friend Flora adds dried lavender and other aromatics to a large jar of potpourri each summer, which she later makes into gift sachets for her friends.

Learning about the lore, history, and uses of herbs is nearly as much fun as cultivating them. Owners of a vintage home, for example, often research the plants in common use when it was built, and feature them in a border; someone in the clergy might design a bed using herbs mentioned in the Bible; a music buff fond of Simon and Garfunkel might plant a bed of "parsley, sage, rosemary and thyme," using the theme from

their song *Scarborough Fair*. Herbalist Adelma Simmons at her mecca for herb lovers, "Caprilands," in Coventry, Connecticut, features such varied historical themes as Shakespeare, medieval and colonial periods, as well as a bride's garden, saints' garden, plots with only silver- or gold-colored plants, one filled completely with fragrant geraniums, a cutting garden for dried bouquets and wreaths, and much more.

DESIGNING AND PLANTING AN HERB GARDEN

Herbs are so versatile that they are at home almost anywhere—along pathways, as landscape plants or ground covers, in rock gardens, terraces, vegetable beds, or containers. But they usually give the most gardening pleasure when planted in a well-designed herb bed. It may be as informal as a tiny plot outside the door of a country cottage, or as formal and elaborate as a classic medieval wheel, knot, butterfly, stained glass window, or some other geometric design.

Look to your surroundings for good locations, as you would in designing any garden. The ideal site for most herbs is in the sun, although a few, such as the mints, watercress, and lemon balm grow well in shade. Some will thrive in almost any type of soil, but most prefer it to be well drained, with a pH that is neutral to sweet, rather than acidic. In a sunny "ell" outside a kitchen door you might plant a small salad garden of culinary perennial and annual herbs, a few radishes, cherry tomatoes, lettuce, and scallions. An open hillside might lend itself to a series of terraced, small circular plots, each with a different type of herb.

In small, informal beds such as these, minimal planning is necessary—primarily the arrangement and proper spacing for the plants you've chosen. Consider the ultimate size of each plant, and arrange it so that the small species, such as parsley and thyme, are not hidden and shaded by lovage, comfrey, or other tall growers.

If you choose to create a larger, more ornamental bed, it is desirable to plan it first on graph paper. To attain the necessary symmetry and balance, the different species must be orderly and neat, colors and sizes arranged to balance each other, and edgings are essential. Pathways, which are integral to the design of most geometric-type gardens, should be in place before any planting is done. Paths of flagstone, brick, pebbles, or mown grass form the skeletons of such beds. Each path should be 3 or 4 feet wide to provide plenty of room to move about and work in each area. If birdbaths, sundials, and statuary are used, they should also be installed before any planting is done.

The different colors of herb foliage make them fun to arrange in interesting patterns. Blooming times are not especially important because most of their flowers are rather inconspicuous. Rows of compact, low-growing plants (chives and parsley, for example) can be used to separate various groupings and to edge the paths.

Whether your garden is formal or informal, position any spreading varieties where they will not become invasive. As we learned from the experience in our first herb garden, the weedy species are best kept within bounds by planting each one in a separate soil "pocket." These can be large plastic pots sunk into the garden or sunken clay tiles such as those used for chimney liners.

Once established, most perennial herbs are hardy and will live for years, but in northern zones tender plants (rosemary and bay) must be treated as annuals or potted and taken in for the winter. In addition to perennials, you may want to reserve spots in your garden to plant some of the many excellent annuals. A culinary herb garden wouldn't be complete without basil, dill, borage, anise, chervil, coriander, sweet marjoram, nasturtium, rocket, and summer savory. Seeds of biennials such as parsley must be resown each spring along with the annuals. The seeds can either be sown directly in the garden, or, for an earlier harvest, seedlings set out.

Most perennial herbs can be started from seed, although it is far easier to buy started plants in order to get quicker results. A few, such as French tarragon and lavender, should be started by division rather than by seed to obtain good plants. Also, the different strains of oregano and the mints can vary so much in flavor that it is best to taste or smell each variety before planting it in your garden.

The more humus, the better, in an herb bed. Mix manure and compost with the soil and prepare it as thoroughly as if you intended to plant a flower or vegetable garden. After the surface is smoothed, take your design in hand and outline the spaces for each herb with white flour or lime. After planting, spread a mulch around each plant to help prevent erosion and to keep the plants clean. It's annoying to find herbs that you intend to use in a salad or potpourri splattered with dirt from the latest rainstorm.

A List of Useful Perennial Herbs

Bay, sweet bay, laurel (*Laurus nobilis*). Slow-growing evergreen shrub with aromatic leaves, frequently used in soups and stews. Sun-loving, it is a tender perennial and must be taken indoors during the winter in cold climates. Difficult to propagate. Can grow to a height of 10 feet.

Boneset, Indian sage (*Eupatorium perfoliatum*). Medicinal herb popular with early colonists who learned of its value from the Indians. Use as a tonic, and for treating colds and fevers. Grows best in marshes and other wet places. Height: 5 feet.

Burnet, salad burnet (*Sanguisorba minor*). Cucumber-flavored leaves are used in drinks, soups, and salads. Easily grown from seed. Grows 1 to 2 feet tall in sun or light shade and slightly alkaline soil.

Camomile, also spelled chamomile (*Anthemis nobilis*). Tea made from the blossoms is used as a soothing tranquilizer; also used as a tonic. Grows easily from seed or divisions. Annual German camomile (*Matricaria chamomilla*) is often confused with the perennial and has similar medicinal qualities, but grows larger—up to 2½ feet tall. *A. nobilis* grows up to 10 inches with a spreading growth habit.

Caraway (*Carum carvi*). Biennial culinary herb used to flavor cheese, rye bread, and pastries. Seeds ripen in fall of second year. Height: 2 feet. Likes sun and ordinary garden soil.

Catmint (*Nepeta cataria*). Beloved by felines and used in tea by humans as a cough remedy and aid to digestion. Height: 2 to 3 feet. Easily grown in sun or light shade, and in most soils.

Chicory (*Cichorium intybus*). The root may be used as a substitute for, or additive to, coffee. Bright blue flowers. Grows so easily that it often becomes a roadside weed, and for this reason is best planted in a location away from the garden. Height: 2 to 3 feet.

Chives (*Allium schoenoprasum*). Small onionlike plants, useful in salads, soups, and egg dishes. Easily grown from plants or seeds. A nice kitchen pot plant that grows to a height of 1 foot.

Comfrey (*Symphytum officinale*). Vigorous herb with large leaves, sometimes used as a poultice to aid in the knitting of broken bones. Once used as a medicinal healing herb, but recent findings suggest it may be harmful if ingested in more than small amounts. Also grown for animal food. Usually started from divisions. Height: 2 to 3 feet. Grows easily in sun and ordinary garden soil.

Costmary, bible leaf (*Chrysanthemum balsamita*). Its fragrant leaves with a minty flavor were pressed and used as bookmarks in Bibles during colonial days. Used today as a garnish, in tea, and for potpourri. Propagated by root division. Height: 2 to 3 feet. Likes a sunny spot and ordinary garden soil.

Fennel, sweet (*Foeniculum*). Short-lived perennial. Florence fennel (*F. dulce*) or finocchio, grown for its anise-flavored foliage, seeds, and fleshy base; is usually harvested as an annual. Common fennel, *F. vulgare*, more weedy, is grown primarily for its seed and foliage. Both are used in salads and stews and, less commonly, as a medicine to reduce appetite and to treat various ailments. Easily grown from seed, but best kept isolated, as it is reputed to adversely affect the growth of other plants near it. Height: 4 to 5 feet. Needs full sun and grows in ordinary garden soil.

Feverfew (*Chrysanthemum parthenium*). Biennial or perennial. Hardy medicinal herb credited with many beneficial characteristics, from treating colic to an overdose of opium. Easily grown from seed or division; grows 2 to 3 feet tall. Best in sun or light shade and a well-drained soil.

Ginseng (*Panax quinquefolium*). Medicinal plant with roots that are said to have many miraculous powers. The Chinese have prized it for centuries as everything from a tonic to an aphrodisiac. In this country it is valued mostly as a cash crop. It needs acidic soil, heavy shade, and frequent applications of fungicides as protection against disease. The plants grow slowly, and it may take up to ten years for the roots to reach harvestable size. Height: 15 inches.

Hops (*Humulus lupulus*). Perennial vine that produces flower pods used for flavoring beer. Propagated easily from seeds, layers, or root division. Likes full sun, grows rapidly, and often becomes rank. The tops may die to the ground over the winter in cold areas, but roots are hardy.

Horehound (*Marrubium vulgare*). Leaves are dried for tea and used fresh in candy and cough syrup. Grown from seed, cuttings, or division. Height: 1 to 2 feet. Needs full sun and dry, sandy soil.

Hyssop (*Hyssopus officinalis*). A hardy ancient herb used as a purifying tea and for medicine, it is said to cure all manner of ailments from head lice to shortness of breath. Started by seed or division. Grows to 3 feet. Prefers full sun and well-drained, alkaline soil.

Lavender (*Lavandula*). Aromatic herb used either fresh or dried, in sachets and pillows. Grows from seeds, cuttings, or divisions. Plant in a protected location in the North. Prefers lime soil. English lavender (*L. vera*) produces the loveliest blossoms and the most fragrant oil. Height: 1 to 2 feet.

Lemon balm (*Melissa officinalis*). Lemon-scented leaves are used for tea, jelly, or flavoring, either dried or fresh. Attracts bees. Start from cuttings or division. Height: 1 to 3 feet. Plant in sun or light shade and well-drained soil.

Lemon verbena (*Aloysia triphylla* or *Lippia citriodora*). Tender, aromatic perennial that cannot stand frost, so must be used as a houseplant during the winter in northern climates. Loses its leaves in the fall, but they promptly return. May be used for culinary purposes, but most often enjoyed only for its fragrance. Height: 10 inches.

Lovage (*Levisticum officinale*). The celery-flavored leaves and stalks are used in soups, salads, and similar dishes. Large plant. Grows well from seed. Height: 4 to 6 feet. Grows best in partial shade and moist, fertile soil.

Mint (*Mentha*). Peppermint and spearmint are the most popular, but orange, apple, lemon, and others are also widely grown. They have medicinal qualities, are also used in teas, jelly, and salads, and are used as flavoring for candy and ice cream. Although they may be grown from seed, buy small plants of your choice to be sure of getting the variety you want. Various heights up to 3 feet tall.

Oregano (*Origanum vulgare*). A perennial, sometimes known as wild marjoram. Often confused with sweet marjoram (*O. majorana* or *Majorana*), also perennial except in the North where it is not hardy and is treated as an annual. Used in soups, salads, meat dishes, and pizza, especially in Italian and Mexican cuisine. Easily grown from seed, cuttings, or division. Because there are many species, test the plants you buy for strength of the flavor. Height: 1 foot. Grows in full sun and ordinary garden soil.

Parsley (*Petroselinum crispum* (curly), *P. hortense* (Italian). A biennial usually treated as an annual. Probably the most commonly grown culinary herb today, used as a garnish, and in salads, soups, and such. Grows easily from seeds, but they are slow to germinate. Height: 1 foot. Prefers full sun or light shade and moist, rich soil.

Pennyroyal (*Mentha pulegium* (English), *Hedeoma pulegioides* (American). Old-time medicinal herbs used for flavoring and to cure a variety of illnesses. The American Indians and early settlers also used it as an insect repellent. Although it grows profusely in the wild, cultivated plants grow to a larger size. Grown from seed, cuttings, or root divisions. Height: 1 foot. Prefers a shady location and moist soil.

Rosemary (*Rosmarinus officinalis*). Used both as an aromatic and flavoring herb, it is useful in sauces, soups, teas, and especially as flavoring for lamb. Too tender to winter over in many areas of the North, it makes a nice potted plant and can be grown as a bonsai. Thrives with moisture, but needs well-drained, alkaline soil and is susceptible to insect pests. Started from seed, cuttings, or layers. Grows to 6 feet in warm climates, but much shorter elsewhere.

Rue (*Ruta graveolens*). A bitter medicinal herb used for thousands of years as an antidote to all kinds of poisons. Often worn as a potion to ward off fevers and fleas; used as a disinfectant as well. Easily grown from seed, but the ancient Greeks believed that a plant stolen from a neighbor's garden had more power than one acquired honestly! Height: 2 to 3 feet. Plant in an alkaline soil, in sun or partial shade.

Sage (*Salvia officinalis*). One of the most common culinary herbs, used by the early settlers who mixed it with pork sausage, poultry, and other meats. It was also regarded as medicinal, and though it is seldom credited now with curing tuberculosis, it is said to counteract the effects of fat in meat, and to be useful for treating sore throats and headaches. Many varieties available; easily grown from seeds, but are short lived. Height: 2 to 3 feet. Grows in a sunny spot and ordinary garden soil.

Scented geraniums (*Pelargonium*). Numerous varieties, each with a distinctive fragrance, flower, and leaf. Not frost-hardy. The leaves of rose geraniums are used in apple jelly or to make tea. Most varieties are grown primarily as scented houseplants. Started from cuttings. Prefers full sun and well-drained soil.

Sorrel (*Rumex*). The leaves have a sour, acidic, citrus flavor and are used in soups and salads. French sorrel (*R. scutatus*) is most often planted, but garden sorrel (*R. acetosa*) is similar. Prefers acidic soil. Grows easily from seeds or division and often becomes a weed. Height: 2 feet. Plant in sun to partial shade.

Sweet cicely (*Myrrhis odorata*). A rather uncommon culinary herb in this country, its anise-flavored leaves are used in soups and salads. Propagated by seed, but not easily; grows in rich soil in a shady spot. Height: 2 to 3 feet.

Sweet woodruff (*Asperula odorata*). Used in Germany for many centuries to flavor May wine, it has also been used as an ointment, in perfume, and as an internal medicine. Placed in drawers, it repels insects and gives sheets and towels a pleasant scent. Likes acid soil. Difficult to grow from seed, so buy plants instead. The top may be cut and dried anytime; the delightful fragrance appears only after drying. Height: 8 inches.

Tansy (*Tanacetum vulgare*). A strong-smelling plant used as a fly and ant repellent, and in tea as an aid to digestion. Use sparingly to flavor salads; too much, it is said, will cause an abortion. Its yellow foliage may be dried for bouquets. Grows well in full sun and ordinary garden soil from seed or divisions; can become weedy. Height: 2 to 3 feet.

Tarragon (*Artemisia dracunculus*). The French variety has the best flavor and is much preferred to Russian tarragon (*A. redowski*). Used in many culinary treats, including salads, eggs, fish, chicken, vegetables, and vinegar. Grows easily from root divisions. Should be mulched for overwintering in the North. Height: 2 to 3 feet. Plant in sun and ordinary garden soil.

Thyme (*Thymus*). Pronounced "time," it is a mainstay of most gardens, often used as a ground cover or rock plant. Most varieties have ornamental, culinary, and aromatic qualities. Used in the kitchen to flavor soups, salads, dressings, omelets, bread, sauces, and vegetables. Easily grown from divisions, seeds, or cuttings. Various heights, up to 1 foot tall.

Wormwood (*Artemisia absinthium*). A bitter, strong-smelling, medicinal herb, it is a perfect example of the ancient belief that a medicine must taste bad to be effective. Used to make aromatic absinthe. It was once widely planted around poultry yards, both for the health of the birds and also as a repellent to wild animals. Toxic in large doses. An attractive plant with gray foliage, it is easily grown from seed and may quickly become a weed, so be wary of planting it in your garden. Height: 2 to 5 feet.

Ordinary garden soil is fine, and so is a location in the sun or light shade.

Watercress (*Nasturtium officinale*). Used for garnish and flavoring. If you have a shallow, slow-moving stream or pond where there is no threat of flood, you may want to try growing this flavorful herb. It is grown commercially in greenhouses under controlled conditions. Watercress can be easily transplanted from one stream to another. Propagated by division. Low-growing.

25

Gardens for Birds and Butterflies

We gardeners may rate plants for their visual appeal, but birds and butterflies are more interested in cuisine. If you provide a yard that offers a lush menu of nectar and insects, and perhaps a hummingbird feeder, it will get a five-star rating from the winged world! Fortunately, it is easy to develop such a border because nectar is secreted by a great many of the colorful flowers we all love.

CREATE A HUMMINGBIRD HAVEN

In the late spring everything comes to a halt when we hear the unmistakable whirring of the first ruby-throated hummingbird and his mate, newly returned to our New England garden after spending the winter in Central America. It seems a miracle that these tiny visitors, weighing one-eighth of an ounce or less, with wings that beat seventy-five times each second and propel them at speeds of 30 miles per hour, should choose our humble yard for their summer vacation.

No matter where you live, some kind of hummingbird may find you. East of the Mississippi, it will be the ruby-throated, but several others, including the rufous, broad-tailed, and black-chinned are found in the West. All are attracted to flowers by sight rather than scent. Their favorite colors are red, pink, and orange because flowers with those hues are most likely to provide nectar, especially those with tubular shapes, such as the fuchsia. Color triggers such an automatic response in these birds that they will curiously inspect even a red umbrella, orange shirt, or red-handled hoe! In a shady spot, bright orange shades appeal most to them, and in dry desert locations where flowers, leaves, and grass are scarce, they are attracted to green flowers.

Obviously, the perennials in a hummingbird garden should feature their favorite colors. Plant plenty of them, because the birds need a great deal of nectar to satisfy their voracious appetites. Try to choose species with blossoming seasons that overlap, to provide a constant food supply. Red-hued annuals, such as petunias, salvia, geraniums, cosmos, scarlet runner beans, and snapdragons can be interspersed to provide nectar throughout the summer when there are gaps in the perennial blossoms. Many flowering shrubs are also attractive to hummingbirds.

The return of the hummingbirds from their winter home is timed to coincide with the blooming of nectar-producing flowers in the spring, but some years blossoms are delayed by cool, wet weather. You can help to ensure the survival of the birds by providing artificial nectar. Place a solution of one part sugar to four parts water, that has been brought to a boil, in a hummingbird feeder, and the birds will quickly find it. Do not use honey, because it can quickly develop bacteria in warm weather. The sweet syrup provides energy, but not much nourishment—for that they'll need nectar from your flowers, as well as aphids, tiny spiders, and other small insects. Avoid using insecticides or other chemicals that might diminish their food supply or poison them.

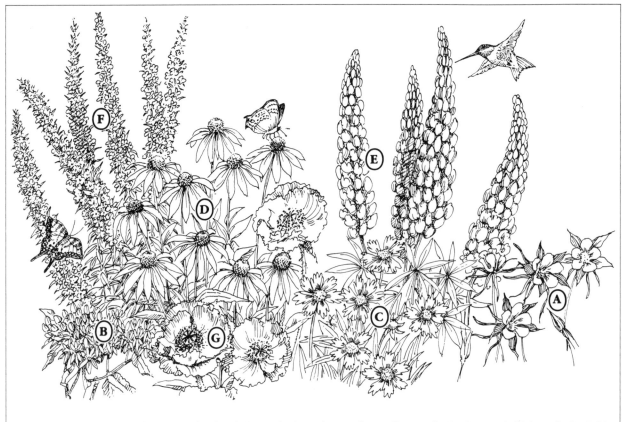

A. *Aquilegia canadensis* (eastern columbine), B. *Asclepias tuberosa* (butterfly weed), C. *Coreopsis* (tickseed), D. *Echinacea purpurea* (purple coneflower), E. *Lupinus* (lupine), F. *Lythrum* (lythrum), G. *Papaver orientale* (Oriental poppy)

Red-hued varieties of the following perennials attract hummingbirds and supply nectar as well.

Althaea, hollyhock
Aquilegia, columbine
Asclepias, butterfly weed
Campanula, bellflower
Delphinium, larkspur
Dianthus, pinks, carnation, sweet William
Digitalis, foxglove
Echinops, globe thistle
Hemerocallis, daylily
Heuchera, coral bells
Iris, bearded kinds
Lilium, lily
Lupinus, lupine
Lychnis, campion
Lythrum, loosestrife
Monarda, bee balm
Nepeta, catmint
Papaver, poppy
Penstemon, beardtongue
Phlox paniculata, garden phlox
Salvia, sage
Saponaria, bouncing bet
Stachys, betony

Red-flowering varieties of the following shrubs and vines are also attractive to the hummers and may be used to complement the perennials.

Buddleia, butterfly bush
Caragana, pea shrub
Chaenomeles, flowering quince
Cotoneaster
Kolkwitzia, beauty bush
Lonicera, honeysuckle
Rhododendron, azalea
Ribes, flowering currant
Syringa, lilac
Weigela

A BED FOR BUTTERFLIES

Most of us cultivate our perennial beds without concern for butterflies and are simply grateful for whatever beautiful lepidoptera happen to drop by. But once, long ago, we saw a garden planted specifically to attract them: the Bok Gardens at Iron Mountain, Florida. We've never forgotten the sight of thousands of beautiful butterflies feeding in the same small area. People who have seen the Monarchs congregate in their Central American wintering grounds report feeling a similar sense of awe.

Butterflies, unlike hummingbirds, are not concerned about the color of the flora, but enjoy feasting on nectar in a sunny spot sheltered from the wind. A true butterfly garden contains plants that provide food for the larvae caterpillars, as well as nectar for the butterfly. Consequently, if you want to attract a specific type, you should consult a good book on butterflies, such as *The Butterfly Garden* by Matthew Tekulsky (Harvard Common Press), to find which foods the larvae of that species prefer. In general, the wildflowers that are part of their natural environment are the best choices for planting in a butterfly garden. The Monarchs, for example, choose milk-weed as the spot to lay their eggs, and they can often be found in the fall on goldenrod.

Perennials that Butterflies Enjoy

Asclepias tuberosa, butterfly weed
Buddleia, butterfly bush
Centaurea macrocephala, globe centaurea
Dianthus, pinks, sweet William
Digitalis, foxglove
Echinops, globe thistle
Eupatorium coelestinum, mistflower
Helianthus, sunflower
Hesperis, rocket
Liatris, gayfeather
Lilium, lily
Lupinus, lupine
Monarda, bee balm
Rudbeckia, gloriosa daisy, golden glow

26

The Cottage Garden

Even if you live in a mansion modeled after Mt. Vernon, you could still create a cottage garden there, but it would seem much more appropriate near a small unpretentious home. The name invokes an image of various annual and perennial flowers, fruits, berries, herbs, vegetables, and shrubs in a variety of colors, sizes, and shapes, all tucked into a small front yard that leads to a storybook cottage with a thatched roof. It would be the kind of haven where you might expect to meet elves, fairies, and nature spirits.

Although cottage gardens exist all over the world, the British have elevated them to an art form, as you know if you have visited rural England. These inveterate gardeners, in a country where land is scarce, plant everything in the smallest of front or backyards. Their skill makes what could be an unsightly hodgepodge into a beautiful and productive garden. Cottage gardens usually occupy only a tiny space, but have been known to approach an acre in size.

Such plantings are rare in North America because we are conditioned to have a well-groomed lawn in front of the house; in certain suburbs, zoning regulations forbid anything as unconventional as an unmanicured cottage garden. This unfortunate attitude causes us to miss out on an unusual kind of gardening. Few styles are more fun to develop and it's convenient to grow a variety of vegetables, fruits, herbs, and flowers in a small space near the house.

The basic requirement for such a garden is a sunny enclosure with well-defined boundaries such as stone walls, picket fences, hedges, or buildings. It should be filled with rich, deeply tilled soil to encourage plant roots to grow downward rather than outward, and have pathways throughout so each section can be reached easily. In most, there is little or no lawn, and plants fill every nook and cranny.

The perennials in a bona fide cottage garden are old-fashioned and informal, including native and near-wild varieties that are the antithesis of modern hybrids. It is rare to see such a garden without vintage plants such as hollyhocks, pansies, and primroses. A clump of staked Pacific hybrid delphinium or a tea rose are "flora non grata," but their predecessors, the larkspur and shrub rose, would be very much at home. Most old-fashioned cottage garden plants have a delicious fragrance, unlike many of their modern descendants.

No hard-and-fast rules exist for designing such a garden, but the underlying concept is that there should be no symmetrical rows of plants or careful arrangement of colors to spoil the patchwork effect. Instead, lavender and lamb's ears, onions, lettuce, and lupine can enjoy each other's company in a conglomeration of little plots. Annual bedding plants may be set amidst the vegetables, herbs, and perennials, and the berry plants grown in clumps instead of orderly rows. Small fruits such as gooseberries, currants, and blueberries are found in a cottage garden, as are dwarf fruit trees, but because you may find it necessary to spray the fruits, keep them apart from the berries, herbs, and vegetables. Although things may appear to be crowded, each plant must still have enough room to get the sun, moisture, and fertility it needs to thrive.

As you would guess, the fixtures most at home in a cottage garden are natural-looking objects such as an arbor to hold climbing roses or a grapevine, a beehive, a swinging gate, and furniture of weathered wood or stone. Natural-looking pathways can be constructed of wooden blocks, flagstone, or similar materials.

CARE

The charm of a cottage garden is due primarily to the frequent attention it receives with hoe and trowel. Not a garden for the dilettante, it is a project for the true amateur in the best meaning of that word: one who loves a pursuit, but is not a professional practitioner of it. Cottage gardeners should be dedicated, though, and have plenty of time and energy to devote to their passion. Because there are no well-defined rows where a tiller could conveniently fit, cultivating must be done by hand, as well as the feeding and weeding. Old-fashioned perennials usually do not require as much spraying and staking as hybrids, but they still need adequate water and nutrient renewal. Such plants tend to grow more profusely than the hybrids, so division and deadheading may take more time than in other gardens. Although this care is demanding, it can reward you with an abundance of colorful blooms, from the earliest spring snowdrops and yellow daffodils to the last fragrant roses of summer.

In addition to bulbs, herbs, vegetables, shrub roses, and fruits, the following old-time perennials are special favorites among cottage gardeners. You will undoubtedly include your own special favorites, and it is permissible to sneak in a hybrid now and then if the spirit moves you. For more complete lists of appropriate plants, see *The Cottage Garden* by Anne Scott-James (Penguin).

Suggested Plants for a Cottage Garden

Anthemis tinctoria, marguerite
Aquilegia, columbine
Aster
Campanula medium, Canterbury bells
Cheiranthus, wallflower
Convallaria, lily-of-the-valley
Dianthus, pinks
Digitalis, foxglove
Helianthus, sunflower
Hemerocallis, daylily
Hesperis, rocket
Lilium, lily (especially 'Enchantment,' Madonna, regal, and tiger lilies)
Lupinus, lupine
Primula, primrose
Viola, pansy, violet

27

A Low-Maintenance Garden

Customers at our nursery often asked, "What looks nice all year and requires no care whatsoever?" Except for recommending a birdbath, flagpole, or plastic flowers, we have never been able to provide a satisfactory answer. The best we could do was suggest plants that thrive with a minimum of care. Easy-care plants are ideal for anyone who wants a nice-looking border, but doesn't want the maintenance that most gardens require—perhaps because of a demanding job, a physical handicap, or simply because golf seems like more fun on a Saturday afternoon.

The design of the garden can determine the amount of labor required nearly as much as the kinds of plants you choose. Formal, symmetrical beds with sheared borders are certain to appear in disarray if anything falls over or gets weedy, but an informal planting or one that's partially wild, can look good even if you haven't tended it for a couple of weeks. Gardens that need a large amount of hand weeding, such as rockeries, are not good choices if you want to avoid time-consuming care.

Most neglected gardens suffer primarily because they are larger than the owner can easily maintain, so the first rule of easy-care gardening is *keep it small*. When you design the beds, keep them relatively narrow so you can reach most of the plants from the front or back without having to pick your way among them. Separate any vigorous ground covers or fast-spreading varieties from less active plants by edgings, paths, or other solid barriers they cannot cross. When you plant, leave more space between your clumps than you ordinarily would to allow them to grow a bit larger before they need dividing. And when frequent watering is necessary, this process can be simplified by installing sprinklers in the bed at planting time and equipping them with a timer valve.

CHOOSING EASY-CARE PLANTS

When you set out to create a low-maintenance garden, look for plants that will stay compact and attractive for years without becoming weedy or invasive. Many perennials fit into this category, but it is difficult to compile a complete list since, as we said before, some that behave well in one section of the country may act quite differently under other climatic conditions.

Easy-care plants have some or all of the following characteristics:

- No need to divide more than every 3 to 4 years.
- Disease and insect resistance.
- Hardiness in your climate—no need to take extra precautions for winter protection.
- Sturdy stems that don't need staking.

- Long blossoming period; you'll need fewer varieties to keep your garden filled with bloom.
- Foliage that remains attractive throughout the season.

Although few perennials fit all the above criteria, it is surprising how many do fulfill the low-maintenance requirement. Below is a list of those perennials which are most appropriate for an easy-care garden.

Achillea, yarrow (especially the 'Coronation Gold' variety)
Aconitum, monkshood
Astilbe, spirea (dwarf varieties)
Chelone, turtlehead
Delphinium, low-growing varieties
Dicentra spectabilis, bleeding-heart
Dictamnus, gas plant
Doronicum, leopard's bane
Geranium, crane's bill
Geum, avens
Gypsophila, baby's-breath
Hemerocallis, daylily
Heuchera, coral bells
Hosta, plantainlily
Iberis, candytuft
Iris sibirica, Siberian iris
Liatris, gayfeather
Lobelia cardinalis, cardinal flower
Lupinus, lupine
Lythrum, loosestrife
Narcissus, daffodil

Paeonia, peony
Phlox
Primula, primrose
Pulmonaria, lungwort
Rudbeckia, gloriosa daisy
Trollius, globeflower
Veronica, speedwell
Yucca, Adam's needle

GARDENS FOR THE ELDERLY AND HANDICAPPED

We'll never forget the day many years ago when we discovered one of our favorite octogenarian friends lying flat on her side in her yard, bracing herself with one hand and pulling weeds with the other. She was crippled with arthritis of the hip, but as a dedicated gardener had no intention of giving up her favorite pastime!

Fortunately, modern medicine has now developed an artifical hip joint for our friend, and provided her and others who have physical disabilities with adaptive tools. Gardening chores are made much easier by such new-fangled products as long-handled weed pullers and shears with a long reach for cutting flowers, these being constructed to hold the object rather than let it drop. Lightweight tools and new types of

HOW TO CONTROL THE WEEDS

After you've chosen the varieties you want, the next important step is to cut down on weeding, the most time-consuming chore in any garden. Take the following steps:

1. Prepare the soil well before planting; remove all quack grass and other perennial weed clumps and roots. If you have very heavy sod, you might want to remove it altogether because otherwise you'll constantly be fighting the weeds. Removal of the sod will take the topsoil with it, so the choice is a tough one.
2. Insert a vertical edging (plastic, aluminum, or steel) in the soil around the bed to prevent adjacent grass roots from creeping into the area.
3. Pave any pathways with bricks or crushed stone rather than maintain them as grass.
4. Examine each new plant you add to the garden to be sure no weeds are clinging to the clump. Most nurseries carefully keep weeds out, but it is best to look over newly purchased plants anyway, as well as gifts

from other gardeners. If you are in doubt about a plant's "cleanliness," carefully wash off the soil before setting it in the ground.

5. If they fit into your gardening philosophy, carefully use herbicides to prevent the sprouting of weed seeds that may subsequently blow in.
6. After planting, carefully spread a generous layer of mulch between the plants to prevent new weeds from getting a foothold.
7. Avoid the use of fresh farm manure, hay, and other organic products that may contain weed seeds. Use dried manure instead, or commercial dry or liquid fertilizers (either organic or chemical). These are weed-free, and if you use slow-release plant foods, or fertilizer spikes or pills, only one feeding per year should be necessary.

See chapter 8 for more on weeds and how to restrict their growth.

spades that require little leverage pressure are also available. Garden centers and catalogs often have these and other labor-saving devices.

If you or a family member find it difficult to bend over, or are confined to a wheelchair, plantings in large pots or boxes set on a railing around a deck or terrace will make gardening easier. Narrow raised planters made of brick, concrete, or stone, built to the height that is best for the gardener, are even better than pots for perennials. If the soil in these planters reaches to the ground, they supply increased space for the roots, and in cold climates they are less likely to freeze solid. For further information, contact the National Council for Therapy and Rehabilitation Through Horticulture, 9220 Whiteman Road, Suite 300, Gaithersburg, Maryland 20879.

A Child's Garden

For many years we led a 4-H club and gardening was one of the most popular group projects. The children always displayed their prize vegetables and flowers at the county fair or local field day with great pride. Although the competition undoubtedly stimulated the care they gave their plots, the sense of accomplishing something on their own, often for the first time, was a great confidence builder. For many of them, growing plants became a lifelong interest. As soon as a child is old enough to know you don't eat the daisies, and disciplined enough to pull weeds rather than flowers, it's a good time to give him or her a small space for a private plot. We have friends only 5 years old who love growing things, but of course not every child is ready at that age.

The young are even more impatient than we are and likely to lose enthusiasm if they can't see results quickly, so a combination garden of annuals, vegetables, and perennials may be best. Children tend to become discouraged if the enterprise seems to be more work than fun, so the plants they select should be sturdy and require a minimum of care. The plot should be small enough so that when other diversions appear, as they will, the weeds will not get out of hand. And even if they may not appeal to you, a few plastic or ceramic ornaments could help a child to enjoy his or her garden more.

To encourage a sense of accomplishment, let the garden belong to the child as much as possible, even though you may need to lend a helping hand from time to time. Involve him or her in the project from the start, including the selection of varieties, preparing and planting the bed, and maintenance. Let the child be in charge of harvesting the bouquets or food, too. A sign, "Eddie's Garden" or "Karen's Plot," may stimulate even more pride of ownership. We know of one couple who provided their son a hedged-in area, hidden from the rest of the yard, for his very own "secret" garden.

A child's garden should stimulate the imagination. A friend of ours, a distinguished adult gentleman, swears that as a child he once saw a small elf dressed entirely in green, dancing about in the family garden. His story is so convincing that we believe him. Children are more attuned to nature than adults, and more ready to accept magic and miracles. A garden can encourage closeness to the earth's myriad phenomena, and give a child adventures and experiences that would otherwise be missed.

Perennials that have legends attached to them are especially fun for children to grow. They also enjoy flowers connected with objects—the large bells of Canterbury and the tiny ones of *Heuchera* and lily-of-the-valley, the valentines of the bleeding-heart (*Dicentra*), the smiling faces of pansies, the growing habits of hen-and-chickens (*Sempervivum*), and the silver dollars of the money plant (*Lunaria*). Fast-growing plants can be compared to the one in Jack and the Beanstalk. Certain flowers can be connected to nursery rhymes:

Mary, Mary quite contrary
How does your garden grow?
With silver bells and cockle shells
And pretty maids all in a row.

Others relate to songs:

Lavender's blue, dilly-dilly, lavender's green.
When I am king, dilly-dilly, you shall be queen.

Spring bulbs are perennial favorites for children, as they wait with excitement for the dead-looking, egg-shaped balls they planted in the fall to push their green tips through the earth and become bright yellow daffodils or red tulips. They may enjoy growing catmint for their feline pets, too, or different kinds of mint for tea parties.

Children love to pick bouquets and are not likely to be impressed greatly by garden design, so forget about arrangement, and encourage them to grow perennials with bright colors and pleasing fragrances. A child will probably find a dandelion patch as beautiful as a clump of trollius. One of the greatest gifts you could give a child is love for the earth and its living things, but if gardening is made to seem a series of chores at an early age, his or her first garden is also likely to be the last. One man told us that in seeking a wife, he always asked each candidate if she liked to garden. If the answer was yes, she was immediately stricken from the list—he remembered his mother's stern discipline in the garden and wanted no more of it!

The perennials below are worth choosing for a child's first garden, because all are easy to grow and each has something about it that is especially intriguing to youngsters.

Achillea, yarrow 'Coronation Gold'
Althaea rosea, hollyhock
Asclepias tuberosa, butterfly weed
Campanula medium, Canterbury bells
Convallaria, lily-of-the-valley
Dicentra spectabilis, bleeding-heart
Heuchera, coral bells
Lunaria, money plant, honesty
Physalis alkekengi, Chinese lantern
Sempervivum, hen-and-chickens
Viola, pansy, violet

A good book on this subject is *Let's Grow! 72 Gardening Adventures With Children* by Linda Tilgner (Garden Way Publishing).

29

The Collector's Garden

Aunt Molly had enough salt and pepper shakers to fill all the shelves in her large dining room from floor to ceiling. We always enjoyed her shakers because each set obviously meant so much to her, either because of its beauty, uniqueness, or because it reminded her of some special person or place.

Just as she collected salt and pepper shakers, and some individuals amass coins, stamps, buttons, or rare books, others collect plants. Most specialize in only one or two species or genera, but they may grow many varieties of the plant group they have chosen. A collection might range from a few kinds of one wildflower species, such as native orchids, to many thousands of named varieties of iris, peonies, or lilies.

Most serious plant collectors belong to the national society that promotes the use, increased knowledge, and continued development of their plant (see the list of plant societies in the appendix). You'll find societies for most of the popular perennials, including cacti, carnations, daffodils, ferns, *Hemerocallis*, herbs, hosta, iris, lilies, peonies, *Primula*, rock garden plants, and wildflowers. Society members usually receive a magazine or newsletter several times a year, attend meetings with other enthusiasts, and tour public and private gardens where they can view old and new varieties. These get-togethers also allow them to swap information, seeds, and plants.

Many of the people who collect a specific plant did not begin growing it with that intent. Instead, they were attracted by its beauty or special characteristics; interest can grow along with the plants and develop into an engrossing hobby. If you decide to specialize, select a species that will do well in your location. We know a man who started a huge collection of chrysanthemums in our county, but gave up the second year when he realized that the short growing season and hard winters were too much for his favorite plant.

Luckily the variety of perennials is so large that wherever you live there will be a wide range from which to select, and if you live in a unique area, you'll have an opportunity to grow special kinds that are denied to gardeners in the rest of the country. In a desert location, cacti and other succulent plants might be a perfect choice; in a coastal area, the seashore plants; and in the cool North, alpine plants and ferns. A woodland location may be the spot for a collection of wild orchids or other native flower species, and a wetland provides an opportunity for unusual water plants.

Just as a tintype collection might be displayed in various ways, so can your perennials. Some specialists plant them in neat rows, scientifically arranged as if they were in a nursery. They can be easily cared for in this kind of grouping and are less likely to become mixed or mislabeled. Others prefer to blend their collection into the landscape by creating attractive garden beds or borders. Often the species is planted with other perennials, shrubs, and trees that not only complement it, but provide color when the primary collection is not in bloom.

However you grow the plants, a collection needs extra care in placement. The small differences in

A variety of *Hemerocallis* (daylily) cultivars.

many varieties appear indistinguishable to the casual observer. For this reason, similar varieties should be placed near each other so that subtle differences are easier to recognize. Otherwise, visitors may doubt your claim to have 120 different cultivars of Siberian iris, or be skeptical when you announce that the triploid bloom of a certain *Hemerocallis* is actually 4 millimeters larger than the diploid!

Labeling each plant carefully becomes extremely important when you have a collection—not only for displaying your varieties, but so you are sure of the name if you sell or swap plants, use them in breeding new hybrids, or exhibit them in shows. Small green or white plastic garden markers inscribed with permanent ink are easy to read without stooping, but aluminum labels, embossed with a ballpoint pen and wired to a metal stake, last much longer. Accurate records are necessary, too, when you are ordering new plants, or else you may buy something you already own. Especially in the case of a collection garden, keep your master plan in a safe place. We have had visiting two-year-olds pull up some of our stakes to use as swords.

One discouraging aspect of amassing a plant collection is the confusion over variety names. Sometimes the same variety may have several names; neither is it unusual to find that the same name is used for a number of quite different varieties. Over the years we have bought many wrongly labeled plants and know now that you cannot always assume, when ordering a certain plant, that you will get exactly what you ordered. Often you may not find out about the mistake for years. Most nurseries are honest, but sometimes in the spring rush, employees are careless and mistakes happen. Buy only from firms you have found trustworthy and report any known error to the company as soon as a flower blooms. If mistakes continue, report the erring firm to your plant society so that others can be alerted.

A plant collection is a rewarding hobby. We have several hundred varieties of *Hemerocallis* and eagerly await the first flower of each newly acquired hybrid. Like many other collectors, we enjoy cross-pollinating our best blooms to see what new surprises the seedlings will produce, always hoping to hit the jackpot and come up with a spectacular beauty.

Plant specialists may gain other rewards in addition to the fun of growing. Besides developing new varieties, they also add to the sum of scientific knowledge. One of our cousins, who collects wildflowers, discovered a native orchid which had not previously been identified and it now bears his name in botanical treatises. Such recognition is gratifying, but we're sure that the many beautiful slides he has taken, as well as the pleasure his avocation has brought him over the years, means much more to him.

30

The Selling Garden

I n our town, and in each of those that surround us, perennial gardeners offer plants for sale on a small scale. Each sells a different assortment of his or her own favorites. One grower divides clumps from his border with customers as they arrive. Another splits up all her plants in the spring and sets them in rows to encourage larger growth, then sells them the following year. Still another grower specializes in potted lilies and other perennials, which makes it easy for customers to serve themselves. A small nursery called "Perennial Pleasures" is known all over Vermont for its fine collection of old-fashioned plants and herbs.

None of these people intended to open a "nursery" when they started to grow perennials. But, like other gardeners, they found that as a result of frequent division, they were often faced with a large quantity of unwanted plants. They hated to throw them away, so decided to cash in on the surplus and operate a bona fide small nursery.

Selling plants is an interesting home business and provides a good opportunity to meet other gardeners. It is nice to know, too, that you are merchandising a product which is nonpolluting, beautifying, and making people happy. A nursery can be demanding, however, especially in the springtime when much of the work must be done. Many customers will probably not be gardening experts, so you will spend a lot of time giving suggestions and information. Working people will want to pick up plants during the early morning or evening hours, as well as on weekends

and holidays. No one will want to drive a long distance and find you unavailable. Unless you have extra help, be prepared to give up such things as regular meals and social events during the growing season.

Before opening, take care of all the legal requirements involved in operating such a business—you wouldn't want your first publicity to be an item in the court news. You will probably need a local zoning permit, and it will be necessary to register with your state department of agriculture and submit to an inspection by them. Sign up with your state's tax department, and get forms for collecting sales tax, and register your trade name with them and with your county or township. In addition, if you want to put up a sign by the roadside, you *may* be required to obtain a permit from the state.

Starting a perennial business does not require a big investment. You can grow thousands of plants on a half acre of land with very little machinery or other equipment. If you grow stock from seed, you'll need cold frames or other types of seed beds and you may even want a small greenhouse. Parking space is necessary for your customers and a shelter as protection on rainy days. Maintain a well-planted perennial border, not only for your own pleasure, but to show prospective buyers how their plants will look when fully grown and in bloom.

If you decide to sell a wider variety of plants than you can conveniently raise, you may be able to buy from wholesale growers. Check with your state's nursery association for a listing of suppliers. Wholesale horticultural supply houses can provide fertilizers, pots, labels, tools, and other products in the quantities necessary to run a nursery business. The appendix has a source list of gardening supplies.

Even if you sell a variety of plants, you may want to specialize in one species. Try to select a species such as iris or hosta, or a collection of plants such as herbs or rock garden plants, all of which have enough named cultivars available for you to offer a wide assortment. In this way you will build a reputation as an expert and people will seek you out for outstanding plants and information.

Some perennial nurseries grow all their plants in rows, dig them up with a ball of soil, and wrap them in wet newspapers for each customer on the spot. Selling "from the ground" takes far less watering time and saves the trouble of potting the plants. It does take longer to wait on customers, however, and a bit of your soil leaves with every order.

Potted plants are not only far easier for customers to handle, but also make quick self-service possible.

The plants are more likely to survive since the root-balls remain intact, and are less likely to dry out when they are taken home and planted. If you buy topsoil and grow plants in containers, however, be prepared to water them daily.

Merchandising is as important as growing. Mark each plant with its variety name and price to make it easy for buyers. If you sell on a large scale, provide a printed price list or catalog that includes a brief description of each plant and directions on how to grow it. Keep a pile in a convenient place, so people can pick up extras for friends and relatives.

Profits in a home perennial business can be good if you keep the overhead low, but the selling season is comparatively short so it would be difficult to make the proceeds amount to more than a modest supplementary income. Gardeners often confess that they are better growers than businesspeople. If you fall into this category, and it is important to you to make a profit, you may want to take some courses on managing a small business before you hang out your shingle.

Paeonia 'Philippe Rivoire.' Peony (double).

Lychnis coronaria. Rose campion.

Lilium. Lily.

Dianthus barbatus. Sweet William.

Heuchera sanguinea. Coral bells.

Dicentra spectabilis. Bleeding-heart.

Lupinus. Russell hybrid lupine.

Thalictrum aquilegifolium. Columbine meadowrue.

Stachys byzantina. Lamb's ears.

Ajuga reptans 'Variegata.' Carpet bugleweed.

Artemisia schmidtiana. Silvermound.

Sedum sieboldii. October Daphne.

Papaver orientale. Oriental poppy.

Hemerocallis 'Autumn Whisper.' Daylily.

Helenium autumnale. Common sneezeweed.

Helenium nudiflorum/H. flexuosum. Sneezeweed.

Gaillardia. Blanketflower.

Geum. Avens.

Rudbeckia. Coneflower.

Rudbeckia fulgida 'Goldsturm.' Coneflower.

Iberis. Candytuft.

Lilium auratum. Gold-banded lily.

Nymphaea. Water lily.

Cerastium tomentosum. Snow-in-summer.

Achillea millefolium 'Coronation Gold.' Milfoil.

Chrysanthemum 'Sun Quill.' Mum.

Coreopsis verticillata 'Zagreb.' Threadleaf coreopsis.

Nymphaea. Water lily.

Leonard P. Perry

Leonard P. Perry

Anthemis tinctoria. Golden marguerite.

Iris pseudacorus. Yellow flag.

Leonard P. Perry

Cindy McFarland

Euphorbia cyparissias. Cypress spurge.

Heliopsis. Heliopsis.

Hosta decorata. Blunt plantainlily.

Hostas in a shade garden.

A border of grasses.

Astilbe. Spirea.

Centaurea montana. Mountain bluet.

Iris sibirica. Siberian iris.

Salvia. Sage.

Iris xiphioides. English iris and white iris.

Platycodon grandiflorus var. *mariesii.* Balloon flower.

Echinops. Globe thistle.

Hosta flower.

Ajuga reptans 'Rosea.' Carpet bugleweed.

Achillea ptarmica 'The Pearl.' Sneezewort.

Phlox paniculata 'Mia Ruys.' Garden phlox.

Chrysanthemum maximum. Shasta daisy.

Gypsophila. Baby's-breath.

Paeonia. Peony.

Echinacea purpurea. Purple coneflower.

Thymus serpyllum. Mother-of-thyme.

Dictamnus. Gas plant.

Nymphaea. Water lily.

Primula. Primrose.

Primula denticulata. Himalayan primrose.

Phlox carolina. Thick-leaf phlox.

Rock garden.

Seven Pines perennial border.

The Levitan garden.

A shade bed.

Peonies.

A pink and lavender garden.

A yellow garden.

An early summer border.

PART III

DESCRIPTIONS OF THE BEST GARDEN PERENNIALS

Except as noted, plants are suitable for gardens in zones 3 through 7, and unless stated otherwise, heights given refer to *total mature* height. Bracketed information indicates blooming season. The symbol ◆ indicates that the plant which follows is a bulb plant, and ✳ means that the plant is shown in the color section starting on page 119.

Illustrations by Mallory Lake

ACANTHUS (a-kan'thus),
bear's breech

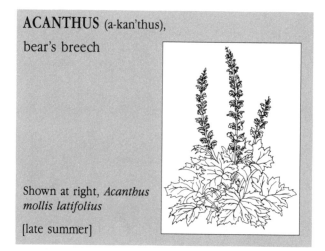

Shown at right, *Acanthus mollis latifolius*

[late summer]

Acanthus are valued for their shiny ornamental leaves as well as their large, showy flower spikes. Unfortunately, they are not reliably hardy where the ground freezes, so are best planted in **zones 8 to 10**. Where they grow well the plants last for years. They thrive in sun, although benefit from light shade on hot summer days. They need a deep, well-drained soil, and should be set at least 3 feet apart since the roots become large. *Acanthus* leaves were used as models in the design of the capitals of Corinthian columns in ancient Greece.

A. longifolius has excellent foliage, and 3- to 4-foot lilac-colored blooms. *A. mollis* (artist's acanthus) has purple or white spiky flowers, similar to those of lupines. *A. perringii* is the most dwarf with 12-inch spikes of rose-toned blooms.

PROPAGATION. *Acanthus* plants may be dug up and divided in early spring. Can be grown from seed, but the seedlings grow slowly and may take years to bloom.

ACHILLEA (a-kil-lee'a),
yarrow

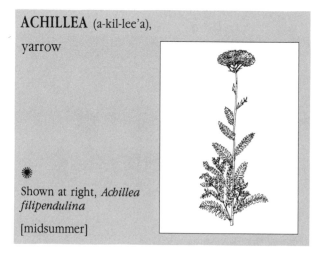

✳

Shown at right, *Achillea filipendulina*

[midsummer]

These easy-to-grow plants with fernlike fragrant foliage have their place in the border, and form nice spots of color, but most species need frequent division so the garden doesn't become filled with them. Species range in size from tiny creeping rock garden plants to 4-foot giants. They grow in nearly any well-drained soil, like a sunny location, and are useful in poor, dry soils.

The hybrid 'Coronation Gold,' (height: 3 feet) is one of the best, with large, golden flower heads which can be dried so successfully that the winter bouquets look nearly as fresh as the summer ones; blooms over a long period. *A. filipendulina* (fernleaf yarrow), 'Golden Plate,' is similar to 'Coronation Gold,' but taller (4 to 5 feet) with larger flowers. The cultivar *A. millefolium* (common yarrow), 'Fire King,' has rosy-pink flowers, and looks best in a wildflower or rock garden (height: 2 feet). *A. ptarmica* 'The Pearl' is called sneezewort because the roots were once dried and used as snuff; grows to a height of 2 feet and is one of the most popular varieties with small, double, pure white blooms that are excellent in arrangements and for drying, but without the lacy leaves. *A. taygetea* (height: 18 to 25 inches), has attractive silvery green foliage and yellow flowers throughout the summer; the cultivar 'Moonshine' is particularly recommended for cutting. *A. ageratifolia* which grows about 6 inches tall with gray-white leaves and white flowers, and *A. tomentosa* (wooly yarrow) are appropriate as rock garden plants.

DISEASES. Crown gall, mildew, rust.

PROPAGATION. *Achilleas* are easily propagated by division in either spring or fall. Common varieties may also be started from seed and root cuttings.

ACONITUM (a-ko-ny'tum),
monkshood

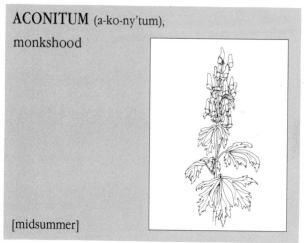

[midsummer]

Like delphinium, these magnificent tall plants (3 to 4 feet tall) add class to a sunny or lightly shaded border with their stately blue or purple flowers. They are not as brittle as delphinium, so need less staking. Once established, they thrive for years without need of division. They grow best in full sun or partial shade, and like moist soil. Useful in the semi-wild garden, a lightly shaded border, or as tall foundation plants between windows. Each individual floweret looks like a little hood, and people enjoy lifting it up to see the two monkeys on sticks. Although used medicinally in small amounts for both humans and animals, *Aconitum* is poisonous, so take care when very small or very curious children are around the plants.

A. napellus (garden or common monkshood) is the common tall-growing variety with dark blue flowers; *A. n.*

bicolor has excellent blue and white flowers. *A. ivorine* has white blooms, blossoms early, and has a height of about 3 feet. *A. autumnale* (autumn monkshood) blooms in September; *A. fischeri* (azure monkshood) grows 3 to 4 feet tall and has dark blue flowers. *A. orientale* grows quite tall, and blooms for most of the summer. *A. alba* has white blooms, is less vigorous than the others, and likely to be shorter lived.

DISEASES. Crown rot, mildew, mosaic, wilt.

PROPAGATION. Easily divided at any time of the year, but early spring or fall is best. Seeds take a long time to germinate and grow.

ACTAEA (ak-tee'a), baneberry

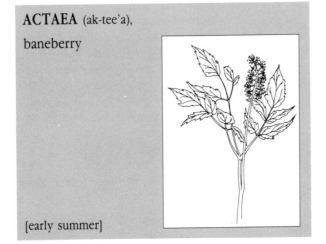

[early summer]

Baneberries, a native plant, are showy in bloom, and even more so when in fruit during late summer. They are especially good in a woods garden, because they like light shade and a soil rich in leaf mold. They also do well on the north side of a building, which gets little sun. Both berries and roots are poisonous when ingested.

A. alba (white baneberry) has white flowers in spring and white fruit with a purple eye later in the summer. *A. rubra* (red baneberry) is shorter with white flowers and red berries. *A. spicata* (black baneberry) is an imported variety with bluish white flowers and purple-black berries. All grow from 1 to 2 feet tall.

PROPAGATION. By seed or by division.

ADAM'S NEEDLE. See *Yucca*

AEGOPODIUM PODAGRARIA (ee-go-po'di-um), goutweed bishop's weed snow-on-the-mountain

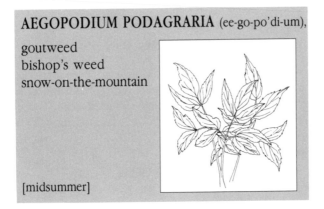

[midsummer]

Aegopodium podagraria (goutweed or bishop's weed) is a ground cover with shiny, dark green leaves that can be attractive in the right place, but it usually becomes a vicious weed and we don't like to recommend it. It does grow well in spots where grass may fail, and succeeds in shaded, worn-out soil. Be sure to keep it under control because it will creep into lawns, flower beds, and vegetable patches. *A. p. variegata* (snow-on-the-mountain), with green and white variegated leaves, is only slightly less vigorous.

DISEASES. Leaf blight may bother in hot weather.

PROPAGATION. Usually by division, but seeds may also be used.

AETHIONEMA (ee-thi-o-nee'ma), stonecress

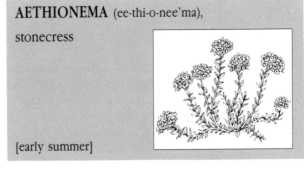

[early summer]

Stonecress are closely related to rockcress, and have attractive candytuft-type flowers in late spring.

Stonecress are ideal for the rock garden because they tolerate warm sunshine and dry soil. They prefer sandy, alkaline soil, and should be cut back after blooming.

A. grandiflorum (Persian stonecress) is the tallest, growing about 18 inches tall with grayish leaves. Lower-growing varieties include the creeping *A. coridifolium* (Lebanon stonecress), usually less than 3 inches tall, with bluish foliage and pink blooms; 'Warley Rose' is one especially fine offspring of this species.

PROPAGATION. By seeds, or by taking cuttings in midsummer.

AJUGA (aj'oo-ga), bugleweed

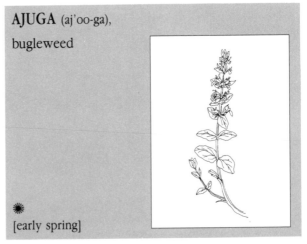

✳
[early spring]

Ajuga is excellent, low-growing ground cover with attractive foliage and blooms, but unless it is used carefully it can crowd out your other garden plants. Ideal for spots where it can be confined such as in rock gardens, the space between a wall and a path, beneath roadside trees, and other places where it's difficult to mow or where other plants do poorly.

A. reptans (carpet bugleweed) 'Rubra' has purple leaves and dark blue flowers; *A. r.* 'Alba' has white flowers; and the foliage of *A. r.* 'Burgundy Glow' changes color as it ages throughout the season, starting out as wine red, then becoming creamy white, then dark pink. *A. pyramidalis*, about 10 inches tall, has dark green leaves and does not spread like the other *Ajugas*, so it is better for a border planting.

DISEASES. Crown rot.

PROPAGATION. *Ajugas* are easily grown from seeds or divisions, and are not fussy about soils.

ALCHEMILLA (al-ke-mill'a), lady's mantle

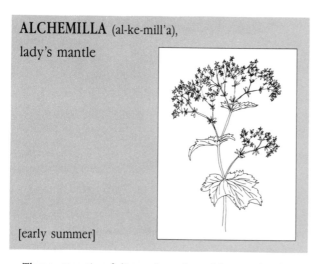

[early summer]

These attractive foliage plants have blooms that last a remarkably long time after cutting. A good ground cover, but they often self-seed and become weedy. They like sun or light shade and grow in nearly any soil that is not wet.

A. alpina (mountain lady's mantle) has gray leaves and yellow flowers. *A. vulgaris* (lady's mantle) grows to 1 foot, has yellow blooms, and rounded leaves, sometimes 6 inches in diameter that resemble those of a water lily.

PROPAGATION. By cuttings in summer, or by planting seeds in spring or fall.

ALLIUM (al'li-um), ornamental onion chives

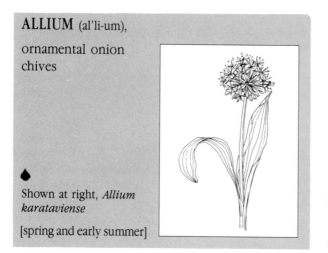

Shown at right, *Allium karataviense*

[spring and early summer]

These easy-to-grow flowering bulb plants are members of the same family as garlic, leeks, onions, and shallots. They need full sun and rich soil that is well drained.

A. schoenoprasum (chives) are usually grown as herbs, but with their attractive pink flowers look nice as an edging plant. Other ornamental alliums are *A. caeruleum*, blue globe onions, with blue flowers (height: 18 inches); *A. cyaneum*, blue flowers (height: 6 inches); *A. moly*, lily leek, yellow blooms (height: 12 inches); *A. neapolitanum*, Naples onion, white blooms (height: 15 inches); *A. ostrowskianum*, Ostrowsky onion, rose-purple flowers (height: 9 inches); *A. rosenbachianum*, Rosenbach onion, rosy-purple blooms that are good for drying (height: 30 inches). Among the largest are *A. roseum grandiflorum*, bigflower rosy onion, which has huge rose-purple flowers on 4-foot stalks; *A. tuberosum*, Chinese chives, with white fragrant blooms (height: 3 feet); and *A. zebdanense*, which has white blooms and reaches a height of 2 feet.

DISEASES. Rot.

PROPAGATION. Easy to start by dividing the clumps in early spring. Plant the bulbs of small-growing plants so the bottoms are about 2 inches below the surface, and the larger ones deeper. *Alliums* may be grown from seed, but many species take a long time to germinate.

ALTHAEA ROSEA (al-thee'a), hollyhock

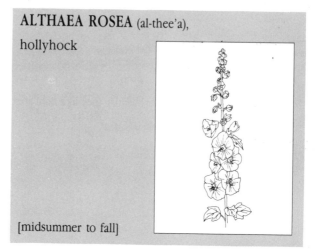

[midsummer to fall]

These tall-growing (4 to 5 feet or more) flowers are prized because they are so stately and bloom over a long period. They are biennials in warm climates and short-lived perennials in the cooler zones. Hollyhocks need full sun, a deep rich soil, and are ideal against a building, fence, or hedge, since they need protection from wind. Otherwise they must be staked. They have been favorites in cottage gardens for generations, and were one of the few flowers grown around American farmhouses a century ago.

The old-fashioned single varieties are slightly more hardy, and often taller growing than the double hybrids, but the latter are more showy and their ruffled, roselike blooms come in a wide range of colors. 'Chater's' is one of the most popular varieties.

DISEASES. Crown rot, leaf spot, mildew, rust, wilt.

INSECTS. Aphids, borers, Japanese beetles, nematodes, slugs.

PROPAGATION. Easy to grow from seed, they often self-sow, assuring a continuous supply of plants.

ALYSSUM SAXATILE (al-is'sum),

goldentuft
basket-of-gold.
Also known as
AURINIA SAXATILIS
(aw-ri'nee-a)

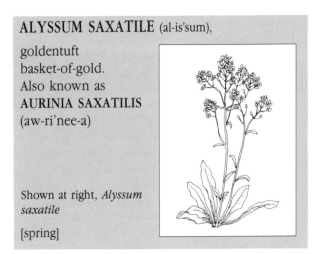

Shown at right, *Alyssum saxatile*

[spring]

For the rock garden, border, and for edging flower beds, shrub borders, or paths, the perennial alyssum has long been popular. It likes ordinary, good garden soil and full sun. Most grow up to 15 inches tall with golden yellow flowers. *A. saxatile* 'Compacta,' dwarf goldentuft, however, does not reach that height, and *A. s.* 'Flora Plenum' has bright yellow double flowers.

DISEASES. Club root, leaf rot, wilt.

INSECTS. Flea beetle.

PROPAGATION. Since alyssums spread freely, they are easy to divide. They also root well from cuttings in early summer, and except for the double varieties, start easily from seed. Sow the seed in August and let it winter over in a protected place, for best results.

AMSONIA (am-soh'ni-a),

bluestar
amsonia

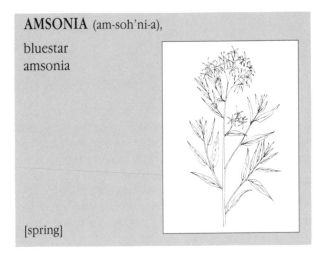

[spring]

The light blue flowers that appear in spring or early summer are a lovely addition to either a sunny border or a wild semishaded garden and it is an easy plant to grow.

A. tabernaemontana (willow amsonia) is hardiest (zone 3), growing from 3 to 4 feet tall with willowlike leaves that turn yellow in the fall. *A. ciliata* (bluestar, zone 6 or

warmer) has darker flowers and attains a height of 2 feet. Both kinds like full sun, but the soil shouldn't be allowed to dry out.

DISEASES. Leaf spot, rust.

PROPAGATION. Start new plants from seed or by dividing large clumps in early spring.

ANAPHALIS (a-naff'a-lis),

pearly everlasting

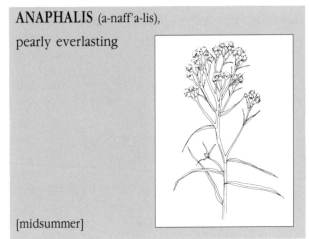

[midsummer]

The hardy everlastings with their gray foliage are valued both as garden flowers and for drying. They grow well in poor, dry soil and like full sun, but *will* grow in partial shade—usually so well they become weedy.

A. margaritacea (common pearly everlasting), a native wildflower, reaches a height of about 2 feet. *A. triplinervis* (pearly everlasting) is more often cultivated. All are useful in sunny rock gardens and wildflower plantings because of their clusters of white flowers. When picked just before the flowers reach their peak, they can be dried naturally for winter blooms, or dyed various colors before drying.

PROPAGATION. By seeds or by division.

ANCHUSA (an-koo'sa),

Italian bugloss

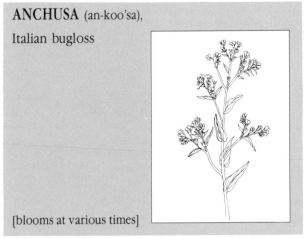

[blooms at various times]

The rich blue color of the forget-me-not-type flowers of *A. azurea* (also known as *A. italica*), Italian bugloss, are greatly prized in the perennial garden, although they tend to be short-lived. They like a deep, well-drained, fairly light soil, and full sun. Grows tall, up to 6 feet in height, so it needs staking. Blooms in June and July. 'Dropmore' is an especially good variety. *A. capensis*, cape bugloss, is a biennial that blooms all summer and is especially good for shady rock gardens.

DISEASES. Mosaic, rust.

INSECTS. Leafhoppers.

PROPAGATION. The plants often self-sow, so propagation by seed is easy. Divide the plants or take root cuttings in early spring.

ANDROSACE (an-dros'a-see), rock jasmine

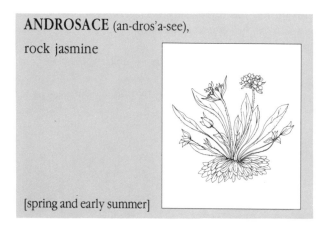

[spring and early summer]

These attractive alpine plants do well in North America in spots where they enjoy dry weather and cold winters. All grow in poor, sandy soil with a little lime, and do especially well in a sunny rock garden.

A. helvetica, from the Swiss Alps, is only an inch tall. *A. lanuginosa*, a trailing plant with silver-gray foliage and pink-lilac blooms, often provides two blooming periods in the same year. *A. sarmentosa*, from the Himalayas, is regarded as best of all: it is more moundlike and has rosette-like leaves with attractive rosy pink flowers. Other varieties come from Spain, Siberia, and the southern Tyrol.

PROPAGATION. By separating the rosettes and planting them.

ANEMONE (a-nem'o-nee), anemone windflower

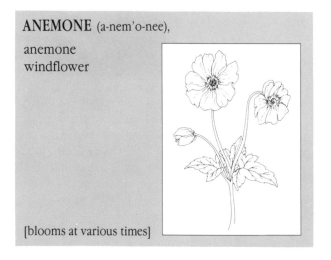

[blooms at various times]

Many of the anemones, including the native wood anemones, are ideal for shady wildflower gardens and rockeries because they look best in natural settings. Blooming in pink, white, and purple, they like loamy soil rich in leaf mold or compost, and a protective mulch during the winter. Most thrive in light shade, except the Japanese varieties which prefer full sun. Some kinds bloom early in the spring, but *A.* x *hybrida* and *A. japonica* both sold as Japanese anemone, (2 to 3 feet in height)—the best and largest flowering variety—and *A. vitifolia* 'Robustissima' (grape-leaved anemone) bloom in the fall and keep blossoming even after light frosts. *A. magellanica*, a native of southern South America, is exceptionally hardy; it grows 12 inches tall and has white flowers. *A. pulsatilla* (pasque flower, 10 inches tall) has fine cut leaves and bluish purple blooms in the spring.

DISEASES. Leaf spot, collar rot.

INSECTS. Blister beetle.

PROPAGATION. The best method is to divide the roots in early spring, although they can be started by root cuttings and seed.

ANTHEMIS (an'them-is), golden marguerite

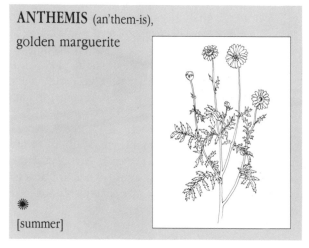

[summer]

These golden bright flowering beauties grow from 1 to 3 feet tall, have aromatic fern-type foliage, and bear an abundance of medium-sized daisies that range from bright yellow to creamy white in color. They grow well in ordinary soil, enjoy full sun, but often spread so rapidly both by seed and underground stems that they require frequent division to keep them in control.

It's a big job, but try to keep the flowers picked so they won't go to seed and start new plants. Seedlings usually are not as attractive as the named varieties and are even more weedy.

A. tinctoria is golden marguerite. *A. tinctoria* 'Moonlight' is one of the best and blooms over a long season. *A. t.* 'Kelwayi' has exceptionally large lemon-colored flowers and grows up to 3 feet tall. *A. montana*, white anthemis, has creamy white flowers.

DISEASE and INSECT troubles are rare.

PROPAGATION. Named varieties by division, others by seed or division.

AQUILEGIA (a-kwee-lee'je-a), columbine

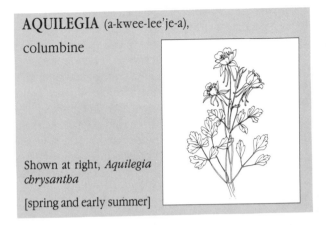

Shown at right, *Aquilegia chrysantha*

[spring and early summer]

These flowers are treasures for the garden, whether you choose the wild varieties, found frequently in rocky pastures and along roadsides, or the new brilliantly colored, large-flowering hybrids. They dance gaily in a light breeze, grow in compact clumps in any good garden soil, like sun or light shade, and most get to be about 20 to 30 inches tall. The natives fit well into a wildflower or rock garden.

A. canadensis (native eastern columbine) has red and yellow flowers with short spurs. *A. caerulea*, Rocky Mountain columbine, is a tall plant (up to 4 feet) with white petals and long blue spurs. *A. chrysantha* (golden columbine) has yellow flowers with long spurs and blooms late. *A. vulgaris* (European columbine) has either blue, purple, white, or pink flowers; *A. flabellata* (fan columbine) is more dwarf, about 18 inches, and has excellent foliage.

Native columbines have been used for developing numerous large-flowering, colorful hybrids, many of which have been named. Some have flowers as large as daffodils, and long showy spurs. All make excellent border plants and cut flowers, but unlike their wild ancestors, need to be replaced every three or four years.

DISEASES. Crown rot, leaf spot, mosaic, root rot, rust.

INSECTS. Borer, leaf miner.

PROPAGATION. Native *Aquilegia* may be propagated by division, but hybrid plants are short-lived, so are mostly grown from seed. It is best to buy seed, rather than save your own, because the flowers will usually be better. Patience is necessary since some varieties germinate irregularly rather than all at once, and the seedlings require at least a year's growth before blooming.

ARABIS (ar'a-bis), rockcress

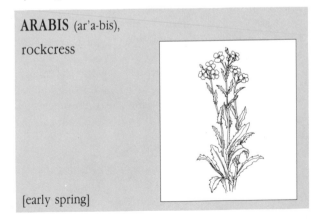

[early spring]

As the name suggests, this plant is excellent for the rock garden, where its pure white flowers completely cover the foliage in early spring. The flowers reach well above the 6-inch gray foliage and the plants form a dense mass. *Arabis* likes full sun and good, loose garden soil. It should be cut back after blooming.

A. albida (also known as *A. caucasica*), wallcress, especially the variety 'Flore Pleno' with double white blooms, is the most common variety. *A. alpina* has smaller flowers, but blooms more heavily; *A. aubretioides* has pink flowers and needs winter protection in the North; *A. billardieri* has rose-colored blooms and gray leaves; *A. blepharophylla* has rosy purple fragrant flowers; and *A. procurrens* has white flowers and is an excellent grower and bloomer.

DISEASES. Club root, leaf spot, mildew.

INSECTS. Aphids.

PROPAGATION. By seeds, division, or cuttings.

ARENARIA (a-re-nay'ri-a), sandwort

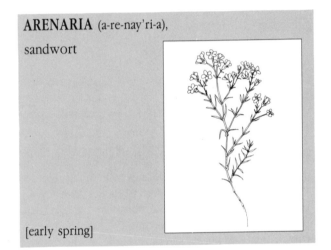

[early spring]

Though not a common plant, the white-blooming sandwort is worthy of a place in any rock garden. It grows easily, likes light soil, and grows to a height of 3 or 4 inches. The sandworts prefer sun, but will tolerate light shade; most kinds need a bit of winter protection in cold climates.

A. balearica, Corsican sandwort, is often used for planting along stone steps because of its tight, compact growth. *A. grandiflora* has more spreading shoots, but fewer blooms. *A. montana*, mountain sandwort, blooms heavily with a great profusion of white flowers in May, and is one of the most widely planted. *A. verna*, moss sandwort, from the Arctic, has small starlike flowers. Although moss sandwort is northern in origin, it should be protected to prevent winter windburn where it isn't covered with snow and because of its vigor should be planted where it won't crowd out weaker plants.

DISEASES. Leaf spot, mildew, rust.

PROPAGATION. Sandworts spread quickly, and may be propagated by seeds, spring division, or by cuttings taken in late summer.

ARMERIA (ar-meer'i-a),

thrift
sea pink

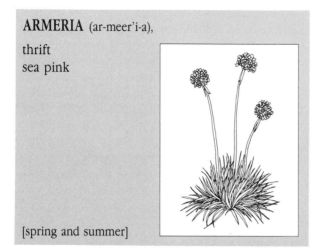

[spring and summer]

These dwarf perennials with grasslike clumps of foliage are mostly evergreen except in severe climates. They like a sunny spot, sandy soil, and are good choices for the seaside or rock garden.

A. *maritima* (common thrift, grows to 1 foot or less) is the most popular, and varieties have been developed with white, red, and pink blooms. A. *m. laucheana*, with crimson flowers, is considered one of the best. A. *pseudarmeria* (plantain thrift) includes taller varieties and has red-toned flowers. A. *gigantea* grows to 2 feet, bears rose-colored blooms, and is good from zone 5 south; 'Ruby' is an outstanding cultivar.

No serious DISEASES or INSECTS.

PROPAGATION. The best varieties of thrift are propagated by dividing the clumps; this should be done every 3 years. Seed planted in the fall and protected over the winter in a cold frame also give good results.

ARTEMISIA (ar-te-miz'i-a),

wormwood
silvermound
Dusty Miller

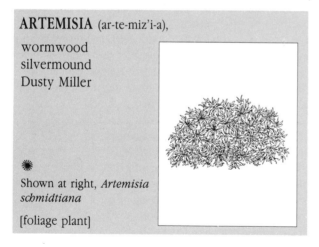

❋

Shown at right, *Artemisia schmidtiana*

[foliage plant]

Most of these plants have inconspicuous flowers and are grown instead for their unique foliage, which is silvery white, silky textured, and sometimes fragrant. They like full sun, ordinary good garden soil, and an occasional cutting back to keep them looking good.

A. *abrotanum*, southernwood, grows about 4 feet tall, is shrubby in growth, and a nice background plant. A. *absinthium*, wormwood, an old-time medicinal herb, is often planted to repel wild animals from gardens and poultry yards. A. *lactiflora* (white mugwort, grows to 4 feet) is the one variety that is grown for its feathery white flowers, but few nurseries carry it. A. *ludoviciana albula*, 'Silver King,' (3 feet tall) is superb for bouquets and drying. A. *schmidtiana* (silvermound) is one of the most popular border varieties, which grows into a strikingly beautiful compact silver mound. A. *stellerana* (beach wormwood, Dusty Miller), 1 foot tall, is a creeping variety used widely in seashore plantings. A. *tridentata* (sagebrush) and A. *vulgaris* (mugwort) are both useful where growing conditions are difficult, but they tend to be weedy, and like the wormwoods, must be kept under control.

DISEASES. Rust.

PROPAGATION. Artemisias are easily divided, and may also be propagated from cuttings and seeds.

ARTICHOKE. See *Helianthus tuberosa*

ARUNCUS (a-run'kus),

goat's beard

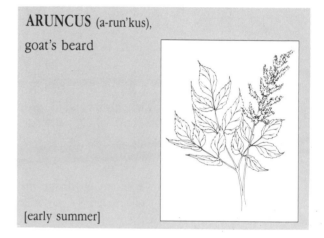

[early summer]

These tall-growing (up to 7 feet) perennials with snow white blossoms make good single specimens or background plants in the border, but are also useful in wild or semi-wild gardens. They will grow in ordinary garden soil and full sun, but do best in moist places that are lightly shaded. The blooming period is rather short. A. *sylvester*, sylvan goat's beard, is the common tall-growing kind; A. *s.* 'Kneiffi,' an improved variety with finer leaves, grows to only 2 or 3 feet.

PROPAGATION. Clumps are easily divided to start new plants, or they may be grown from seeds. The plant is dioecious, with the male and female blossoms on separate plants, so don't be surprised when you don't find seeds on the male ones.

ASARUM (ass'a-rum),

wild ginger

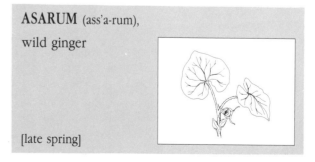

[late spring]

Large-leaved, low-growing (6 inches), attractive, aromatic plants. Both the native *A. canadense* (Canadian wild ginger) and the European *A. europaeum* (European wild ginger) are worthwhile plants for the wild garden. The latter is better, but grows only where winters are not too severe. Both thrive in light shade, a loamy, well-drained soil rich in leaf mold, and prefer plenty of moisture.

DISEASES. Leaf spot, rust.

PROPAGATION. Plants may be divided in early spring.

ASCLEPIAS (as-klee'pee-as),

butterfly weed
milkweed

[midsummer to early fall]

Members of the Milkweed family grow wild in many areas. *Asclepias* start to grow late in the spring, and should be marked so the underground sprouts won't be damaged by early cultivation. They have long roots and are difficult to divide or transplant.

A. tuberosa, butterfly weed, the variety usually grown, has bright orange flowers on 24-inch stems. True to its name, it attracts butterflies and if it weren't so easy to grow, it would probably be much more appreciated. It likes full sun and isn't particular about soils. Although most grow well only in dry soils, *A. incarnata* (swamp milkweed) is good for planting in wet places. It has pink flowers and narrow leaves. *A. curassavica* (bloodflower, 3 feet tall) has red-orange flowers and is widely planted in the South.

DISEASES. Leaf spot, mosaic, rust.

INSECTS. Aphids, caterpillars, scales.

PROPAGATION. *Asclepias* is usually propagated from seeds. Since they are difficult to transplant, plant the seed in pots and let them become well established before transplanting them outside. Division is also possible.

ASPERULA (as-per'oo-la),

woodruff

[spring]

Woodruff makes a good ground cover; it grows best in moist, acid soils in light shade. May need winter protection in the North. Be sure it is confined, because if you are permissive it may turn into a bad weed in your border.

In the Latin nomenclature, sweet woodruff is known by the names *Asperula odorata* and *Galium odoratum*. A small, fragrant herb with white flowers and graceful dark green whorled foliage, it grows to 1 foot. The fresh leaves are traditionally used to flavor May wine, and the dried leaves laid among clothes for their pleasant scent and to repel insects. *A. hexaphylla* is similar, but grows to about 2 feet or more.

PROPAGATION. By division. Seeds, although much slower, may also be used.

ASTER (as'ter),

Michaelmas daisy
aster

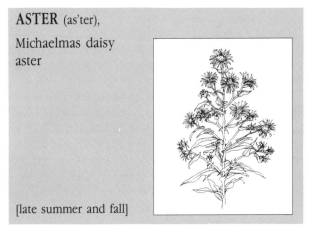

[late summer and fall]

Because asters bloom at the end of summer when flowers are few, they would be appreciated even if they weren't particularly beautiful. The hundreds of varieties range in height from a few inches to nearly 6 feet. The range of color includes not only the common lavender and purple, but also pink, red, white, rose, and deep blue. All grow well in full sun and ordinary garden soil, although many bloom too late for the short growing season of the far northern states. Asters need little special care beyond regular dividing, but pinching back several times in early summer will help develop more compact, bushy plants.

Although in England all asters are called Michaelmas daisies, in the States the term is commonly applied only to such old standbys as *A. novae-angliae*, the tall-growing New England aster, which is prolific along the roadsides in early fall, and *A. novi-belgii*, New York aster, with its wide range of colors. Both are worth planting in natural gardens and borders; the new hybrids of both species with their brilliant colors and larger blooms are ideal for any perennial border. 'Barr's Blue,' 'Harrington's Pink,' 'Red Star,' and 'September Ruby' are a few of the *A. n.-a.* named varieties; 'Boningale White,' 'Coombe Violet,' 'Crimson Violet,' and the white 'Mt. Everest' are among the New York hybrids. There are so many new cultivars that listing them all would be nearly impossible. Buy only those that you are sure will do well in your climate.

The native *A. puniceus* (purple-stemmed aster) does well in damp places; *A. patens* (late purple aster) thrives in poor soils and blooms earlier than most.

DISEASES. Leaf spot, mildew, rust.
INSECTS. Japanese beetles, lace bugs.
PROPAGATION. Divide the clump in early spring.

ASTILBE (as-til'be), spirea

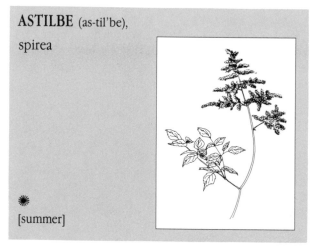

[summer]

The *Astilbes* are a group of feathery-plumed flowers. They range in height from a few inches to several feet, and come in many shades of pink, red, and cream, as well as white. *Astilbes* grow well in full sun or light shade, in ordinary garden soil. One gardener friend of ours found that the flowers will look better and last longer in partial shade. Most varieties behave nicely in the border, although a few of the older types are known to spread quickly and outgrow their spot. They are heavy feeders, so additional fertilizer is necessary if the plants are to thrive. All varieties should be dug up and divided every two to four years.

The hybrids of *A. arendsii* (false spirea) are the most popular and come in many varieties. Among them are 'Avalanche,' white with 30-inch stems; 'Fanal,' bright carmine red, 2 feet tall; 'Peach Blossoms,' light pink, 26 inches high; 'Red Sentinel,' bright red, 30 inches; and 'Rheinland,' bright pink, also 30 inches high. By choosing varieties that bloom at different times, you can have blossoms for most of the summer.

DISEASES. Mildew, wilt.
INSECTS. Aphids, Japanese beetles, mites.
PROPAGATION. By division in early spring. New varieties are originated by planting seeds.

AUBRIETA DELTOIDEA (oh-bree'ta), purple rockcress

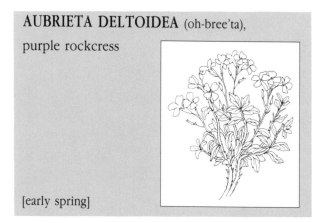

[early spring]

Although they are called purple, the *Aubrietas* have been hybridized into a wide range of colors including pink, crimson, lavender, and red-purple.

These rock garden plants, 3 to 6 inches high, are not widely grown, possibly because they are not reliably hardy except from zone 6 south, and are difficult to transplant except in fall or early spring. They grow best in light, well-drained soils, in full sun, and should be cut back heavily directly after blooming.

PROPAGATION. By dividing the plants in late fall or by planting seed. Cuttings taken in late summer root well in a greenhouse.

AUTUMN AMARYLLIS. See *Lycoris*

AUTUMN CROCUS. See *Colchicum*

AVENS. See *Geum*

BABY'S-BREATH. See *Gypsophila*

BALLOON FLOWER. See *Platycodon*

BANEBERRY. See *Actaea*

BAPTISIA (bap-tis'i-a), false indigo

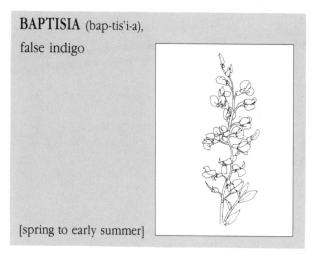

[spring to early summer]

Baptisias deserve a spot in the border, especially the color garden. These unusual pea-shaped flowers grow on spikes, do best in full sun, and grow well in dry soil.

B. australis (blue false indigo, 3 to 5 feet tall), hardiest of the *Baptisias*, has blue flowers and prominent seedpods. It makes a nice hedge, but dies back immediately after even a mild frost. *B. tinctoria* (yellow false indigo, 3 to 4 feet) is less hardy, has yellow blooms, and like *B. australis*, is a good plant for either the border or a wildflower bed.

DISEASES. Leaf spot, mildew, rust.
PROPAGATION. By dividing the plants or by planting seeds in spring or fall.

BASKET-OF-GOLD. See *Alyssum*

BEARDTONGUE. See *Penstemon*

BEAR'S BREECH. See *Acanthus*

BEE BALM. See *Monarda*

BELAMCANDA (bel-am-kan'da), blackberry lily

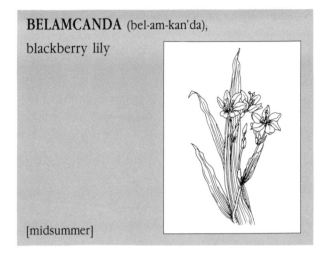

[midsummer]

B. chinensis, blackberry lily or leopard flower, has small red-spotted, orange lilylike blooms on 24- to 30-inch stems. The pods may be dried for use in bouquets. Plants need full sun, do best in good soil, and require some winter protection in the North.

DISEASES. Leaf spot.

INSECTS. Borers.

PROPAGATION. By dividing the fleshy tubers in the spring, or by planting seed at that time. They also self-seed prolifically.

BELLFLOWER. See *Campanula*

BELLIS (bel'lis), English daisy

[spring and summer]

B. perennis, the English daisy, has been praised for centuries in song and poetry, and it is a welcome addition to North American as well as English gardens. Its low height (6 inches) makes it ideal for the rock garden or for edging paths and the perennial border. They like full sun, but will tolerate light shade, and prefer a cool location in good garden soil. In zones 3 to 5 they may need some winter protection. The flowers, both single and double, begin in early spring in reds, pinks, and whites, with some of the better cultivars being 'Dresden China,' 'Giant Rose,' 'Longfellow,' and 'Snowball.'

The name suggests they are perennials, but they are usually grown as biennials and seed is sown each year. They are also often started under glass in late winter like bedding plants, and grown as annuals.

DISEASES. Blight, leaf spot, rot.

INSECTS. Nematodes.

PROPAGATION. *Bellis* grow easily from division, or from seeds that are generally planted during summer in a sheltered place to bloom the following summer. In some places they self-sow enough to become weedy.

BERGAMOT. See *Monarda*

BERGENIA (ber-jeen'ee-uh), bergenia

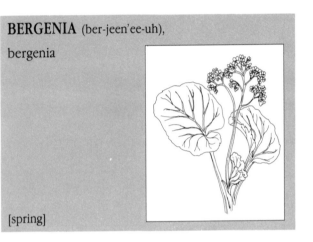

[spring]

These fleshy-leafed natives of Asia are grown at the front of perennial borders not only for their ornamental leaves, which can grow to 1 foot in width, but also for the showy pink, white, or purple-pink flower clusters that appear in early spring. They will grow in most soils, but prefer a sandy soil with some lime, afternoon shade, and winter protection in zones 3 to 6. Most grow from 12 to 18 inches tall. In cool climates, the leaves turn bronze in fall. The *Bergenias* were formerly classed in the *Saxifraga* genera.

B. cordifolia, heartleaf bergenia, is from Siberia and the one most often found in catalogs, but *B. crassifolia*, leather bergenia, is more popular on the West Coast. *B. stracheyi*, an Indian native, is less hardy, shorter (about 12 inches in height) and has less crinkly leaves.

DISEASES. Leaf spot.

INSECTS. Slugs.

PROPAGATION. By seed, or by dividing the plants in early spring or fall.

BETONY. See *Stachys*

BISHOP'S HAT. See *Epimedium*

BISHOP'S WEED. See *Aegopodium*

BLACKBERRY LILY. See *Belamcanda*

BLANKETFLOWER. See *Gaillardia*

BLEEDING-HEART. See *Dicentra*

BLUESTAR. See *Amsonia*

BOLTONIA (bol-toh'nee-a), boltonia

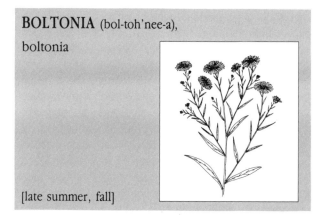

[late summer, fall]

BUGBANE. See *Cimicifuga*

BUGLEWEED. See *Ajuga*

BUGLOSS, ITALIAN. See *Anchusa*

BUGLOSS, SIBERIAN. See *Brunnera*

BUNGE. See *Ceratostigma*

BUTTERCUP. See *Ranunculus*

BUTTERFLY WEED. See *Asclepias*

CACTUS, HARDY. See *Opuntia*

These tall-growing, asterlike plants bloom late in the season, and produce an abundance of daisy-shaped, 1-inch pink, white, or lavender flowers, making them a valuable background plant for the border. The grow well in full sun and are not fussy about soils. The canes must be thinned out in early summer, so the remaining ones will be sturdier. Even so, staking is advisable. Regular division is necessary to keep the clumps from getting too large.

B. asteroides, white boltonia, can grow up to 8 feet and has white flowers. 'Snowbank,' a shorter cultivar (4 feet), is the most popular variety. Other shorter-growing varieties include *B. latisquama*, violet boltonia, which has lavender blooms, and *B. latisquama* 'Nana' (2½ feet high) that bears large pink flowers.

DISEASES. Leaf spot, mildew, rust.

PROPAGATION. By seed, but dividing the plants in the spring is easier and faster.

BONESET. See *Eupatorium*

BOUNCING BET. See *Saponaria*

BRUNNERA MACROPHYLLA (brun'er-a), Siberian bugloss

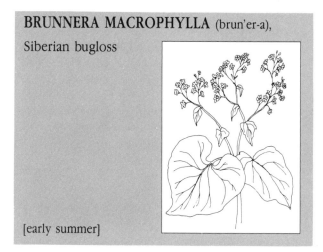

[early summer]

Also sold as *Anchusa myosotidiflora*, this perennial is a native of Siberia, grows about 18 inches tall, and does well in semishade. It is a member of the Borage family and has clusters of small, intense blue flowers that resemble forget-me-nots.

PROPAGATION. By seed, division, or root cuttings.

CALLIRHOË (kal-lir-o'ee), poppy mallow

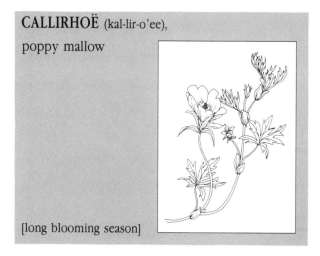

[long blooming season]

These low-growing plants (6 to 8 inches in height) with 2-inch, poppy-shaped blossoms, are good for small borders, rock gardens, on top of banks, and other sunny places as long as the soil is well drained. Their stems are trailing, and their deep carrotlike roots, which can withstand drought conditions, make them especially useful for **seashore plantings**. Abundant—as well as summer-long—purple, red, pink, and white blossoms are especially valued. They grow rapidly, but are sometimes short-lived, and in some locations are biennial. Mature plants are difficult to transplant.

PROPAGATION. Plant the seeds to propagate, or take 4-inch stem cuttings in early summer.

CALTHA (kal'tha), marsh marigold cowslip

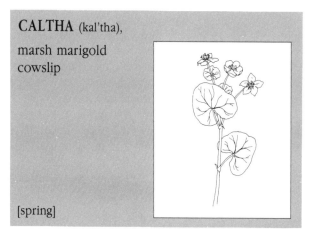

[spring]

The bright yellow wildflowers, *C. palustris*, are well known to those who explore bogs and wet places. Their attractive, bright green, heart-shaped leaves are often eaten as "boiled greens." *Calthas* are ideal for a wet natural garden, but they may also be worth a try in normal soil if it isn't too dry. They grow about a foot tall and need little care.

PROPAGATION. By dividing the plants in early spring.

CAMPANULA (kam-pan'you-la),

bellflower
Canterbury bells

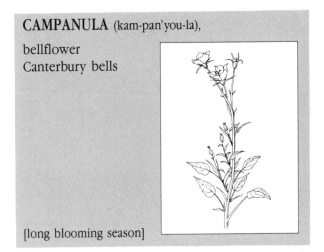

[long blooming season]

An entire book could be written on the many species of this large group of perennial and biennial plants. The bell-shaped flowers come in a wide variety of colors, and grow anywhere from a few inches to several feet high. Most are extremely attractive in a border or rockery, but some, such as *C. persicifolia* (peach bells), are better for wild gardens or country roadside plantings because they can get weedy and overrun a cultivated garden. These plants are so durable they can be completely neglected and still live for centuries.

Campanulas like full sun, but can grow in light shade. If given plenty of room to grow, and good garden soil, they will show their appreciation by blooming heavily. The taller varieties should be staked. A winter mulch of evergreen boughs over the plants will help keep the crowns from being crushed by the snow, which can make them susceptible to early spring rot.

There are a number of low-growing species. *C. caespitosa* (6 inches tall) is ideal for the rock garden and has blue flowers. *C. carpatica* (Carpathian harebell) is another useful rockery or border plant with a height of 8 inches and blue or white blooms all summer. *C. cochleariifolia* is a dwarf variety from Europe; it is long blooming with blue or lavender flowers. *C. garganica* grows to 6 inches, has bright blue star-shaped blooms, and likes light shade. *C. persicifolia* (peach bells) grows from 2 to 3 feet tall, has blue, pink, or lavender flowers, and is best in the wild border.

Taller varieties include common *C. glomerata* (clustered bellflower), 30 inches in height, with white, purple, or blue

flowers and large leaves; blooms in early summer. *C. lactiflora* (milky bellflower) has bright blue flowers, grows to 36 inches, thrives in either sun or partial shade. *C. poscharskyana* (Serbian bellflower), a 10-inch tall variety, grows into a compact plant, blooms all summer, and is often planted in hanging baskets. *C. rotundifolia* (bluebell or harebell) have blue or purple flowers, and a full height of 12 inches. Brought to this country by English and Scottish settlers, it has now become naturalized in some places.

C. medium (Canterbury bells) the most spectacular and well known of campanulas, are the garden bellflowers often featured in children's books and animated cartoons. They are biennial, in white, pink, blue, and purple, and grow in a pyramid shape to a height of about 2 feet. *C. medium calycanthema* (cup-and-saucer) also biennial, is closely related. Both bloom in early summer.

DISEASES. Crown rot, leaf spot, root rot, rust.

INSECTS. Aphids, slugs, thrips.

PROPAGATION. Perennial campanulas may be divided in early spring, or started from seed. To assure a continuous supply of the biennial varieties, seed must be planted every year.

CANDYTUFT. See *Iberis*

CANTERBURY BELLS. See *Campanula*

CANYON POPPY. See *Romneya*

CARDINAL FLOWER. See *Lobelia*

CARNATION, BORDER. See *Dianthus*

CASSIA (kash'a),

senna

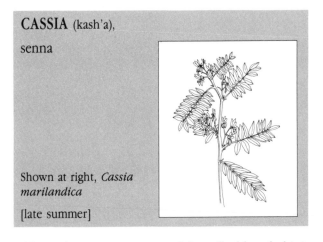

Shown at right, *Cassia marilandica*

[late summer]

These plants may grow up to 8 feet tall, although this is more the exception than the rule. Still, they are not the best choice for a doorway garden, but are ideal for the back of a border. The attractive leaves are fernlike, and the clusters of yellow pea-shaped flowers bloom in late summer.

C. marilandica, about 3 feet tall, the perennial *Cassia* known as wild senna, is related to a group of tropical plants and shrubs, but it is hardy even as far north as zone 4, and fast-growing enough to be used as a herbaceous hedge. It prefers sun, and grows well in moist soil. It is best not to disturb it for many years.

DISEASES. Dieback, rot.

INSECTS. Lace bugs, nematodes, scale.

PROPAGATION. By seed that should be sown as soon as it is ripe. Large clumps may be divided in the spring with a saw or hatchet.

CATANANCHE (cat-a-nan'chee),

cupid's dart

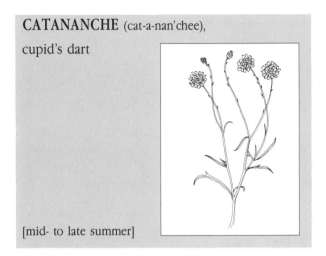

[mid- to late summer]

For all but the coldest sections of the country this rich blue, daisylike flower, 2 feet tall, is a good addition to the garden. It blooms from mid- to late summer, likes sun and sandy garden soil. *C. caerulea* (blue cupid's dart) is most commonly planted; *C. c.* 'Alba' is a white cultivar. Both should be massed to make an effective display, and both make good dried flowers.

PROPAGATION. Start seeds indoors in late winter for blooms the same year, or propagate by division or root cuttings.

CATCHFLY. See *Lychnis*

CATMINT. See *Nepeta*

CENTAUREA (sen-tor'ree-a),

knapweed
mountain bluet
perennial bachelor's
   button

✳

Shown at right, *Centaurea montana*

[early to midsummer]

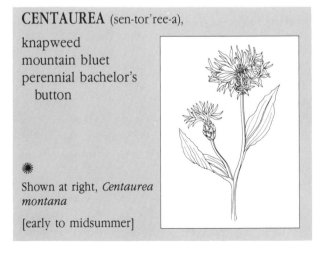

Of the hundreds of different *Centaureas* only a few are regularly planted in perennial borders. Most varieties came from Europe or Asia, but some have become naturalized (and occasionally overpowering) in North American gardens. The *Centaureas* like ordinary garden soil, full sun, and are useful additions to the border, wildflower, or rock garden, and in planters. The flowers are long lasting and good for cutting. All are very hardy, easy to grow, and need to be kept under control—prevent the plants from going to seed and divide them frequently.

C. babylonica (Babylonian centaurea) has yellow flowers and grayish leaves and grows to 12 inches. *C. dealbata* (Persian centaurea) has pink, white, or red flowers, grows about 18 inches tall, and blooms for most of the summer. *C. macrocephala* (globe centaurea) becomes nearly 4 feet tall and has large, thistlelike yellow flowers that attract butterflies in midsummer. *C. montana* (mountain bluet) grows to 18 inches, and has bright blue spidery flowers for over a month in early summer; tends to spread rapidly. *C. m.* 'Alba' has white flowers.

DISEASES. Stem rot, rust, wilt, yellows.

INSECTS. Aphids, leafhoppers.

PROPAGATION. By seeds, or division in early spring.

CENTRANTHUS (sen-tran'thus),

valerian

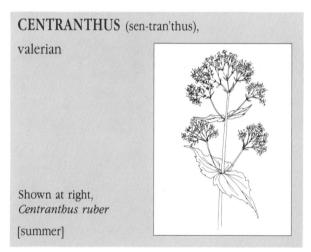

Shown at right,
Centranthus ruber

[summer]

Hardy and easy to grow, but needs good garden soil and excellent drainage in order to survive the winter. It looks good either in a border or wild garden, and is a good cut flower. More blooms are produced when it is cut frequently.

C. ruber, red valerian, is sometimes called Jupiter's beard, and grows to a height of 3 feet. It has large clusters of red, pink, or white (*C. r.* 'Albus') flowers that are tiny but fragrant. Usually blooms in early summer, but may continue off and on throughout the season.

PROPAGATION. Divide in early spring, take cuttings in early summer, or plant seeds. The red and pink varieties often self-sow and must be weeded out.

CERASTIUM (see-ras'tee-um),
snow-in-summer

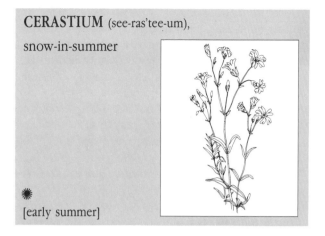

✳

[early summer]

Its name derives from the great mass of small white flowers that completely cover the silvery foliage of this low-growing plant in early summer. All varieties are useful for a rock garden or terrace, garden steps, and on steep banks. It grows easily in most soils.

C. tomentosum (snow-in-summer, 6 inches tall), the variety usually planted, has gray foliage. *C. biebersteinii* (Taurus cerastium) looks much the same with greener foliage; it is a bit taller. *C. arvense* (field chickweed) is better for a hot dry location, but it can become weedy.

INSECTS. Spider mites.

PROPAGATION. By seed, dividing the plant in early spring, or by taking cuttings directly after flowering.

CERATOSTIGMA (ser-rat-o-stig'ma),
bunge
leadwort
plumbago

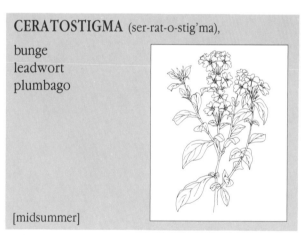

[midsummer]

Ceratostigma is often called plumbago, which it closely resembles. It spreads quickly in areas with long growing seasons, and can be used as a ground cover. Also useful as a rock garden plant, or as edging in the border. It likes full sun, but will tolerate light shade; needs good, well-drained soil.

C. plumbaginoides (leadwort) grows well in **zones 6 to 10**, and with winter protection in zone 5. It provides blue flowers when flowers of that color are scarce late in the season. Grows about 12 inches tall, and forms a mound of dark green leaves, covered with long-lasting, cobalt-blue

flowers. When the flowers die the foliage turns a reddish bronze.

PROPAGATION. New plants are started by dividing the clumps in the spring.

CHEIRANTHUS (ky-ran'thus),
wallflower

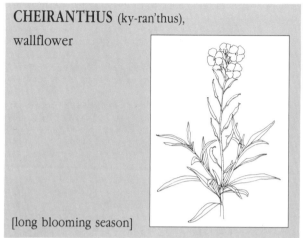

[long blooming season]

The fragrant biennials are related to the annual stock, but the leaves are greener. They grow up to 2 feet tall, in a variety of colors, and are attractive in the border or wild garden from zone 5 south. They prefer an alkaline soil that is well drained.

C. cheiri, English wallflower, comes in many shades, but is not always hardy in northern U.S. gardens. Those who love it often overwinter the plants in cold frames or cool root cellars. Planting them in containers or raised beds of rich, sandy soil with a bit of lime, in partial shade, gives them the growing conditions they like and the good drainage they need to survive the winter outside. *C. allionii* (also *Erysimum bieraciifolium*), Siberian wallflower, is a hardier biennial. By keeping the flowers picked, the plants will keep producing bright orange flowers all summer in zone 3.

PROPAGATION. Generally started from seeds. Take cuttings in early summer to get plants that replicate the parents.

CHELONE (kel-lo'nee),
turtlehead

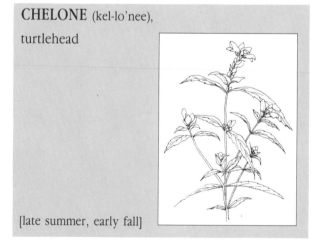

[late summer, early fall]

The turtleheads are unusual plants for the wild garden, perennial border, or alongside a stream. Their odd-shaped flowers, resembling a turtle head with its mouth open, add interest. The bitter tasting leaves were formerly used to make medicinal tea.

C. glabra (white turtlehead) has white to pale pink blooms, and those of *C. lyonii* (pink turtlehead) are rose-pink. *C. obliqua* (rose turtlehead) has red blooms. All grow from 1 to 3 feet tall, bloom in late summer, and are most at home in moist or swampy places. They can tolerate full sun, but grow best when shaded from afternoon sun.

DISEASES. Leaf spot, mildew, rust.

PROPAGATION. By seeds, cuttings, or dividing the clumps in the spring.

CHINESE FORGET-ME-NOT. See *Cynoglossum*

CHINESE LANTERN PLANT. See *Physalis*

CHIVES. See *Allium*

CHOLLA. See *Opuntia*

CHRISTMAS ROSE. See *Helleborus*

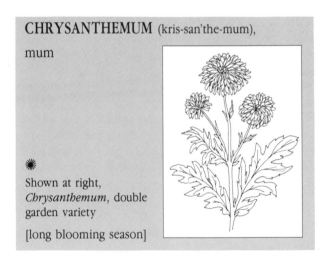

CHRYSANTHEMUM (kris-san'the-mum), mum

Shown at right, *Chrysanthemum*, double garden variety

[long blooming season]

The numerous varieties of plants in this large family take so many different forms and bloom at so many different times that they are invaluable in the perennial border. All are good for cutting, too.

C. x morifolium, the garden mum, has long been the mainstay of the fall garden because it blooms for a long time and in many different colors.

Mums need sun and rich soil to flourish. Young plants should be pinched back several times in late spring and early summer to make them bushy and well branched. In zones 3 and 4 all pinching should cease by July first, or blooming will be delayed. In warmer zones, continue pinching until mid-July, or until the plant is well branched and bushy and appears capable of producing lots of blooms later.

Other than the pinching, garden mums need no special care, except to keep the faded blooms picked for best appearance and longer flowering. To get the best blossoms on the larger flowering kinds, pick off all buds except for one at the end of each stem. All the plant's energy will then go into developing a few big, long-stemmed flowers.

In the past, *C. x morifolium* (the garden mum) could be grown only from zone 5 south because it couldn't withstand subzero temperatures; only a few of the cushion and pompom kinds bloomed before early northern frosts. Fortunately, both hardier and earlier-blooming varieties have been developed in recent years. Now even zone-3 gardeners can grow many of the cushion and pompom mums, and even some of the larger flowering kinds, successfully. Most of the spoon, daisy, and quill mums still bloom too late and are too tender for planting in zone 5 or colder. The same applies to the exhibition mums, including the giant football-types, which were once popular as decoration at college football tailgate parties. These "florist" mums are primarily raised in greenhouses or by southern growers. Even without these beauties, gardeners still have thousands of varieties from which to make a selection, and the full-color pictures in perennial catalogs can make planning a fall garden a real delight.

Northern gardeners find that even the hardy mums benefit from a winter mulch of evergreen boughs or similar material. Some people dig up and pot their plants and store them in a cold frame or root cellar for the winter. Because mums are so susceptible to winter injury and disease, many people do not try to save their old plants at all, but instead order new rooted cuttings each spring. Still others prefer to wait until late summer and buy potted blooming plants to use around the foundation of their homes, or to set near spots in their border where some of the earlier-flowering perennials have died back.

To help prevent disease, the clumps should be split apart early each spring, and the small divisions replanted. Better yet, if you have a greenhouse pot up some of the divisions from which you can take cuttings to root and plant outside later. Whether you save your plants or buy new, you can better control disease if you set mums in a new place each time, so any virus that might have wintered over in the soil around old plants will not easily find your new ones.

C. parthenium, feverfew, has tiny white flowers that are good fillers in bouquets. The plant was used in the past as a medicinal herb.

C. coccineum, pyrethrum or painted daisy, has pink, red, or white flowers in singles or doubles. It starts blooming in early summer, and if cut back after the flowers fade, it will often bloom again. Pyrethrums do well in sun or light shade, and ordinary garden soil, but tend to be short-lived in wet places. They are hardy to zone 3, but putting a light mulch over them for the winter is good insurance. Organic gardeners should be familiar with the insecticide made from these plants.

The shasta daisy (*C. maximum* and the *C. x superbum* hybrid) is one of the most desirable garden perennials for many reasons. It is vigorous, hardy, prolific, easy to grow, and flowers in a variety of ways including single, double, fringed, and dwarf blossoms. Never plant them in a wet place. They can be grown from seed, or purchased from a nursery or catalog if you want some of the named cultivars. Like other chrysanthemums, they should be divided often, perhaps even every other year if they are growing well. They do not need pinching, but the double, fringed, and semidouble varieties benefit from winter protection. 'Little Miss Muffet' is a shorter version of the shasta daisy. *C. arcticum* (arctic daisy) is similar, but even smaller and is ideal for rock gardens. *C. uliginosum* (giant daisy) grows to 6 feet or more.

DISEASES. Leaf spot, mildew, wilt, and yellows.

INSECTS. Aphids, borers, miners, mites, nematodes, and plant bugs.

PROPAGATION. Divide the plants, or root the tops you pinch off in spring and early summer in moist, sandy soil. Shasta daisies and pyrethrums are easily grown from seed, and new varieties of garden chrysanthemums are originated by seed.

CIMICIFUGA (sim-mi-siff'you-ga),

bugbane
snakeroot

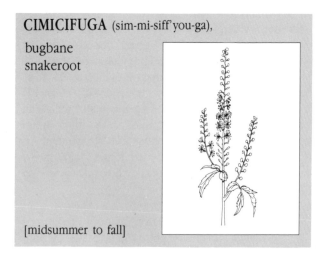

[midsummer to fall]

These tall plants with white bottle bush-type flowers go well at the back of a border. Although the unpleasant odor of the bugbanes repels insects, a person has to get real close to find it offensive. They are not difficult to grow, but are hard to propagate which makes them hard to find in nurseries.

The bugbanes like a shady location with moist soil, but they will grow in full sun if given moist soil rich in leaf mold. It takes several years for them to reach their best, so don't disturb them once planted.

The native variety, *C. americana* (American bugbane), grows about 3 feet tall and is well known to wildflower lovers. *C. racemosa* (black snakeroot), another native plant, is the most commonly cultivated kind. It has creamy white blooms in midsummer, grows to a height of 6 feet or more, and is a good background plant. *C. dahurica* also grows tall with white flowers; and it blooms in September. *C. simplex* (Kamchatka bugbane) is only 3 feet tall, and blooms very late, usually in October.

DISEASES. Leaf spot, rust.

INSECTS. Nematodes.

PROPAGATION. By seeds or division, neither of which is easy.

CINQUEFOIL. See *Potentilla*

CLEMATIS (klem'a-tis or klem-mat'is),

bush clematis

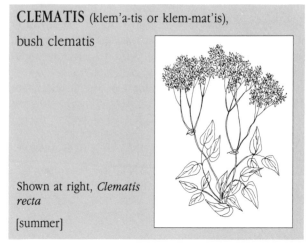

Shown at right, *Clematis recta*

[summer]

Perennial bush clematis is quite different from the large, flowering vine species. The garden types are dense, shrubby bushes about 2 to 5 feet tall with lacy flowers. Most bloom over a long period and the flowers are attractive for cutting. They do best in loamy, cool garden soil which is neutral or slightly acid, and like afternoon shade.

C. heracleifolia (tube clematis) grows to 4 feet and has blue flowers which are attractive in a "blue and white" garden. *C. integrifolia* (solitary blue clematis) is probably the best variety. It also has blue flowers and grows with vinelike stems from 18 inches to 2 feet tall. *C. recta* (ground clematis) reaches 4 to 5 feet, has fragrant white flowers, and blooms most of the summer.

DISEASES. Blight, crown gall mildew, rust.

INSECTS. Caterpillars, mites, nematodes.

PROPAGATION. By dividing the plants, or by stem cuttings or seeds.

COLCHICUM (col'chik-um),

autumn crocus

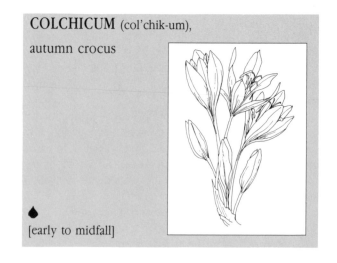

[early to midfall]

The common name is misleading because *Colchicums* are members of the Lily family. They blossom in the fall on 1-foot stems, although their foliage (which appears in spring) dies back in early summer. They are excellent in the rock garden, at the front of the border, or at the base of trees. They like sun, ordinary garden soil, and most need a protective mulch in order to survive winter in the North, but otherwise they are easy to grow.

Plant the corms about 3 inches deep in late summer, and fertilize them in the spring so they will make lush growth before they die down. The corms are extremely poisonous.

C. autumnale, meadow saffron, is the most common, but there are numerous other named varieties available. Most *Colchicums* are low-growing with pink or rosy purple flowers, although *C. luteum*, yellow autumn crocus, has yellow blooms.

DISEASES. Leaf spot, rot.

PROPAGATION. Usually by dividing the corms, but seed is also possible.

COLUMBINE. See *Aquilegia*

CONEFLOWER. See *Rudbeckia*

CONVALLARIA (kon-va-lair'ee-a), lily-of-the valley

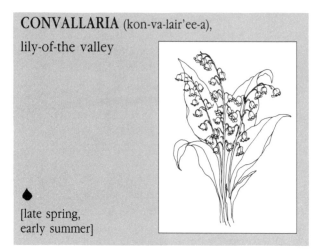

◆

[late spring, early summer]

Nearly every garden has a place somewhere for the delightfully fragrant and old-fashioned lily-of-the-valley (*C. majalis*). They insist on partial to heavy shade, and although they will grow under large trees, the results will be much better where there is less competition for moisture and nourishment. Rich, somewhat acid soil is preferred. When the conditions are right, they quickly naturalize and cover a large area with a rich green carpet. The plants grow about 8 inches tall with broad leaves and fragrant white bell-like flowers. They need little care, but the clumps should be dug up and separated whenever the blooms become sparse.

The cultivar 'Rosea' has pinkish blooms. 'Giant Bells' is taller and has larger flowers. Cultivars with double white blooms are also available.

The stems and roots of *Convallaria* are poisonous, so both the growing plants and cut flowers should be kept

away from small children who might want to taste them.

DISEASES. Leaf spot, stem rot.

INSECTS. Weevils.

PROPAGATION. Propagate by dividing the plant clumps which easily fall apart. The small sections of the rhizomes are called "pips."

COPPERTIP. See *Crocosmia*

CORAL BELLS. See *Heuchera*

COREOPSIS. (kor-ee-op'sis), tickseed

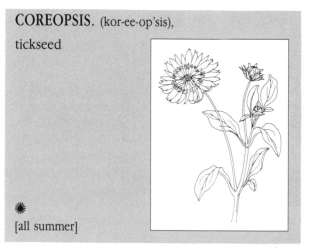

✳

[all summer]

Tickseed was so named because its seed resembles a tick, which belies the beauty of its bright, daisylike, yellow-toned flowers. They are a delight in any garden, blooming early and for most of the summer in cool areas. They may self-sow and become weedy, however, although perennial varieties are less troublesome than the annuals.

Coreopsis grows easily in sunshine and moist garden soil. They are excellent cut flowers. The fading blooms should be kept picked to maintain blossoms over a long time. Because they are somewhat susceptible to frost, a mulch is recommended in northern zones.

C. grandiflora (big-flowered coreopsis) is a popular species. It grows to a height of 3 feet, with single or semi-double yellow flowers. It is often short-lived, and must be planted frequently or allowed to self-seed in order to guarantee subsequent growth. *C. lanceolata* (lance coreopsis) is one of the hardier species, growing from 12 to 30 inches tall; there are several named varieties which have both single and double blooms. 'Brown Eyes' has yellow flowers with a dark center. *C. verticillata* (threadleaf coreopsis) grows 1 to 3 feet tall and blooms throughout the summer; has lacy foliage. It spreads by underground stems, and is very drought-resistant.

DISEASES. Fungus, rot, virus.

INSECTS. Leaf miners, mites.

PROPAGATION. New plants are easily started by division. Seeds planted early will often bloom the first year, making it possible to grow them as annuals.

CORONILLA (cor-ro-nil'la),
crownvetch

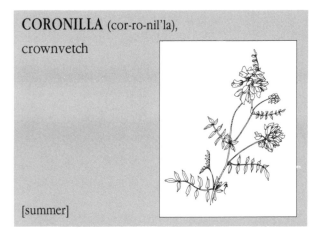

[summer]

C. varia (crownvetch) has increased in popularity in recent years as a ground cover and for erosion control on roadsides and banks. It grows about 2 feet tall, has fernlike foliage, pink and white blooms, and grows rapidly. Though a European native, it has become a wildflower in much of the country, and if let loose in a flower border it can quickly become a weed, spreading both from seeds and underground stems similar to quack grass. It is an ideal plant for a sunny steep bank. Space them 3 feet apart in each direction.

PROPAGATION. By dividing clumps. For large numbers of plants, sow the seed as soon as it is ripe; or store them in a tight container for the winter, then soak in hot water the night before planting in the spring. They may also be grown from cuttings or layers.

CORYDALIS (cor-rid'a-lis),
corydalis

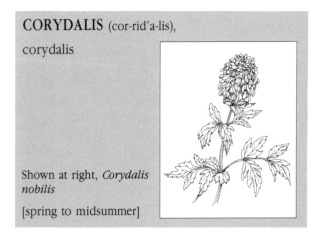

Shown at right, *Corydalis nobilis*

[spring to midsummer]

Corydalis resembles its relative, the *Dicentra* (bleeding-heart), both in leaf and flower, but the plant and bloom are smaller. They are good for the rock or wildflower garden, grow well in sun or light shade, and prefer rich soil. In some locations the conditions are such that they self-seed and spread rapidly.

C. cheilanthifolia, Chinese corydalis, is 10 inches high and has yellow flowers in spring. *C. lutea*, yellow corydalis, has gray foliage, yellow blooms, a height of 15 inches, and is often treated as an annual. *C. nobilis*, Siberian corydalis, up to 30 inches in height, has white blooms with purple edging, and the plants die down soon after flowering. *C. sempervirens*, Roman wormwood, grows 2 to 4

feet in height and is a familiar eastern wildflower with small pink flowers; it is often transplanted into the perennial border, but with little success since it is usually biennial.

PROPAGATION. By dividing the roots in the fall or by planting seeds as soon as they are ripe in the summer. Stem cuttings are also possible.

COWSLIP. See *Caltha*

CRANE'S BILL. See *Geranium*

CROCOSMIA (cro-cos'mee-a),
montebretia
coppertip

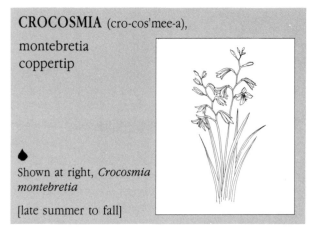

Shown at right, *Crocosmia montebretia*

[late summer to fall]

Originally from South Africa, this delightful plant was little noticed for years because most books described it as hardy only in the warmest parts of the country. It has become naturalized in England, however, and a plant given to us several years ago is still thriving in our zone-3 garden. Apparently they don't like the soil around them to freeze for long periods, and ours seldom does because of our snow cover.

Crocosmia grow from corms. The plants have iris-type leaves, reach a height of 2 feet or more, and in late summer produce scarlet, orange, orange-yellow, or orange-red blooms over long periods. They like a sunny location, light afternoon shade, and good garden soil. Several beautiful named hybrids are available.

PROPAGATION. Easily propagated by dividing the corms in early spring, but beautiful flowers also sometimes result when plants are grown from seed sown as soon as it is ripe.

CROCUS, COMMON. See *Crocus vernus*

CROCUS, VERNUS (kro'kus),
common crocus

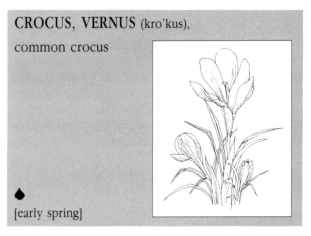

[early spring]

These perennials, grown from bulblike corms, are often hailed as the first harbingers of spring. They grow in ordinary soil as long as the have full sun. Although they are often set in lawns, this is not the best spot for them since their foliage should not be mowed until it dies naturally. Plant the corms in late fall, pointed side up, 4 inches deep. Divide your old clumps in the fall every 3 to 4 years, if you can remember where they are.

There are a great many different kinds of crocus in a wide range of colors, both striped and plain, but the species from southern Europe or Asia are not always hardy in the North. A winter mulch is advisable, unless constant snow cover is certain.

DISEASES. Rot, rust, scab.

INSECTS. Aphids, mites.

ANIMAL PESTS. Chipmunks, mice, and squirrels sometimes eat the bulbs.

PROPAGATION. By dividing and replanting the bulbs in fall. They reproduce so fast that they are quite inexpensive.

CROWNVETCH. See *Coronilla*

CUPID'S DART. See *Catananche*

CYNOGLOSSUM (sin-o-gloss'um),

hound's tongue
Chinese forget-me-not

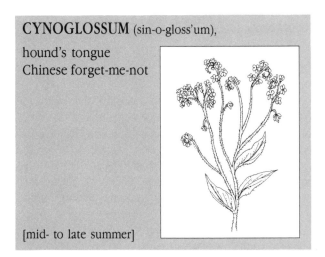

[mid- to late summer]

These small, intensely blue flowers, on 20- to 30-inch stems, grow with so little trouble in ordinary garden soil, in sun or light shade, that they deserve a place in the border. *C. amabile* (Chinese forget-me-not) has white, pink, or blue flowers, and is a biennial. *C. nervosum* (great hound's tongue), a perennial from the Himalayas, has deep, gentian blue flowers.

PROPAGATION. Divide perennial varieties in early spring. Both biennial and perennial kinds may be grown from seed sown in the spring.

DAFFODIL. See *Narcissus*

DAISY (daz'ee),

daisy

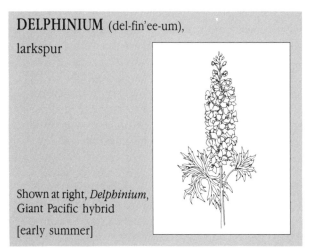

Shown at right,
Chrysanthemum maximum

Few flowers are more beloved than the daisies. Small children gather handfuls of the wild kind as gifts, teenagers pull out the petals to check the status of their love life, and florists shape them into beautiful arrangements. They are perennial favorites for everyone. Originally called "day's eye," a day seldom passes over the course of the summer when one species or another is not in bloom.

The label "daisy" refers to members of the large Compositae family that have flowers with flat petals extending from a central disklike center. Many are in the chrysanthemum genus. Other daisy-type flowers include *Anthemis*, aster, *Bellis*, coreopsis, *Doronicum*, *Echinacea purpurea*, *Erigeron*, *Gaillardia*, *Helenium*, *Helianthus*, *Heliopsis*, inula, pyrethrum, and *Rudbeckia*.

DAYLILY. See *Hemerocallis*

DEAD NETTLE. See *Lamium*

DELPHINIUM (del-fin'ee-um),

larkspur

Shown at right, *Delphinium*,
Giant Pacific hybrid

[early summer]

The majestic delphinums, with their tall, spirelike flowers, in blue, purple, lilac, pink, and white, have long been important accent plants in a proper border. Once the advice given to a beginning gardener was, "Plant the delphinium first, then designing the rest of the border will be easy." The new hybrids have made delphiniums even more desirable, and though they may need more care than many other plants, they are worth the trouble.

Delphiniums like a sunny location, but don't mind a little light afternoon shade and need rich garden soil with a little lime. Give the plants plenty of space to allow the good air circulation necessary to prevent mildew. The tall-growing ones should be protected from the wind by a hedge, fence, wall, or building, and each stalk may need to be staked separately. After blooming the stalks should be cut down, and in areas where the growing season is long enough, they will bloom again in September.

The hybrid delphiniums do best in the cool North where they grow to their full beauty and last for years. We have seen ten-year-old Pacific hybrids reach a height of 10 feet in northern gardens. In the South they are likely to be short-lived, and are sometimes treated as annuals.

Overgrown clumps of the long-lived species should be split up every four or five years to keep them thriving, and if the divisions appear healthy, these can be replanted. If you buy hybrid plants get those grown from seed rather than division because they are more vigorous, and set them in the spring. Potted plants, or those dug with a ball of soil are preferable, because bare-rooted ones are difficult to transplant.

Check your perennial catalogs for the varieties of delphinum currently available. *D. formosum* (garland delphinium, 3 to 4 feet tall) includes such favorite hybrids as the light blue-flowered 'Belladonna,' dark blue 'Bellamosum,' and the white-blooming 'D. Moerheimii' and 'Casa Blanca' cultivars. Hybrids of *D. elatum*, candle larkspur, which range in height from 3 to 6 feet, are also commonly grown, including the Kelway hybrids, Wrexham, Blackmore and Langdon hybrids, and many others, including the Pacific hybrids.

The Giant Pacific hybrid series add gigantic size and spectacular color, which compensates for the fact that they are short-lived, fragile, and difficult to stake. Most come fairly true from seed and have large, semidouble blooms in a wide spectrum of colors. 'Galahad' is clear white; 'Astolat' comes in shades ranging from a pale pink to raspberry rose; and 'Black Knight,' a superb, very dark purple has cultivars in many shades of blue. The Connecticut Yankees, a shorter-growing hybrid strain, come in blue, white, lavender, and purple. Dwarf Pacific hybrids include 'Blue Heaven,' clear blue in color, and the 'Blue Fountains,' which are available in a variety of colors.

Several delphinium species are shorter in height and longer-lived than the hybrids; some are quite susceptible to diseases such as mildew and rust. Among them are *D. cardinale*, scarlet larkspur, 2 to 3 feet tall, with bright scarlet flowers; it is a California native, and not hardy in the North. *D. grandiflorum*, Chinese or Siberian delphinium, is a low, spreading plant with bright blue flowers. *D. tricorne*, dwarf larkspur, gets only 3 feet high, and is a native of the Midwest.

DISEASES. Unfortunately the best varieties of delphinium seem to have the most troubles. Botrytis, blight, leaf spot, mildew, and rot are the most common diseases, and it may be necessary to make frequent applications of fungicide throughout the season.

INSECTS. Aphids, cutworms, cyclamen mites, slugs.

PROPAGATION. Delphiniums are easy to grow from seed, and this is the best way to get vigorous, healthy plants. Plant only fresh seed because those over a year old are not likely to grow. Sow seeds during the summer in a shady spot, and mulch the seedlings over the winter; or store the seed in sealed plastic bags in the refrigerator. Then plant in midwinter in a greenhouse, under grow lights, or in a seedbed in the spring. Delphiniums may also be started from stem cuttings taken in early summer.

DESERT CANDLE. See *Eremurus*

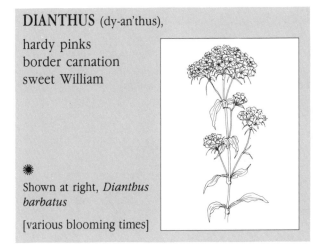

DIANTHUS (dy-an'thus),

hardy pinks
border carnation
sweet William

✱

Shown at right, *Dianthus barbatus*

[various blooming times]

Dianthus is derived from the Greek for divine flower, and so it is. The carnation is but one member of this large family of hundreds of species, most of which have a spicy fragrance similar to clove, and grasslike foliage. The greenhouse carnation is not hardy enough to be grown in northern gardens, but the pinks make excellent border plants and cut flowers. Nearly all are dwarf growing, although some get up to 2 feet tall.

The plants grow well in rich garden soil with a little lime added, and unless otherwise noted, each species needs full sun, good drainage, and good air circulation. Perennial varieties should be divided each year to keep them healthy. Biennials need replanting every year, and even though they may live more than two years, the second blooming is not usually as good. Avoid mulching because the stems need air circulation.

D. barbatus, sweet William, a biennial or short-lived perennial, is one of the best known species. It lacks the spicy fragrance of other pinks, but is popular because of its wide range of colors and habit of blooming for a long period in early summer when brightly colored perennials are scarce. Plant these in masses of the same color for best effect. They come in regular (12 to 18 inches) and dwarf (4 to 6 inches) varieties: 'Newport Pink' is a popular one of regular height; 'Wee Willie' and 'Indian Carpet' are colorful dwarf mixtures.

D. arenarius (sand pink, 6 to 12 inches tall) has pink or white flowers and grows well in partial shade. *D. deltoides,* maiden pink, forms a tight low mat of green foliage with pink or red flowers 6 to 12 inches tall in early summer; a strong grower and bloomer, it is good for rock and semi-wild gardens. *D. plumarius,* grass pink, has white, pink, or red flowers, gray-green, grasslike foliage, and grows to a height of 6 to 12 inches. It is excellent for edging. 'Pink Princess' is a popular cultivar. *D. superbus,* lilac pink, 2 to 3 feet tall, has lilac-pink flowers, is very fragrant, and is best grown as a biennial. *D.* x *winteri* (12 inches tall) is classed as a border carnation, and the hybrids come in a wide range of colors and color combinations, including yellow.

Besides the available species, many hybrids are offered by nurseries, including the *D. allwoodii* cultivars such as 'Alpinus,' 'Blanche,' and 'Ian.'

DISEASES. Leaf spot, stem rot, root rot, rust.

INSECTS. Aphids, mites, slugs.

PROPAGATION. Perennial *Dianthus* can be propagated by division in spring, stem cuttings in midsummer, or by seed. Biennial varieties can be propagated from seed. *Dianthus* seed is easily gathered, and the plants often self-sow, but if you grow more than one color, the colors of the seedlings will often vary because of cross-pollination.

soil, in a spot with morning sunshine and light afternoon shade, to obtain the longest period of bloom. The east side of a building is ideal. Leave plenty of room for the plant to grow—3 to 4 feet is not too much.

D. canadensis, squirrel-corn, is a wildflower that grows from a small bulb. It has greenish white flowers with red tips in early spring, grows about a foot high, and is good for the rock garden or wild garden if rich, woodsy soil is provided. *D. cucullaria,* Dutchman's breeches, is similar to *D. canadensis,* except the white flowers have yellow tips, and it is more likely to flourish in lime-rich soils.

D. eximia, fernleaf or fringed bleeding-heart, is a dwarf species (12 to 18 inches high) that makes an excellent edging plant with its lacy leaves and pink flowers that appear throughout the summer. It likes full sun or light shade and ordinary good garden soil. Because fernleaf bleeding-heart spreads rapidly by underground stems, it must be pulled or divided ruthlessly to keep the clumps or borders neat. *D. formosa,* Pacific bleeding-heart, similar to *D. eximia,* is more often grown on the West Coast where the climate is better suited to its growing habits. Several named cultivars of both *D. eximia* and *D. formosa* have better blooming habits than the species.

DISEASES. Stem rot, wilt.

INSECTS. Aphids.

PROPAGATION. The plants may be grown from seed, but division is much faster and produces excellent plants. Dividing directly after blooming or in very early spring gives best results. Stem and root cuttings are also possible.

DICENTRA (di-sen'tra), bleeding-heart

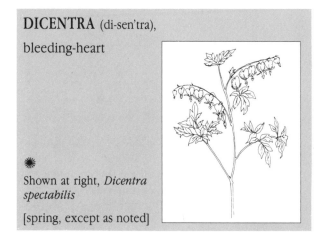

Shown at right, *Dicentra spectabilis*

[spring, except as noted]

Bleeding-hearts have been gardening favorites for centuries, and few plants attract more attention when they are in full bloom. They do best out of full sun, which makes them attractive to gardeners with shady spots.

The most spectacular is *D. spectabilis,* old-fashioned bleeding-heart (2 to 3 feet tall), which is especially popular because it is beautiful in both flower and foliage. The heart-shaped flowers hang gracefully from long arching stems, and range in color from pink to bright red. Except in shady spots in the cool North, *D. spectabilis* dies down after blooming. *D. s.* 'Alba' has white flowers and is somewhat less vigorous than the pink variety. Plant deep in rich, moist

DICTAMNUS (dick-tam'nus), gas plant

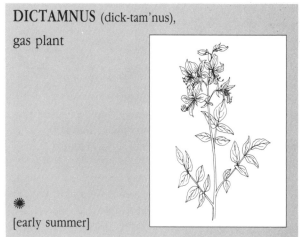

[early summer]

There is no middle ground—either you like or dislike the gas plant and its unusual odor; but either way you must admit it is interesting. Its growth habit resembles that of a shrub because it has a mound of leathery-textured, glossy green foliage.

Gas plants will grow in sun or light shade, but they like rich soil, and once planted, should not be disturbed since they bloom best only when the plant is well established.

They are attractive either as single specimens or in groups of three or more, and have no serious pests. Leave a space of at least 3 feet between them.

The pungent odor that gives the plant its name can be better appreciated if, on a hot summer evening when the air is quiet, you hold a lighted match next to the ripe seedpod and watch it ignite the volatile oils in a flash of light. People with delicate skin sometimes get a rash from this oily substance when they touch the plant.

D. albus (gas plant) has white flowers, and two available cultivars: *D. a.* 'Ruber' with purplish pink blooms, and *D. a.* 'Purpureus' with purple ones. Blooms appear on spikes 2 to 3 feet tall in early summer; the scent is somewhat like an old-fashioned stomach tonic mixed with lemon. These are followed by clusters of attractive, but equally strong-smelling, seedpods.

PROPAGATION. If you don't mind waiting three or four years, the best way to propagate the plants is by seed. The clump of woody, carrotlike roots can be divided, but it is not easy and the new plants become established slowly. Root cuttings made in early spring are sometimes successful.

and benefit from a light winter mulch where there is little snow cover.

D. grandiflora (also known as *D. ambigua*) is the yellow foxglove from Europe, 30 inches tall, and shorter than most *Digitalis*. *D. lanata* (Grecian foxglove, 3 feet tall) has small grayish flowers with yellow markings. *D.* x *mertonensis* (Merton foxglove, 3 to 5 feet high) has red blossoms and is perennial.

D. purpurea is common foxglove. Reaching a height of 2 to 4 feet, this biennial has been hybridized into many different varieties with spectacular blooming habits. Among these are the 'Excelsior' hybrids, on which florets come out from the stalk at right angles, rather than in the normal downward position.

DISEASES. Anthracnose, leaf spot, mildew, root and stem rot.

INSECTS. Aphids, Japanese beetles, mealybugs.

PROPAGATION. All *Digitalis* are easy to grow from seed. Thin seedlings to 1 or 2 feet apart if the plants have self-sown. Perennial kinds can be divided in spring or fall.

DIGITALIS (dij-i-tal'lis), foxglove

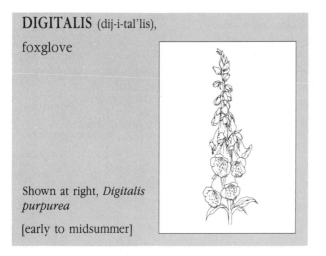

Shown at right, *Digitalis purpurea*

[early to midsummer]

DORONICUM (do-ron'i-kum), leopard's bane

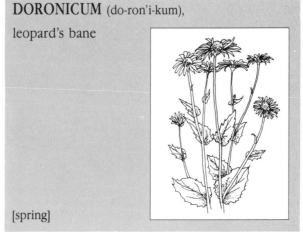

[spring]

Those suffering from heart maladies may be familiar with the name *Digitalis* because, although the leaves are poisonous, they are used as a heart stimulant in small amounts. Gardeners plant them for their tall showy clumps of bell-like flowers.

No one could have admired foxglove more than we until one day a clump dropped its seeds over the fence, and the plants spread so rapidly that in a few years our entire orchard was a sea of brightly colored blooms. Beautiful, yes, but still a weed, and we strongly advise picking the flowers before they go to seed, except for a very few of the best ones from which you may want to grow seeds for replacements—foxgloves are biennials or short-lived perennials.

The plants are most effective when planted in masses of the same color, and are equally attractive in the perennial border or the semiwild garden. They grow in any ordinary soil that is not wet over the winter, and will respond better with extra fertilizer. They thrive in sun or light shade,

The leopard's banes are the earliest daisy-type plants to bloom; the flowers grow on long stems above the heart-shaped leaves, making them good cut flowers. They add a bright spot to the border before most other garden perennials are started. *Doronicum* grows best in moist, rich garden soil; it likes a sunny spot in cool climates, light shade in warm areas. Even though their height ranges from 2 to 3 feet or more, they are good for the middle of the border because so few other plants bloom at the same time. The plants may even be dug up in late fall, potted, stored in a cool root cellar, and then brought into a warm sunny room for late winter bloom.

D. austriacum (Austrian leopard's bane) reaches a height of 4 feet and is somewhat hairy; it has several flowers on each stem, unlike most other *Doronicums*. *D. caucasicum* (Caucasian leopard's bane, 2 feet high), especially the 'Madam Mason' and 'Magnificum' cultivars, are popular because of their showy 2-inch flowers. *D. plantagineum* (showy leopard's bane) has 3- to 5-inch flowers on 3-foot stems, but its size makes it useful only in large gardens.

DISEASES. Mildew.

INSECTS. Aphids, Japanese beetles, mealybugs.

PROPAGATION. Divide every two or three years just after flowering. This is also the best way to start extra plants, although they can be raised from seed.

DRABA (dray'ba),
draba

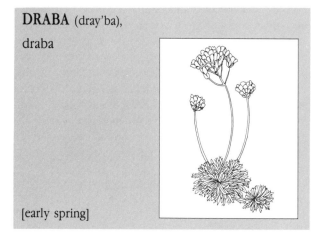

[early spring]

These dwarf alpine plants form a grasslike mat and are suitable for the rock garden or steep slopes. They originally come from several mountainous regions of the world, grow easily in sandy, loamy, well-drained soil, and like full sun. The plants often grow in tight rosettes and produce clusters of small yellow or white flowers. *D. alpina*, *D. densiflora* (rockcress draba), and *D. sibirica* (Siberian draba) are all natives of the arctic or subarctic region, so are the most hardy. *D. aspera* is a better choice for the warmer parts of the country.

DISEASES. Mildew, rust.

PROPAGATION. From seeds or by dividing the plants in spring after they flower.

DRAGONHEAD, FALSE. See *Physostegia*

ECHEVERIA (esh-eve-ee'ri-a)
echeveria

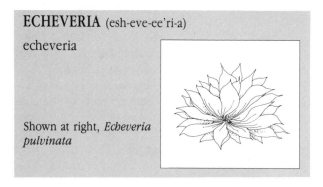

Shown at right, *Echeveria pulvinata*

These succulent plants are suitable only for the warmest sections of the country. They grow mostly in rosettes resembling the *Sempervivums*, and are commonly planted in rock gardens, terrace gardens, and in formal carpet beds found in parks. In the North, they are mostly grown in greenhouses and sunny windows.

E. agavoides, molded-wax echeveria, is 6 inches tall, and has red flowers with yellow tips. *E. amoena*, baby echeveria, has coral red flowers on 6-inch stems. *E. coccinea*, scarlet echeveria, has gray-green leaves that turn red as they mature, and red flowers. *E. gibbiflora*, fringed echeveria, from Mexico, is 2 feet tall and has yellow flowers; some varieties have bronze-colored leaves. *E. secunda* is considered slightly hardier than most of the other varieties; it has red flowers and red-edged leaves.

PROPAGATION. By division, since plants grown from seed usually have blooms of inferior color.

ECHINACEA (ek-in-ay'see-a),
purple coneflower

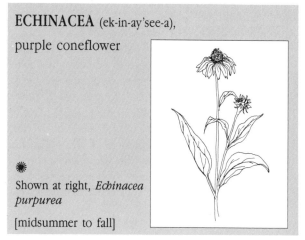

Shown at right, *Echinacea purpurea*

[midsummer to fall]

Coneflowers are a worthy addition to the garden because they offer a large daisy-type, cone-shaped flower in late summer. The plants like a sunny spot, but will tolerate light shade, and grow in ordinary good garden soil. They are long-lived, but need to be divided whenever the clumps get too large—usually every three or four years.

Although the rose-purple blooming species *E. purpurea* (purple coneflower) is the most common, newer cultivars bearing white, red, and pink blooms are also available. Because the plants grow to a height of 3 to 4 feet, they are very much in evidence. The more vibrant shades should be separated from other strong colors by paler shades.

DISEASES. Leaf spot, virus.

INSECTS. Japanese beetles.

PROPAGATION. Best done by division because plants grown from seed usually do not come true.

ECHINOPS (ek'in-ops),
globe thistle

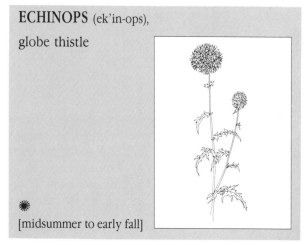

[midsummer to early fall]

These hardy plants with their unusual globelike blue flowers are as attractive to people as to the bees that cluster around them. If picked before they reach full bloom they make excellent dried flowers. As children, we used to try to fool the other kids into thinking the unopened buds were porcupine eggs.

Globe thistles are easy to grow in nearly any soil, and they can withstand dry conditions better than most other perennials. They like full sun or light shade, and should be divided frequently to keep them under control and in a healthy condition.

Largest of all is *E. exaltatus*, Russian globe thistle. A neighbor has one that grows to the size of an old-fashioned lilac bush every year. It makes a spectacular sight when in bloom, and fortunately, it doesn't crowd out anything else since it is used as a corner plant. *E. ritro* (glove thistle, 1 to 3 feet tall) is a far more reasonably sized plant for the garden border, but unfortunately *E. exaltatus* is often sold under that name, and a takeover of the border is inevitable. 'Taplow Blue' (Taplow Blue globe thistle), one of the best, is a commonly grown cultivar of 3 to 4 feet, but *E. exaltatus* has been widely sold under that name, too.

DISEASES. Crown rot.

INSECTS. Japanese beetles.

PROPAGATION. By dividing the clumps or by root cuttings. They are easy to grow from seed, but the plants may differ in growth habit from the parent.

EDELWEISS. See *Leontopodium*

ENGLISH DAISY. See *Bellis*

EPIMEDIUM (ep-i-mee'dee-um),
bishop's hat

[late spring]

This low-growing (12 inches high) plant has heart-shaped leaves and delicate flowers in shades of red, yellow, and white that look like bishops' hats. It is one of the finest dwarf perennials available for the border, rock garden, or as a ground cover in a zone 5 climate or warmer. It will grow in full sun and poor soil, but prefers light shade and

good soil. Never let it dry out. Mulch around the plants rather than cultivate because the roots are shallow and can be easily damaged.

Experts do not agree on the scientific names for the various species of this plant, so we list those that are most frequently used.

E. alpinum (alpine epimedium, 12 inches high) has gray, red, or yellow flowers. Hybrids have been developed—among them is 'Rubrum,' which has bright crimson blossoms. *E. grandiflorum*, (long-spurred epimedium) from Japan and Korea, grows slightly taller with pink and white flowers that bloom in early summer. *E. pinnatum* (Persian epimedium) is the least hardy of all; it has yellow blooms from late spring through early summer. The variety 'Sulphureum,' grows only about 8 inches tall; and where it is hardy, zone 5 or warmer, it makes a fast-growing ground cover that has few pests.

PROPAGATION. By dividing the clumps in either fall or spring.

EREMURUS (e-ree-mew'rus),
desert candle

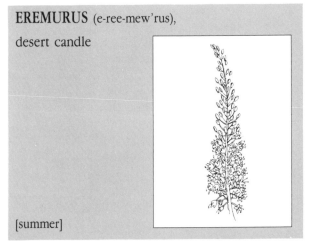

[summer]

These tall-growing perennials from Asia have a growth habit similar to that of yucca, with spikes of colorful flowers that reach 4 to 8 feet above short, succulent foliage. And like yucca, once established, they should not be disturbed. They like well-drained soil, sun, protection from high winds, and a winter mulch.

Most are too tender for the North, but *E. himalaicus*, Himalayan desert candle (8 feet high), from the Himalayas is worth a try in zone 4; it produces white or pale pink flowers on tall spikes in June. *E. aurantiacus* (also known as *E. stenophyllus*) orange dessert candle, grows to 5 feet, has orange flowers, and blooms in July.

PROPAGATION. Although the desert candles are interesting perennials, few catalogs carry them. Propagate by dividing the plants in late fall, or by planting the seed as soon as it is ripe. Protect the young plants over the winter in a cold frame or greenhouse.

ERIGERON (ee-rij'er-on),

fleabane

[all summer]

These easy-to-grow annuals and perennials produce 2-inch, asterlike flowers, most in shades of pink and lavender, with yellow centers. They are not fussy about soils or location, and will grow in full sun, although they bloom better if they get some afternoon shade.

E. speciosus, Oregon fleabane, is the most commonly grown species, and several of its hybrids are offered by nurseries. *E. s.* 'Azure Fairy' has semidouble lavender blooms and grows about 30 inches tall; 'Foerster's Darling' is a bright pink with semidouble blossoms; and 'Pink Jewel' grows to about 24 inches with flowers in various shades of pink. *E. glaucus*, beach aster, a native of West Coast shorelines, is salt-tolerant.

DISEASES. Leaf spot, mildew, rust, yellows.

INSECTS. Aphids.

PROPAGATION. *Erigeron* are easily grown from cuttings, seed, or by dividing the plant in the spring.

ERINUS (ee-ry'nus),

liver balsam

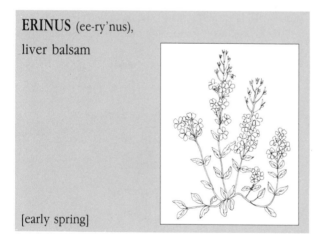

[early spring]

E. alpinus, alpine liver balsam (6 inches in height), is a small alpine plant with tiny leaves and rosy purple flowers that blossom in May. They are ideal rock garden or edging plants, and like a rather dry location, partial shade, and a lime soil.

PROPAGATION. By dividing the plants in spring, although they also grow easily from seed.

ERODIUM (ee-ro'di-um),

heron's bill

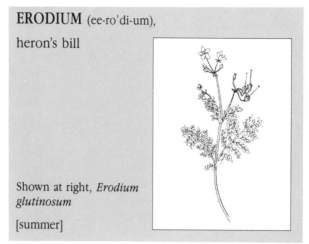

Shown at right, *Erodium glutinosum*

[summer]

Although the name implies great height, heron's bill is a dwarf plant which grows from 3 to 18 inches tall, with long seedpods that resemble a heron's bill. They are good rock garden or edging plants (related to the geraniums), prefer full sun and dry, gravelly soil. All benefit from some winter protection in the North.

E. chamaedryoides (alpine geranium, 3 inches in height) has large, wavy leaves and white flowers with pink veins that blossom all summer long. *E. c.* 'Roseum' has deep pink flowers in singles and doubles. *E. manescavii* (Pyrenees heron's bill) is a bit taller at 12 inches and has purple flowers.

PROPAGATION. By seeds, dividing the plants in early spring, or by taking small offshoots with a bit of root attached in midsummer.

ERYNGIUM (er-rin'ji-um),

sea holly

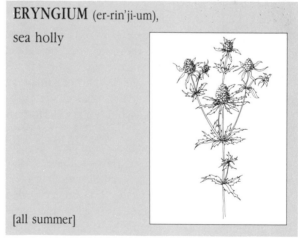

[all summer]

The sea holly is a thistle-type plant—even the flowers are surrounded by prickers. It grows from 2 to 4 feet tall, with blue or white flowers and blue-gray foliage, which is one of its most attractive features. It grows wild on sand dunes, as the name implies, and the hybrids are interesting in the perennial or wildflower border. The leaves and flowers make good fillers in bouquets, and both may be dried easily. They like sandy, loamy soil with a bit of lime and full sun. Once planted, they should not be disturbed.

E. amethystinum (amethyst eryngium) is one of the best available species, growing about 2 feet tall, with steel gray leaves and blue-purple flowers that bloom from June to late August. *E. planum* (flat-leaved eryngium) is often sold as *E. amethystinum*. It is less attractive than *E. amethystinum* and better suited to the wildflower border; it has small blue flowers that come out in mid- to late summer. *E. maritimum* is the true sea holly; 12 inches in height, it has white or pale blue flowers.

PROPAGATION. *Eryngiums* can self-sow and spread over an area with alarming speed so keep the fading flower heads picked. To have the best luck starting them from seeds, imitate the plants in nature and sow the seeds as soon as they are ripe. The clumps may also be divided, but not easily because of their fleshy roots. Root cuttings grow well.

EUPATORIUM (you-pa-toe'ri-um),

boneset
Joe Pye-weed

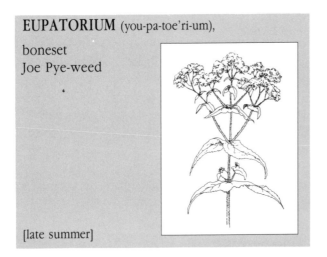

[late summer]

Many of the native *Eupatoriums* were valued as medicinal herbs—boneset, hemp agrimony, wild hoarhound, and white snakeroot, for instance. Some of these flowering plants deserve a place in the wildflower garden, and possibly even the perennial border. All like full sun, but tolerate light shade, and will grow in nearly any soil. Most have a tendency to become weedy.

E. coelestinum (mistflower, hardy ageratum, 24 inches in height) has coarsely toothed leaves and tiny blue or violet-blue flowers in flat 2- to 4-inch clusters. It thrives in light, sandy soil, but is a bit tender for northern gardens, preferring zones 5 to 8. *E. maculatum*, Joe Pye-weed, grows best in wet places, to a height of 5 to 9 feet. It has purplish flowers that appear in late summer and early fall. Tea made from the plant was used by the Indians and the early settlers as a cure for fevers.

DISEASES. Crown rot, mildew.

INSECTS. Aphids, leaf miners, scales.

PROPAGATION. By seed, or by dividing the clumps in spring.

EUPHORBIA (you-for'bee-a),

spurge

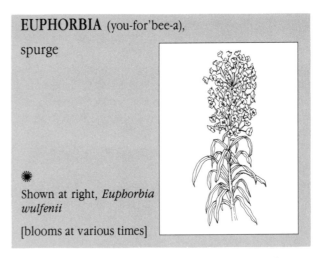

✳

Shown at right, *Euphorbia wulfenii*

[blooms at various times]

This large group of plants contains a collection of annuals and perennials, many of them weeds, and one important flowering shrub, the Christmas poinsettia. The *Euphorbias* usually found in perennial borders grow from 1 to 3 feet tall, have a milky sap in their stems, and grow best in full sun and dry, sandy soils. Like poinsettias, they have colored upper leaves called bracts (that look like flowers) which surround a small, inconspicuous bloom. Watch them carefully as they can easily grow out of control.

E. corollata (flowering spurge, 3 feet in height) is a European wildflower that has showy white bracts and small white flowers which blossom in mid- to late summer. *E. cyparissias*, cypress spurge, has leaves resembling conifer needles and brilliant yellow bracts; it has become so much at home in this country that it has often spread through cemeteries and abandoned farms. *E. epithymoides*, cushion spurge, gets about 3 feet wide, grows to 1 or 2 feet in height, and is often found in catalogs and perennial nurseries. It has golden yellow top bracts that resemble flowers in spring, and turn rose colored in fall. *E. myrsinites*, myrtle euphorbia, is a trailing plant, spring flowering, with bright yellow bracts; it's a good rock plant because it does well in difficult, dry places.

PROPAGATION. By division in early spring, or by seeds or cuttings.

EVENING PRIMROSE. See *Oenothera*

FALSE DRAGONHEAD. See *Physostegia*

FALSE INDIGO. See *Baptisia*

FALSE LUPINE. See *Thermopsis*

FALSE MALLOW. See *Sidalcea*

FERNS

See the chapter on shade gardening for more information about the culture of ferns, and descriptions of those usually grown in borders, woodland plantings, and rock

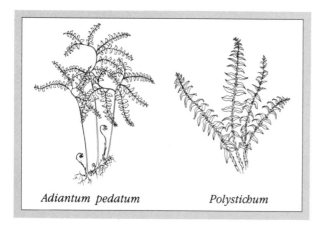

Adiantum pedatum   *Polystichum*

gardens. They are listed below by their common names to enable you to choose the kinds most likely to fit your location, and to more quickly determine the scientific names.

In evolution, the ferns are a notch below the plants that produce seeds, since they bear neither seeds nor fruit. They reproduce by spores usually located on the underside of their leaves, which are called fronds.

BLADDER FERN, *Cystopteris bulbifera.* Moist, rich soil; 2 to 3 feet high; prefers shade. Has bulblets on fronds.

BRACKEN FERN, *(Pteris) Pteridium aquilinum.* Grows well in poor soil, but in deep, rich soil it may reach 6 or 7 feet. Sun or shade, likely to become weedy.

CHAIN FERN, *Woodwardia.* Likes acid, swampy soil and partial shade; 12 inches in height. *W. virginica* grows to 60 inches and likes wet soil.

CHRISTMAS FERN, *Polystichum acrostichoides.* Evergreen foliage, 10 to 30 inches in height. Sun or shade; moist soil, rich in leaf mold.

CINNAMON FERN, *Osmunda cinnamomea.* Four to 6 feet tall; sun or light shade; moist soil. Provides edible fiddleheads in spring.

CLIFF-BRAKE FERN, *Pellaea atropurpurea.* Semievergreen foliage; 4 to 12 inches high. Likes most soil, sun, or light shade. Good in rock gardens.

CLIMBING FERN. See Hartford Fern

CRESTED SHIELD FERN, *Dryopteris cristata.* Likes moist soil; shade; grows to 30 inches. Has dark green leathery fronds.

GLADE FERN, *Athyrium pycnocarpum.* Cool, moist, lime soil; shade; grows to 3 or 4 feet.

GOLDIE'S WOOD FERN, *Dryopteris goldiana.* Likes most soils; cool, shady spots; 4 to 5 feet high.

HARTFORD FERN, *Lygodium palmatum.* Vinelike, climbs to 5 feet. Moist, acid soil; shade. Not common, and not easy to grow.

HAY-SCENTED FERN, *Dennstaedtia punctilobula.* Will grow in most soils; sun or light shade; 24 to 30 inches in height. Can be weedy.

HOLLY FERN, *Polystichum brauni.* Deep green and leathery; 1 to 2 feet tall. Likes a deep, moist soil with a mulch and light shade.

INTERRUPTED FERN, *Osmunda claytoniana.* Massive beauty that grows to 4 feet or more. Moist soil, light shade. Easy to grow.

LADY FERN, *Athyrium filix-femina.* Moist soil; sun or light shade; 2 to 3 feet high.

LONG BEECH FERN, *Thelypteris phegopteris* (also known as *Dryopteris phegopteris*). Eighteen-inch fronds, 7 inches wide. Likes rich, moist, acid soil and full shade.

MAIDENHAIR FERN, *Adiantum pedatum.* Moist soil; shade; 8 to 20 inches tall. One of the prettiest ferns, with near-circular fronds that are horizontal to the ground.

MARGINAL SHIELD FERN, *Dryopteris marginalis.* Evergreen foliage; 12 to 30 inches tall. Moist soil; shade.

NEW YORK FERN, *Thelypteris noveboracensis.* Moist soil; shade; 2 feet tall.

OSTRICH FERN, *Matteuccia struthiopteris pensylvanica.* Grows to 6 feet. Moist, rich, wet soil; shade.

PURPLE CLIFF-BRAKE FERN. See Cliff-Brake Fern

RATTLESNAKE FERN, *Botrychium virginianum.* Early spring foliage; 12 to 30 inches high. Slightly acid, moist soil; shade.

ROYAL FERN, *Osmunda regalis.* Grows from 2 to 6 feet. Wet, acidic soil; sun or light shade. Will even grow in water.

SENSITIVE FERN, *Onoclea sensibilis.* Moist soil; sun or light shade; 6 to 24 inches high. Ornamental spore stalks.

VIRGINIA CHAIN FERN, *Woodwardia virginica.* Moist to wet soil; partial shade; 2 to 4 feet high.

WALKING FERN, *Camptosorus rhizophyllus.* Creeping plant that layers itself. Moist, lime soil; 5 to 12 inches in height. Rocky slopes or shade.

WOODSIA FERN, *Woodsia obtusa.* Medium dry soil; shade; 6 to 18 inches high. Good edging fern.

FEVERFEW. See *Chrysanthemum*

FILIPENDULA (fil-i-pen'dew-la), meadowsweet

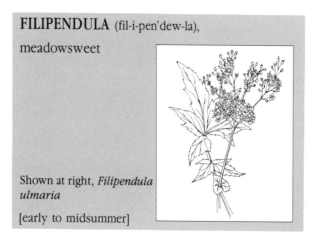

Shown at right, *Filipendula ulmaria*

[early to midsummer]

Fragrant white or light pink clusters of small flowers grace the tops of the hardy *Filipendulas*. Although there are many species, only a few are commonly found in catalogs or grown in gardens. They do well in any rich garden soil, but appreciate moisture and need extra water during the blooming season. They benefit from light shade.

F. hexapetala (also known as *F. vulgaris*), dropwort, 'Flore Pleno,' has tiny double roselike white flowers, and a height of 18 to 24 inches. *F. palmata* 'Elegans' has pale pink flowers and grows from 2 to 3 feet tall. *F. rubra* 'Venusta,' queen-of-the-prairie, is a giant at 6 feet, and has large plumes of pink flowers.

DISEASES. Leaf spot, mildew, rust.

PROPAGATION. By seed or by dividing the plants in early spring.

FLAX. See *Linum*

FLEABANE. See *Erigeron*

FLEECEFLOWER. See *Polygonum*

FORGET-ME-NOT. See *Myosotis*

FOXGLOVE. See *Digitalis*

FUNKIA. See *Hosta*

GAILLARDIA (gay-lar'dee-a),

blanketflower

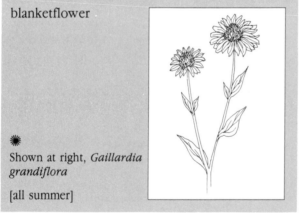

Shown at right, *Gaillardia grandiflora*

[all summer]

These showy flowers with their large daisylike blooms are a worthy addition to any garden not only because of their beauty but because they stay in bloom all summer. They are available in annual, biennial, and perennial forms, can have both single and double blooms, and various color combinations of red, yellow, and gold. Dwarf varieties start at 8 inches, but most grow from 15 to 24 inches tall. *Gaillardias* like full sun, and a rich, warm, sandy, well-drained soil. They are fairly hardy, but appreciate a heavy mulch for winter protection in the North.

G. aristata is common blanketflower, and numerous hybrid named varieties have been developed. Among the *G.* x *grandiflora* hybrids are 'Goblin' and the 'Monarch' strain.

DISEASES. Leaf spot, yellows.

INSECTS. Beetles, leafhoppers.

PROPAGATION. The common kinds and 'Monarchs' by seed. Other named varieties should be started by dividing the roots in early spring, or by taking cuttings in late summer from the new shoots that appear at the base of the plant. It is also possible to start a large number of plants by digging the entire clump in the fall, cutting the roots into small pieces, and planting them in flats in a warm greenhouse over the winter.

GALANTHUS (gay-lan'thus),

snowdrop

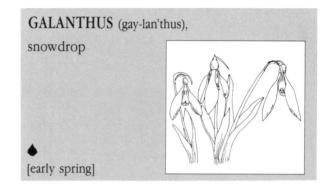

[early spring]

The white snowdrops with their droopy 1-inch blossoms are one of the first flowers of spring and are not fazed even by snow falling on them when they are in full bloom. They grow from bulbs, get 6 to 10 inches tall, and should be planted 3 inches deep in ordinary garden soil. They bloom best in light shade and their foliage disappears by summer. Most naturalize easily. *G. elwesii*, giant snowdrop, has the largest flowers, but many gardeners prefer the smaller-flowering *G. nivalis*, common snowdrop.

DISEASES. Blight.

INSECTS. Bulb flies, nematodes.

PROPAGATION. Either by separating the offsets after the foliage disappears in the spring, or by planting seeds.

GARDEN HELIOTROPE. See *Valeriana*

GAS PLANT. See *Dictamnus*

GAYFEATHER. See *Liatris*

GENTIAN. See *Gentiana*

GENTIANA (jen-she-a'na),

gentian

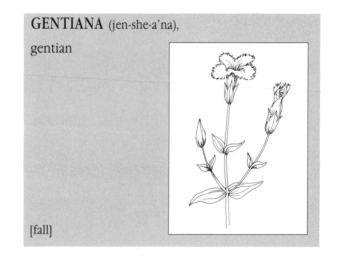

[fall]

Hailed in poetry and paintings, these rich blue flowers of the woods, blooming barely before the start of winter, have always delighted nature lovers. To grow them in the garden, their natural habitat should be duplicated as much as possible. Moist, woodsy, acid soil, partial shade, and a mulch of leaves all help create this environment, but even so, gentians are not easy to grow. They are difficult to transplant, and if grown from seed, the seed should be very fresh. This is not easy because the flowers bloom so late in the season that the seed often doesn't fully mature before it freezes. Even when seed is available, the resulting seedlings are often small and delicate, and easily lost.

The most attractive gentian, *Gentianopsis crinita*, the famous fringed gentian, is a biennial which makes its growth the first year, blooms the next, and then dies. Both the fringed gentian and the bottle or closed gentian (*Gentiana andrewsii*) are on the endangered list in most states, so if you choose these varieties, buy them from a nursery rather than dig them from the wild. *G. andrewsii* grows to about 18 inches and the blooms look like tight purple-blue buds. *G. septemfida* var. *lagodechiana*, crested gentian, has deep blue, bell-shaped blooms, attains a height of 6 to 12 inches, and is one of the easiest gentians for any gardener to grow.

DISEASES. Blight, leaf spot, rust.

PROPAGATION. Grow from seed or divide in early spring.

GERANIUM (jer-ray'ni-um),
crane's bill

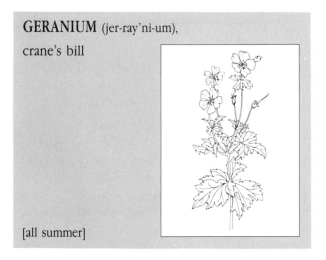

[all summer]

Don't confuse this hardy garden plant with the plants commonly called geraniums, which are used for houseplants, window boxes, and bedding plants. Officially those are the *Pelargoniums*, related to the geranium, but not hardy enough to be included here.

The term crane's bill refers to the bill-like extension beyond the seeds. The plants form mounds of deep green foliage up to 2 feet in diameter, with small 1- to 2-inch pink, red, lavender, white, or purple blossoms that appear over the surface. Their size and shape makes them good plants for the front of a border, or along garden paths.

In recent years many named varieties have been developed that are especially good for the perennial border, and many of the wild species are ideal for the rock or wildflower garden. The garden kinds like sun, the wild ones prefer light shade. Ordinary garden soil that never becomes too dry suits them, and they must be divided frequently to keep them under control.

The assortment carried by each catalog and nursery varies. *G. cinereum* grows to 8 inches; the 'Ballerina' cultivar has deep pink flowers, and those of 'Splendens' are crimson-red. *G. dalmaticum* grows about 6 inches tall with pink flowers; *G. endressii* (Pyrenean crane's bill) 'Wargrave Pink' is an improved European cultivar, 15 inches high, with clear, deep, pink flowers. *G. grandiflorum* (lilac crane's bill) is 12 inches high and has lavender-blue flowers that appear in early summer. *G. sanguineum* is called blood red crane's bill because it has magenta flowers that blossom for most of the summer; it grows to 15 inches and self-sows so easily that it may become weedy. *G. s. lancastrense* has a profusion of pink flowers in midsummer.

DISEASES. Leaf spot, mildew, rust, virus.

INSECTS. Plant bugs.

PROPAGATION. Species grow easily from seed. Divide named cultivars in early spring.

GEUM (jee'um),
avens

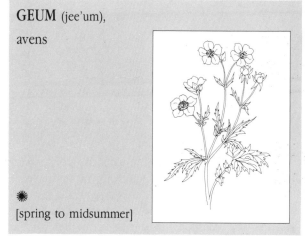

✳
[spring to midsummer]

The *Geums* are bright spots of orange, red, and yellow in either the border or rockery. They are low growing, usually less than 15 inches tall, and many have flowers up to 3 inches across. They prefer full sun or light shade, and ordinary soil that holds moisture well but doesn't stay wet over the winter. None do well in hot climates, but thrive instead where summers are cool and the winters fairly mild, although even in the best habitat they are often short-lived.

G. quellyon, also known as *G. chiloense* (Chilean avens), is a popular variety, but it needs winter protection in the North. Many improved varieties have been developed including 'Lady Stratheden,' a double yellow; and 'Mrs. Bradshaw,' a semidouble scarlet, 24 inches high. *G. x borisii* (Boris avens, 12 inches high) is a dwarf grower and a good ground cover, with cultivars that include 'Dolly North,' an orange yellow; 'Fire Opal,' which is bright flame-colored; and 'Red Wings,' a semidouble red.

INSECTS. Spider mites.

PROPAGATION. By division in spring, by cuttings taken in early summer, or by seed.

GLOBEFLOWER. See *Trollius*

GLOBE THISTLE. See *Echinops*

GLORIOSA DAISY. See *Rudbeckia*

GOAT'S BEARD. See *Aruncus*

GOLDEN MARGUERITE. See *Anthemis*

GOLDENROD. See *Solidago*

GOLDENTUFT. See *Alyssum*

GOUTWEED. See *Aegopodium*

GRAPE HYACINTH. See *Muscari*

GRASSES, ORNAMENTAL

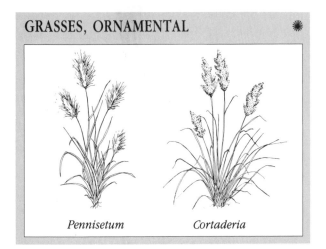

Pennisetum   *Cortaderia*

Many years ago we tested a new quack grass herbicide that worked by removing the chlorophyl from the leaves and turning the clumps perfectly white. In the next few weeks we were surprised how many people asked if they could buy the beautiful ornamental grass for their gardens! Up until that time, like most gardeners, we had felt that grass was suitable in fields and lawns, but certainly did not belong in a garden. After seeing showy varieties in city parks and arboretums, we realized we were wrong and that grasses can be as lovely as flowers. Unfortunately, their use is limited because many need a great deal of room, can grow to a height of 20 feet, some are not hardy, and a few are fussy about soils.

Propagate grasses by dividing the clumps in spring or by planting seed. When using seed, give the plants plenty of space at each stage of their development—seedling bed, transplant bed, and final planting—or poor growth will be the result. Grasses with variegated foliage should only be propagated by dividing the clumps, since they won't ordinarily come true from seed.

ARRHENATHERUM (ar-ren-a'ther-um), oat grass. An early summer, low-growing grass (8 inches high) with green and white leaves. Later, the plants die to the soil, and then re-sprout. It makes an attractive white edging for a perennial border or as an occasional contrasting single clump.

ARUNDO (a-run'doh), giant reed. Most spectacular of the ornamental grasses, sometimes reaching a height of 20 feet. Growing from the stem, which is similar to a cornstalk, are long, bright green leaves. In late summer, reddish plumes over a foot tall bloom at the top of the stalk; they turn a silvery gray later in the season. *Arundo* is useful as a single specimen in a large bed, as a background plant, or in a natural garden. It likes deep, rich soil and sun, but needs protection in the colder climates. There are also variegated species.

BAMBOO (bam-boo'). Most of the hundreds of bamboos are tropical plants, and even many of the so-called hardy ones need some winter protection in the North. All are more branchy than the tropical species that produce garden stakes and fishing poles. In the East, most bamboos grow best near the coast from Long Island south and along the Gulf of Mexico. On the West Coast they grow best in California, Arizona, and close to the coast of Oregon. They like deep, fertile moist soil that is well drained.

Bamboos have woody stems that are sometimes hollow, and are the same diameter at the top as at the base. They grow rapidly, and many are attractive, but the running types which spread from underground rhizomes can become very weedy and difficult to eradicate.

Three main genera are considered hardy in the temperate United States: the *Arundinarias* (running types), the *Bambusas* (clump types), and the *Phyllostachys* (both clump and running types).

Arundinaria variegata (dwarf whitestripe bamboo) has green and white leaves and is hardy to southern New England. It grows about 30 inches tall, and like other running types spreads rapidly and must be kept under control. It is often used for contrasting effect in the border. *A. simonii* (Simon bamboo) grows very tall, often more than 15 feet, with narrow green leaves that sometimes have white stripes. It spreads less rapidly than most other sorts; the young shoots are edible.

Most of the *Bambusa* group are natives of China, India, and Burma, and are hardy only in the South. *B. palmata* (also known as *Sasa palmata*) gets to be 8 feet tall, with leaves over a foot long and 3 inches wide.

Phyllostachys aurea, fishpole or golden bamboo, grows to 20 feet, with light green canes that turn yellow as they mature. The young shoots are edible in early spring.

Propagate clump bamboos by dividing the clumps in late winter. The running bamboos can be propagated by taking 12-inch root cuttings when the plants are dormant. Do not allow new plants to dry out during the first year of growth.

CORTADERIA (kor-ta-der'ee-a), pampas grass. Pampas is one of the most showy of the grasses—it can grow from

10 to 20 feet tall and has long, white, silky plumes that appear in late summer. It is widely planted in parks and large borders. Available at many perennial nurseries, it grows well in ordinary soils, in full sun. The plants are either male or female, but only the females produce plumes. It is too tender for northern areas, and must either be mulched heavily or dug up and wintered over in a cold frame or root cellar. A mature clump of these grasses creates such a striking effect that they are well worth the trouble.

C. selloana (pampas grass) grows to 10 feet or more, and has an abundance of white showy plumes in late summer. *C. s.* 'Rosea' has pink plumes.

Propagate by division.

ERIANTHUS (er-ri-anth'us), ravenna or plume grass. Ravenna grass (*E. ravennae*) resembles pampas grass, but is shorter (5 to 12 feet) and less showy. It is hardier, however, and looks nice in either the perennial or shrub border. Like full sun and ordinary garden soil.

FESTUCA (fes-tew'ka), fescue. There are many species of this grass. *F. ovina glauca*, blue fescue, is a popular kind. Grows only 12 inches tall with plumes reaching well above it. The silvery blue foliage is evergreen. Quite hardy; doesn't become rank in the border, so it is useful as an edging plant.

MISCANTHUS SINENSIS (mis-kan'thus), eulalia grass. Several cultivars of this 10-foot grass make excellent ornamentals; they increase in size slowly, and grow well in good garden soil and full sun. Among them are *M. s.* 'Gracillimus,' maiden grass, 4 to 5 feet tall, with silvery green leaves, and feathery plumes; *M. s. purpurascens*, 3 to 4 feet in height, purple-red foliage in late summer; *M. s.* 'Zebrinus,' the well-known zebra grass, which has yellow and green leaves that are marked crossways, and pink or beige plumes; and *M. s.* 'Variegatus,' striped eulalia grass, its white and yellow leaves are marked lengthwise.

Miscanthus is best propagated by cutting apart and planting the large clumps of roots while they are dormant in early spring.

PENNISETUM SETACEUM (pen-i-see'tum), fountain grass. *P. setaceum*, 3 to 4 feet in height, is a native of Ethiopia, with narrow leaves and foot-long plumes that vary from copper color to rose red in different cultivars. Grows in good garden soil, full sun, and should be protected over the winter in northern regions. Colored varieties are best propagated by root division in spring; others grow easily from seed.

PHALARIS ARUNDINACEA PICTA (fal'a-ris), ribbon grass. Of the *Phalaris*, this particular green and white striped species, 2 to 4 feet in height, is one of the hardiest and easiest to grow. It can get weedy, so is more appropriate to a grass garden than a perennial border. The best color appears where the soil is moist and not too fertile. When planted along brooks and ponds it spreads rapidly by underground stolens, but in dry soil it grows more slowly and is easier to control.

STIPA PENNATA (sty'pa), European feather grass. This one reaches a height of 3 feet and is grown for its feathery plumes that are sometimes a foot long. Needs winter protection in northern zones. Likes sun and ordinary soil, and is propagated by seeds or division.

GYPSOPHILA (jip-sof'fill-a), baby's-breath

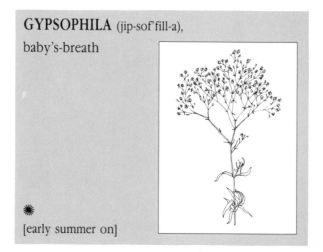

✳
[early summer on]

Lovely in the garden, as a filler in bouquets, and excellent as a dried flower, the *Gypsophilas* are important additions to any border. The clouds of tiny, lacy, white flowers are familiar to most anyone who has seen a floral arrangement. The taller kinds (3 to 4 feet) fit into the border nicely, and the dwarf varieties are useful as an edging or in the rock garden. They like full sun, lots of water, and well-drained, lime (the word *Gypsophila* derives from the Greek, meaning fond of lime) garden soil. They need space to grow to their full size and beauty without being moved because their long taproot does not like to be disturbed.

The best varieties of *Gypsophila* are grafted and these should be planted so that the graft union is set 1 to 2 inches below the soil surface, to encourage root formation above the graft. Pick the flowers as soon as they fade and the plants will keep blooming. Stake them, if necessary.

G. paniculata (baby's-breath) has single flowers, but some of the improved varieties are double. 'Perfecta' grows 3 feet tall and just about as wide, producing large double-white flowers for several weeks in midsummer. 'Bristol Fairy' is 4 feet tall, has smaller double-white flowers that also bloom over a long period. 'Pink Fairy' grows about 18 inches tall and has large double-pink flowers in profusion almost until frost.

G. repens (creeping baby's-breath) is a creeping variety, 4 to 6 inches high, that spreads rapidly; it is best for the rockery or to trail over a wall. 'Alba' is the white variety, and 'Rosea' a fine pink.

DISEASES. Botrytis, crown gall, yellows.

INSECTS. Leafhoppers.

PROPAGATION. Ordinary forms of *Gypsophila* are grown

from seed or by cuttings. *G. repens* can be divided, but the best kinds are difficult to obtain from cuttings and do not come true from seed, so are cleft grafted on seedlings of *G. paniculata*. Grafting is done in midwinter on potted seedlings in a greenhouse.

Plants may also be grafted in summer, and the new plants sheltered in a tight, shaded cold frame over the winter until the graft has healed. Then they should be hardened off by gradually opening the frame a bit more each day before being planted outdoors. Young plants should be protected over the winter.

HEATHS AND HEATHERS

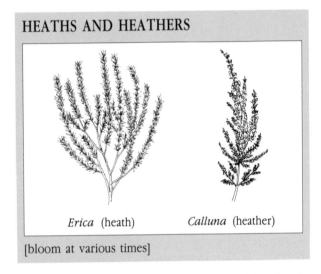

Erica (heath)   *Calluna* (heather)

[bloom at various times]

Along a path, in a rock garden, as an edging for the border, along a foundation, but especially on a gentle sloping bank, the heaths and heathers with their lavender, pink, and white blooms are a welcome sight from early summer on. When cut, the flowers last a long time and dry beautifully. The foliage comes in various shades of green, red, and gray. The plants thrive in acid soil that is well supplied with compost or peat moss, and do best when sheltered from drying winds in both winter and summer. Most need regular pruning in early spring to keep them in good form. Given all this, and a bonny bit of protective covering for the winter, they warm the heart of even a non-Scot.

The heath and heather family is so huge that only a voluminous work could describe them all. Therefore, only a few of the most readily available kinds are described below.

The true Scotch heather, *Calluna vulgaris*, are shrubby plants that bloom in summer with small purple flowers that last for the rest of the season. A large number of improved hybrids have been developed, most of which grow from 12 to 15 inches tall, and also bloom in mid- to late summer. Among these fine cultivars are:

'Blazeaway'—light lilac blooms and golden foliage
'County Wicklow'—double pink blooms
'Gold Haze'—white blooms, yellow foliage
'Golden Carpet'—only 2 inches tall, pink blooms, yellow foliage that turns to orange-red for the winter
'H. E. Beale'—24 inches tall, a spreading type with double pink blooms

'Kinlochruel'—15 inches high, double white blooms
'Martha Herman'—12 inches in height, white blooms
'Mrs. R. H. Gray'—3 inches in height, lavender blooms
'Silver Queen'—12 inches in height, pink flowers, silvery foliage

Daboecia cantabrica, Irish heath, grows from 15 to 18 inches tall, with tiny white, pink, or purple flowers in mid- to late summer. It grows well only in very acid soil with plenty of peat. Named varieties include 'Alba,' white; 'Bicolor,' white and purple; 'Nana,' a dwarf variety; and 'Pallida,' pink blooms.

Erica (heath) is similar to heather in appearance and culture. A native of the Mediterranean region and South Africa, it benefits from a sheltered location and winter protection. All grow best in areas where the frost-free season is long and the soil rich in peat moss.

E. carnea (spring heath) prefers acid soil but is slightly more tolerant of lime than most of the others. *E. c.* 'Aurea' has pink blooms in early spring; 'Pink Spangles,' is 10 inches high, has large pink flowers, blooms in early spring; 'Springwood Pink,' a low-growing pink; 'Springwood White,' a low-growing white; 'Vivelli,' dwarf and spreading, red blooms early in the season, red foliage in fall; 'Winter Beauty,' pink blooms during late winter and early spring in mild climates.

E. cinerea, twisted or gray heath, common in Scotland, grows to 2 feet, must have acid soil, and blooms in mid-summer. Cultivars include: 'Atrorubens,' dwarf with red flowers; 'C. D. Eason,' red flowers with a pleasant fragrance; 'Golden Drop,' dwarf with pink flowers and yellow foliage; and 'P. S. Patrick,' purple flowers.

E. vagans, Cornish heath, is a spreading plant, 12 inches high, that blooms from mid- to late summer. The cultivar 'Lyonesse' has white flowers, 'Mrs. D. F. Maxwell,' has bright red flowers, and 'St. Keverne' has pink flowers.

DISEASES. Mildew, mold, rot, rust.

INSECTS. Mites, scales.

PROPAGATION. Heaths and heathers are not easy to propagate. The best varieties are started from cuttings that are treated with a root-promoting chemical and rooted in a greenhouse. Seeds can be germinated in a shaded cold frame in early spring, or during the winter in a greenhouse.

HELENIUM (hell-lee'ni-um), sneezeweed

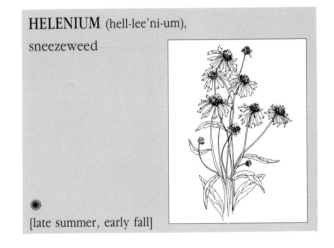

[late summer, early fall]

This plant gets its scientific name from Helen of Troy, and the common name arose because the dried flowers were formerly ground into a dust that stimulated sneezing.

The *Heleniums* are closely related to the sunflower and the blooms are similar. They grow from 1 to 6 feet tall, with large flat blossoms of yellow, crimson, bronze, or various combinations thereof, and produce an abundance of attractive, long-lasting cut flowers. They are excellent plants for a large border, and bloom at a time when their colors complement the chrysanthemums and autumn leaves. Most soil types are acceptable, even wet ones; they need full sun, and should be divided every spring for best results.

H. autumnale (common sneezeweed) is most commonly planted. Some popular varieties include: 'Brilliant,' 36 inches high, a heavy bloomer in a variety of colors; 'Butterpat,' clear yellow, about the same height; 'Golden Youth,' 36 inches high, light yellow blooms; 'Riverton Beauty,' an old favorite, grows to about 4 feet with yellow flowers and a dark center; and 'Pumilum,' 24 inches in height, yellow and red blossoms. *H. hoopesii*, orange sneezeweed, is clear yellow or orange, a native of the Rocky Mountains, and blooms in early summer. It grows about 24 inches tall.

DISEASES. Leaf spot, mildew, rust.

INSECTS. Beetles.

PROPAGATION. Division is possible, but because the plants tend to be short-lived, it is better to plant seeds in summer as soon as they are ripe. Cuttings taken in spring root well.

HELIANTHEMUM (he-li-an'thee-mum), sun rose

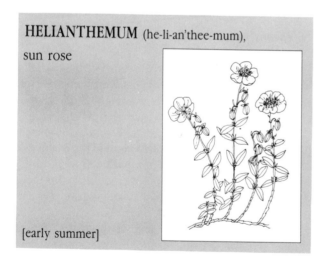

[early summer]

The sun rose is a shrubby evergreen plant, grows 8 to 20 inches tall, with yellow flowers resembling those of a single rose. They like full sun and light, dry, lime soil. They do best if severely cut back after blooming, and all varieties benefit from winter protection in the northern states.

H. appeninum, Apennine sun rose, has cultivars known as 'Roseum' (clear pink flowers on 8-inch stems) and 'Wendle's Rose' (bright pink flowers and wider leaves). *H. nummularium*, common sun rose, has single or double flowers in early summer, and grows about a foot high. Among the *H. n.* cultivars are 'Buttercup' which has golden yellow flowers and blooms later; 'Fire Dragon' that has coppery red ones, and 'St. Mary's' that has white blooms in mid- to late summer. *H. n. multiplex* is best for rock gardens since it is a trailing plant with small leaves, and can withstand the rigors of rock garden life.

PROPAGATION. By division. But cuttings taken in early summer root so easily that this method is common when large numbers of plants are wanted.

HELIANTHUS (he-lee-an'thus), sunflower

[midsummer to fall]

This large genus includes the familiar annual sunflower, as well as a wide variety of perennials with yellow and gold blossoms—some are valuable for the border, others are ugly weeds.

Some *Helianthus* grow 10 or more feet tall, but even the shorter ones are so coarse and conspicuous that they are really only suitable for planting in the back of the border. Easy to grow as long as they have full sun and rich, deep, moist garden soil. For best results, add generous amounts of manure. The clumps should be divided every year. Some varieties need winter protection in the North.

H. angustifolius, swamp sunflower, is native to southeastern swamps, has purple petals on small flowers, and a height of 3 to 7 feet. *H. decapetalus*, thinleaf sunflower, is most often found in catalogs because of its height, 4 to 5 feet, and is appropriate for most plantings. It blooms in mid- to late summer; both 'Flora Pleno' and 'Soleil d'Or' have double blossoms.

H. maximiliani, Maximilian sunflower, grows to 10 feet in a favorable location. Native to the Midwest, it has 3-inch flowers, and can grow in dry soil; it blooms later than other sunflower species, often as late as October. *H. mollis*, ashy sunflower, is 4 feet tall, has grayish, heart-shaped leaves covered with hairs, and pale yellow blooms with dark centers.

H. tuberosus, Jerusalem artichoke, has sunflowerlike flowers, but is seldom used in perennial plantings because it is too large and too vigorous. The tubers are eaten both raw and cooked, and are especially popular as diet foods.

DISEASES. Crown gall, leaf spot, mildew, stem rot.

INSECTS. Aphids, beetles.

PROPAGATION. By dividing the roots in early spring or late fall, or take cuttings in early summer.

HELIOPSIS (he-li-op'sis), sunflower heliopsis

[all summer]

Another sunflower-type flower, but one that has lost favor because so many similar flowers are better. The 3- to 5-foot plants are sun-loving, hardy, and easy to grow (they will tolerate even poor soils). Resembling zinnias, the large orange and yellow flowers, both single and double, are produced for a long period throughout the summer, and are good for cutting.

H. helianthoides (sunflower heliopsis) has single flowers of thick texture with single leaves. *H. h.* 'Pitcherana,' an improved variety, has larger blooms and better color. *H. h. scabra* (rough heliopsis) has, predictably, rough leaves. Improved varieties include 'Golden Plume,' with large double yellow blooms, and 'Karat' with large single blooms of clear yellow on 4-foot stems.

DISEASES. Crown gall, leaf spot, mildew, stem rot.

INSECTS. Aphids, beetles.

PROPAGATION. By division, seeds, or cuttings taken in early summer

HELIOTROPE, GARDEN. See *Valeriana*

HELLEBORUS (hell-e-bor'us),
Christmas rose
Lenten rose

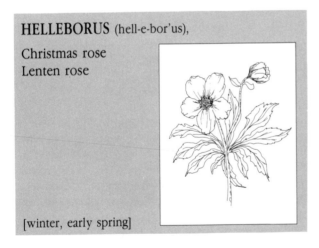

[winter, early spring]

Although it doesn't always live up to its name by blooming on December 25th, *H. niger* (Christmas rose) flowers at various times during the winter in mild climates, and in early spring in the North. The greenish white or pinkish 2- to 4-inch buttercup-shaped flowers come on 12-inch

stems and last a month or more. It likes winter sun and summer shade, but may take years after it has been moved to become established enough to bloom well again. In the North, winter precautions are recommended, and some gardeners build a protective frame covered with plastic that is placed over the plants. They need rich, well-drained soil, and should be set with the crowns 1 inch beneath the soil. The 'Altifolius' cultivar has somewhat larger blooms. In mild climates, *H. lividus corsicus* may be grown—it is 18 inches high, has pale green flowers, and interesting grayish foliage. *H. orientalis* (Lenten rose), blooms later than *H. niger*, has white and purple blooms and grows to 18 inches.

DISEASES. Leaf spot, mildew, rot.

INSECTS. Slugs.

PROPAGATION. By dividing the roots or by planting seed in a cold frame or greenhouse as soon as it is ripe. Seedlings take two or more years before they bloom.

HEMEROCALLIS (hem-mer-o-kal'lis), daylily

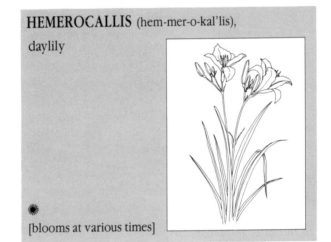

[blooms at various times]

Forty years ago an entry on the rather ordinary daylily would have merited only a short description, but since that time the rust-colored tawny, the yellow lemon lily, and the common early orange daylily have been hybridized into thousands of gorgeous flowers that deserve a prominent place in every garden. Fortunately, most of the qualities of old-time daylilies, including vigor, hardiness, dependability, and ease of culture and propagation, have not been greatly diminished. At present, they are probably the perennial most planted in American gardens.

The daylily has been described as the perfect flower because it grows so easily, multiplies well, is easy to care for, and is not susceptible to insects or disease. It can be used in nearly any landscape plan, and comes in a wide variety of heights, forms, and colors. The lilylike shape fits well in a formal border, yet is natural enough to plant along paths, fences, pools, and foundations, and the dwarf varieties are excellent for rock gardens and even under trees. For the more practical gardener, the buds and blossoms are delicious stir-fried, and the roots can be peeled and cooked or sliced into salads.

Each flower lasts only a day. Some open in the morning and fade at dusk, but others stay open until midnight. A few open in the evening and last through the next day. In spite of the short life of individual flowers, the *Hemerocallis* blooming season is longer than for many other perennials. Each plant produces many buds, and since the numerous varieties bloom at different times, it is possible to enjoy blossoms for the entire summer and early fall. As a bonus, if a storm wrecks all the blooms one day, the new flowers that appear the next morning will be fresh and undamaged!

Daylilies like to grow in full sun, but most don't mind some light afternoon shade. The red and pink varieties sometimes have better color if they are shielded somewhat from the hot afternoon sun.

Daylilies like soil that is fertile, well drained, and slightly acid to neutral in pH. The soil should be loose and deep because their root system becomes very large, and most years they need to be watered during the growing season in order to get the best blooms. They need dividing every six to ten years.

Hemerocallis are classified as dormant, evergreen, or semi-evergreen. Dormants are usually hardy and will do well throughout the country. Evergreens and semi-evergreens vary widely in frost resistance, and these varieties should be planted experimentally in the North since very few have been able to adapt to northern conditions.

Presently there are more than 45,000 named cultivars of *Hemerocallis*. This mind-boggling assortment resulted from thousands of crosses among Oriental wild species, including the following:

H. altissima—very clear yellow, night blooming, and very tall

H. aurantiaca (orange daylily)—an orange evergreen

H. dumortieri (early daylily)—a vigorous early orange

H. fulva (tawny daylily)—the tawny roadside daylily that has gone wild in much of the country. 'Europa,' the best-known variety of this, is an excellent ground cover and is used in shady, wild gardens.

H. lilioasphodelus, also known as *H. flava* (lemon daylily)— quite fragrant, was a favorite of our ancestors

H. middendorffii (Middendorff daylily)—a pale orange dwarf

H. multiflora (mayflower daylily)—has a great many orange flowers on each scape (flower stalk)

The remarkable cultivars available today have come about because plant breeders recognized the many possibilities in these and other species. The discovery that the alkaloid known as colchicine could increase the number of plant chromosomes made even larger blooms and new color combinations possible, and these showy tetraploid mutations increase in popularity each year.

DISEASES. Leaf spot.

INSECTS. Daylilies are bothered by few pests, but Japanese beetles, mites, and thrips are possible problems.

PROPAGATION. By dividing the roots in early spring or in late summer after they finish blooming. The small pro-liferations, or slips, that develop on the flower stalks can also be rooted in moist sand or sandy soil. Plants grown from the seed of hybrids will vary greatly, but are often quite good.

BUYING DAYLILIES. Because of the huge number of varieties available, selecting a few of the best plants for a small border can be difficult. Besides the wide range of colors, there are trumpet shapes, flat forms, miniatures, giants, talls, dwarfs, night-bloomers; those with fragrance; double blooms and large loose blooms called "spiders."

If possible, before ordering from a catalog, visit a nursery, perhaps one that specializes in daylilies, or tour a display garden or arboretum when the plants are in bloom. Don't be too anxious to order all the newest creations. New cultivars can cost up to $200 each, and though many are truly outstanding, sometimes only an expert can distinguish the expensive ones from those costing $5 or $10.

What kinds you buy should depend on where you want to plant them. For mass plantings, you may want to consider some of the inexpensive, older, vigorous kinds that have withstood the test of time.

'Autumn Red'
'Bell Tel,' yellow
'Formal Affair,' peach
'Green Ice,' pale yellow
'Gusto,' red
'Sandalwood,' orange-pink
'Talisman,' orange
'Tijuana,' orange-yellow
'Winning Ways,' yellow-green

Dwarf varieties for the front of the border or rock garden include:

'Ed Murray,' red
'Little Butterfly,' yellow
'Little Delight,' pink
'Renee,' yellow
'Sleigh Ride,' red
'Stella D'Oro,' a yellow that blooms nearly all summer

For extra tall background plants, use the 5- to 6-foot *H. altissimas* 'Autumn Minaret,' 'Challenger,' and 'Statuesque.' If you want a giant-sized, loose-petaled spider-type, try 'Kindly Light.'

Beautiful choices for border or foundation plants appear below. These are proven cultivars and are suitable for gardens in both the North or South. Note that only the predominating color is listed, and many blooms are combinations of two or more shades. Check catalog descriptions for further information about size, flower shapes, and height of plant. Blooming times are indicated by E (early in the growing season), M (midseason), and L (late in the season).

'Abstract Art'—buff with coral (M)
'American Revolution'—one of the darkest reds (M)

'Astolat'—near white (M)
'August Flame'—red (L)
'Bold Baron'—purple with white stripes (L)
'Chicago Brave'—yellow (L)
'Chicago Royal'—purple tones (M)
'Disneyland'—blend of pink, orchid, and yellow (M)
'Double Gold'—rich yellow (M)
'Firecup'—bright red (E)
'Grandfather Time'—red (M)
'Grandways'—lavender-rose (E)
'Helen Connelley'—pale orchid (M)
'Hudson Valley'—yellow (M)
'Ice Carnival'—creamy white (M)
'Lovely Dancer'—rose-peach (M)
'Peppermint Lounge'—rose-pink (M)
'Pink Snow Flakes'—pale pink (M)
'Prairie Charmer'—pink with purple eye (M)
'Prairie Moonlight'—light yellow (M)
'Radiant Greetings'—orange-yellow, red halo (M)
'Rocket City'—bright orange-yellow (M)
'Royal Flair'—purple-lavender, wine eye (M)
'Silver Circus'—yellow with pink (E)
'World of Peace'—pink-white (L)

HEN-AND-CHICKENS. See *Sempervivum*

HERBS. See chapter 24

HERON'S BILL. See *Erodium*

HESPERIS (hes'per-is),
sweet rocket

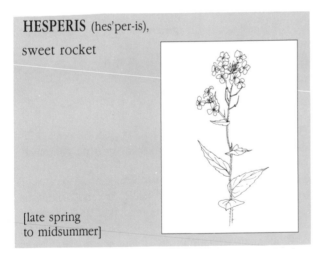

[late spring
to midsummer]

For the fragrant or wild garden, *H. matronalis* (sweet rocket) with its lavender, pink, or white phloxlike blooms, is a good choice (3 feet high). It can even be planted in the regular border if you pick off the flowers before they go to seed; otherwise it will take control. Because it is a short-lived perennial, you may want to leave a bloom or two to get replacement seeds, but be sure to keep an eye on those blossoms. Keeping the flowers picked also encourages the plants to bloom all season.

DISEASES. Club root, mildew, mosaic, rust.

HEUCHERA SANGUINEA (hew'ker-a),
coral bells

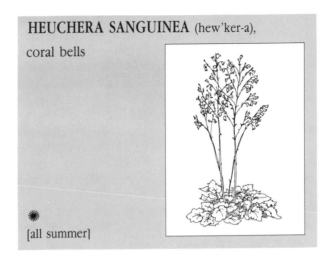

✳
[all summer]

We have seen large flower borders completely edged with red or pink coral bells—it was an impressive sight. The leaf clumps of this dainty plant are compact and grow only a few inches tall; the brightly colored stalks of tiny bell-shaped flowers are borne on 15-inch flower spikes. *Heuchera* likes rich, moist soil, full or nearly full sun, and requires some winter protection in northern areas where snow cover is uncertain. They are good rock plants, and a clump tucked here or there along a border is always effective because of their long blooming season.

Numerous named varieties of *H. sanguinea* (coral bells) have been developed. Pink shades include 'Edge Hall,' 'Pride of Nancy,' 'Rhapsody,' and 'Rosamunde." Among the bright reds are 'Grenade,' 'Matin Bells,' 'Mt. St. Helens,' 'Pluie de Feu,' and 'Queen of Hearts.' 'Alba,' 'June Bride,' 'Virginale,' and 'White Cloud' are among the white cultivars.

DISEASES. Stem rot.

INSECTS. Mealybugs, weevils.

PROPAGATION. Coral bells may be grown from seed that are best sown inside during late winter; they will bloom in two years. Propagate named varieties by dividing the plants just about any time, but if done in late summer or fall overwinter the plants in a cold frame until they develop a good root system.

HIBISCUS (hy-bis'kus),
rose mallow

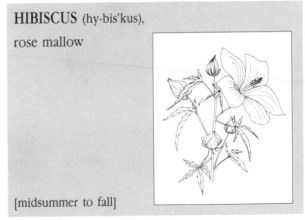

[midsummer to fall]

The Mallows are a large family that includes many plants, from small wildflowers to tropical trees that are grown inside as houseplants in the North.

For a real conversation stopper, grow a few *H. moscheutos* (common rose mallow) hybrids in your garden and cut them for a mammoth bouquet. The flat, 6- to 12-inch flowers come in a wide range of colors, but their size and the plant's 3- to 6-foot height make them suitable for only large gardens. In the right location they make an impressive display, as they do when planted as small shrubs in the landscape. *H. moscheutos* grow well in sun or light shade, and because they should be set 3 or 4 inches deep in rich, moist soil, they are slow to sprout in the spring. Unfortunately for northern gardeners, they bloom late and are not easy to cover, so often get caught in an early frost. The roots are tender, which makes a protective mulch over the winter necessary.

Perennial nurseries sell named varieties, and seed catalogs offer seed in both mixtures and separate colors. 'Frisbee' is a new, early-blooming variety.

DISEASES. Leaf spot, gall, rust.

INSECTS. Aphids, Japanese beetles, scales.

PROPAGATION. Usually from seed; if started inside in midwinter, the plant will produce blooms the first year making it possible to grow them as annuals. With care, the roots of named varieties can be divided in the spring.

HIMALAYAN BLUE POPPY. See *Meconopsis*

HOLLYHOCK. See *Althaea*

HONESTY. See *Lunaria*

HOSTA (hos'ta), plantainlily funkia

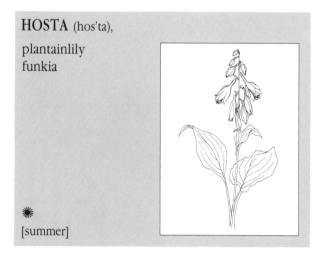

✳
[summer]

The hardy hostas produce blue, lavender, or white blooms on long leafless stalks, but the plants are grown as much for their beautiful foliage clumps and because they prosper in shady locations. Hundreds of hybrids have been developed that range in size from small dwarfs to giant-sized specimens, with leaves of all shapes in white, yellow,

blue, and variegated shades. Even those who have always regarded hostas as weeds have to admit the colorful new hybrids bear little resemblance to the uninteresting plants of a few decades ago, and thousands of varieties make them a collector's dream.

Hostas are low-maintenance plants that often thrive where other desirable plants refuse to grow. They look nice on a shady bank, along a woodland path, and as an edging for a shrub or wildflower garden. They are also useful under trees, and as foundation plants on the shady side of buildings, hedges, or high fences. Although they much prefer light shade, they will grow in full sun if the soil is moist, deep, and well supplied with humus and nutrients.

The many named cultivars have not always been well classified, and you may find the same plant being sold under several different names. The numerous hosta species are better defined, however. They are listed below according to the species name.

H. decorata (blunt plantainlily) is a dwarf variety, usually less than 18 inches tall. Because of a compact growth habit, it makes a good edging plant. It has green and white leaves, dark blue flowers, and spreads quickly.

H. fortunei (fortune's plantainlily) has flower spikes that can grow to 3 feet; blooms in July with flowers that are lavender to white. *H. f.* var. *gigantea* (also known as *H. elata*) has huge green leaves and grows quickly to an impressive clump. *H. f.* 'Hyacinthina' has blue-green leaves and lavender flowers; 'Marginato-alba' has green leaves with a white margin.

H. lancifolia (narrowleaf plantainlily, 2 feet high) has narrow green leaves, lavender flowers, and blooms later than most others. *H. plantaginea* (fragrant plantainlily) blooms in late summer and fall, has fragrant white flowers on 2-foot stems, and makes a good ground cover. It needs winter mulch in northern locations where a heavy snow cover is uncertain. The hybrid 'Royal Standard' has pale green leaves and fragrant white blooms on 30-inch stems that appear in late summer and fall.

H. sieboldiana (Siebold plantainlily, 18 to 30 inches high) from Japan, has blue-green leaves and many hybrid descendants. *H. s.* 'Frances Williams,' for example, has bluish leaves with gold edges and is one of the most popular hostas.

H. undulata (wavyleaf plantainlily) has wavy leaves and variegated foliage that is most attractive in shade; it blooms in July and the flowers range from lavender to blue. *H. u.* 'Univittata' has green and creamy white leaves. *H. ventricosa* (blue plantainlily) has shiny green leaves and large purple blooms.

Other popular varieties include many of uncertain ancestry, but they are usually hybrids of several species. Blue foliage types include 'Hadspan Blue,' 'Love Pat,' and 'Elegans.' Those with gold or variegated yellow leaves are 'Ginko Gold,' 'Gold Standard,' 'Piedmont Gold,' 'Sum and Substance,' and 'Kabitan' (this particular variety grows less than a foot tall and is especially good for edging and for planting in moist rock gardens). Among white variegated kinds are 'Francee,' 'Fringe Benefit,' 'Medop-pica,' and 'Thomas Hogg.'

DISEASES. Crown rot, leaf spot.

INSECTS. Caterpillars, slugs.

PROPAGATION. By dividing the clumps in early spring. Or you can experiment with seeds and see what develops.

HOUND'S TONGUE. See *Cynoglossum*

HOUSELEEK. See *Sempervivum*

HYACINTH. See *Hyacinthus*

HYACINTHUS (hi-a-sin'thus), hyacinth

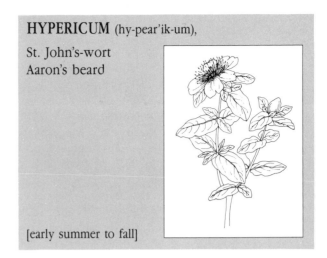

[spring]

H. orientalis (common garden hyacinth) is the most commonly planted species of these popular spring-flowering bulbs. Plant them about 6 inches deep in good, light garden soil during late fall, and then mulch them heavily in the North. The fragrant flowers come in various shades of pink, blue, red, yellow, and white. They are often grown inside for late winter blooms.

Be sure the bulbs are not planted where they may be exposed to prolonged wetness over the winter because they tend to rot quickly. The plants do best in full sun, and are hardy to zone 5, although they will survive in colder regions if there is good snow cover all winter.

DISEASES. Gray mold, blight, mosaic, rot.

INSECTS. Bulb flies, mites, nematodes.

PROPAGATION. Although home gardeners usually have the best results if they buy commercially grown bulbs, old clumps may be separated after blooming and the small bulblets pulled off and replanted to extend the planting. Most hyacinths are grown commercially in Holland, where large bulbs are dug up, the bases are scooped out slightly, and then replanted. This "wounding" stimulates the bulb to produce many bulblets inside the scooped out portion. They are dug up the following year and grown to a larger size before selling.

HYPERICUM (hy-pear'ik-um),
St. John's-wort
Aaron's beard

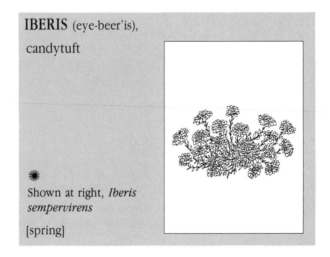

[early summer to fall]

These low-growing, shrublike plants have bright golden flowers that are 2 to 3 inches in diameter, and are ever-green or semi-evergreen in mild climates. They bloom profusely, and although they like a sandy soil and a warm location, the flowers bloom longer if they are lightly shaded from the afternoon sun.

H. calycinum (Aaron's beard) has bright yellow flowers 3 inches across, and blooms over a long season. *H. cerastoides* (St. John's-wort), 5 inches tall, has smaller yellow blooms and is good for rock gardens. *H. kalmianum* (kalm St. John's-wort), 3 feet in height, is the hardiest of the species, and grows wild in most of the East. *H.* x *moseranum* (goldflower) is 2 feet tall, has an abundance of attractive golden yellow flowers with red anthers, but should be grown only in mild climates. *H. patulum henryi* (Henry St. John's-wort), 3 to 4 feet tall, is an attractive variety with large cuplike flowers, and even when the tops suffer winter-kill, the roots sometimes survive without protection. 'Hidcote' is a popular variety.

DISEASES. Mildew, root rot.

PROPAGATION. By dividing the roots, by cuttings in early summer, or by seeds.

IBERIS (eye-beer'is),
candytuft

Shown at right, *Iberis sempervirens*

[spring]

Iberis is a low-growing perennial, often with a woody stem, and one of the best spring-blooming plants. Many of them originated in Iberia, hence the name. They grow from 6 to 12 inches tall, forming dense mats, and white blooms that sometimes fade to lavender, cover the plants. After candytuft becomes well established, the plant should not be disturbed. It likes sunshine, rich soil, and frequent watering. Usually planted in the flower border and rock garden, it also looks nice in hanging baskets and window boxes.

I. saxatilis, rock candytuft, grows 6 inches tall and is popular in rock gardens. *I. sempervirens* is edging candytuft, of which 'Little Gem,' 'Purity,' 'Pygmea,' 'Autumn Snow,' and 'Snowflake' are popular varieties. 'Autumn Snow' blooms again in the fall. *I. gibraltarica* (Gibraltar candytuft) grows to a height of 15 inches, has rose-pink flowers, and is a good rock garden plant in mild climates.

DISEASES. Club root, mildew, rust.

INSECTS. Caterpillars, scales.

PROPAGATION. Candytufts can be divided, or cuttings taken in early summer will root easily. Common varieties may be raised from seed, but the plants grow slowly.

INDIGO, FALSE. See *Baptisia*

IRIS (eye'ris), iris

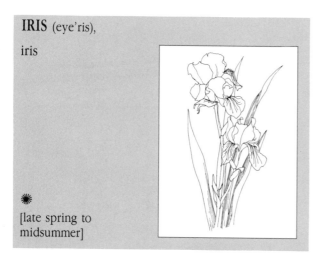

[late spring to midsummer]

Iris should be considered an important part of every garden because they fill a void between spring bulbs and summer flowers. But even if they did not fill this need, their beauty is too startling to miss. Iris take their name from the Greek goddess of the rainbow and come in a wide variety of lovely colors. All have flat, sword-shaped foliage, and a flower form consisting of three outer petals (falls), and three inner petals (standards), which are often upright. Some iris species also have beards, or fuzzy appendages that hang from the throat of the flower over each of the falls. So many thousands of bearded iris cultivars have been originated that identifying a variety in an inherited garden is nearly impossible.

All iris prefer full sun, but each variety has specific soil and moisture requirements. None of the garden varieties can tolerate a winter in wet soil, and all need to be divided periodically so the roots do not become crowded.

Iris were once called by the name "flag," but the term is now used mostly to identify blue flag, *I. versicolor*, a blue-flowering plant, and *I. pseudacorus*, yellow flag, a similar one with yellow blooms. Although both thrive in shallow water, they will grow in moist soil, too.

Of the many spectacular bearded species, *I. germanica* (German iris) 2 to 3 feet tall is the most popular because it grows well in ordinary soil with no unusual moisture requirements. The huge list of hybrids developed from this species attests to its reputation, and the blooms come in many colors and color combinations. The rhizomes are shallow growing and should be planted nearly level with the surface of the soil. Taller and heavier blooming-types may need to be staked in windy locations.

The discouraging thing about growing bearded iris is the various blights, leaf spots, rusts, rots, borers, and thrips that bother them. Cut off any diseased foliage or borer damage as soon as it appears and spray with a garden fungicide once or twice early in the season. And cut off all foliage before winter to prevent pests from lingering. Problems increase when large masses of iris are grown together, so consider placing other plants among them to make it harder for pests to spread.

I. kaempferi, Japanese iris, are beardless with large flat-topped blooms in many different colors; they grow from 2 to 3½ feet tall. They like slightly acid soil and additional moisture during the growing and blooming season, but do not allow the roots to be wet over the winter. Japanese iris have an abundance of spectacular blooms in midsummer. More tender than most other iris, they need winter protection in exposed northern locations.

I. sibirica, Siberian iris, 2 to 3 feet in height, don't mind a year-round moist place. They prefer an acid soil. They are hardy, easy to grow, and are particularly good for planting in wild areas and around water. In the past the flowers were usually blue in color and rather small, but many new hybrids have large blooms in purple, white, pink, and other colors.

Because both Japanese and Siberian iris increase rapidly, small new plants grow quickly into heavy blooming and established clumps.

I. xiphium is a blue iris, commonly called Spanish iris. It has been crossed with *I. tingitana*, the Tangiers iris, to create many hybrids known as Dutch iris, which are widely grown by florists for early spring bouquets. When grown outdoors they are best in regions where winters are not too severe, although in colder regions the bulbs can be dug up in the fall and stored for spring planting like *Gladiolus*. Some cultivars include 'Blue Ribbon,' lavender-blue; 'Hildegarde,' pale blue; 'Ideal,' deep violet; 'Royal Yellow,'

yellow; 'Symphony,' white with yellow; and 'White Wedgewood,' a creamy white.

Several dwarf iris are worthy of a place in the front of the border or rock garden. *I. chamaeiris*, Crimean iris, 10 inches tall, and *I. cristata*, crested iris, 3 to 5 inches in height, are two of the best known. Both have blue, red-purple, or white blooms in late spring and early summer.

PROPAGATION. By dividing the root clumps in late summer. Divisions with three or more sprouts should bloom the following year. Plants grown from seed vary widely.

VARIETIES. Listing even a tiny percentage of iris varieties is impossible here, and no matter what we choose, we're sure to omit someone's favorite. Here are some excellent ones, and their predominant color(s), now being listed in catalogs and sold in garden centers.

Bearded or German Iris

'After All'—ivory-cream
'Art Shades'—yellow with lavender-pink
'Autumn Leaves'—brown with yellow and rose
'Baroque'—orange shades
'Black Bart'—glossy black
'Blue Luster'—bright medium blue
'Camelot Rose'—silvery orchid and red-orange
'Carnaby'—pink and rose
'Christmas Time'—white with red beard
'Close Up'—creamy pink and brown-toned rose
'Cloverdale'—rose-lilac with white
'Dancing Bride'—white with yellow
'Desert Song'—purple and white
'Dutch Chocolate'—chocolate and red-brown
'Elysian Fields'—buff and pink
'Frost and Flame'—red and white
'Gingerbread Castle'—brown
'Glacier Sunset'—white with orchid shades
'Gold Burst'—white with yellow
'Heavenly Angels'—white with greenish cast
'Holiday House'—pink and buff blend
'Laced Cotton'—white
'Lemon Mist'—yellow shades
'Monaco'—lavender with pink and white
'New Moon'—lemon yellow
'Olympic Torch'—bronze shades
'Pretty Nancy'—pink with white
'Prosperity'—yellow shades
'Raspberry Ripples'—red shades
'Sable Night'—deep purple
'Taste of Honey'—yellow and brown
'Toll Gate'—pale blue with dark purple
'Winter Dreams'—white

Japanese Iris

'Apple Blossom Cascade'—pink
'Cobra Dancer'—purple
'Gold Bound'—double blooms, white with gold band
'Nikko'—purple-blue

'Pink Frost'—light pink, double blooms
'Red Titan'—red-purple
'Tinted Cloud'—blue-lavender and violet

Siberian Iris

'Amelia Earhart'—blue
'Anniversary'—white
'Blue Moon'—violet-blue
'Dark Circle'—purple
'Dear Delight'—light blue
'Dreaming Spires'—lavender and deep blue
'Harpswell Haze'—light blue
'Mountain Lake'—blue
'Red Emperor'—red-purple
'Shadowy Lake'—blue
'Wing on Wing'—white

JACOB'S LADDER. See *Polemonium*

JOE PYE-WEED. See *Eupatorium*

JONQUIL. See *Narcissus*

KNAPWEED. See *Centaurea*

KNIPHOFIA (ni-fo'fi-a),

tritoma
torch lily
red-hot poker

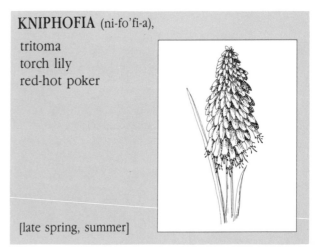

[late spring, summer]

The red-hot pokers, as these plants were once called, are not commonly grown because not many garden centers carry them. They have a straight-as-a-poker form, and tight little flowers in brilliant red, orange, white, and yellow combinations (as well as solid colors), that cluster around the stem, adding brilliance to the garden. The hummingbirds love them. Most grow to about 3 feet, do well in ordinary, well-drained garden soil, prefer sun, and in the North should be heavily mulched or moved into a cold frame for the winter.

K. uvaria is the common torch lily, so-called because of its orange-red flowers. It is a South African native, and its numerous cultivars include 'Bee's Sunset,' orange; 'Coral Seas,' red; 'Maid of Orleans,' white; 'Primrose Beauty,' yellow; 'Springtime,' red and yellow; 'Summer Sunshine,' bright red; and 'White Fairy,' cream colored.

DISEASES. Leaf spot.

INSECTS. Nematodes.

PROPAGATION. Best propagated by division in spring, or basal cuttings (those made near the base or bottom of a stem or branch) in early summer. Seedling plants may take years to bloom.

LADY'S MANTLE. See *Alchemilla*

LAMB'S EARS. See *Stachys*

LAMIUM (lay'mi-um), dead nettle

Shown at right, *Lamium maculatum*

[late spring, summer]

Though this genus includes some terrible weeds, dead nettles don't bite when touched, like stinging nettles. They grow to 1 foot, do well in light shade and most soils, and their snapdragon-type pink or white flowers blossom over a long period. Some make nice ground covers.

L. maculatum (spotted dead nettle) is the only recommended species. Its leaves are spotted with white and it blooms in late spring and summer. Cultivars include 'Album,' creamy white blooms; 'Beacon Silver,' pink flowers and variegated leaves; and 'Chequers,' violet flowers.

The plants are relatively **PEST FREE**.

PROPAGATION. By dividing the plants in spring.

LANTERN PLANT, CHINESE. See *Physalis*

LARKSPUR. See *Delphinium*

LATHYRUS (la'thi-russ), perennial pea vine sweet pea

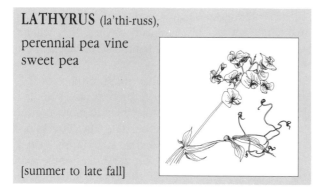

[summer to late fall]

Although the annual sweet pea (*L. odoratus*) is an annual garden favorite, the perennial pea is not nearly as well known. It likes sun, thrives in good soil, and needs support for its climbing vines. Once planted, it is long-lived and does not like to be disturbed. The pink, lavender, red,

and white blooms should be cut frequently to prevent seed formation and promote a longer blooming season.

The most commonly grown species are *L. grandiflorus*, everlasting pea, a 6-foot tall climbing perennial with rose-purple flowers; it is not hardy in the North. *L. latifolius*, perennial pea vine or sweet pea, is hardier, has rose-pink flowers, and can grow to 9 feet. 'White Pearl' (white) and 'Rose Queen,' (bright pink) are named cultivars of *L. latifolius*. *L. japonicus*, maritime pea, grows wild along eastern beaches, and is useful for seaside plantings.

DISEASES. Anthracnose, mildew, root rot.

INSECTS. Aphids, spider mites.

PROPAGATION. By seeds, and since seedlings transplant poorly, it is best to start them in peat pots.

LAVANDULA (lah-van'dew-la), lavender

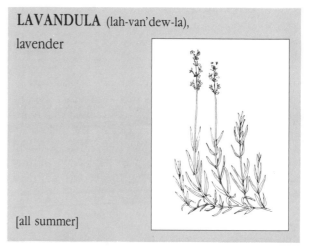

[all summer]

Although not as popular today, this fragrant herb was once grown in nearly every garden, and its special fragrance was prized in the border as well as in soaps and lotions. The flowers were cut for bouquets, and also dried and used in potpourri or placed among stored linens.

These shrubby, low-growing plants with light gray or green needle-shaped foliage, and purple, lavender-blue, or white flowers, add interesting textures to the front of the border and rock garden. They can also be used as foundation plants or grown as compact, untrimmed hedge. They need full sun, and do best in light soil. Lavender doesn't entirely die back during the winter, and since it is somewhat tender, it does best in a sheltered location and may need winter protection when grown in the North.

Depending on which book you read, English lavender, *L. angustifolia*, may also be identified as *L. officinalis*, *L. vera*, or *L. spica*. It can grow up to 3 feet tall, but is usually shorter, especially in the North. Many cultivars are available, including dwarf forms that are less than a foot tall.

DISEASES. Leaf spot, root rot.

INSECTS. Caterpillars, plant bugs, nematodes.

PROPAGATION. Named varieties should be propagated by cuttings taken in early summer or by carefully dividing the plants in early spring. Seeds of species plants may be started inside in late winter and the young plants set outside in a shaded bed after the danger of frost is past.

LAVENDER. See *Lavandula*

LAVENDER, SEA. See *Limonium*

LEADWORT. See *Ceratostigma*

LEONTOPODIUM ALPINUM (lee-on-to-poh'di-um),
edelweiss

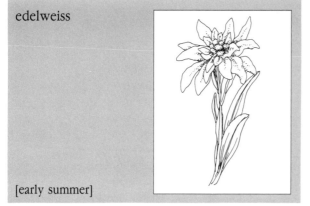

[early summer]

This tiny flower is beloved in the Alps where it hangs precariously onto rock cliffs. Since they are easy to grow in the garden, it is not necessary to risk life and limb to get a glimpse of this legendary specimen. The plants are extremely hardy, and since they need dry, poor soil, and full sun, are ideal for a rock garden. By themselves, the tiny yellow flowers would be rather inconspicuous, but their enchantment springs from the silvery white, wooly upper leaves, called bracts, that cluster around each blossom and appear to be part of it.

PROPAGATION. Easily grown from seed, or increased by dividing the plants.

LEOPARD'S BANE. See *Doronicum*

LIATRIS (ly-ay'tris),
gayfeather

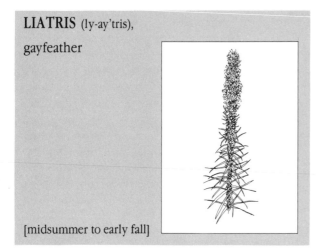

[midsummer to early fall]

Because of the unusual pink-lavender color of most liatris cultivars, it is sometimes difficult to find the right place for this spiky perennial, either in a garden or a bouquet. Placement near white flowers or among a lot of green is advisable for best color coordination. They make good cut flowers in every other way, though.

Liatris have the unusual habit of starting to bloom at the top of the spike instead of the reverse, as is common with most spiky plants. They like light soils, are annoyed by fertilizer, grow well in sun or light shade, and are excellent butterfly attracters.

L. pycnostachya (Kansas gayfeather) has pink-purple flowers, blooms in midsummer, and reaches a height of 4 feet; 'Alba' is a white cultivar. *L. scariosa* (tall gayfeather) also has pink-purple blooms, but doesn't get quite as tall; the cultivar 'White Spire' has white blooms. *L. spicata* (spike gayfeather) is 3 feet tall and has reddish purple flowers; 'Kobold' is an improved cultivar.

DISEASES. Leaf spot, rust, rot.

PROPAGATION. By seeds, best sown in the fall, or by division of the roots in early spring.

LILIUM,
lily

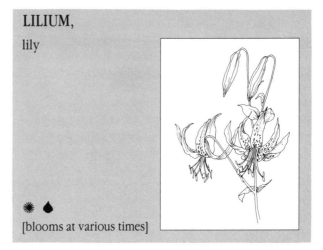

[blooms at various times]

The lily is one of the most loved of all garden perennials. Whole borders are grown of these beautiful, fragrant plants that range in size from miniatures to showy, tall specimens that sometimes hold 20 to 30 flowers at a time. Blooms may be recurved (like the turk's cap lily), trumpet-shaped, upward facing, or hang like bells, and be as much as 8 inches in diameter. They come in every imaginable color except pure blue. Although requirements of the many lily species differ, the garden varieties all demand well-drained soil and a location that won't permit the bulbs to become waterlogged for any length of time. Bloom colors are often best if the bulbs are planted where they will be exposed to full sun, but receive light shade during the heat of the afternoon.

Lily bulbs are more fragile than those of tulips or daffodils, and should never be allowed to dry out. If you can't plant the bulbs immediately, store them in moist peat in plastic bags, and plant as soon as possible. Put a little bonemeal in the bottom of the hole and set each one so the top of the bulb is about 5 inches below the surface of the soil. Apply a small amount of garden fertilizer around them each spring, but be careful not to give them excessive amounts of manure or nitrogen.

Most varieties over 3 feet tall need staking, but it's surprising how rugged their stems are, given the weight of the blooms. Begin to stake the plants as soon as buds form. The stems should not be cut immediately after blooming, but be allowed to die down naturally so nutrients can return to the bulb before winter. Because they are planted deep, most lilies are hardy throughout the continental United States and southern Canada, although the Madonna types should be mulched in the North.

It would be difficult to list all the lily species, to say nothing of the myriad varieties which have been developed. Even dedicated collectors find that they cannot begin to amass all the named cultivars now in existence, to say nothing of keeping up with new introductions. Most nursery catalogs carry only a few of the most popular species, so if you want others it will be necessary to buy from lily specialists, a few of which are listed in the appendix.

Among the popular species often used for mass plantings are *L. lancifolium*, also known as *L. tigrinum* (tiger lily), one of the earliest Oriental introductions, which has adjusted so well it has become naturalized in many places; *L. regale* (regal lily), another early introduction and a garden favorite, it has fragrant rose-purple (outside) and white (inside) blossoms; *L. candidum* (Madonna lily) has pure white flowers that are traditionally planted to bloom along with the blue delphiniums. Set the bulbs only 1 or 2 inches deep and mulch them heavily before winter.

L. longiflorum, the traditional Easter lily, is too tender for outdoor northern gardens. But if you get one for Easter you can plant it outside that summer, pot it up in the fall, store it in a cool root cellar until midwinter, then place it in a greenhouse or sunny window. With luck, you may be able to get it to blossom the day before Easter!

Hundreds of hybrids have been developed from the many *Lilium* species. Some of the better known hybrids include the Asiatic group, which are early bloomers; the Aurelians with their large trumpet flowers; Imperials have attractive red and gold markings on white blooms; Olympics with fragrant white blooms; and the Oriental hybrids, late bloomers with fragrant flowers.

Vigor varies widely not only among the different hybrids, but also in different locations. Among our favorite vigorous lilies are the Midcentury hybrids, which include cultivars such as 'Burgundy' and 'Enchantment,' considered by many to be one of the best with its orange-red blooms.

One disappointing thing about growing the recent hybrids is that so many of them are short-lived. This isn't a reason for not growing them, however, because their spectacular beauty can outweigh the trouble and expense of frequent replacement. Many gardeners prefer to grow species and varieties that will prosper for years. Some of these are 'Bright Star,' 'Corsage,' 'Elegans,' 'Enchantment,' 'Henryi,' 'Paisley,' 'Regal,' 'Sutter's Gold,' 'Thunderbolt,' and 'Tiger Lily.'

Some popular lily species and cultivars are listed below.

Early Bloomers

'Burgundy'—dark red
'Campfire'—red
'Candlelight'—light yellow
'Elegans'—red
'Enchantment'—red-orange
'Firecracker'—scarlet
'Juliana'—creamy white
'Nova'—bright yellow
Regal hybrids—white with dark outside, very fragrant
'Sentinel'—white with yellow throat

Midseason Bloomers

'Black Dragon'—white inside, dark red outside
'Golden Splendor'—golden yellow
'Golden Sunburst'—clear yellow
'Green Magic'—large white with green throat
'Moonlight'—light yellow
'Pink Perfection'—various shades of pink
L. speciosum, showy lily hybrids including 'Imperial Gold,' 'Imperial Silver,' 'Imperial Crimson'

Lilies for the Wild Garden

Canada Lily (*L. canadense*)—yellow to red
Wood lily (*L. philadelphicum*)—orange to red, spotted, grows best in the shade
Turk's cap lily (*L. superbum*)—yellow-red, dark spots

DISEASES. Blight, botrytis, crown rot, mold, rust.
INSECTS. Aphids, borers, nematodes, thrips.
PROPAGATION. Lilies can be propagated in several ways:

- Planting seeds works well to propagate species that come true from seed (the tiger and regal lilies are examples) and to originate new varieties. Some lily seeds sprout easily and grow rapidly, such as those of the Regal and Mid-century hybrids, but others may take many months to start.

- Large bulbs often split in the middle, and can be pulled apart and replanted. Although such bulbs usually bloom the first year after planting, they need an additional year to reach their potential.

- Small bulblets form around the main bulb (the underground stem) and along root stolens which roam through the surrounding soil. These can be broken off and planted in spring or fall. A few varieties spread rapidly in this way, including 'Enchantment' and other Midcentury hybrids, and such clumps need dividing regularly or they will deteriorate into a lot of tiny plants that bloom sparingly, if at all.

- The outside scales of a bulb can be peeled off and planted in light soil. In a short time they will form a new bulb that will grow into a plant. These new bulbs can be set to the proper depth the following fall or spring.

- Small bulbils form along the stalk of certain lilies such as the tiger (*L. tigrinum*) and sargent (*L. sargentiae*). If a lot of plants are wanted, pull off the flower buds before they open so more energy can be directed into the production of bulbils. Plant these as soon as they are fat and begin to fall from the plant.

LILY. See *Lilium*

LILY-OF-THE-VALLEY. See *Convallaria*

LILY-TURF. See *Liriope*

LIMONIUM (ly-mo'ni-um),

sea lavender

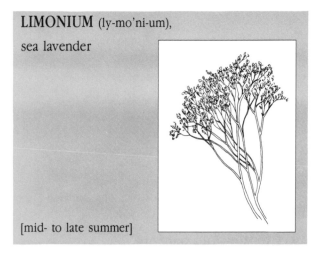

[mid- to late summer]

These plants with low, leathery, rosettelike foliage have lavender-hued flowers on 12- to 18-inch stems. They are suitable for perennial borders, and rock gardens, or can be used as fillers in floral arrangements and for dried bouquets. They like full sun, light garden soil, and are ideal for shore plantings because they are not damaged by ocean spray.

L. latifolium (sea lavender), the most commonly cultivated species, has lavender flowers, and blooms for a long period in midsummer. Plants listed as *L. tataricum* (Tatarian sea lavender), actually belong to the related genus *Goniolimon*. They are 12 inches tall and easier to grow than *L. latifolium*, but hardy only in mild climates. It has red and white flowers. One cultivar, 'Nanum,' is only 9 inches high.

The species often used in floral arrangements is *L. sinuatum* (notch-leaf sea lavender), an annual.

DISEASES. Leaf spot, rust.

INSECTS. Aphids, mites, nematodes.

PROPAGATION. *Limonium* sometimes self-sows, so it is easily propagated by seed, although it may take three years to flower. It can also be started from root cuttings, but division must be done with care because the plant does not like to be disturbed.

LINARIA (lin-ay'-ri-a),

toadflax

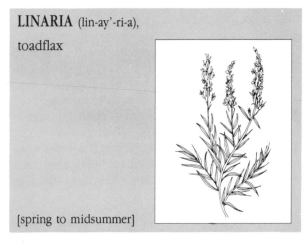

[spring to midsummer]

Although butter-and-eggs, *L. vulgaris*, is a common wildflower and a bad weed on roadsides and in waste areas, the garden varieties are much more respectable and desirable.

These snapdragon-like flowers are easy to grow, don't mind poor rocky soil, and prefer full sun.

L. alpina, 6 inches, alpine toadflax, is a fine rock plant, with tiny purple, yellow, and white blooms. *L. genistifolia*, 30 inches, has bright yellow flowers in early summer, and although it self-sows, it seldom becomes weedy.

DISEASES. Crown rot, leaf rot, root rot, mildew.

INSECTS. Aphids, mites, nematodes.

PROPAGATION. Grows well from seed, which is best planted in the fall. Or divide the spreading tuberous roots in early spring.

LINUM (lie'num),

flax

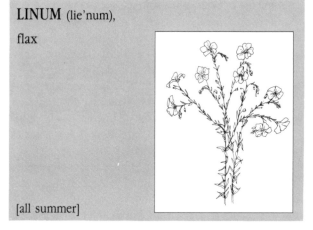

[all summer]

Several of the perennial flax, with their small golden, blue, or white flowers, are worth a spot in the flower border or the rock garden. The blossoms last only a day, and if they are picked before they go to seed, they'll keep blooming all summer. Most grow a bit over a foot tall and need full sun. The plants do not like their roots disturbed by cultivation, so a permanent mulch around them is advised.

L. flavum, golden flax, has yellow flowers; *L. perenne*, perennial or blue flax, grows to a height of 2 feet, has lovely blue flowers that blossom all summer, and feathery blue-green leaves; *L. p. album* has white blooms. All are evergreen, a bit woody, and somewhat tender in the North, so need winter protection.

PROPAGATION. By seeds, cuttings, or by dividing the plant in early spring.

LIRIOPE (li-ri-o'pee),

lily-turf

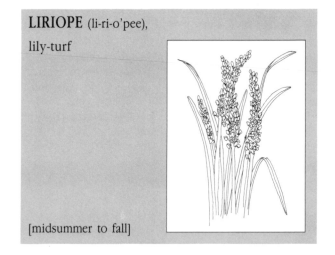

[midsummer to fall]

Native to the Orient, these small evergreen plants are excellent for warm climates (zone 6 and warmer) and can withstand exposure to saltwater spray. Their blooms resemble grape hyacinths and rise above grasslike leaves growing from tubers or bulbs.

L. muscari (blue lily-turf) grows to a height of 2 feet in tight clumps, and is often used as an edging for paths, as a ground cover, or in rock gardens. The flowers resemble grape hyacinths and come in lavender and white shades; they grow in sun or shade and require no care. *L. spicata* (creeping lily-turf) has light lavender blooms in midsummer. It grows to 1 foot, is hardy to zone 4, and although it's not particularly competitive with grass, can still become invasive in its favorite spots.

INSECTS. Slugs.

PROPAGATION. By division in early spring.

LIVER BALSAM. See *Erinus*

LOBELIA (lo-bee'li-a),

cardinal flower
lobelia

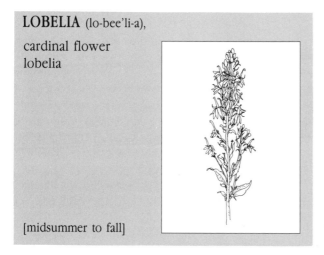

[midsummer to fall]

The *Lobelias* include many varieties, both annual and perennial. *L. cardinalis*, the scarlet-red cardinal flower, grows 3 to 4 feet tall and is wild in many moist spots in the East. It's ideal for naturalizing in the wildflower garden, but will also make a good perennial border plant, especially if the soil is damp. It thrives in sun, but prefers light shade. Plant in a protected location, and mulch heavily for the winter unless you are certain of a deep snow cover. Many hybrids have been developed in shades of bright pink, purple, or rose-red that blossom throughout the summer.

L. siphilitica, blue cardinal flower, grows from 1 to 3 feet tall and has blue flowers; the 'Vedrariensis' cultivar has purple flowers on spikes which, when cut, last for many days. *L. x speciosa*, sweet lobelia, is a tetraploid developed in Canada with larger blooms and shorter stalks.

DISEASES. Blight, leaf spot, rot, rust.

INSECTS. Aphids, leafhoppers, nematodes, wireworms.

PROPAGATION. By seeds sown in early fall in a cold frame. Roots are easily divided in spring.

LOOSESTRIFE. See *Lysimachia*

LUNARIA (loo-nay'ri-a),

honesty
money plant

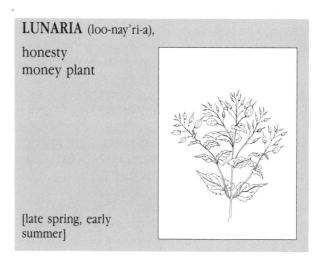

[late spring, early summer]

These 3-foot tall biennials have sweet-scented flowers of white or purple-magenta, which is not everyone's favorite shade, but are grown mostly for their 1- to 2-inch coinlike, silvery seed pods. Thought to resemble the moon as well as coins, the plant thus acquired the names *Lunaria* and money plant. They are used in dried arrangements and children like them for play money. To get the coins after the pods turn brown, remove the outer covering, and find the treasure within.

Lunarias are not fussy about soils, though they do better with a little lime, and in partial shade. A good spot to grow them is in the wild garden, where they sometimes self-sow.

DISEASES. Canker, club root, leaf spot.

PROPAGATION. Plant seed in early spring where you want them to grow permanently, since they are not easy to transplant. They should bloom and make "money" the next year.

LUNGWORT. See *Pulmonaria*

LUPINE. See *Lupinus*

LUPINUS (loo-pie'nus),

lupine

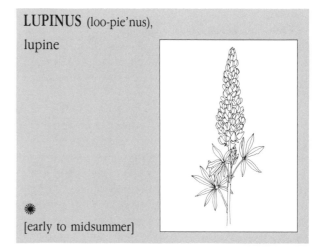

✳
[early to midsummer]

Even though they have gone wild in some places and become rather common, lupines are some of the best garden perennials, especially the brightly colored 'Russell' and other hybrids. They come in brilliant shades of red, pink, purple, yellow, white, and blue, often with bicolor shades on the same 18-inch flower spike that tops the 3-to 4-foot stem. They bloom in early summer and may bloom again later in the season if you don't let them go to seed.

Set lupines at least 2 feet apart because the clumps get large, and once established, it is best not to move or divide them. Where they are happy, they are easy to grow. Never plant them in a swampy spot—a moist, but well-drained soil is much preferred. They also need full sun, and especially enjoy the cool, dewy nights of the Northeast and Pacific Northwest.

Although the colorful hybrids are less vigorous than the common *L. perennis* (sundial lupine), they are best for the perennial border; the common strains are good for natural gardens, to cover slopes, and for planting on banks near streams.

DISEASES. Blight, mildew, virus.

INSECTS. Aphids, plant bugs.

PROPAGATION. The clumps can be separated, or stem cuttings can be taken from them in spring, but we much prefer to raise the 'Russells' and other hybrids from seed by planting them in peat pots for easier transplanting.

LYCHNIS (lick'nis),

rose campion
Maltese cross
catchfly

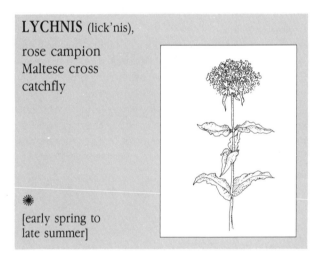

✳
[early spring to late summer]

There are many *Lychnis* species—including annuals, biennials and short-lived perennials—and several cultivars, each quite different and worth planting in the perennial border. All like full sun, sandy rich soil, and are tolerant of dry conditions.

L. coronaria, rose campion, grows 2 to 2½ feet tall, is a short-lived perennial, with silvery gray leaves and crimson-pink flowers in early summer. *L. chalcedonica* is the Maltese cross, which has bright orange-red blooms on 3-foot stems. Each floret in the round head resembles a small cross; it is long-lived, easy to grow, and some catalogs also offer 'Alba,' a white variety. *L.* x *haageana*, Haages campion, is 18 inches tall, comes in various red and pink shades, blooms in early summer, and then (in some localities) immediately goes dormant. *L. viscaria*, German catchfly, grows to a foot, has brilliant magenta blooms, and has a sticky substance on its stems just below the flower. *L. v.* 'Splendens' is a dazzling rosy crimson. The foliage grows in a compact green mound and turns a reddish color in the fall.

DISEASES. Leaf spot, rot, rust.

INSECTS. Whiteflies.

PROPAGATION. *Lychnis* are easy to grow from seed which, when planted early in the spring, will bloom the second year. Or divide plants in early spring.

LYCORIS SQUAMIGERA (ly'ko-ris),

magic lily
autumn amaryllis

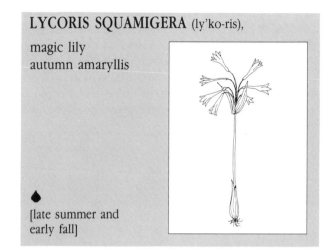

◆
[late summer and early fall]

These plants are members of the Amaryllis family, with daffodil-like leaves that come up early in the spring. By summer these turn yellow and disappear, and nothing shows until the sudden appearance in early fall of the 3-foot stalks, each with several rose-colored, amaryllis-type blooms. Although it is not considered hardy in the North, it has grown for nearly four decades here in northern Vermont, withstanding occasional temperatures of -40°F, sometimes with little snow cover.

Plant the bulbs 5 inches deep, in summer or very late fall when they are dormant. Make sure they have full sun, and they'll need little care.

DISEASES. Leaf scorch.

INSECTS. Nematodes.

PROPAGATION. To start new plants, separate the small bulblets from the bulbs and plant them in summer or late fall.

LYSIMACHIA (ly-sim-ak'i-a),

loosestrife

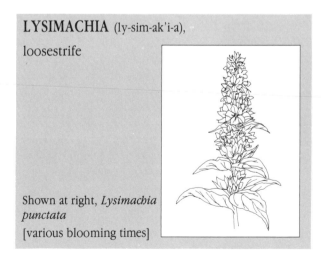

Shown at right, *Lysimachia punctata*
[various blooming times]

Many of these plants of the Primrose family are wild and rather weedy. The varieties that follow are all useful in wild gardens, and especially in spots where it is difficult to grow other perennials. But make sure they are kept under control or they may decide to inherit your earth. *Lysimachia* do best in moist, sunny locations, but will tolerate light shade, especially in hot climates.

L. clethroides, Japanese loosestrife, has various other common names including shepherd's crook and gooseneck loosestrife. It grows from 2 to 3 feet, has hairy leaves, and white flowers in midsummer that are good for cutting. *L. nummularia*, creeping Charlie, is 2 feet in height, vinelike in growth, with yellow blooms throughout the summer; it is useful in wet places, such as along streams. *L. punctata*, yellow loosestrife, is a European native, but has made itself so much at home in the Colonies that some people wonder why it was ever invited. Three feet in height, its yellow blooms on leafy upright stems are attractive in early summer, however, and it grows well where better behaved perennials will not.

PROPAGATION. By dividing the roots in late fall or in early spring.

LYTHRUM (lith'rum or ly'thrum),

purple loosestrife
lythrum

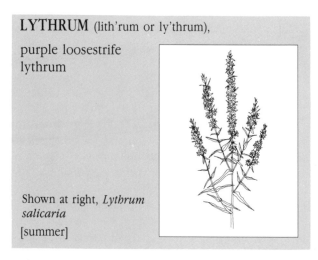

Shown at right, *Lythrum salicaria*
[summer]

This bright magenta-colored flower has long been admired where it grows naturally and abundantly along Quebec roads. The 4- to 6-foot, almost woody stalks with willowlike leaves produce a prolific number of blooms. They like full sun and ordinary garden soil, but reach full beauty in soils with more than average moisture. Lythrum are ideal for a wild garden, and for naturalizing along streams or ponds.

L. salicaria, purple loosestrife, is the most familiar species because it has become naturalized in many places. Several improved cultivars have been introduced, including 'Dropmore Purple,' a rich deep purple; 'Morden's Gleam,' a bright carmine; and 'Robert,' a clear rose-red. All bloom for a long period in midsummer, are attractive for the back of a border, and have no serious pests.

Although purple loosestrife can become very weedy in certain areas, cultivated varieties are not as invasive. The 'Robert' cultivars in our back border have stayed compact for many years. Remove the fading flower heads if you notice that self-sowing is a problem.

PROPAGATION. By dividing the plants in spring or fall, or by root cuttings taken in early summer. Native species may be grown from seed.

MACLEAYA (mac-lee'ah),

plume poppy
(formerly *Bocconia cordata*)

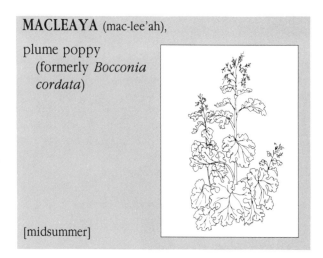

[midsummer]

M. cordata (plume poppy) grows too large for most small borders and perennial islands, but it is an impressive plant for backgrounds and large natural plantings. It grows from 6 to 10 feet tall with very large, deeply cut, lobed leaves with silver gray undersides. Pinkish-white flowers appear on long plumes around midsummer.

The plant is useful where a mass of attractive foliage is wanted, or as a background plant. It needs lots of sunlight in cool places, but in a warm location prefers light shade. Grows well in moist places and is not fussy about soil. It can send out an enormous number of suckers in some locations, so it is more suitable as a single isolated specimen plant, or for a wild garden, where there is less likelihood of its becoming weedy.

PROPAGATION. By seed or division.

MAGIC LILY. See *Lycoris*

MALLOW. See *Malva*

MALLOW, ROSE. See *Hibiscus*

MALTESE CROSS. See *Lychnis*

MALVA (mal'vah),

mallow

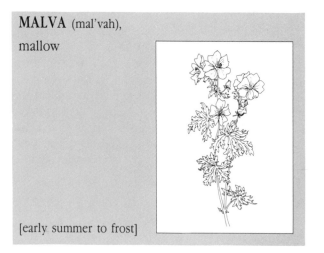

[early summer to frost]

Many of the mallows are common weeds, both annual and perennial, but a few of the hardy perennials are good for the border, where the 2- to 3-foot plants produce pink, lavender, and white flowers. They have petals with irregular edges that vaguely resemble a single rose. In fact, some common names for *Malva* are skunk rose, musk rose, or musk mallow. They need a sunny spot and well-drained soil; in hot climates, partial shade is recommended.

Both *M. alcea*, hollyhock mallow, and *M. moschata*, musk mallow, are similar in appearance, each with white to lavender pink blooms, but *M. alcea* is slightly shorter (2 feet) and a bit less hardy. Both bloom in early to midsummer. *M. alcea fastigiata* has deep pink flowers and grows to 3 feet.

DISEASES. Leaf spot, mildew, rot, rust.

INSECTS. Caterpillars.

PROPAGATION. By seeds, but named varieties should be divided to get plants that are true to the parent.

MARGUERITE, GOLDEN. See *Anthemis*

MARSH MARIGOLD. See *Caltha*

MEADOWRUE. See *Thalictrum*

MEADOWSWEET. See *Filipendula*

MECONOPSIS (mek-on-op'sis),
Himalayan blue poppy,
Welsh poppy

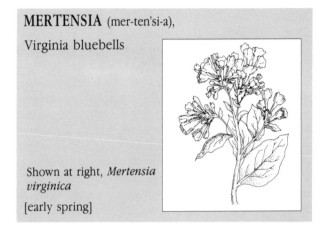

Shown at right, *Meconopsis cambrica*

[summer]

These relatives of the true poppy (*Papaver*) are outstanding in Great Britain, but most of this country is not suitable for them. Only the Pacific Northwest seems to provide the cool summers and high humidity they like. Most of the species are biennials or short-lived perennials, and many originated in the high mountains of Asia. *M. betonicifolia*, Himalayan blue poppy, is 2 to 5 feet tall and the best known species. Blue is a rare color in a poppy, a fact that makes these 2-inch flowers with golden centers so alluring. *M. cambrica*, Welsh poppy, is 12 to 18 inches tall, has smaller yellow or orange flowers, and is easier to grow. Both kinds like light shade and a deep, rich, well-drained loam, and frequent watering. They are difficult to transplant because of their long taproot.

DISEASES. Mildew, rot.

PROPAGATION. By planting the seeds in pots so they can be transplanted easily. Keep seedlings away from direct sunlight, and pick the first buds off to conserve the plant's strength. Welsh poppies can be divided when dormant.

MERTENSIA (mer-ten'si-a),
Virginia bluebells

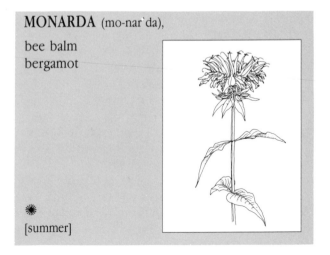

Shown at right, *Mertensia virginica*

[early spring]

M. virginica (Virginia bluebells) is the best kind and most commonly grown—a delightful wildflower and a lovely border perennial that looks well with daffodils. Virginia bluebells are chosen not only because they bloom early and can thrive in light shade, but also for the unique colors of their bell-like blossoms. The flower clusters are a bright reddish purple in bud, and a deep blue in full bloom, so the plant seems to have two completely different kinds of flowers at once. They grow from 1 to 2 feet high, do best in moist, deep, rich soil, and in a location where they can enjoy spring sunshine and summer shade. They naturalize well under deciduous shrubs or trees, if the shade is not too deep, and are good for the wildflower garden or the front of a shady border. After blooming, they die back for the summer, so mark the spot with a stake if you intend to dig in the area or move or divide the plants later.

DISEASES. Leaf spot, mildew, rot.

INSECTS. Slugs (if they are a problem in your area).

PROPAGATION. By dividing the plants while they are dormant in the summer, or by seed which should be planted immediately after gathering.

MICHAELMAS DAISY. See *Aster*

MILKWEED. See *Asclepias*

MONARDA (mo-nar'da),
bee balm
bergamot

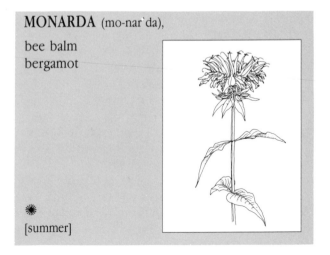

✳

[summer]

Although one sometimes sees a neglected garden where the bee balm has gone on a rampage, in a well-kept border they provide satisfaction and a bright spot of summer color. The leaves have a minty scent, and bees and hummingbirds are enticed by their tubular flowers. From 2 to 3 feet tall, colors range from white and pinky lavender through clear pink to bright red; the flowers bloom for most of the summer. They like moist soil, sun or light shade, and are ideal for naturalizing or a wildflower garden. Cut them back after blooming, and divide each spring to keep them within bounds if they are planted in the garden border because they send out runners and can easily take over.

M. didyma (bee balm or Oswego tea) is the best garden species. Good cultivars include 'Adam,' red; 'Blue Stocking,' violet-purple; 'Cambridge Scarlet,' scarlet; 'Croftway Pink,' light pink; 'Mahogany,' deep red; and 'Snow White,' creamy white. *M. fistulosa*, wild bergamot, is a native plant with smaller lavender flowers. It tolerates dry soil, but can rapidly become weedy.

DISEASES. Leaf spot, mildew, rust.

INSECTS. Stem borers.

PROPAGATION. Usually by seed, but the best varieties should be reproduced by division.

MONEY PLANT. See *Lunaria*

MONKSHOOD. See *Aconitum*

MONTEBRETIA. See *Crocosmia*

MOUNTAIN BLUET. See *Centaurea*

MUGWORT. See *Artemisia*

MULLEIN. See *Verbascum*

MUM. See *Chrysanthemum*

MUSCARI (mus-kay'ree), grape hyacinth

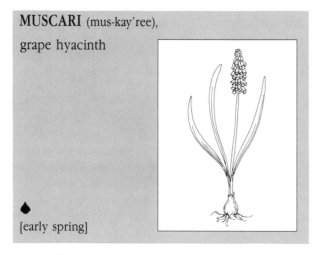

[early spring]

Much like the crocus, these little flowering bulbs herald the coming of spring. They grow only 6 inches tall, with bunches of blue or purple flowers at the end of each stalk that look like tiny grape clusters. Excellent in a rock garden or to edge a border. They grow easily, spreading both by offsets and seed, and are so competitive that they can even fight it out with grass. Since they can become weedy in some places, however, be careful where you plant them or be prepared to keep them under control.

Plant the bulbs in early fall, cover them with 2 inches of soil, and space them 3 inches apart. They grow in full sun or light shade, and need little care, but don't mow off the leaves until they have died down.

M. armeniacum (Armenian grape hyacinth), the most-planted species, is a native of Asia Minor and several varieties are available; 'Blue Spike,' double blue flowers; 'Early Giant,' fragrant light blue flowers; 'Heavenly Blue,' light blue; and 'Cantab,' later-blooming, light blue. *M. botryoides* (common grape hyacinth) is slightly hardier; its flowers are usually blue, but white and pink varieties are also available.

DISEASES. Rot.

INSECTS. Nematodes.

PROPAGATION. By digging the bulb clumps and separating them. Common kinds can be grown from seed.

MYOSOTIS (my-o-so'tis), forget-me-not

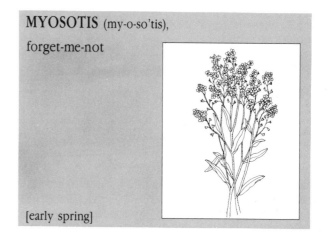

[early spring]

The forget-me-not has been described as an adventuresome adolescent because it continually wants to break away from home and join the wild bunch. It particularly enjoys dampness such as that beside a stream, but it also likes compost piles and mulch heaps. It seeds so freely that in late spring many perennial borders are covered with these familiar dainty blue flowers that have a tiny gold circle in the center. *Myosotis* are annuals, perennials, and biennials. The biennial kinds must be planted every year unless they self-sow, but perennial kinds live for several years.

M. sylvatica, woodland forget-me-not, at a mere 2 feet high, is the most common. *M. alpestris*, alpine forget-me-not, grows from 4 to 10 inches and is less common, but available in some seed catalogs. Both are biennial. *M. scorpioides*, 15 inches high, is true perennial forget-me-not. It is a blue or pink flowering European variety, and is now frequently seen growing in large masses near ponds and streams.

DISEASES. Gray mold blight, mildew, rot, rust.

INSECTS. Aphids, caterpillars, flea beetle.

PROPAGATION. Plant *Myosotis* seeds where they will grow permanently. Divide perennial kinds in early spring.

MYRTLE. See *Vinca*

NARCISSUS (nar-sis'us),

daffodil
jonquil

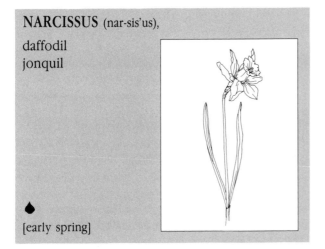

[early spring]

Narcissus have long been celebrated by both poets and peasants as harbingers of spring. They are easy to grow, and it's nearly impossible to have too many of these bulb plants. Botanists have classified the various kinds according to their flower form: trumpet, large cupped, small cupped, flat cupped, double, and those with several flowers in a single stem. In size they range from miniatures under 10 inches, to large flowering kinds that may grow over a foot and a half tall. Many are very fragrant.

The terms narcissus, jonquil, and daffodil are often used interchangeably, which can be misleading. A daffodil is a trumpet-type of narcissus, so although all daffodils are narcissus, the reverse is not true. Likewise, jonquil correctly refers only to varieties of the species *N. jonquilla* and similar plants. Even the plural of the word narcissus has been debated, but the American Daffodil Society has decreed that the same word should be used for both the singular and plural.

Fortunately it is easier to grow narcissus than to figure out their names. Most are hardy and easy to grow; and if provided with sun and good garden soil, they bloom faithfully for years. They are appropriate for the border, rock garden, and for naturalizing in masses. To create the best color effect, arrange them in groups of a dozen or more of the same variety.

Plant them in early fall 5 to 7 inches deep and about the same distance apart. This timing gives the bulbs a period before the ground freezes to form the mass of fibrous roots necessary to supply extra energy for spring blooming. Place some bonemeal, dried manure, or other slow-acting fertilizer in the bottom of the hole before planting.

Named varieties of narcissus should be divided every five or six years to keep them flowering well, but many older kinds such as the double yellows or pink-cupped whites will keep blooming for generations without attention, so these are some of the best to choose for naturalizing. Lift and separate the bulbs directly after the leaves have died down in early summer. Additional application of garden fertilizer each year helps them retain their blooming size and vigor.

It is important to let the leaves of the narcissus die down naturally after blooming. Since their yellowing leaves are not attractive, it *is* tempting to mow or cut them off too early, but it's essential that all the nourishment in the leaves return to the bulb before it goes dormant for the summer.

DISEASES. Blight, leaf scorch, leaf spot, rot, virus.

INSECTS. Aphids, bulb flies, mites, caterpillars, mealybugs, nematodes, thrips.

Although this list seems imposing, it is likely that none of these may ever bother your plants, and if they do, an all-purpose garden dust will probably correct the problem.

PROPAGATION. To propagate narcissus, dig the bulbs after they have died down completely and separate them. Replant at once, or dry in the sun a few hours, store in a cool dry place, and plant them in early fall. For the fastest increase of bulbs, plant them less deep than usually recommended. Their energy then goes into creating new bulbs, but don't expect them to bloom as well. New varieties are started by planting seeds.

NEPETA (nep'et-a),

catmint

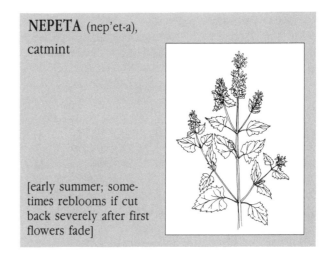

[early summer; sometimes reblooms if cut back severely after first flowers fade]

Many gardeners don't realize how attractive flowering catmint is, and how well it fits into the perennial border, rock garden, or path border. Dainty blue flowers cover compact mounds of mint-green foliage. It grows beautifully in ordinary garden soil and full sun, and needs little care.

N. mussinii (often confused with the sterile hybrid *N. x faassenii*), Caucasian or flowering catmint, is a very different plant from *N. cataria* (catmint), the herb that our feline friends go wild about, or *N. hederacea* (also *Glechoma hederacea*), the weedy gill-over-the-ground or ground ivy, that infests lawns and gardens. Since many different strains of *N. mussinii* have been developed, you may want to visit a nursery when the plants are in bloom to be sure of getting the most attractive ones. 'Blue Wonder' is one popular cultivar growing about a foot tall.

DISEASES. Leaf spot, stem rot, virus.

INSECTS. Caterpillars, leafhoppers.

PROPAGATION. Division of the clumps. If more plants are wanted, layer them or take root cuttings in late spring. Common kinds can be grown from seed.

NYMPHAEA (nim-fee'a),

hardy water lily

✳

[different times throughout the summer]

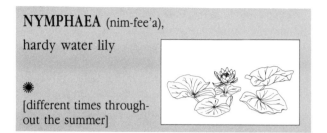

Among floating plants, the water lily is certainly the queen. They grow beautifully in shallow ponds, pools, tubs, or slow-moving streams, and all like full sun.

N. odorata (fragrant native water lily) is very attractive with its waxy white blooms, and is one of the easiest to grow. It can be dug from shallow ponds and transplanted nearly any time. *N. gigantea* (Australian water lily) has larger flowers and is more showy. *N. tuberosa aquatic* (magnolia water lily) is also a native, has white flowers, but is not fragrant. It blooms mostly in the morning and closes tight during the afternoon and evening. The Marliacea hybrids are among the best of the hardy water lilies, and include various shades of red, pink, yellow, and apricot.

For frost-free southern gardens, and for inside pools, there are many tropical species, including both day-blooming varieties such as brilliant red 'Director,' 'George T. Moore,' and those that open only at night. These come in a wide range of vivid colors as well as white, and many are fragrant.

DISEASES. Leaf spot, rot.

INSECTS. Aphids, beetles.

PROPAGATION. By dividing the roots in early spring. For cultural methods and more information, see chapter 19 on water gardens.

OENOTHERA (ee-no-thee'rah),

sundrop
evening primrose

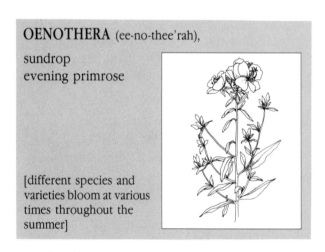

[different species and varieties bloom at various times throughout the summer]

Bright yellow is always a cheery color in the garden, and it's hard to find a brighter shade than that provided by the sundrop.

The genus *Oneothera* includes both day-flowering and evening-flowering species. If your *Oneothera* opens in the morning, "sundrop" is probably the proper term, even though it may be incorrectly called "evening primrose."

Whatever you call them, these hardy plants are easy to grow, asking only for full sun and good garden soil, although they will tolerate poor soil.

Sundrops are useful in a rock garden, as edging along steps or paths, and for a bright spot at the front of the border. They need occasional division to keep them healthy and prevent them from spreading too much.

O. fruticosa and *O. tetragona* are similar and often mislabeled. Both are sundrops, and the most popular species because they are 18 to 24 inches tall. Most have rich yellow blooms for the majority of the summer. *O. missourensis*, Ozark sundrop, is a bit shorter (12 inches) with large, golden blooms, and attractive seedpods that can be dried. It has a trailing growth habit. *O. biennis*, 3 to 4 feet in height, the native evening primrose, is a biennial that blooms in late afternoon and evening. Sometimes gardeners move a few of these roadside plants into their perennial borders, but promptly regret it because they quickly become fast-spreading weeds. *O. speciosa*, white primrose, a weedy biennial, is 18 inches high, and gradually turns a not-very-attractive pink. Not recommended for a border because it is so invasive.

DISEASES. Leaf spot, rust.

INSECTS. Aphids.

PROPAGATION. By separating the clumps in early spring, or by seeds.

ONIONS, ORNAMENTAL. See *Allium*

OPUNTIA (o-pun'ti-a),

prickly pear
cholla

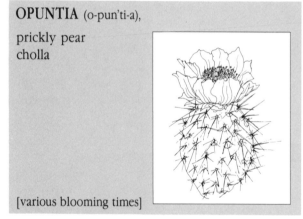

[various blooming times]

Most members of the large Cactus family are suitable only for southwestern deserts or sunny northern windows, but there are some that are hardy even in the North for use in rock gardens and borders. The *Opuntia*, or prickly pear, are most common, and although they do not resemble their desert cousins, they nevertheless have lovely flowers and some attractive-colored spines.

The *Opuntias* like full sun and a sandy soil. For this reason, they are especially happy at the seashore, and are ideal for sunny rock gardens. If grown in a border, that part of the bed should be raised a few inches to ensure good drainage since they cannot tolerate wetness over the winter.

Among the numerous species are *O. arenaria*, which has red flowers; *O. compressa*, yellow flowers; and *O. imbricata*, purple flowers.

DISEASES. Crown gall, rot.

INSECTS. Aphids, mealybugs, mites, nematodes, scales.

PROPAGATION. By seeds and by cuttings taken from the older parts of the stem. Some of the unusual varieties are occasionally grafted.

PACHYSANDRA (pack-iss-and'ra),

pachysandra

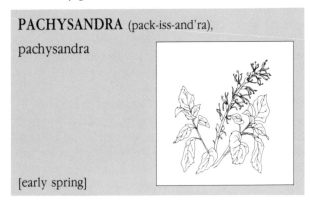

[early spring]

Although it has masses of white flowers in early spring, low-growing *Pachysandra* is not a plant for the flowering border. Instead, it is prized for the handsome, glossy foliage that makes it an excellent ground cover, particularly on shady banks, along woodland paths, and for covering forest floors where other plants will not grow. It needs shade to thrive, likes deep, moist, slightly acid soil, and spreads rapidly by underground stolens. Set the plants 8 inches to 2 feet apart, depending on how quickly you want an area covered.

Neither of the common varieties are hardy in exposed northern locations, but do grow when sheltered in zone 4. *P. procumbens*, Alleghany pachysandra, is evergreen in the South, but the leaves die to the ground in the North. *P. terminalis*, Japanese pachysandra, is 6 to 10 inches tall, evergreen, and the most planted kind. The variety 'Variegata' has green and white leaves.

DISEASES. Blight, leaf spot.

INSECTS. Mites, nematodes, scales.

PROPAGATION. By dividing the plants in spring, or by cuttings taken in early summer.

PAEONIA (pee-oh'nee-a),

peony

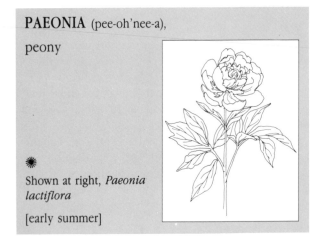

✳
Shown at right, *Paeonia lactiflora*

[early summer]

Even people who can't get excited about spring violets and forget-me-nots, admire the giant flowering peony. In Colonial America, the only landscaping many homes had was a lilac bush and a dark red Memorial Day "piney" near the front door. Gardeners today can choose from the hundreds of new peony varieties that have since replaced the old *P. officinalis* (common peony), which invariably fell apart soon after blooming, and had a strong, unpleasant odor. Some of the modern red, pink, white, and even yellow blooms can be 10 inches or more across, and the shrublike foliage, up to 3 feet in height and width, looks nice throughout the summer and fall.

In addition to their beauty, peonies are attractive in other ways. They are hardy, fragrant, long-lived, need only infrequent dividing, and are superior cut flowers. They can be grown as focal points in a border, or as hedges, and they are especially good foundation plants in northern areas where woody shrubs may suffer badly under the weight of heavy snow.

Peonies deserve the extra care it takes to grow the most spectacular blooms. Begin by buying good-sized plants (3 to 5 eyes or sprouts on each bare-rooted clump) from a reliable firm, and plant them carefully in the right spots. They like full sun, but also grow well on the southeast side of a building where they will get light afternoon shade, but plenty of skylight. Allow 3 feet in diameter for each plant.

Bare-rooted plants should be set out in early fall in deep, very rich, well-drained soil. Dig a hole the size of a bushel basket, and prepare the soil by thoroughly mixing in several large shovelsful of well-aged manure or compost, and a few handfuls of dried manure or a half cup of slow-acting commerical plant food. Put most of the soil back in the hole, and set the root clump so the spot where the red sprouts emerge from the root is only an inch (2 inches in light soil) below the surface, as shown in the drawing. If put in any deeper, the plant could struggle and it may be many years before it blooms properly. Planting too deep is the most common cause of failure with peonies.

More manure heaped over the plant each fall will keep it growing and blooming well, or if that's not available, a cup of commercial fertilizer sprinkled around it in early spring will suffice. As soon as the buds begin to develop, the plant will need to be staked. Or place one of the wire or plastic hoops specially made for this purpose around it to hold the heavy blooms up off the ground. Each branch will produce several buds, so to obtain the largest flowers, pinch off all the buds except for the terminal one. Don't pick off any of the flowers for the first year or two, but after that the plant won't be harmed if half the flowers are cut for bouquets.

Once peonies are planted, don't disturb them. They like stability, and will get bigger and more productive each year. Once every eight or ten years they may need dividing, but certainly not more often unless you need to start new plants, or the old ones begin to deteriorate in the center.

Although ants often roam over the plants, they do no apparent damage and are merely attracted by the sweet sub-

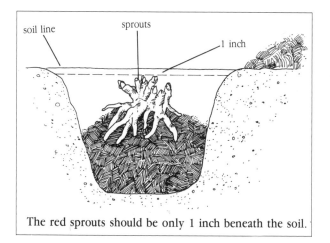

The red sprouts should be only 1 inch beneath the soil.

Red Shades

'Aucturas'—red, single-type
'Big Ben'—dark red, bomb-type
'Cherry Hill'—maroon-red, semidouble-type
'Constance'—red, Japanese-type
'Felix Crousse'—bright red, double-type
'Highlight'—dark red, double-type
'Kansas'—bright red, double-type
'Karl Rosenfield'—dark red, double-type
'Longfellow'—bright red, double-type
'Nippon Beauty'—dark red, yellow edge, Japanese-type
P. officinalis—old-fashioned, Memorial Day red, double-type
'Philippe Rivoire'—deep red, double-type
'President Lincoln'—red, single-type
'Red Charm'—deep red, bomb-type
'Robert W. Auten'—dark red, semidouble-type

White Blooms

'Ann Cousins'—double-type
'Ethel Mars'—white with pink tint, semidouble-type
'Festiva Maxima'—white with red flecks, double-type
'Isani Gidui'—buff center, Japanese-type
'Le Cygne'—one of the most famous white double-types
'Lillian Wild'—double-type
'Minnie Shaylor'—yellow stamens, semidouble-type
'Moon of Nippon'—yellow center, Japanese-type
'Northland'—bomb-type
'White Wings'—single-type

Pink Shades

'Doreen'—bright pink, Japanese-type
'Doris Cooper'—light pink, double-type
'Dresden Pink'—medium pink, double-type
'M. Jules Elie'—bright pink, double-type
'Mrs. Franklin D. Roosevelt'—rose-pink, double-type
'Nice Gal'—rose-pink, semidouble-type
'Sarah Bernhardt'—deep pink, double-type
'Seashell'—pink, single-type
'Solange'—buff-pink, double-type
'Therese'—bright pink, double-type

DISEASES. Botrytis, red spot, rot, wilt, virus.
INSECTS. Scales, thrips.

stance in the buds. The old wive's tale that ants must be present or the flowers won't open, is not true. Botrytis is the most common cause for buds not opening, and the disease can cause new growth to turn brown and rot. Apply a fungicide throughout the summer to control it.

The three main species of peonies are *P. albiflora* (or *P. lactiflora*), Chinese peony, from which a great many of our double flowering beauties have been created; *P. officinalis* (common red peony), the so-called Memorial Day peony from which come many single and double varieties; and *P. tenuifolia* (fernleaf peony), which also has numerous cultivars.

The tree peony, *P. suffruticosa*, is a small shrub rather than an herbaceous perennial.

Peonies are ordinarily classified according to the shape of their blooms as described below, although many new hybrids don't fit these classifications exactly.

- *Single flowering*—a single row of petals
- *Japanese*—a double row of petals with an airy, petal-like center. Anemone-types are similar.
- *Bomb-type*—a ball-like center and petal-like stamens
- *Semidouble*—wide petals, stamens are mixed in with petals
- *Double- or rose-type*—these very double forms are the most popular

Listed by color below are a few of the many popular peony varieties.

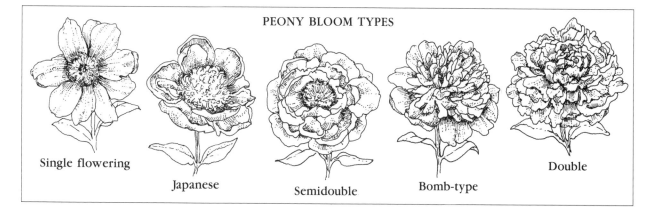

PEONY BLOOM TYPES

Single flowering   Japanese   Semidouble   Bomb-type   Double

PROPAGATION. By dividing the root clumps. Make sure there are three or more "eyes" (red sprouts) on each division. By dividing the plant in midsummer, just after the blooms have faded, they may have a small bloom or two the next year.

PAINTED DAISY. See *Pyrethrum*

PAMPAS GRASS. See *Grasses, ornamental*

PANSY. See *Viola*

PAPAVER (pap-ay'ver), poppy

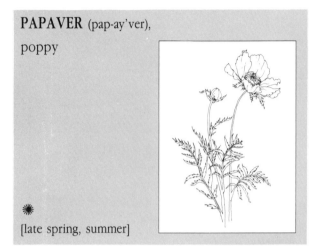

[late spring, summer]

Like the peony, the Oriental poppy, *P. orientale*, is a spectacular flower in the early summer garden. These long-lived plants grow from 2 to 4 feet tall, on stems that tend to sprawl. Although brilliant orange is their most common color, the huge blooms are also available in shades of red or pink, and sometimes in white or pale pink with a dark blotch. The colors are rather unstable, though, and if you let hybrids go to seed, the vigorous seedlings are likely to produce mostly orange flowers that will crowd out the weaker hybrids.

Plant Oriental poppies in full sun and rich soil. If possible, put them in a spot where other plants can camouflage them in midsummer, because after blooming they die down and become dormant, and look messy for a time. New growth appears soon after the old leaves have died, and this is the only good time to divide them, if you want to start new plants.

Some popular Oriental varieties include 'Apricot White,' 'Barr's White,' 'Cavalier' (red), 'Cheerio' (pink), 'Mahony' (red), 'Perry's White,' 'Scarlet Glow.'

Iceland poppies, *P. nudicaule*, are less showy than the Orientals, grow to a height of 12 inches, and come in shades of yellow, white, and orange in both single and double blooms. Most are fragrant, and make nice edging plants. If kept picked, they will bloom all summer. Plant Iceland poppy seeds in a permanent location since they do not transplant well. Usually the plants self-sow, so all that's necessary is to thin out the seedlings in the spring.

DISEASES. Botrytis, blight, leaf spot, mildew, virus.

INSECTS. Aphids, leafhoppers, nematodes, plant bugs.

PROPAGATION. Oriental poppies, by dividing the plants when they are dormant, just after blooms are passed. Start Iceland poppies from seeds.

PEARLY EVERLASTING. See *Anaphalis*

PEA VINE, PERENNIAL. See *Lathyrus*

PENSTEMON (pen-stee'mon), penstemon beardtongue

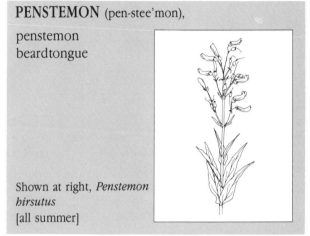

Shown at right, *Penstemon hirsutus*
[all summer]

About 250 species of the brightly colored penstemons grow throughout their native North America. Most need protection in northern regions where there is no certainty of snow cover. Their common name comes from the tubular-type flower that appears to have whiskers protruding from its open mouth. Throughout most of the summer, the showy small flowers borne on thin, 1- to 2-foot stalks, burst forth in many colors. The plants like full sun, good deep soil, well-supplied with leaf mold and mixed with a little sand for good drainage. Like many perennials they require adequate moisture, but don't like their roots to be wet for long periods. The blossoms make good cut flowers.

P. barbatus (bearlip penstemon), 3 to 6 feet tall, has bright red flowers throughout the summer. 'Rose Elf,' 18 inches high, and 'Prairie Fire,' a bright orange-red, 2 feet high, are two popular cultivars. *P. alpinus* (alpine penstemon) is a shorter growing, but slightly more hardy, species with purple flowers in early summer. *P.* x *gloxinioides* (gloxinia penstemon) hybrids have large red or pink flowers in summer, grow 2 to 3 feet high, and are suitable only in the warmer parts of the country. Among the fine cultivars are 'Firebird,' 'Garnet,' and 'Ruby King.'

DISEASES. Rust, root rot.

INSECTS. Aphids, caterpillars, nematodes.

PROPAGATION. By seed planted in early spring, or by division, best done in the fall. Also started from cuttings taken in late summer.

PEONY. See *Paeonia*

PERENNIAL BACHELOR'S BUTTON. See *Centaurea*

PERIWINKLE. See *Vinca*

PHLOX (flocks), phlox

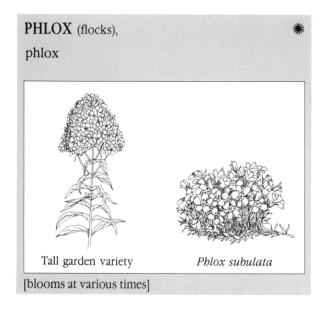

Tall garden variety   *Phlox subulata*

[blooms at various times]

'Prime Minister'—white with red eye
'Progress'—light blue with purple eye
'Red Glory'—red
'Sir John Falstaff'—large pink flowers
'Starfire'—red
'The King'—purple
'White Admiral'—late-blooming white

When phlox is mentioned, most people think of the tall-growing, brightly colored *P. paniculata* (sometimes called *P. decussata*), known as garden phlox, which forms the foundation of perennial borders in July and August. But other important members of this family are also worthwhile additions to the garden. Moss pink or moss phlox (*P. subulata*) is only 5 inches high, and it covers banks and rock gardens in early spring with carpets of tiny pink, lavender, red, white, or blue flowers. *P. canadensis*, Canadian phlox (also called *P. divaricata*, wild blue phlox), is 12 inches high and blooms in late spring, covering the plant with flowers in white or shades of blue. *P. carolina* (also called *P. suffruticosa*), thick-leaf phlox, reaches a height of 3 feet and has pink or white blossoms that appear about a month earlier than those of garden phlox.

Like daylilies, delphiniums, lilies, and peonies, the summer-flowering *P. paniculatas* are aristocrats of the garden, and well worth the care it takes to grow them. They all thrive in rich, deep garden soil, need adequate moisture (especially at blooming time), plus a little extra fertilizer and lime. They prefer full sun, but will tolerate light afternoon shade. Because of their stiff woody stems, phlox do not need staking, and all the common varieties are hardy in the North. Clumps should be set 2 to 3 feet apart.

Because their colors are so vivid, plant garden phlox carefully. Separate clashing hues with plants of white or pale colors. Always cut off the fading flower heads before any seeds form. Phlox grown from self-sown seed, even from the best plants, almost always produce flowers of a muddy magenta color.

Popular varieties of *P. paniculata*, and their colors, are listed below.

'Bright Eyes'—pink with red eye
'Caroline Vandenberg'—lavender-blue
'Elizabeth Arden'—pink
'Mount Fuji'—white
'Orange Perfection'—salmon-orange
'Pinafore Pink'—low-growing pink

P. carolina/suffruticosa grow well under the same conditions as *P. paniculata*, and are worth planting because they bloom earlier and extend the phlox season. 'Miss Lingard,' a white, is one of the best known cultivars, and makes a nice contrast to the blue delphiniums that bloom at the same time. *P. canadensis/divaricata* (wild blue phlox) is a native species, especially good for planting in wildflower gardens and in rockeries; 'Alba' is a white variety. *P. subulata* (moss pink) grows best in slightly acid, sandy soil. Among the attractive cultivars are 'Alexander's Surprise,' pink; 'Brilliant,' red; 'Emerald Cushion,' pink; and 'Blue Hills,' light blue.

The biggest weakness of phlox is its susceptibility to powdery mildew, which is encouraged by high humidity. Because the disease is difficult to treat, prevention is the best cure. Good air circulation is essential, so space the plants at least 2 feet apart and away from moisture-retaining walls, buildings, and hedges. Thin out the phlox stems while they are still small; leave only 4 or 5 stems in a clump if mildew is a problem. This will permit the plants to dry out quicker after a rain or dewy night, but still provide a good display of flowers. Thinning also encourages stronger stems and larger flowers.

DISEASES. Mildew, leaf spot, rot.

INSECTS. Beetles, mites, plant bugs.

PROPAGATION. All types of phlox can be propagated by dividing the clumps in fall or early spring, or by taking stem cuttings in early summer. *P. subulata* layers easily. *P. paniculata* can be grown from root cuttings, which is the method nurseries use to start large numbers.

We know of an easy method for home gardeners to start new plants from root cuttings in early summer. With a knife or spade, cut straight down a foot or so into the soil, completely around a mature phlox plant about an inch from the stems. This will sever all the exterior roots, but leave them in place: they will grow up into new little plants that can be dug and transplanted the following spring.

PHYSALIS (fiss'a-lis), Chinese lantern

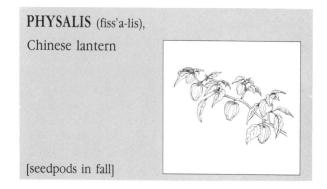

[seedpods in fall]

Of the many species of *Physalis*, those cultivated in gardens are the types with 2-inch, orange, lantern-shaped seedpods that are good for drying. *P. alkekengi* (also known is *P. franchetii*) is most common. Unfortunately, because it spreads by both long underground stolens and seeds, it can become a wretched weed, so plant it where it can be contained. It is hardy, gets to be about 2 feet tall, and has tiny white blooms in summer. *Physalis* likes sun or light shade, and grows in ordinary soil. It needs little care except for preventing it from going to seed, and cutting back the clump to keep it under control.

For winter bouquets, pick the stems just after the pods turn orange, and hang them upside down in a shaded dry spot with good air circulation until they are dry.

DISEASES. Wilt.

INSECTS. Striped beetle, flea beetle.

PROPAGATION. By seed or division.

PHYSOSTEGIA (fy-so-stee'ji-a),
false dragonhead

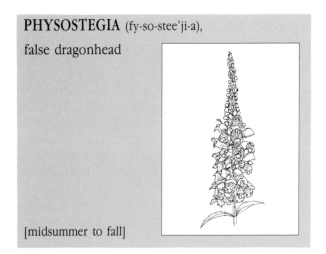

[midsummer to fall]

The flowers of *P. virginiana* (false dragonhead) are striking: 6- to 10-inch flower spikes covered with small snapdragon-type, rosy pink, lilac, or white blooms arranged in rows on four sides of the stem. Other names given to these colorful flowers are obedient plant (because the florets stay in whatever position they are placed) and American heather. They grow from 2 to 4 feet tall, do well in shady borders, and are also attractive along streams and in wildflower gardens. These hardy plants like moist soil, but also do well in dry soils, though they don't get as tall. Under the right conditions, they can spread rapidly.

DISEASES. Mildew, rust.

INSECTS. Aphids.

PROPAGATION. By dividing the plants or from seeds.

PINCUSHION FLOWER. See *Scabiosa*

PINKS, HARDY. See *Dianthus*

PLANTAINLILY. See *Hosta*

PLATYCODON (plat-i-ko'don),
balloon flower

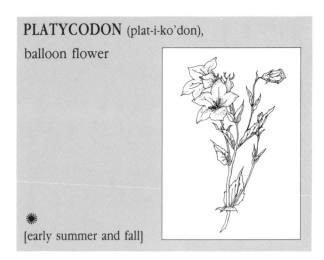

✳

[early summer and fall]

P. grandiflorus (balloon flower) gets its name from the partly opened flower that looks like a small balloon. In full bloom it resembles the campanula, with blue, white, or pink star-shaped flowers on 1- to 3-foot stems. Light, well-drained garden soil and sun pleases them, and a winter mulch is beneficial. They are an excellent border plant, long-lived, not invasive, and easy to care for. Because they always sprout late in the spring, mark the spot so you won't accidentally plant something else there or dig them up by mistake. After planting try not to move them, because their long taproot makes it difficult to transplant them successfully.

The popular variety, *P. g. mariesii* (Japanese bellflower), is 18 inches in height and has deep blue or white flowers that are bell-shaped.

They are good cut flowers, but will last longer if their stems are singed with a match before being placed in water.

DISEASES. Root rot.

PROPAGATION. *Platycodons* are best grown from seed because the plant is difficult to divide.

PLUMBAGO. See *Ceratostigma*

PLUME POPPY. See *Macleaya*

POLEMONIUM (po-lee-mo'ni-um),
Jacob's ladder

Shown at right, *Polemonium boreale*
[late spring to midsummer]

Jacob's ladder is excellent when used as a blue spot in the border, or for planting in a blue and white garden. Clusters of small, flat, or bell-shaped flowers grace the top of fernlike leaflet pairs that have been compared to the rungs on a ladder. They grow easily, needing only moist, but well-drained, garden soil. They like afternoon shade, but will grow in full sun. All the species listed below are hardy to zone 3.

P. boreale (also known as *P. humile*), a dwarf alpine plant with purple-blue flowers, is suitable for rock gardens and shady banks. *P. caeruleum*, Jacob's ladder, is 1 to 3 feet high and commonly planted in borders; 'Blue Pearl' is one of the better cultivars. 'Album' has white flowers. *P. reptans*, creeping Jacob's ladder, reaches a height of only 6 or 8 inches, grows wild in many places, and has light blue or white flowers in May. It is a good plant for the wildflower garden.

DISEASES. Leaf spot, mildew, rust, wilt.

PROPAGATION. By dividing the plants in early spring, by stem cuttings, or by sowing seed in the fall.

POLYGONUM (po-lig'o-num), fleeceflower

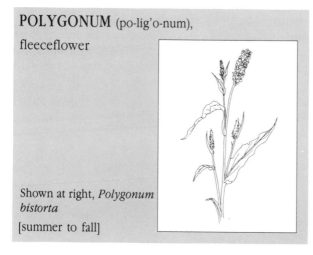

Shown at right, *Polygonum bistorta*

[summer to fall]

This group of plants with numerous tiny red or white flowers on spikes or heads are highly ornamental, and most have foliage that turns an attractive red color in the fall, but they can also turn into some of the worst weeds imaginable. Bindweeds, knotweeds, smartweeds, and snakeweeds are all part of the aggressive *Polygonum* family.

P. affine (Himalayan fleeceflower) is a hardy dwarf plant used as a ground cover, but recommended only where other plants don't grow well; it has small red flowers in late summer. *P. amplexicaule* (mountain fleece) is an attractive 3-foot border plant, with red or white flowers, but it is hardy only to zone 6. *P. cuspidatum* (Japanese fleeceflower or Mexican bamboo) has white flowers and can grow to 8 feet in one season, even in the North. Never plant it except in a natural setting far away from other cultivated plants. It spreads by underground stems and is nearly impossible to keep under control or to eradicate. Both *P. cuspidatum* and *P. sachalinense* (originally from Sakhalin Island in

Russia) are known as bamboos, but gardeners who have had them escape and move into other plantings use far less flattering names to describe them. As sold in this country, *P. reynoutria* (Reynoutria fleeceflower) is considered by experts to be a form of *P. cuspidatum compactum*. Three feet high, it has white to pink flowers, is a good ground cover, but can also be invasive.

DISEASES. Leaf spot.

INSECTS. Aphids, Japanese beetles.

PROPAGATION. By dividing the fleshy roots.

POPPY. See *Papaver*

POPPY, CANYON. See *Romneya*

POPPY, HIMALAYAN BLUE. See *Meconopsis*

POPPY MALLOW. See *Callirhoë*

POPPY, PLUME. See *Macleaya*

POPPY, TREE. See *Romneya*

POPPY, WELSH. See *Meconopsis*

POTENTILLA (po-ten-till'a), cinquefoil

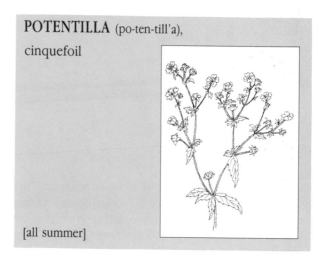

[all summer]

Although the native creeping potentilla, *P. canadensis* (oldfield cinquefoil), is a common weed all over the East, the garden varieties bear little resemblance to it. Nor do they much resemble the shrubby potentilla (*P. fruticosa*) often used as a foundation plant or a low-growing hedge. Herbaceous garden varieties do not like extreme heat, are less hardy than either the wild or shrubby forms, and need winter protection when grown from zone 4 north. The 12-to 18-inch plants resemble the strawberry in their trailing growth habit and leaf shape, but are more colorful with their red, yellow, and white blossoms. A good addition to the perennial border or rockery, and a fine edging plant, potentilla grows best in light, rich, loamy soil, sunshine or light shade, and needs to be divided often.

P. atrosanguinea (Himalayan cinquefoil) grows to 18 inches, and has cultivars which produce a wide variety of single and double flowers in bright orange, red, and yellow.

P. nepalensis (Nepal cinquefoil) has cultivars similar to the Himalayan, such as 'Miss Willmott,' which grows to 1 foot and has magenta-rose flowers. *P. tridentata* (three-toothed cinquefoil) is a low-growing variety often planted in rockeries; it has white strawberrylike blossoms that appear throughout the summer.

DISEASES. Leaf spot, mildew, rust.

INSECTS. Aphids, weevils.

PROPAGATION. By dividing the spreading plants. All varieties can be grown from seed, and some, such as 'Miss Willmott,' will come true.

PRICKLY PEAR. See *Opuntia*

PRIMROSE. See *Primula*

PRIMULA (prim'you-la), primrose

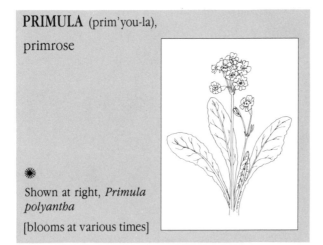

❋

Shown at right, *Primula polyantha*

[blooms at various times]

A border of *Primulas* in bloom is a joyous sight. They will reward you if you provide the special conditions they prefer. These cheery, low-growing plants have been hybridized into hundreds of forms, colors, and color combinations.

They like a somewhat heavy, slightly acid soil, which is rich in peat moss, compost, and other humus. The conditions that best suit them are those found in Great Britain and the Pacific Northwest, because they enjoy cool weather and moisture. They thrive in partial shade, especially during the hottest part of the day, but will not flower in deep shade, and are averse to deep cultivation or other root disturbance. Frequent division, perhaps every year, is essential, and should be done directly after blooming. The plants like a deep mulch, and appreciate a covering of evergreen boughs during the winter.

P. auricula, auricula primrose, grows to 8 inches, has evergreen leaves, and clusters of fragrant, single petal blooms in many colors, often with contrasting centers. *P. denticulata*, Himalayan primrose, is 10 to 12 inches tall, less hardy, has foliage with whitish flecks, and globelike flower heads of violet or white. *P. japonica*, Japanese primrose, is the candelabra-type with pink, red, purple, or white whorls of flowers on 18- to 24-inch stalks; it is a favorite

with gardeners because it is so easy to grow and propagate, and blooms over a long season. 'Millar's Crimson' and 'Postford's White' are two popular varieties. *P. juliae*, Julia primrose, has tiny, 3-inch tall flowers that are excellent in masses, particularly the Juliana cultivars. *P. x polyantha*, the well-known polyantha primrose group, are some of the largest flowering varieties at 12 inches, with huge umbels of single or double, often ruffled, blossoms in bright and pastel shades. *P. sieboldii*, Japanese star primrose, is 8 to 12 inches tall and will grow in more sunlight than others. Excellent Barnhaven hybrids with starlike blossoms in shades of pink, purple, blue, and white, have indented petals; petals in shades of pink, purple, blue and white; they go dormant and the foliage disappears in summer. *P. vulgaris*, English primrose, is 6 inches in height, has evergreen foliage, and the blooms come in many colors.

DISEASES. Anthracnose, leaf spot, rot, rusts, yellows.

INSECTS. Aphids, beetles, mealybugs, mites, red spiders, slugs.

PROPAGATION. Except for the cultivars that must be divided, *Primulas* are easily grown from seed which may be planted during late winter in a greenhouse, under grow lights, or in spring in a shaded outdoor bed. Some varieties take a long time to germinate, and the delicate, young plants must be handled and transplanted with special care. Established clumps can be divided in spring after they have finished flowering, or in late summer after they start to go dormant.

PRUNELLA (pru-nell'a), self heal

[early summer]

This member of the Mint family is often listed in catalogs, but we do not recommend it for most locations. Although most species are garden weeds, it probably has a place in rock gardens, or as a ground cover in places where nothing better will grow.

P. grandiflora, self heal, is a 12-inch high creeping plant that forms a thick evergreen mat with cylindrical spikes of purple flowers. Among the cultivars are 'Alba,' white; 'Rosea,' pink; and 'Rubra,' red. *P. webbiana*, 9 to 15 inches high, has attractive rosy purple, pink, and white blooms, and is not as invasive as most other species.

PROPAGATION. By seeds or division.

PULMONARIA (pul-mo-nay'ri-a),

lungwort
troutflower

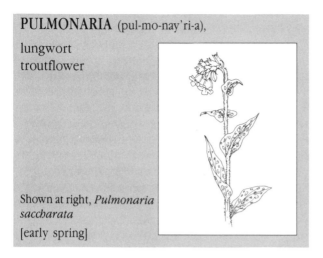

Shown at right, *Pulmonaria saccharata*

[early spring]

Pulmonaria are one of the first perennials in the border to bloom. Their tiny bell-shaped flowers decorate low-growing clumps of 6-inch leaves that may be spotted like a trout or, as early physicians pointed out, diseased lungs. All are very hardy, easy to grow, and form a clump rapidly, yet do not become weedy. They grow in full sun or light shade, in rich moist soil, and do especially well under deciduous trees.

P. angustifolia, blue or cowslip lungwort, is 6 to 10 inches tall, has green leaves, and blue, trumpet-shaped flowers that are pink as they open, but change to blue. *P. officinalis*, common lungwort, has light green leaves with white spots, small rose-red flowers that gradually turn blue-purple, and grows to a height of 12 inches. *P. saccharata*, Bethlehem sage, 6 to 15 inches in height, has pointed leaves dappled with white, and cultivars that come in red, white, blue, and pink. 'Mrs. Moon' has large pink flowers that fade to an attractive blue, and nice foliage.

PROPAGATION. By division in summer after they finish blooming, or by seed.

PURPLE CONEFLOWER. See *Echinacea*

PYRETHRUM. See *Chrysanthemum coccineum*

RANUNCULUS (ra-nun'kew-lus),

buttercup

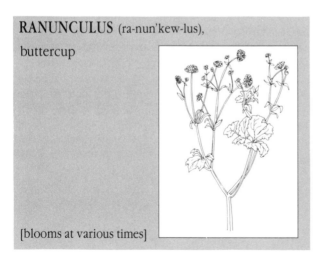

[blooms at various times]

There is a great variety of *Ranunculus* from which to choose and at least three species are worth planting in the perennial border—especially their new hybrids which have bright colors. They grow well in sun or light shade.

R. aconitifolius, aconite buttercup, 2 to 3 feet tall, is hardy from zone 5 south. Its leaves resemble those of *Aconitum* (monkshood), and the tall flower stalks have rounded blossoms. It likes moist, rich, well-drained soil. 'Flore Pleno' is an attractive double white and 'Luteus Plenus' is a double yellow.

R. asiaticus, the tuberous-rooted Persian buttercup, has large double and semidouble yellow flowers that appear in midsummer. It needs well-drained soil, and can survive the winter outdoors only in warm sections of the country. Can be grown as an annual in severe climates, or the tubers may be dried and stored inside over the winter like *Gladiolus* corms. The strain 'Superbissimus' (height: 1 foot), has a good chance of survival outdoors in zones 7 to 9 if planted in a raised bed with the roots buried 2 inches deep.

R. montanus, mountain buttercup, at only 3 to 6 inches in height, is good for a rock garden. It has large single yellow flowers in late spring, does not spread rapidly, and is hardy to zone 5.

DISEASES. Mildew, mold, rot, rust, virus.

INSECTS. Aphids, caterpillars, mites.

PROPAGATION. By dividing the roots or tubers in early spring. Seeds are also possible.

RED-HOT POKER. See *Kniphofia*

ROCKCRESS. See *Arabis*

ROCKET. See *Hesperis*

ROCK JASMINE. See *Androsace*

ROMNEYA (rom'nee-a),

canyon poppy
tree poppy

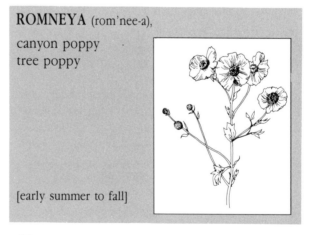

[early summer to fall]

The name canyon poppy suggests the southwestern desert, but this plant will grow in **zones 6 and 7**. Light, sandy, not-too-fertile loam and full sun, with a heavy mulch, are the preferred growing conditions. The large (4 to 6 inches) silky, single peony-type white flowers with yellow centers appear in early summer and continue to bloom for a long time on tall, 4 to 6 feet shrubby-looking branches. The blooms are fragrant and last only a few days. *R. coulteri* (California tree poppy) is the most commonly grown, but *R. trichocalyx* is very similar. Both are natives of California and Mexico.

PROPAGATION. Since plants grown from seed may take up to three years before flowering, root cuttings are better. Cut parts of the root into 3-inch pieces and plant horizontally about one-half inch deep in sandy soil in a greenhouse or hot bed during early spring. After sprouting, the plants should be transplanted and grown in pots until well established.

ROSE CAMPION. See *Lychnis*

ROSE MALLOW. See *Hibiscus*

RUDBECKIA (rood-beck'i-a),

coneflower
gloriosa daisy

☀

[midsummer to frost]

This large genus of the Daisy family includes annuals, biennials, and perennials, many of which are valuable border plants. They are easy to grow and need only full sun and ordinary garden soil to thrive.

Gardeners often dig up bright black-eyed Susans (*R. hirta*) from beside the road, and move them to their flower border without realizing that they are annual or biennial and will die shortly after blooming. (They are ideal plants for a wildflower garden, however, if allowed to reseed.) Golden glows (*R. laciniata hortensia*), on the other hand, are so durable that after decades of neglect, they still bloom beside the cellar holes of old farms and abandoned country schoolhouses.

R. hirta gloriosa (gloriosa daisy) with bright blooms in orange, yellow, and red tones, give the garden a full-of-bloom look in midsummer when other flowers are scarce. They come in double, semidouble, and single blooms. Since the plants are short-lived, they must be replaced every few years. They grow easily from seed, and if started early, bloom the same year.

Many hybrids of *R. fulgida* are offered by perennial nurseries including 'Goldsturm,' a large golden yellow, which grows about 2 feet tall. *R. laciniata* and *R. speciosa* are the

cutleaf and showy coneflowers respectively, which grow wild in moist woodlands. *R. l. hortensia* (golden glow), needs staking and grows too tall for most small borders at 6 to 8 feet, but new hybrids are shorter, and better for backyard plantings; 'Gold Drop' is only 2 to 3 feet tall.

DISEASES. Crown rot, leaf spot, mildew, rust.

INSECTS. Aphids, beetles, plant bugs, sawflies.

PROPAGATION. Biennial kinds are started from seed only. Perennial varieties can be propagated either by division or seed.

SAGE. See *Salvia*

ST. JOHN'S-WORT. See *Hypericum*

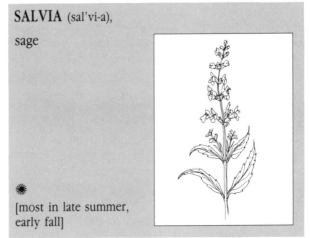

SALVIA (sal'vi-a),

sage

☀

[most in late summer, early fall]

The salvia genus not only includes the herb *S. officinalis* (garden sage), and the familiar brilliant red *S. splendens*, (scarlet sage, cultivated as an annual), but also perennial varieties good for the border that grow from 2 to 5 feet tall with masses of small blue or lavender flowers on long spikes. Salvias are vigorous growers and many have aromatic foliage. They like full sun and sandy, dry garden soil that is not too fertile. Most need winter protection in zones 3 and 4.

Quite a few of them are suitable for the garden. *S. azurea* (blue sage) one of the hardiest, is 3 to 4 feet tall, has leaves that are bluish green on the underside, and light blue flowers. *S. farinacea* (mealycup sage) is less leggy in appearance at 2 to 4 feet, but so **tender** it is often grown as an annual north of zone 8. The tiny white hairs that cover the flowers produce a mealy look; 'Blue Bedder,' a Wedgewood blue, and 'Victoria,' a vivid purple-blue, are attractive cultivars. *S. pratensis*, also listed as *S. haematodes*, (bloodvein sage) is usually biennial, 1 to 3 feet in height, has lavender-blue blooms that come early, and leaves with red veins.

The salvia hybrids are superior to the species. *S. x superba* (violet sage) hybrids, for example, bloom early, but if kept picked will continue to bloom all summer.

DISEASES. Leaf spot, mildew, wilt.

INSECTS. Aphids, beetles, plant bugs, whiteflies.

PROPAGATION. Perennial salvia grows readily from seeds. Cultivars should be propagated by cuttings, or can be divided in early spring.

SANDWORT. See *Arenaria*

SAPONARIA (sap-o-nair'i-a),

soapwort
bouncing bet

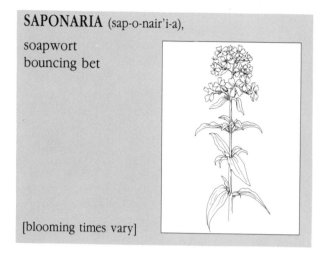

[blooming times vary]

This plant is named because the juice from crushed leaves and stems of some species can be used to create a soaplike lather. All thrive in full sun and well-drained garden soil.

S. ocymoides, rock soapwort, is 8 inches tall covered with small pink flowers in early summer, and is ideal for rock gardens. 'Splendens' has deep rose blossoms, and those of 'Rubra' are deep red. Needs cutting back after flowering to keep it compact and attractive. *S. officinalis*, bouncing bet, grows to a height of 30 inches. A European native, it has become a weed in much of the United States. The plants have pink blooms, which appear throughout the summer, most abundantly at night; it's best in a wildflower garden, where it can be kept under control. Like the other *Saponarias*, it has no serious pests.

PROPAGATION. By seed, division of the plants in early spring, or cuttings taken in late summer.

SAXIFRAGA (sax'iff-rag-a),

saxifrage

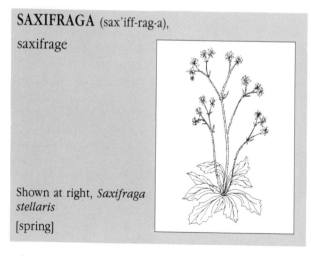

Shown at right, *Saxifraga stellaris*

[spring]

An entire book could be written describing the immense Saxifrage family, which consists of hundreds of named species. In Latin, *Saxifraga* means "rock breaking," and as the name implies most are small plants suitable for the rock garden. One exception, *S. stolonifera* (strawberry geranium or mother of thousands) is a favorite houseplant, although it's often planted outdoors for the summer. *Saxifraga* need well-drained, sandy, limestone soil, and prefer partial shade. Their forms and growth habits vary from succulent to mossy types, and the flowers come in many different colors.

A few hardy species can be grown in the North. *S. caespitosa*, 6 inches in height, is a native plant that produces white blooms in spring. *S.* x *geum*, kidney leaf saxifrage, grows in broad rosettes of round, shiny, leathery leaves with small white flowers to a height of 1 foot. *S. paniculata*, aizoon saxifrage, 12 inches or more, an Arctic alpine, has yellow flowers with purple markings in May. Its many cultivars include 'Alba,' white; 'Balcana,' white with red spots; 'Densa,' a compact-growing variety with silvery foliage; and 'Paradoxa,' bluish leaves and white flowers. *S. virginiensis*, Virginia saxifrage, is a native of the eastern United States that grows from the Carolinas to Canada; it grows from a few inches to a foot tall, does well in rocky soils, and forms an attractive rosette of leaves with white or greenish white blooms.

In addition to the above hardy varieties, there are many others suitable for rockery plantings in warmer parts of the country. *S. cotyledon*, Jungfrau saxifrage, grows about 2 feet tall, and bears interesting white flowers with red veins in May and June. *S. longifolia*, longleaf saxifrage, is another 2-foot species that produces a rosette of silvery green leaves and white flowers in May. *S.* x *macnabiana*, MacNab saxifrage, are hybrids with white flowers that have purple spots. *S. umbrosa*, or *S.* x *urbium*, 'London Pride,' 1 foot high with small pink flowers, is widely grown in England and in similar moist climates.

DISEASES. Blight, gray mold, leaf spot, mildew, rust.
INSECTS. Aphids, mealybugs, mites.
PROPAGATION. By dividing the plants in early spring.

SAXIFRAGE. See *Saxifraga*

SCABIOSA (scab-i-o'sa),

pincushion flower
scabiosa

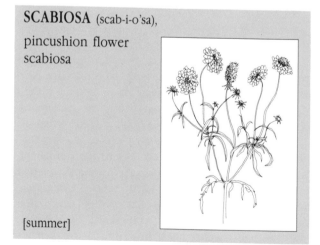

[summer]

These plants were given the botanical name *Scabiosa* because they were once considered a cure for the itch, and called pincushion flower because the dark stamens stand out like pins in a cushion. But we think such a beautiful specimen deserves more elegant nomenclature. Delicate petals surround the "cushion" of these long-stemmed, 3-inch wide flowers, in shades of light blue, lavender, and white. At least three of the many perennial scabiosa species are worth planting in the border and they are described below. They bloom for several weeks, especially if the flowers are kept picked, like full sun, and well-drained limestone or neutral soil. They don't appreciate extreme heat or cold. Because they bloom sparsely, plant them in a group to create an effective clump in the border. Plants grow to 2 feet tall.

S. caucasica (pincushion flower) has blue or white flowers, and the Isaac House hybrids come in a wide range of blue shades; it is an excellent cut flower. *S. columbaria* (dove scabiosa) has pink or lilac ball-shaped blooms in midsummer, which are smaller than those of *S. caucasica. S. ochroleuca* (cream scabiosa) has yellow, globelike, 1-inch blooms for most of the summer; it is too tender for planting in the far North, and is often short-lived in hot climates.

DISEASES. Blight, leaf spot, mildew, rust.

INSECTS. Aphids, mealybugs, mites, slugs.

PROPAGATION. By division for cultivars, to be sure of getting the same variety. Seed produces the strongest plants, however, and a large proportion will closely resemble the parent.

SCILLA (sill'a), squill

[early spring]

This group of dwarf-growing, spring-flowering bulbous plants is native to southern Europe and Asia. Most like a sunny location and good garden soil. The bulbs spread rapidly, both by offsets and from seed, so are excellent for planting in a wildflower garden. Plant 3 inches deep.

S. bifolia, twinleaf squill, is early flowering, with starlike blue, pink, or white flowers, 3 to 6 inches in height, and hardy to zone 5. *S. hispanica* (also listed as *Endymion hispanicus*), Spanish bluebell, 12 to 15 inches tall, is longlived, and unlike many other species, prefers a shady spot; cultivars have blue, pink, and white flowers. *S. siberica,* Siberian squill, 6 inches tall, is the most widely grown; it's hardy, and has deep blue or white flowers.

DISEASES. Blight, mosaic, rot.

INSECTS. Aphids.

PROPAGATION. By seed, or by digging the clumps after blooming and separating the bulbs.

SEA HOLLY. See *Eryngium*

SEA LAVENDER. See *Limonium*

SEDUM (see'dum), stonecrop

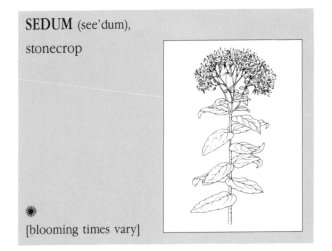

[blooming times vary]

Nearly 400 species are reputed to be in this genus of low-growing succulents. Some are well suited to the rock garden, some are good ground covers, but others are ugly weeds. Only a few are suitable for the perennial border.

Sedums are easy to grow. In fact, one of their common names is "live forever." They like dry, infertile soil, and grow in sun or light shade. Their flowers come in a wide range of colors, and one or another is in bloom throughout the season. They are also very hardy.

One of the best for the border is *S. spectabile*, showy stonecrop, 18 to 24 inches high, and its cultivars. As children we carefully rubbed the slippery leaves to separate the membranes, so we could blow them up as tiny balloons. It has lavender-pink flowers in late summer, but like other sedums can become a weed that is hard to eradicate. There are several similar species of fleshy-leaved sedums and among the cultivars that deserve a place in the border are 'Autumn Joy,' which is considered one of the best fall flowers, with light pink blooms that darken to red and then russet in autumn; 'Brilliant,' with bright red blooms; 'Meteor,' crimson-red; and 'Stardust,' a creamy white with bluish foliage.

Low-growing wide-leaved sedums suitable for rock gardens or as ground covers include *S. kamtschaticum,* Kamschatca sedum, a favorite for planting in walls where it can trail over rocks. It has tiny yellow-orange blossoms and leaves that turn an attractive bronze during the fall. *S. sarmentosum,* from the Orient, is known as stringy stonecrop, and is often planted as a prostrate ground cover. It has bright yellow flowers in summer and evergreen leaves. *S. spurium,* two-row stonecrop, is 6 inches tall, has pink-white flowers, and foliage that turns bronze red; among the cultivars are 'Dragon's Blood,' which has bright crimson flowers and 'Album,' a white. *S. ternatum,* mountain stonecrop, a native of the United States, is found in the eastern regions of the country. It grows in tight rosettes, has blue-white flowers in early summer, and seeds itself freely.

There are a number of narrow-leaved sedums worthy of consideration as ground covers or for rockeries. *S. acre*, goldmoss stonecrop, has a mat-growing habit that makes it a favorite in the rockery, although it can become weedy if not controlled. It has bright yellow flowers in late spring, and is good for planting between flagstones in paths and terraces. Cultivars of interest are 'Aureum,' which has leaves with yellow tips; 'Elegans,' with silver-tipped leaves; and 'Minus,' an extremely low-growing type. *S. anglicum*, English sedum, is a 2-inch tall creeping plant with white flowers. *S. dasyphyllum*, leafy stonecrop, also very dwarf, has pink flowers in June, is good in rock gardens and for planting in the dirt crevices of stone walls. *S. lydium*, Lydian stonecrop, grows slightly higher, has white flowers in June, and reddish foliage. *S. sexangulare*, hexagon stonecrop, is a creeper, 3 inches in height, with dark yellow flowers in midsummer. *S. stahlii*, coral beads, 8 inches tall, also has yellow flowers, but is hardy only in states below the Mason-Dixon line.

DISEASES. Crown rot, leaf spot, rot, rust.

INSECTS. Aphids, mealybugs, nematodes, scales.

PROPAGATION. By cuttings. Nearly every piece will root and grow into a new plant in practically no time. The plants may also be divided, layered, and grown from seed.

SELF HEAL. See *Prunella*

SEMPERVIVUM (sem-per-vy'vum),
hen-and-chickens
houseleek

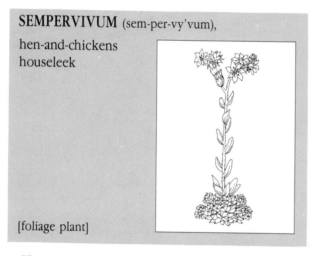

[foliage plant]

These neat-looking, rosettelike succulent plants have long been favorites in terraces, rock walls, stone paths, and rock gardens, as well as edgings for foundation plantings and perennial borders. Some grow so densely they can be used as ground covers. The different species and varieties grow from a few inches to about a foot tall, with red, yellow, or greenish flowers that are not particularly attractive. The plants are valued instead for their colorful foliage, which has made them popular in the creation of intricate plant mosaics in formal gardens and parkway median plantings.

Sempervivums are easy to grow and will survive in small amounts of poor soil, although they do better in sandy,

well-drained, fertile garden soil. They enjoy nuzzling around rocks and need full sun. A little dryness is okay since they are able to store moisture in their succulent stems. A plant will die after it blooms, but since the rosettes multiply so fast around the base of the old plant, this usually goes unnoticed. If a lot of them seem ready to bloom at one time, however, cut the buds from most of them before they open.

Although they like warmth, the hardy varieties need a cool dormant period, so if you pot them up in the fall to bring them in over the winter as houseplants, leave them outdoors for several weeks before bringing them inside.

S. tectorum, hen-and-chickens, is the most frequently grown of the *Sempervivums*, and is also one of the hardiest; in zones 3 and 4 it should be grown in a sheltered location. It has 1-inch-wide pink flowers, and some varieties have leaves with red edging. *S. arachnoideum*, spiderweb houseleek, is another popular variety. It is less hardy than hen-and-chickens, with showy, bright red flowers, and leaves connected by light threads. *S. montanum*, houseleek, 6 inches in height, from the European Alps, grows in dark green rosettes that are covered with thick hairs; flowers are purplish blue. *S. m. braunii* grows slightly taller and has yellowish blooms.

DISEASES. Rot, rust.

INSECTS. Mealybugs.

PROPAGATION. By separating the offsets any time of the year, or by seed.

SENNA. See *Cassia*

SHASTA DAISY. See *Chrysanthemum maximum*

SIDALCEA (sy-dall'see-a),
false mallow
wild hollyhock

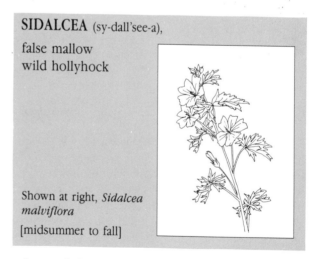

Shown at right, *Sidalcea malviflora*
[midsummer to fall]

Some of these short-lived perennials resemble hollyhocks, but do not grow as tall. Natives of the western United States, they grow from 2 to 3 feet tall, on spikes with pink or white mallow-type blooms that are good for cutting. They are not weedy, and will bloom far into the fall if kept cut. Well-drained garden soil and full sun are necessary for their success. Two species and several varieties are worthwhile in the border or natural garden in zones 5 through 9. *S. candida* is the hardiest and tallest species with small white flowers, and is often called wild hollyhock. *S. malviflora* (checkerbloom) is best in zone 8 or warmer, and has pink flowers.

Perennial catalogs often list the following cultivars: 'Elsie Heugh,' pink; 'Pink Beauty'; 'Rosy Gem'; 'William Smith,' salmon pink; and 'Starks Hybrids,' a mixture of pinks.

DISEASES. Leaf spot, rust.

INSECTS. Aphids, mites.

PROPAGATION. Native species by seeds, named varieties by dividing the plants in spring.

SILVERMOUND. See *Artemisia*

SNAKEROOT. See *Cimicifuga*

SNEEZEWEED. See *Helenium*

SNOWDROP. See *Galanthus*

SNOW-IN-SUMMER. See *Cerastium*

SNOW-ON-THE-MOUNTAIN. See *Aegopodium*

SOAPWEED. See *Yucca*

SOAPWORT. See *Saponaria*

SOLIDAGO (sol-i-day'go),
goldenrod

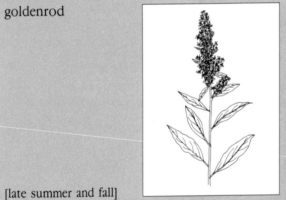

[late summer and fall]

Since over 100 native species of these hardy plants bloom in abundance every fall, few people ever think of planting them in their gardens. Some new hybrids, however, are worthy of a spot in the regular garden, as well as a natural border. Some species have been crossed with asters (x *Solidaster*, hybrid goldenrod, also called *S. luteus*) and others, or are developments from European species. These cultivars range from 1 to 3 feet in height, with plumes sometimes nearly a foot in diameter. They are easy to grow in ordinary soil with a bit of lime, and like full sun, although most will tolerate some light shade. The plant's bad name among hay fever sufferers has been greatly exaggerated. Ragweed, which blooms at the same time, is the real culprit.

DISEASES. Rust (but are relatively pest free).

PROPAGATION. By dividing the plants anytime. Seeds are likely to produce inferior plants because good varieties are easily pollinated by any wild species growing nearby.

SPEEDWELL. See *Veronica*

SPIDERWORT. See *Tradescantia*

SPIREA. See *Astilbe*

SPURGE. See *Euphorbia*

SQUILL. See *Scilla*

STACHYS (stack'iss),
betony
lamb's ears

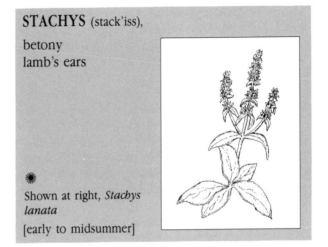

✳ Shown at right, *Stachys lanata*
[early to midsummer]

The betonies are European in origin, but hardy in the North when sheltered. Some are grown for their interesting silvery foliage, which makes a nice contrast in the perennial garden, and others for their blooms. They like sun or light shade and are not fussy about soils.

The familiar *S. byzantina* (also sold as *S. olympica* and *S. lanata*), lamb's ears, is 18 or more inches tall, and is grown for its soft, furry, gray-white foliage; the pink or lavender flowers are insignificant. 'Silver Carpet' is a nonflowering cultivar that makes an effective ground cover. *S. grandiflora* (also sold as *S. macrantha*), big betony, has green scalloped, heart-shaped leaves, and spikes of attractive lavender-pink flowers that grow to a height of 18 inches.

PROPAGATION. By dividing in fall or spring, or by seed.

STOKES' ASTER. See *Stokesia*

STOKESIA (stoke'see-a),
Stokes' aster
cornflower aster

[summer to fall]

A native of the southern states, this perennial, usually with light blue blooms, can be grown in sheltered northern locations, but only with winter protection. *S. laevis* is an easy-care plant, about 18 inches tall, and thrives on light, warm soil in full sun. The blooms are excellent for the front of the border, and make good, long-lasting cut flowers. Some cultivars of note are 'Alba,' white; 'Blue Danube'; 'Cyanea,' blue; and 'Silver Moon,' white.

PROPAGATION. By seed which, if planted early, will bloom the first year.

STONECRESS. See *Aethionema*

STONECROP. See *Sedum*

SUNDROP. See *Oenothera*

SUNFLOWER. See *Helianthus*

SUNFLOWER HELIOPSIS. See *Heliopsis*

SUN ROSE. See *Helianthemum*

SWEET PEA. See *Lathyrus*

SWEET ROCKET. See *Hesperis*

SWEET WILLIAM. See *Dianthus*

THALICTRUM (tha-lick'trum),
meadowrue

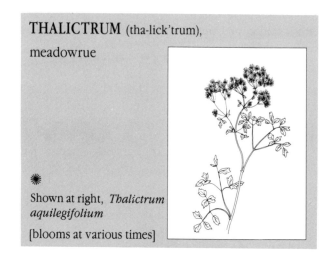

✳
Shown at right, *Thalictrum aquilegifolium*

[blooms at various times]

These plants, with foamy pink, white, yellow, or lavender blooms, are good for the back of the border, the wild garden, or alongside streams and other moist places. They like damp soil and light shade, but most will also grow well in ordinary soil and full sun.

T. aquilegifolium, columbine meadowrue, grows from 3 to 4 feet tall, and has feathery white, pink, or blue flowers in late spring; the name refers to its columbinelike foliage. *T. dipterocarpum*, Yunnan meadowrue, 3 to 5 feet tall, has lavender flowers in late summer; 'Hewitt's Double' is a double cultivar. *T. rochebrunianum*, lavender mist meadowrue, 5 to 6 feet tall, is a superior species with lavender-violet blossoms in mid- to late summer, and nice foliage; needs staking. *T. speciosissimum* (also sold as *T. glaucum*), dusty meadowrue, has bluish green leaves, and fragrant

yellow flowers in early summer; it may grow as tall as 6 feet, and needs staking.

Several low-growing *Thalictrums* are suitable for the rock garden. *T. minus*, low meadowrue, grows 1 to 1½ feet tall with fernlike leaves and yellow flowers. *T. alpinum*, alpine meadowrue, 4 to 6 inches in height, has white blooms.

DISEASES. Leaf spot, mildew, rust.

INSECTS. Aphids.

PROPAGATION. By division, or by seeds which will grow readily.

THERMOPSIS (ther-mop'sis),
thermopsis
false lupine

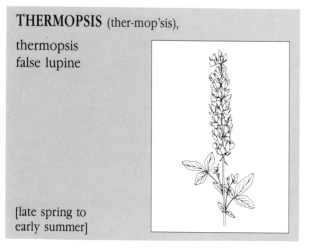

[late spring to early summer]

A few of these native North American plants are suitable for planting in the border. They belong to the Pea family and the common name derives from their tall spikes of yellow lupinelike flowers. *Thermopsis* are easy to grow in full sun, and will tolerate low-fertility soil better than most perennials.

T. caroliniana, Carolina lupine, is one of the most popular, and most showy at 4 to 5 feet in height; it is hardy to zone 3, and has deep roots, so is quite drought-resistant. *T. montana*, mountain thermopsis, is much the same except that it is shorter (2 feet tall) and has smaller blooms. *T. rhombifolia*, prairie thermopsis, is native to the western United States and Canada, and is even more dwarf (1 foot high).

PROPAGATION. By division in spring, or by seed sown in late summer, as soon as it has ripened.

THRIFT. See *Armeria*

THYME. See *Thymus*

THYMUS (tie'mus),
thyme

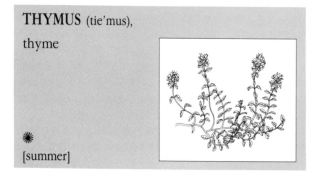

✳
[summer]

The thymes (pronounced times) are a remarkable group of herbs and ornamental plants. Their creeping habit and attractive blooms make them perfect, not only for herb and rock gardens, but for planting between the stones on terraces, and along paths where footsteps will release their minty fragrance.

Thyme does well in garden soil, but can also grow in poor, dry ones. They like full sun or light shade, and prefer shelter from the wind.

There are far too many species to mention here, but the ones that follow are most often planted. *T. serpyllum* (other species are also sold under this name), mother-of-thyme, a 3-inch high creeping plant, is excellent as a ground cover or for terraces; it is covered with purple-pink flowers for much of the summer. The variety *T. s. albus* has white flowers early in summer, and *T. s. coccineus* has red blossoms. *T. s. lanuginosus*, wooly thyme, stands only 2 inches high and has gray fuzzy leaves. *T. x citriodorus*, lemon thyme, 6 to 8 inches in height, so named for the lemony fragrance it exudes when the leaves are crushed, has tiny pink flowers in early June. *T. vulgaris*, common thyme, blooms in May with small lavender or purple flowers, and is often dried and used as a culinary herb.

DISEASES. Rot.

INSECTS. Mealybugs.

PROPAGATION. By division, layering, or by seed.

TICKSEED. See *Coreopsis*

TOADFLAX. See *Linaria*

TORCH LILY. See *Kniphofia*

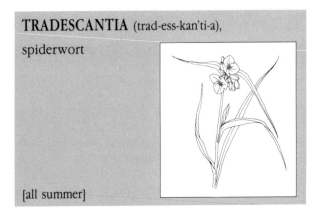

TRADESCANTIA (trad-ess-kan'ti-a),
spiderwort

[all summer]

The *Tradescantia* being offered by up-to-date nurseries have been transformed by hybridizers from a rather uninteresting native into an attractive garden perennial with blue, purple, pink, red, or white flowers on 2½-foot stems. Although each blossom lasts only one day, the petals will disappear, and new flowers open daily throughout the summer. It thrives in rich, moist, woodsy soil, light shade or full sun.

T. virginiana, Virginia spiderwort, 1 to 3 feet in height, is a native species with grasslike foliage, and purple, white, and deep blue flowers. Crosses of this and *T. bracteata*, another hardy *Tradescantia*, have produced *T. x andersoniana*, common spiderwort; lovely cultivars include 'Iris Pritchard,' white with blue; 'Pauline,' pink; 'Red Cloud,' rosy red; and 'Snowcap,' pure white.

PROPAGATION. By division in spring or fall.

TREE POPPY. See *Romneya*

TRITOMA. See *Kniphofia*

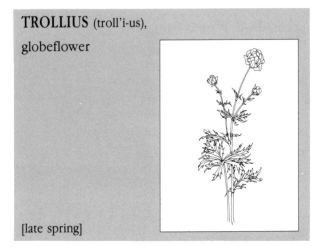

TROLLIUS (troll'i-us),
globeflower

[late spring]

This member of the Buttercup family has been a beloved garden flower for years, and is one of our special favorites. Its large (2 to 3 inch) bright yellow or orange, globe-shaped, buttercuplike blooms on 2-foot stalks, brighten the spring garden, and make excellent cut flowers. Recently introduced cultivars in various shades of orange, pale yellow, and red-orange are even more enticing. A good cut flower.

Trollius do best in moist soils that are rich in humus, and like sun or light shade. The clumps always stay nicely compact and within bounds. Once planted, let them grow undisturbed for several years to obtain the best effect. In the North, it's best to give the plants some winter protection.

T. europaeus, common globeflower, 2 feet tall, is yellow and the most widely planted; it blooms for a long season, and numerous named cultivars are offered by nurseries. *T. ledebourii*, Ledebour globeflower, 3 feet in height, blooms in early summer, has semidouble orange blooms, and is a native of northern Asia; plants sold under this name are likely to be *T. chinensis*.

Some of the cultivars of the various species being offered are 'Etna,' orange; 'Goldquelle,' orange-yellow; and 'T. Smith,' yellow.

DISEASES. Leaf spot.

PROPAGATION. Trollius may be grown from seed, but this is rather tricky because the seeds germinate slowly and unevenly. Older plants may be divided as soon as they finish flowering, but because the plants spread slowly, it cannot be done often.

TROUTFLOWER. See *Pulmonaria*

TULIP. See *Tulipa*

TULIPA (tew'lip-a),
tulip

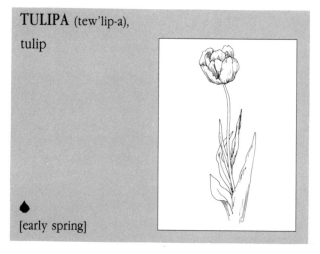

◆

[early spring]

Everyone knows these brightly colored popular bulb plants—they are a welcome sight after the dark cold days of winter. Gardeners who take time to plant a few dozen, or a few hundred of these relatively inexpensive bulbs in the fall have every right to congratulate themselves the next spring. It's hard to become bored with them because there are many tulip species, and some species have thousands of named varieties.

Tulips need a spot that gets either full, or nearly full sun, and the soil should be light, well-drained, and rich. Dig holes 8 inches apart, and deep enough so that the top (pointed end) of the bulb will be at least 4 inches below the surface of the soil, but still have several inches of loose soil beneath it to encourage root development. Place a tablespoon of bonemeal beneath each bulb, and mix a few mothballs in to discourage rodents from using them as winter rations.

The best time to plant bulbs is in late fall, between the period when the weather cools (so the bulbs won't start to grow), and a few weeks before the ground starts to freeze (so the bulbs can form roots to give them the nourishment they need to bloom well in the spring).

Most tulips, unfortunately, do not continue to bloom year after year, or increase in numbers like daffodils. They may survive and produce flowers again the second year if left in the ground, but the blooms will be less satisfactory, and the third year they may not bloom at all. Most gardeners treat them as annuals and buy new bulbs each year. We dig up the old tulips in early summer, after the foliage has died down. We then dry the bulbs for a few days and store them in a cool, dry, dark place, and replant them in late fall, provided we remember where we stored them, which we rarely do.

Luckily for absent-minded gardeners, a new perennial-type tulip is available that produces blooms for several years when left in the ground. The care of these is different, so if you buy them, be sure to follow the accompanying cultural directions.

Sometimes gardeners pot tulip bulbs and store them in a cool basement, until they are brought up to be forced into bloom in late winter. This is successful where temperature and humidity can be controlled as in a greenhouse, but the results in a home atmosphere may not be the same, and it is better to buy plants already started by a florist, instead.

Tulips are sold under the following classifications.

- **COTTAGE** tulips have petals that are rounded at the top, and include the lily-flowered kinds which have petals with pointed tips.
- **DARWINS** and **DARWIN HYBRIDS** are known for their wide variety of rich colors, squarish flowers, and strong stems.
- **EARLY SINGLES** are lower growing, and are prized for their early blooming habit and for potted blooms.
- **EARLY DOUBLES** are used in the same way as the singles; the flowers are not only double, but longer lasting than the singles.
- **LATE DOUBLES**, or peony-flowering tulips, are good choices both in the border and as cut flowers. Because the blooms are so heavy, double tulips should be protected from the wind, and staked if necessary.
- **REMBRANDTS** have flowers that are streaked or variegated.
- **MULTIFLOWERED** have several flowers on the same stem.
- **PARROT** tulips produce large brightly colored, loosely-formed flowers with ragged-edged petals that tend to open wider than most tulips.
- **TRIUMPH** tulips are tall growing and showy, blooming just after the early kinds.
- **FOSTERIANA HYBRIDS** are large, brilliant, early flowering, and include the 'Holland's Glory' and 'Red Emperor' varieties.
- **KAUFMANNIANA HYBRIDS** are often called water lily tulips because they open so wide. Early flowering.

In addition to the many hybrids found under these classifications, there are numerous wild species, many of them miniatures, that are appropriate for the rock garden or wild-flower border.

DISEASES. Anthracnose, blight, crown rot, virus.

INSECTS. Aphids, bulb flies, millipedes, mites, nematodes, wireworms.

PROPAGATION. Tulips are not easy to propagate, and except for favored places in Holland, and North American locales such as Long Island, Michigan, and the Pacific Northwest, the climate is not conducive to starting new plants. For most gardeners it's better to leave this job to the professionals, and buy the bulbs.

TURTLEHEAD. See *Chelone*

VALERIAN. See *Centranthus*

VALERIAN. See *Valeriana*

VALERIANA (val-ee-ri-an'a),

valerian
garden heliotrope

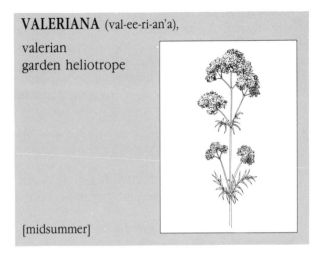

[midsummer]

Valerians are easy-to-grow plants and are not choosy about soils. *V. officinalis*, common valerian, grows to a height of 4 feet in sun or partial shade, has fernlike foliage, and white, pinkish, or lavender blooms. Cultivars also have red blossoms. It is often called garden heliotrope and has a pungent fragrance. Whether it is worthy of a place in the manicured garden is questionable, because of its tendency to spread. The wildflower or fragrant garden is probably a better place for it.

DISEASES. Leaf spot, mildew, rot, rust.

INSECTS. Japanese beetles.

PROPAGATION. By seeds or by division.

VERBASCUM (ver-bas'kum),

mullein

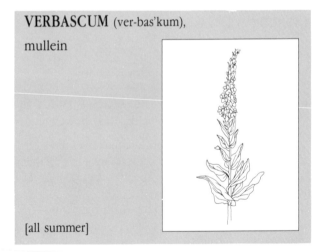

[all summer]

Although moth mullein (*V. blattaria*) is a yellow-blooming, tall biennial weed with wooly leaves—it's a familiar sight in dry country pastures—several more refined species are used as garden plants.

Two perennial species are *V. chaixii* (chaix mullein) with long, 3-foot-tall white flower spikes, hardy to zone 5; and *V. phoeniceum* (purple mullein), 5 feet tall, which has available some excellent purple, pink, and red cultivars. Most are hardy to zone 5, but need protection farther north.

V. thapsus (flannel mullein), is 4 feet tall, a biennial, has yellow- and bronze-colored blooms, and is hardy to zone 3. Good in a natural planting, but it is too invasive for the garden border.

DISEASES. Mildew, leaf spot, rot.

INSECTS. Nematodes.

PROPAGATION. Perennial mulleins are easily propagated by division, and biennial kinds by seed.

VERBENA (ver-bee'na),

verbena

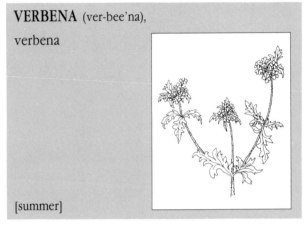

[summer]

Although most of the commonly grown *Verbenas* are annual flowering plants, *V. hastata*, blue verbena, is a hardy perennial even in the North; it grows to 5 feet, which is a bit tall for most borders, but it is useful in a moist woodland garden and along streams. *V. canadensis*, rose verbena, is usually treated as an annual, although it is perennial in the South and survives in the North with protection; a prostrate plant, it grows in ordinary garden soil, full sun, and blooms for most of the summer. A point in its favor is the fact that the profusion of rose-colored blooms so completely covers the old fading blooms that grooming the plant is unnecessary.

DISEASES. Blight, mildew, rot, rust.

INSECTS. Aphids, beetles, caterpillars, leaf miners, mites, nematodes, scales, thrips, whiteflies.

PROPAGATION. By division in the spring, or by seed.

VERONICA (ver-on'i-ka),

speedwell

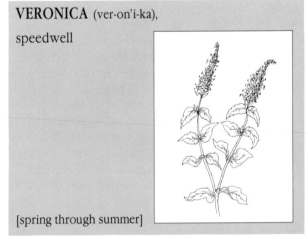

[spring through summer]

Although this plant is seldom called speedwell anymore, it's interesting to note that it was named for the ship that left England with the *Mayflower*, but returned shortly because it was not seaworthy. Whatever it is called, the icicle-shaped flowers of this large genus of annuals and perennials are favorites, especially among those who love blue. The plants vary from low-growing prostrate varieties to large, 2-foot, spiky specimens in shades of blue, pink, red, purple, and white. They grow easily in most garden soils, but prefer those that are somewhat moist. A location in full sun is their first choice, but they will grow well in light shade.

If you are familiar with the weedy, creeping speedwell that takes over lawns, you may be reluctant to choose it for your border or rock garden. Fortunately, there are many other species that are well behaved.

V. gentianoides, gentian speedwell, grows from 6 to 18 inches tall, has pale blue flowers in early summer, and is a good rock garden plant. *V. incana*, wooly veronica, 18 inches high, has clear blue flowers, but is grown mostly for its silvery gray foliage. The cultivar *V. i.* 'Rosea' has pink blooms. *V. latifolia* (also sold as *V. teucrium*), Hungarian speedwell, has a cultivar known as 'Crater Lake Blue' that grows 12 to 18 inches high and is one of the deepest blues you'll ever find. It may sprawl around somewhat, but can be staked if it becomes a problem (we have never staked it, and it looks just fine). *V. longifolia*, 2 feet in height, has lavender-blue flowers, and many good hybrids have been developed in white and pink. *V. l. subsessilis*, clump speedwell, grows into a beautiful 2-foot clump with deep blue blooms. *V. pectinata*, comb speedwell, is a prostrate rock garden plant that has deep blue flowers with white centers. *V. repens*, creeping speedwell, is a good ground cover with blue, pink, or white flowers that blossom in early May; it grows only a few inches tall, and needs winter protection in the North. *V. spicata*, spike speedwell, has many cultivars in different sizes and colors, including the newly developed rose shade *V. s.* 'Red Fox,' 15 inches high.

DISEASES. Leaf gall, leaf spot, mildew, rot.

INSECTS. Caterpillars, nematodes.

PROPAGATION. By dividing the plant in spring. Creeping kinds can be layered. Some are easily rooted from cuttings. Seed is also possible, but the plants may not come true.

VINCA (vin'ka),
myrtle
periwinkle

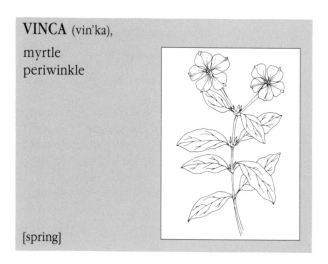

[spring]

These evergreen vines, with shiny, oval, mostly evergreen leaves, are excellent ground covers, and useful for planting along shaded woodland paths or for covering a forest floor.

V. major (big periwinkle) is grown mostly as a pot or window box plant in the North, but is a useful perennial vine from zone 7 south; the cultivar 'Variegata' has green and white leaves. *V. minor* (myrtle, common periwinkle) is hardy nearly everywhere, grows well in the sun in northern climates, but does best in the shade even there, spreading rapidly by layers from a multitude of runners. It is not fussy about soils, but seems to do best in moist soils that are rich in potash. Myrtle has been a favorite for covering banks and cemetery plots for generations. The common species has lavender-blue flowers, but named varieties have shades of white, light blue, and purple flowers.

DISEASES. Canker, dieback, gray mold blight and other molds, rot, yellows.

INSECTS. Aphids, beetles, leafhoppers.

PROPAGATION. By separating the matted clumps into rooted plants. If kept watered after division, this can be done anytime.

VIOLA (vy-o'la),
violet
pansy

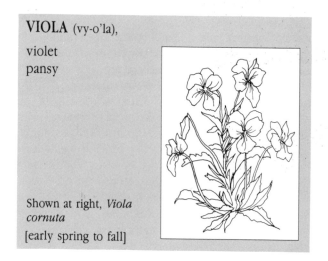

Shown at right, *Viola cornuta*

[early spring to fall]

Many adults can remember the delight they felt as children when they first discovered a patch of purple, white, or yellow violets growing in a park or woodland. These tiny, fragile, colorful blooms have enchanted people for centuries. Lovers present them as a symbol of their devotion, and poets pen their praises.

A wide variety of violas, both annual and perennial, ensures there is one that will thrive in nearly any location. From the tiny roadside violets to the giant pansies, they offer an enormous range of sizes and colors. Prized for their early-blooming, brightly colored flowers, and because they flower over a long period, they are versatile as well: charming in the rock garden, good edging plants for the border, or in front of larger perennials or shrubs in a foundation planting. Violas grow best in rich garden soil, and partial shade, and it may be necessary to pinch back the stems from time to time, to keep the plants from getting leggy during the summer.

V. cornuta, tufted pansy or horned violet, is 6 to 10 inches high, and looks like a large violet or a small pansy. The colors are most often solid red, blue, yellow, or whatever, rather than in combination. If the fading flowers are kept picked, they will bloom for most of the summer. May be somewhat tender in zones 3 and 4, and are worth planting as annuals where they are not winter-hardy. Ordinarily *V. cornuta* lives longer than pansies, but they still are likely to need occasional replacement unless they self-sow. Of the many cultivars, *V. c.* 'Jersey Gem,' a deep blue, is especially attractive.

V. tricolor, Johnny-jump-up, has gone wild in pastures, fields, and occasional lawns. At 6 to 12 inches in height, it looks like a miniature pansy, and makes a good rock garden plant, except for the fact that it is difficult to control since it produces seeds prolifically. It is one of the parents of *V. t. hortensis*, the common garden pansy. *V.* x *wittrockiana* is a group which includes some uncommon beauties such as the popular face-types and solid colors. Usually 6 to 12 inches high, the flower size and color combinations vary greatly, and some are fragrant. Most will bloom all season if they are not allowed to go to seed, and although they are short-lived perennials, gardeners usually treat them as biennials.

V. odorata, sweet violet, is used by florists or grown as a potted plant in cold climates; can be raised outdoors in zones 6 to 10. The long-stemmed flowers (8 inches in height) come in a wide range of colors and are very fragrant.

Native violas are often used in a wildflower bed. To do this successfully, choose kinds that grow naturally in soil and light conditions similar to those in which you will plant them. Some species are biennial or short-lived perennials, and depend on regular seeding to reproduce themselves. *V. canadensis*, the white Canada violet, has white flowers with a lavender tint and yellow center, and likes light shade. *V. pedata*, birdfoot or purple violet, one of the most popular native types grown in wildflower gardens, needs slightly acid soil, spring sun, and summer shade.

DISEASES. Anthracnose, mildew, rot.

INSECTS. Aphids, beetles, caterpillars, cutworms, mites, nematodes, sawflies, slugs.

PROPAGATION. Both violets and pansies are best grown from seed which, if started inside in late winter, will bloom the same year. Seeds may also be sown outside in well-drained raised beds during late summer, but seedlings should be protected by a heavy mulch for the winter. Propagate *V. cornuta* and *V. odorata* by division.

VIOLET. See *Viola*

VIRGINIA BLUEBELLS. See *Mertensia*

WALLFLOWER. See *Cheiranthus*

WATER LILY, HARDY. See *Nymphaea*

WELSH POPPY. See *Meconopsis*

WILD GINGER. See *Asarum*

WILD HOLLYHOCK. See *Sidalcea*

WINDFLOWER. See *Anemone*

WOODRUFF. See *Asperula*

WORMWOOD. See *Artemisia*

YARROW. See *Achillea*

YUCCA (yuck'a), Adam's needle soapweed

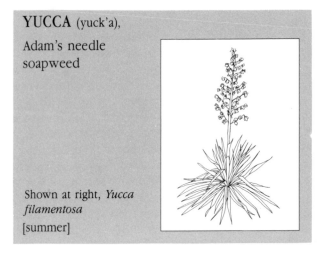

Shown at right, *Yucca filamentosa* [summer]

A yucca plant grows on a bank near our home and when it's in bloom it always creates a lot of interest, since most visitors don't expect to see a desert plant growing in the northern Green Mountains.

Y. filamentosa and *Y. smalliana* are similar, and both called Adam's needle. Some have acclimated beautifully to colder regions, and if you are lucky enough to get a hardy strain, as we did, it will grow well even in zone 3 and still keep its Arizona look. The large, creamy white, bell-like flowers are spectacular on the 5- to 7-foot sturdy stalks that rise from sword-shaped leaves. The threads, or filaments, on the edge of the leaves give the species its name. Cultivars have variegated leaves, which make them interesting foliage plants. Although it may take years for the first blooms, they are well worth waiting for.

Y. glauca, soapweed, is another hardy yucca, with green-white flowers. Three feet in height, the leaves are gray-green with a white margin. The roots are sometimes used for making soap.

Both of these are really shrubs that look like perennials. They are remarkably drought-resistant, but can withstand a damp climate.

DISEASES. Blight, leaf spot, mold, rust, stem rot.

INSECTS. Aphids, mealybugs, mites, scales, stalk borers.

PROPAGATION. By seeds, or by separating the suckers or offsets that form around the main plant. Plant these where they won't have to be moved or disturbed for decades, because they bloom best after they become deeply rooted.

Planting Chart

(for perennials shown in color section)

GENUS	MATURE HEIGHT (INCHES)	SPACING (INCHES)	MONTHS OF BLOOM	COLOR	SOIL	pH	SUN EXPOSURE
Achillea	18–36	12–18	7–9	r,w,y	g	N	s/ps
Ajuga	5–10	10–15	5–6	b,w	g	N	s/ps
Anthemis	24–36	12–18	7–9	y	g	N	s
Artemisia	5–48	12–24	foliage		d	N/A	s
Astilbe	24–48	12–18	6–8	p,r,w	g/m	N	s/ps
Centaurea	18–36	10–18	6–8	b,p	g/d	N	s
Chrysanthemum	6–36	12–24	7–11	p,r,w,y	g	N	s
Coreopsis	12–36	12–15	6–8	y	g	N	s
Dianthus	4–18	12–15	6–8	p,r,w	g	N	s
Dicentra	12–30	12–20	5–8	p,w	g/m	N	ps
Dictamnus	24–36	12–20	6	p,w	g/d	N	s
Echinacea	30–36	12–24	7–9	p	g/m	N	s
Echinops	24–48	12–24	7–8	b	g/m	N	s/ps
Euphorbia	24–36	12–15	4–6	y	d	N	s
Gaillardia	15–30	12–20	6–9	r,y	g/d	N	s
Geum	15–24	12–18	6–8	r,y	g	N	s
Gypsophila	6–48	12–36	6–8	p,w	g/d	N	s
Helenium	24–48	12–18	8–9	r,y	g	N	s
Heliopsis	36–48	15–24	7–9	y	g/d	N	s
Hemerocallis	24–40	18–24	7–9	p,r,y	g/m	N	s/ps
Heuchera	12–18	10–15	6–9	p,r,w	g	N	s/ps
Hosta	18–36	12–24	7–9	p,w	g/m	N,A	sh/ps
Iberis	6–15	10–15	4–9	w	g	N	s/ps
Iris pseudacorus	30–36	18–20	6–7	y	m	N	s
Iris sibirica	24–36	12–18	6	b,p,w	m	N	s
Iris versicolor	30–36	18–20	6–7	b	m	N	s
Lilium (Oriental hybrids)	24–84	30–36	8	r,p,b	g	N	s/ps
Lupinus	30–48	12–18	6–7	b,r,w,y	g	N	s
Lychnis	12–36	12–18	6–8	y,r	g	N	s
Nymphaea	12–18 across	24–30	6–9	b,p,r,w,y	wp	—	s
Paeonia	20–24	18–20	5–6	r	g	N	s
Papaver	36–40	16–18	6	p,y	g	N	s
Phlox paniculata	24–40	12–18	6–8	b,p,r,w	g	N	s
Platycodon	15–24	12–18	6–9	b,p,w	g	N	s/ps
Primula	5–24	10–15	4–6	b,p,r,w,y	g/m	A	ps
Rudbeckia	24–36	18–24	7–9	y	g	A	s
Salvia	36–60	12–18	6–8	b	g	A	s
Sedum	6–24	8–15	7–9	p,r,w,y	g	A	s
Stachys	8–18	9–15	6–7	foliage	g/d	A	s/ps
Thalictrum	36–60	12–18	5–8	p,w,y	g/m	A	s/ps
Thymus	3–8	9–12	6–8	p,r,w	g/d	A	s

COLORS: b = blue, purple shades; p = pink, lilac shades; r = red shades; w = white; y = yellow and orange shades.
SOIL: g = general, loamy garden soil; d = dry soil; m = moist soil; w = wet soil; wp = water plant.
pH: N = normal (6 to 6.5); A = more acid (below 6.0); L = prefers some lime.
LIGHT: s = full or mostly full sun; ps = part sun or light shade; sh = medium to dense shade.

Glossary

Annual plant. One that blooms, produces seeds, and dies the same year.

Asexual reproduction. The propagation of a plant by cuttings, division, grafts, layers, tissue culture, or other vegetative means, rather than by seeds.

Bare rooted. A plant that is transplanted without soil attached to its roots.

Basal. The bottom or base of a plant. A basal shoot is a sprout or branch that grows near the ground. A *basal cut* is one made near the base or bottom of a stem or branch.

Biennial. A plant that grows from seed the first year, and in the second year blooms, bears seeds, and dies.

Border. A flower bed, usually consisting of a variety of plants.

Bract. Leaves that surround or grow so close to a flower that they appear to be part of the bloom.

Bulb. The fleshy root of plants such as lilies, tulips, and similar plants.

Bulbil. Small bulbs that form along the stems of certain plants such as tiger lilies and bladder ferns.

Bulblet. Baby bulbs that develop around a larger bulb below the ground.

Callus. A fleshy tissue growth that forms on a plant while a wound is healing. On cuttings it often, but not always, precedes the development of roots.

Calyx. The outermost group of floral parts, usually green.

Clone. New plant that is started asexually, especially one started by tissue culture.

Cold frame. An outside seed or plant bed enclosed by a frame with a removable transparent cover, that is used to grow plants in a protected environment with no artificial heat.

Compost. Rich, porous soil made of thoroughly decom-posed organic matter. Excellent for building up soil.

Corm. Fleshy root similar to a bulb, but solid. *Gladiolus* plants grow from corms.

Cormels. Small corms that form around the parent. These can be removed and planted to create new plants.

Cultivar. Named variety. A plant that is usually an improvement from the species and unique among other varieties. It is usually, but not always, necessary to propagate cultivars by asexual means.

Cutting. A piece of branch, leaf, or root that is separated from a plant, and rooted to create a new plant with the same characteristics.

Dicotyledon. A plant that produces two seed leaves at germination.

Dormancy. The period of a plant's life during which it is not growing or showing signs of life. Also refers to seeds before they sprout.

Edging. Dwarf, compact plants that are used along the front of a border, or for planting along paths or steps.

Eye. A bud. With perennials it usually refers to a dormant bud growing on the root.

Germination. The sprouting of seeds.

Ground cover. Low-growing plants that spread rapidly either by seed, underground stems that form new plants, or long horizontal top growth that layers into new plants.

Harden off. The process by which perennials and annuals that have been started inside, are gradually exposed to outdoor conditions.

Herbaceous plant. A plant with a stem above the ground which does not become woody.

Herbicide. A chemical used to kill unwanted plants, or to prevent seeds in the ground from sprouting.

Humidity. The amount of moisture in the air.

Hybrid. A new plant developed by the successful cross-pollination of two plants that are genetically different.

Insecticide. A chemical used to control insects.

Island. A flower bed, surrounded by lawn or water.

Lath. A frame or cover with narrow slats to provide shade for plants.

Mature plant. A plant that is old enough to produce blooms and seeds.

Monocotyledon. A plant that produces only one seed leaf. Grasses, lilies, and *Hemerocallis* are examples of monocotyledons.

Named variety. See Cultivar

Offshoots. Small plants growing from the main stem of a perennial, just under the ground. Often these can be taken as cuttings from the parent and grown into new plants.

Peat pellets. Small pellets of peat that swell up when watered. They are often used to root cuttings or start seeds.

Petal. The outer parts—sometimes called the leaves—of a flower which show the color of the bloom.

Perennial. A plant that lives for more than two years. Commonly refers to herbaceous, flowering plants, which may or may not be winter hardy.

pH. A measure of the alkalinity or acidity of the soil, with the higher numbers indicating increased alkalinity, 7 being neutral, and numbers below 7 indicating acidic soil. Most garden soils range from 5 to 6.5 in pH, and the majority of perennials grow well within this range. Some plants, however, demand soil that is more acidic or alkaline than normal.

Pinching. The removal of the tips of new sprouts by the fingers, for the purpose of creating a tight, bushy, and heavier-blooming plant, as is done with chrysanthemums, or to prevent a plant from growing larger, as is often done with houseplants. Extra flower buds are also pinched off in order to increase the size of the remaining blooms. This is a common practice on peonies and other large-flowering plants.

Pollen. The dustlike particles produced by the male stamens on a flower. Usually brown or yellow in color, and spread from flower to flower by bees. The pollen of ornamental grasses is transferred by the wind.

Pollination. The fertilization of the female ova of a plant by the transfer of pollen from the male portion of the same kind of plant on a different flower, resulting in a seed. Besides insects and wind, pollination can also be accomplished by artificial means, and gardeners often do their hybridizing with a small paintbrush and cup.

Rhizome. The fleshy roots of plants such as iris.

Rock garden. Usually a garden of low-growing, spreading perennials grown among rock, often on a slope. Also called rockeries.

Root cutting. Some plants can be propagated by cutting a portion of their roots into small pieces and planting them. The roots then grow tops and additional roots.

Rooting chemical. A chemical in powder or liquid form, into which a cutting is dipped before planting in order to stimulate faster and heavier root growth.

Runner. Vinelike growths on certain plants, which produce new plants by layering or rooting where offsets or offshoots touch the soil.

Scaling a bulb. Peeling off the outer scales of a bulb to start new plants.

Scape. The leafless stalk on which the flowers of some plants such as *Hemerocallis* are produced.

Selection. Choosing the best of a group of seedlings or wild plants for propagation or breeding.

Sepal. The calyx or leaflike back row of petals behind the main showy petals.

Shade. A lower degree of sunlight, which is preferred by some perennials. *Light shade* usually refers to a few hours of morning or late afternoon sun, but considerable skylight all day long. *Moderate shade* is filtered light, such as that coming through trees with light foliage, but little or no direct sun at any time. *Heavy shade* is that under trees with thick foliage.

Succulent. A plant that is capable of storing large amounts of moisture for long periods.

Sucker. A shoot or branch growing from the base of a plant, either above or below ground level. Plants growing from the roots of a parent plant, sometimes even a considerable distance from the parent plant, are also called suckers.

Systemic. Chemicals that a plant absorbs which then permeate it. Some kinds of insecticides, herbicides, and fungicides are being produced as systemics.

Tissue culture. The asexual propagation of plants by the rapid increase of cell growth under carefully controlled conditions of temperature, nutrition, pH, and sanitation in a laboratory.

Transpiration. The process by which a plant loses moisture, usually through its leaves.

Tuber. Fleshy root of a plant in which food is stored. *Helianthus tuberosa* is one of the perennial plants that form tubers.

Turgid. A term used to describe a plant that is well supplied with water. Cuttings from turgid plants root better, and seedlings and mature plants can be more safely transplanted if they are turgid.

Viability. The ability of a bulb to grow or a seed to germinate.

Water stress. The condition whereby a plant loses water faster than it absorbs it.

Wild garden. A planting purposely planned to look natural and uncultivated. It may consist completely of native plants, or natural-looking exotics may also be included.

Appendix

Some of the books listed may be out of print, but still available in libraries, and at used book sales.

Books for Further Reading

Alpines for Your Garden, Alan Bloom, available from International Specialized Book Services, Inc., Portland, Oregon

The Book of Dried Flowers, Malcolm Hillier and Colin Hilton, Simon & Schuster

The Bug Book, John and Helen Philbrick, Storey Communications, Inc. Garden Way Publishing

The Butterfly Garden, by Mathew Tekulsky, Harvard Common Press

The Color Dictionary of Flowers and Plants for Home and Garden, Roy Hay and Patrick M. Synge, Crown Publishers, Inc.

Color In Your Garden, Penelope Hobhouse, Little, Brown & Co.

The Complete Shade Gardener, George Schenk, Houghton Mifflin Co.

Crockett's Flower Garden, James Underwood Crockett, Little, Brown & Co.

Encyclopedia of Ferns, David Jones, Timber Press, Inc.

Flower Arrangements: Month by Month, Step by Step, Julia Clements, David & Charles

A Garden of Wildflowers, Henry W. Art, Storey Communications, Inc./Garden Way Publishing

Gardening With Perennials, Joseph Hudak, Timber Press, Inc.

Gertrude Jekyll on Gardening, Penelope Hobhouse, Ed., David R. Godine

Growing and Using Herbs Successfully, Betty E. M. Jacobs, Storey Communications, Inc./Garden Way Publishing

Herbs Through the Seasons at Caprilands, Adelma Grenier Simmons, Rodale Press, Inc.

Hillside Gardening, William Lake Douglas, Simon & Schuster, Inc.

Keep Your Gift Plants Thriving, Karen Solit with Jim Solit, Storey Communications, Inc./Garden Way Publishing

Let's Grow! Linda Tilgner, Storey Communications, Inc./Garden Way Publishing

Perennials, Pamela Harper and Frederick McGourty, HP Books

The Perennial Garden, Jeff and Marilyn Cox, Rodale Press, Inc.

The Pleasure of Herbs, Phyllis V. Shaudys, Storey Communications, Inc./Garden Way Publishing

Rock Gardening, H. Lincoln and Laurie Louise Foster, Timber Press, Inc.

Rodale's Color Handbook of Garden Insects, Anna Carr, Rodale Press, Inc.

Rodale's Illustrated Encyclopedia of Herbs, Claire Kowalchik and William H.Hylton, Eds., Rodale Press, Inc.

Roses Love Garlic, Louise Riotte, Storey Communications, Inc./Garden Way Publishing

Secrets of Plant Propagation, Lewis Hill, Storey Communications, Inc./Garden Way Publishing

Time-Life Book of Perennials, James Underwood Crockett and others, Time-Life Books, Inc.

Tools and Techniques for Easier Gardening, National Gardening Association (Burlington, Vermont)

The Wildflower Gardener's Guide (regional editions), Henry W. Art, Storey Communications, Inc./Garden Way Publishing

Wildlife in Your Garden, Gene Logsdon, Rodale Press, Inc.

The Wise Garden Encyclopedia, HarperCollins Publishers, Inc.

Wyman's Gardening Encyclopedia, Donald Wyman and others, Macmillan Publishing Co.

Your First Garden, Jack Kramer, The Scribner Book Companies, Inc.

Magazines for Gardeners

Alpine Plants
Box 245
Tahoe Vista, California 95732

Flower and Garden
4251 Pennsylvania
Kansas City, Missouri 64111

Harrowsmith Magazine
The Creamery
Charlotte, Vermont 05445

Harrowsmith Magazine
Camden House Publishing Ltd.
7 Queen Victoria Road
Camden East
Ontario
Canada K0K 1J0

Horticulture
755 Boylston Street
Boston, Massachusetts 02116

Rodale's Organic Gardening
33 East Minor Street
Emmaus, Pennsylvania 18098

Sources of Perennial Seeds and Plants

Arthur E. Allgrove
North Wilmington, Massachusetts 01887
Water plants, etc; catalog, 50

W. Atlee Burpee Co.
5395 Burpee Bldg.
Warminster, Pennsylvania 18974
Seeds and supplies

Beaverlodge Nursery Ltd.
P.O. Box 127
Beaverlodge
Alberta
Canada T0H 0C0
Hardy fruits and ornamentals

Busse Gardens
635 East 7th Street
Route 2, Box 13
Cokato, Minnesota 55321
Daylilies, hosta, iris, wildflowers, rock plants

Carroll Gardens
P.O. Box 310
Westminster, Maryland 21157
Wildflowers, shrubs, and trees

Far North Gardens
16785 Harrison
Livonia, Michigan 48154
Primrose seeds and plants

Harris Seeds
P.O. Box 432
Gresham, Oregon 97030
Flower and herb seeds

Lilypons Water Gardens
P.O. Box 10
Lilypons, Maryland 21717, or
P.O. Box 188
Brookshire, Texas 77423
Water lilies and plants: catalog $4.00

Oregon Bulb Farm
39391 S.E. Lusted Road
Sandy, Oregon 97055
Lily bulbs

Park Seed Co.
P.O. Box 46
Greenwood, South Carolina 29647
Seeds and growers' supplies

Peter Paul's Nurseries
Canandaigua, New York 14424
Water plants and others; catalog, 25

Pinetree Garden Seeds
New Gloucester, Maine 04260
Perennial and Herb Seeds

Putney Nursery, Inc.
Putney, Vermont 05346
Wildflowers and perennials; catalog $1.00

Slocum Water Gardens
1101 Cypress Gardens Road
Winter Haven, Florida 33880
Water lilies, etc; catalog $2.00

Spruce Brook Nurseries
Route 118
Litchfield, Connecticut 06759
Wildflower seeds

Thompson and Morgan, Inc.
Jackson, New Jersey 08527
A large variety of seeds

Van Borgondien & Sons, Inc.
P.O. Box A
245 Farmingdale Road
Babylon, New York 11702
Specializing in spring or summer bulbs and perennials

Van Ness Water Gardens
2460 N. Euclid
Upland, California 91786
A good selection of water plants

Vesey's Seeds Ltd.
York
Prince Edward Island
Canada C0A 1P0
Seeds for short growing seasons

Wayside Gardens
Hodges, South Carolina 29695
Perennials

White Flower Farm
Litchfield, Connecticut 06759
Perennial plants, some shrubs

Gilbert H. Wild and Son, Inc.
Sarcoxie, Missouri 64862
Daylilies, iris, peonies

Plant Societies

Annual dues, society secretaries, and addresses are subject to change.

American Daffodil Society
Miss Leslie Anderson
R#3, 2302 Byhalia Road
Hernando, Mississippi 38632
Dues: $10.00

American Fern Society
Pringle Herbarium
Department of Botany
University of Vermont
Burlington, Vermont 05405
Dues: $8.00

American Hemerocallis Society
c/o Elly Launius
1454 Revel Drive
Jackson, Mississippi 39211
Dues: $12.50

American Hosta Society
c/o Peter Ruh
9448 Mayfield Road
Chesterland, Ohio 44026
Dues: $12.50

American Penstemon Society
Orville M. Steward
P.O. Box 33
Plymouth, Vermont 05056
Dues: $7.50

American Primrose Society
c/o Larry Bailey
1570 Ninth Avenue, North
Edmonds, Washington 98020
Dues: $10.00

American Rock Garden Society
c/o Carole Wilder
221 West Ninth Street
Hastings, Minnesota 55033
Dues: $15.00

Cactus and Succulent Society of America
c/o Charles Glass
Box 3010
Santa Barbara, California 93130-3101
Dues: $20.00

Delphinium Society
Mrs. Shirley E. Bassett
Takakkaw Ice House Wood
Oxted Surrey
RH8 9DW England
Dues: £2

National Chrysanthemum Society, Inc.
c/o Galen L. Goss
10107 Homer Pond Drive
Fairfax Station, Virginia 22039
Dues: $8.50

New England Wild Flower Society, Inc.
Bee Entwise
Garden in the Woods
Hemingway Road
Framingham, Massachusetts 01701
Dues: $25.00

North American Heather Society
Alice E. Knight
62 Elma-Monte Road
Elma, Washington 98541
Dues: $10.00

North American Lily Society, Inc.
Mrs. Dorothy B. Schaefer
P.O. Box 476
Waukee, Iowa 50263
Dues: $12.50

Perennial Plant Association
Dr. Steven Still
217 Howlett Hall
2001 Fyffe Court
Columbus, Ohio 43210
Dues: $35.00

Sempervivum Fanciers Association
Dr. C. William Nixon
37 Ox Bow Lane
Randolph, Massachusetts 02368
Dues: $12.00

Sources of Gardening Supplies

Gardener's Eden
P.O. Box 7307
San Francisco, California 94102
Garden fixtures, tools

Gardener's Supply Co.
128 Intervale Rd.
Burlington, Vermont 05401
Garden tools, frost protectors, food processing equipment

Green River Tools, Inc.
P.O. Box 1919
Brattleboro, Vermont 05301
Tools, cultivators

Melinger's
2310 West South Range
North Lima, Ohio 44452
Tools, natural pest controls, seeds

Park Seed Co.
Greenwood, South Carolina 29647
Garden supplies, seeds, plants, seed starters

Sandoz, Inc.
Crop Protection Division
480 Camino Del Rio South
San Diego, California 92108
Thuricide and other natural controls for insects

Smith and Hawken
25 Corte Madera
Mill Valley, California 94941
Imported tools, garden furniture

Index

Boldface numbers indicate that drawings or photographs appear on that page.

Other Garden Way Publishing Books You Will Enjoy

A Garden of Wildflowers, by Henry Art. How to propagate 101 native species. Art's lucid text is complemented by botanically accurate drawings, maps, tables, $12.95, order # 405-0.

Tips for the Lazy Gardener, by Linda Tilgner. An engaging and enjoyable volume for those who want to cut down on the chores and enjoy their gardens more. $4.95, order # 390-9.

Carrots Love Tomatoes and *Roses Love Garlic,* by Louise Riotte. These two gardening classics tell how to prevent disease and pests naturally by employing the companion planting method. $6.95 (each), order # 064-0 (Carrots); order # 331-3 (Roses).

Keep Your Gift Plants Thriving, by Karen Solit with Jim Solit. Botanist Karen Solit tells how to keep your favorite gift and house plants healthy and happy. You will notice dramatic improvement! $6.95, order # 379-8.

Pruning Simplified, Updated Edition, by Lewis Hill. Professional nurseryman gives you the knowledge and confidence to do a good and proper pruning job. He discusses the pruning of trees, shrubs, flowers, vines, house and garden plants, and more. $12.95, order # 417-4.

The Pleasure of Herbs, by Phyllis V. Shaudys. Growing, harvesting, preserving, cooking, and crafting with herbs—all year long! Drawings, index, $12.95, order # 423-9.

Cold-Climate Gardening, by Lewis Hill. How to extend your growing season and get the most out of your vegetable and landscape plants. Photographs, drawings, index, $9.95, order # 441-7.

Sleeping With a Sunflower, by Louise Riotte. Gardening lore, knowledge, and decades of experience from a popular garden writer. Drawings, charts, recipes, index, $6.95, order # 502-2.

The Wildflower Gardener's Guide, Northeastern edition, by Henry W. Art. An authoritative guide to the 32 native species found in the northeastern quarter of North America. Color photographs, drawings, appendixes, index, $9.95, order # 439-5.

Let's Grow!, by Linda Tilgner. Seventy-two garden projects to enjoy with children of all ages and abilities. Wonderful photographs, drawings, index, $10.95, order # 470-0.

Blue Corn & Square Tomatoes, by Rebecca Rupp. Little-known facts about 20 common garden vegetables makes for enjoyable and fascinating reading. Drawings, index, $9.95, order # 505-7.

The Beautiful Food Garden, by Kate Rogers Gessert. How to landscape with vegetables, herbs, fruit, and flowers; judged the best general gardening book in 1983 by the Garden Writers of America. Color photographs, drawings, photographs, charts, index, $12.95, order # 461-1.

These books available at your bookstore, farm store, garden center, or directly from Garden Way Publishing, Dept. 8600, Schoolhouse Road, Pownal, Vermont 05261. Please enclose $2.00 for Fourth Class or $3.00 for U.P.S. per order to cover postage and handling.